A Twentieth-Century Surgeon

My Life in the
Massachusetts General Hospital

The Bulfinch Building, Massachusetts General Hospital, 1821. It now is a National Monument.

The New Massachusetts General Hospital, 1991. The Ellison Tower is in the left and the White Building on the right.

CLAUDE E. WELCH

A Twentieth-Century Surgeon

My Life in the Massachusetts General Hospital

Boston, Massachusetts
MASSACHUSETTS GENERAL HOSPITAL

1992

Distributed by:

Science History Publications/USA
a division of
Watson Publishing International
P.O. Box 493
Canton, Massachusetts 02021

ISBN 0-88135-181-4

*This book is dedicated
to those who have made my life worthwhile—
my patients, colleagues, family and,
above all, to my devoted wife, Phyllis.*

Table of Contents

List of Illustrations

Preface

Several years ago my sons suggested to me that I should combine my memories and diaries in a brief biography. This relatively simple assignment shortly developed into a formidable task. Medicine and surgery had expanded their frontiers enormously during my lifetime, and the public had become increasingly excited with these developments. Because of my association with many national organizations, personal memories of hundreds of individuals had to be abbreviated severely.

It is a personal record; hence major emphasis is given to the Massachusetts General Hospital about which my life has revolved for many years. Some readers may judge the result too brief and superficial or parochial. Others may find it too long and detailed; for this reason, much factual material has been placed in the appended notes rather than in the narrative.

I am indebted to a countless number of teachers and friends who have guided or accompanied me on my life's journey and in the production of this book. I would like to pay special tribute to my wife, Phyllis Paton, and to my sons, Claude Jr. and John, who for many years had urged me to write these memoirs and who have aided in the development and correction of the manuscript. I also want to honor many individuals, including my teachers Drs. Arthur Allen and Edward Churchill; my other Chiefs of Surgery in the Massachusetts General Hospital, Drs. Paul Russell and W. Gerald Austen; the many residents who worked closely with me; my special associates, Drs. Gordon Donaldson, Grant Rodkey, Glenn Behringer, John Burke, Chiu-An Wang, George Richardson, Stephen Hedberg, Randall Gaz and Ronald G. Tompkins; my secretary Evelyn Hall who tolerated my idiosyncrasies for a quarter of a century; and my nurse assistants of whom I shall mention only two who spent long years with me in the operating room—June Carroll Boehmer and Barbara Masse Connor. Great credit is due to Richard J. Wolfe, Curator of Rare Books in the Countway Library, to Jodi Simpson, and to Elin Wolfe for careful editing of the text.

Perhaps the most valuable contribution these recollections can afford
the reader is a description of life as it actually transpired—with its
comedies, tragedies, aspirations, accomplishments, and failures as they
were played upon the stage of the twentieth century. Above all, I
want to convey the sense of curiosity and excitement that has permeated my life and suggest that future disciples of Aesculapius may
have similar rewards.

Claude E. Welch
Boston, January 1, 1992

Abbreviations
For Organizations Cited in the Text

AAMC   American Association of Medical Colleges
ABMS   American Board of Medical Specialties
ABS   American Board of Surgery
ACCME   Accrediting Council for Continuing Medical Education
ACGME   Accrediting Council for Graduate Medical Education
ACS   American College of Surgeons
AHA   American Hospital Association
AMA   American Medical Association
ASA   American Surgical Association
BCH   Boston City Hospital
CME   Continuing Medical Education
CMSS   Council of Medical Specialty Societies
COBRA   Consolidated Omnibus Budget Reconciliation Act
COGME   Council on Graduate Medical Education
DHHS   US Department of Health and Human Services
FSMB   Federation of State Medical Boards
FDA   Food and Drug Administration
FTC   Federal Trade Commission
GMENAC   Graduate Medical Education National Advisory
            Committee
HEW   Department of Health, Education and Welfare
HCFA   Health Care Financing Association
HMO   Health Maintenance Organization
HMS   Harvard Medical School
IPA   Independent Practice Association
JCAH   Joint Commission on Accreditation of Hospitals
JCAHO   Joint Commission on Accreditation of Health Care
            Organizations (succeeded JCAH in 1987)
LCME   Liaison Committee for Medical Education
MGH   Massachusetts General Hospital
MMS   Massachusetts Medical Society

NEJM	New England Journal of Medicine
NESS	New England Surgical Society
PPRC	Physician Payment Review Commission
PRO	Peer Review Organization
PSRO	Professional Standards Review Organization
RBRVS	Resource-based Relative Value Scale
SIC	International Society of Surgery (Société Internationale de Chirugie)
SOSSUS	Study of Surgical Services of the United States
SSAT	Society for Surgery of the Alimentary Tract
US or USA	United States of America
WHO	World Health Organization

A Twentieth-Century Surgeon

My Life in the
Massachusetts General Hospital

1

Growing Up in Nebraska 1906–1923

My life for the past sixty years has been centered in the Massachusetts General Hospital. When I left Nebraska and arrived in Boston for the first time in 1928, I knew very little about Harvard Medical School where I would spend four years. The Massachusetts General Hospital meant even less to me. As an embryonic surgeon, I would have been very pleased to have had an introductory volume to acquaint me with the unknown world of surgery that has changed dramatically in this century, and of the MGH, where the necessary skills would be taught.

Today, many students and residents who come from far away have the same problem as I had then. Some will complete a five-year training period in the MGH with little spare time to inform themselves of the history and traditions of this great institution, or of its relation with other professional organizations.

To help fill this void, I decided to describe what I had learned during my many years in the MGH. Through these reminiscences interns, residents, and a curious public can be stimulated by the history of the hospital and its staff. They can learn about certain events that made the MGH one of the great hospitals of the world, as it emphasized patient care, research, and education. They will discover certain physicians and surgeons who helped shape modern medicine not only inside the walls of the hospital but elsewhere in other important ways. They will appreciate the exciting advances that have occurred in medicine and surgery during my lifetime and promise to continue in the future.

Here is my story.

*   *   *   *   *

I was born in the town of Stanton, Nebraska, the eldest child of John and Lettie Phelan Welch on March 14, 1906, the same year that Harvard dedicated its new medical school buildings in Boston.[1]

My father and mother had moved to Stanton the year before. For them and for me it was the center of our universe until 1922 when I left for college. They lived there for nearly another decade until they moved to Massachusetts because of the double catastrophes of the Great Depression and the severe drought.

The town essentially was isolated. It was connected with the outside world by the Chicago and Northwestern Railroad and by dirt roads that after heavy rains were impassable. A trip to Norfolk, a larger town twelve miles away, required a full day by horse and buggy even when the weather was propitious.

Stanton was (and still is) the county seat of Stanton county. Located about a hundred miles northwest of Omaha, it contained nearly 1,500 inhabitants and was surrounded by a prosperous agricultural community that was watered by the Elkhorn river. Many of the farmers were of German descent and bilingual. The town contained a typical mixture of different nationalities and cultural variations.[2]

Streets ran directly east–west and north–south. The business section, located in the center of the grid of streets, was formed by strings of buildings extending a hundred yards in each direction. The streets consisted of dirt or of mud, depending on the season. Sidewalks were made of wood. There was a twelve-grade school, seven small churches and a similar number of saloons, large livery stables, and blacksmith shops. The tallest buildings were two grain elevators which were located beside the tracks of the Chicago and Northwestern Railroad. Above one of the largest department stores was the Opera House with large plush seats for several hundred people.

The county court house was a simple building in a square of its own. Behind it was the jail that contained two cells; if it ever contained any customers they were not noted in the two weekly papers—the *Register* and the *Picket*.

For the first ten years of my life, before automobiles became much more common and gravel roads were made, the railroad provided the only dependable connection with other communities. Several Chicago and Northwestern passenger trains with their bright yellow coaches would pass through every day. One, the Flyer, every evening at 8:20, dashed by with steam whistles blowing, stopping only for extreme emergencies. Long freight trains bearing cattle and pigs to the Chicago stockyards were very common. It is not surprising that all the young boys growing up in Stanton wanted to become engineers or conductors on the C and NW.

Winters were severe. Winds blew at gale force, and snow sifted through cracks in windows and under doors. Father was the official recorder of temperature and rainfall for the town. The coldest temperature I can remember occurred one night when, under the twinkling stars, the thermometer stood at 37 degrees (Fahrenheit) below zero. The house was warmed by the kitchen range and a hard-coal burner in the living room. On the back of the stove a plate of goose grease was kept warm for rubbing on our backs to prevent colds. Hot water bottles were taken to bed at night. When colds were prevalent we were given a few drops of turpentine on a sugar cube.

Spring always came with a rush. The melting snows produced floods a mile wide along the Elkhorn river plain, and little creeks swelled to unbelievable proportions. Soon the birds came. My younger brother Ronald and I knew them all. There were huge numbers of red-headed woodpeckers, which now are rare. There were almost equal numbers of bluebirds and robins. Baltimore orioles called from treetops. Rose-breasted grosbeaks sang in anticipation of their favorite potato bugs which appeared a few months later. Dickcissels were on every fence post. Western meadow larks made music in the sky.

One May morning we would return home and sniff a peculiar, lovely odor in the air. A horse-drawn plow had come to the garden. New-turned earth produces a delightful fragrance that rivals new-mown hay in its significance for those who have been raised on the Great Plains.

May was the most beautiful month of all. Vetches appeared in profusion beside the railroad tracks; pasque flowers bloomed on the prairies. In a few years I had collected all of our local flora, classified them and made a large collection of pressed flowers that lasted for fifty years before it crumbled into dust.

In June, summer heat descended like a blanket over the entire state. The temperature inside many houses became unbearable, and many families slept in tents placed in their yards. Crops grew prodigiously. The school year had ended in late May so all hands could do summer work on the farms. South winds blew green ripples and waves over the seas of wheat. With the advent of automobiles, Father was able to take us in our Ford for a Sunday evening ride through the cooler countryside. After a spectacular sunset, flashes of sheet lightning in the distance brought promises of rain. Occasionally huge thunderstorms darkened the sky and poured buckets of water or hail, turning streets into quagmires.

In the autumn it was time for husking corn and gathering pumpkins and squash. Boys set their trap lines. Often, when Ronald and I made the afternoon rounds to discover what we had caught, the brisk winds and the late hour combined to make us so hungry we ate field corn from a few scattered husks. Our traps usually were empty. I only recall some mice and one memorable civet cat, because I was so proud of the catch, I went to school without changing clothes afterward.

The self-contained community of Stanton had its own band, its own orchestra, a famous Gesangverein, a golf club (with sand greens), a Chautauqua in the summer, and a county fair in the fall. Despite the small size of the high school, the teams did very well against formidable opponents. Once a team from Omaha Technical School came to our gymnasium to play basketball. The stands were filled by a raucous crowd that extended onto the playing floor. After what might better have been termed an organized wrestling match, the Stanton team was declared the winner by a score of 17 to 15.

The majority of families in Stanton maintained a garden. Many, including our family, for a time kept a cow that had to be milked morning and night. A pig would be slaughtered every fall and the meat either salted or smoked by the butcher to be eaten throughout the winter. A barrel of apples was placed in the cellar for the same purpose. Transportation in my early youth was by a rented horse and buggy for long trips or later by a Model T Ford, but usually we walked everywhere we wished to go in the town. Major purchases were made from catalogs mailed by Sears and Roebuck or Montgomery Ward; they came after a long delay by freight train from Chicago. These catalogs also acquired another use, for they eventually became standard equipment for the outdoor privies. Water for drinking was pumped from an outside well; rain water for baths or washing was collected from the roof in a large barrel and carried inside to be heated.

My father was the superintendent of schools in Stanton for a decade. He taught classes both in the high school during the week and in Sunday school in the New England Congregational Church; supervised athletic teams; maintained discipline in school and at home; directed and sang tenor in the church choir; and, during summer vacation, worked on his brothers' farms in Iowa. This was not a trivial assignment for a person who was to raise a family of four children, particularly since his salary probably never was more than $1800 a year.[3]

His wife Lettie was just as remarkable a person. She did all of the housework—cooking, cleaning, making clothes for the children—without complaint. She was an active member of the Ladies' Aid of the church. She had a fine voice and sang continuously while she was working. I can still remember such lugubrious tunes as "Give me three grains of corn, Mother"—a ballad that we believed came from the great Irish potato famine—and "In the baggage coach ahead". When Ronald and I were small she would fill two large tin tubs, and put them on the kitchen floor; we would sit in the tubs, stir up bubbles and smell the delightful twin aromas of Jap Rose soap and savories cooking on the kitchen stove.

I can only recall once that mother cried. One night after supper, we criticized some of the food she had prepared. She burst into tears. Thereafter, she became irritable and lost weight. A few months later her condition was found to be due to a toxic thyroid. This event was before the days of iodide supplementation, and there was no good way to prepare a patient safely for an operation. She was referred to a surgeon in Sioux City for this delicate procedure. I was told at the time that he was highly recommended because he prayed before every operation. Although this statement did not exactly inspire confidence, the thyroidectomy could not have been done in a more professional manner. My mother never had any trouble thereafter and never required further medication.

John and Lettie had four children. Ronald was born two years after me. One Sunday when I was seven years old, one of our neighbors took my brother and me out for a drive in the country. When we returned we found, much to our surprise, that we had a new baby sister. We immediately named her Dorothy and she became the queen of the home. Two years later Harold arrived as the last member of the family.

Both John and Lettie were very happy and proud of their children. I received very little oral advice from my father although what he said always was very valuable. For example, he told me that it is easy to make a speech if one has something to say.

As a boy, I lived the usual happy-go-lucky life except that the brotherly affection between me and my younger brother Ronald frequently culminated in minor degrees of physical entanglement. For this and other peccadillos father had a temporary cure, namely, a many-tailed whip that he used very frequently but less effectively than he would have liked, on various parts of my anatomy. This instrument always hung in a very visible location on the dining room wall.

There were no kindergartens when I was young; rather, home

instruction for small children was the rule. As a result of my excellent preschool education, I advanced through the first three grades in the city school in nine months. From that time onward my physical development lagged behind that of my classmates. It was a great disappointment to be unable to qualify for various athletic teams. Only once was I called upon to play in a scheduled basketball contest with a rival school. I quickly made three baskets. Unfortunately at that moment the officials discovered that our team had six players on the floor rather than the five required by regulations. I was ejected, dejected.

My mother also decided it was more important for me to practice each day on the piano for an hour than to develop skills equal to those of Ty Cobb. The hour would drag by. When we finally had a recital I remembered only half of my short piece and ended in a mishmash of notes that were totally original but suggested a Russian overture complicated by vodka. I never participated in a recital again, but did continue to play, even though I still cannot memorize anything more difficult than Peter, Peter, Pumpkin Eater. Many years later, my wife Phyllis and I forced our boys to practice in the same way. First they hated it but now they love playing the piano. One of our greatest pleasures is to play duets.

As soon as school was over in May we would throw our shoes into the closet and run barefoot until September. For about five years from my sixth to eleventh year, it was customary to go to northwestern Iowa to visit relatives. In the earliest days, when the trip had to be made by train, we opened the windows and stuck our heads out into the smoke and flying cinders. From Sioux City to Cherokee pink wild roses were massed along the tracks.

The farms were beautiful and very exciting. We would wade in the creeks, jump in the new-mown hay, milk the cows, turn the handle of the separator that divided milk and cream, gather eggs, play tennis, and eat prodigious meals. Nothing tasted better than huge, red-ripe tomatoes served with cream and sugar.

When automobiles became available we could drive all the way to Cherokee. At times, however, the roads were muddy; and if the car fell into one of the deep ruts in the sticky black loess soil, it was impossible to get out of the rut for many miles. A strong push by husky males, or putting hay under the wheels was required for relief.

Life was dictated by the weather. Usually there were weekly thunder storms throughout the summer. One evening at suppertime, lightning hit and set afire a barn that stood just a hundred yards away from where we were eating. The lightning and thunder were frightening and we wanted to follow the cowering dogs under the beds. I was close to a tornado only once; the funnel passed immediately overhead and struck down less than a half mile away.

Summer brought new adventures that greatly expanded my knowledge of the world. There were no sessions in schools from late May until September so my father, the superintendent of schools in Stanton, was free of academic duties. Either by train or in a wheezy Model T Ford we traveled to northwestern Iowa where all of my paternal and maternal relatives lived. It was there, for the first time, I learned about the history of my family. These facts, in conformance with Thomas Gray's "short and simple annals of the poor," can be recounted in a few brief paragraphs.

I learned that both my paternal grandparents came from relatively undistinguished families of Dorset in southwestern England. Grandfather William Welch had been a soldier and sailor of fortune. He crossed the Atlantic some seventeen times in sailing vessels and had fought in the Sepoy rebellion in India. After leaving the Navy he had moved to Illinois where he met his future wife, Martha Thayer, another emigrant from England. Shortly after the Civil War, when the fertile western prairies were opened for settlement by the Homestead Act, my Grandfather Welch packed his young wife, two children and their few belongings into a covered wagon and headed from Washburn and Bunker Hill, Illinois for O'Brien county in northwestern Iowa. This region was to be their home until they died, "of old age".

The young parents must have lived originally in a sod house cut from the vast prairie. Thereafter the Welch family for many years built and lived in a boxlike home made of wood. Architecturally depressing, it must have been at least utilitarian. I saw it once when, unpainted and tattered, it was in an advanced state of decay. There were a few dilapidated out buildings and some broken box elder trees which were the remnants of the small grove that still typically surrounds an Iowa farm house. It was here that Grandma Welch bore her seven children. Five of them, all sons, grew to maturity.

In the early days, the sole wealth of the family resided in the family horse. With it, the black earth could be plowed and acres of prairie grass and wild roses converted to grains, and then to pigs, cattle, and poultry. If the horse died, disaster was imminent. These hardy pioneers were on their own if an animal became ill. When a horse's abdomen became immensely distended they knew how to spear the rumen with a pitchfork and relieve an otherwise fatal disease.

Later, after the sons had scattered, my grandparents retired from the farm and moved to the small town of Primghar.[4] They owned a small, trim house with a large vegetable garden, surrounded by hollyhocks and petunias. I met our paternal grandparents there for the first time. Grandfather Welch was a taciturn, retiring person, who must have been the bearer of many exciting tales. However he never paid much attention to his grandchildren or told us anything of his past life. He once showed my brother Ronald and me how to splice a rope as he had done for many years in the British navy. Other than that, about the only contacts I can recall were at meal times. As soon as we sat down he uttered unintelligible words of grace. After eating, he would pour the tea from his cup into the saucer and noisily slurp it down. Thereafter he would bury his head in the Chicago *Tribune*.

Grandma Welch was a person of enormous physical, mental and moral strength. After they had retired to Primghar she kept her husband busy at odd jobs. He earned enough money to support them in comfort, though far from luxury. Distrustful of banks, he kept his hard-earned cash in a cigar box on the stairs to the second story bedroom in their home which, of course, never was locked.

Every Sunday Grandma shepherded her unwilling husband to sit in the front pew in the Congregational church. She worked every minute of the day but enjoyed games at night. In the long summer evenings everyone joined in croquet. Playing cards, however, was forbidden. Grandma had an old pump organ on which we played hymns, a Victrola with a large horn, and a library of beguiling books. Listening to *Dardanella* on the talking machine, we would time and again read the *Horrors of the Sea,* with its grisly tales of shipwrecks.

I recall one night when Grandma became extremely ill with severe abdominal pain and vomiting. I was still a small boy. I felt certain she was about to die. The following morning, however, she had recovered from her gallbladder colic and was as spry as ever. This episode made a tremendous impression on me. My inability to help her in such a catastrophe may well have been one of the reasons I finally decided to become a doctor.

Only two of the five Welch boys had more than elementary schooling. However, they compensated by industrious tilling of the fertile land. Will, the eldest, bought a large farm and built what was for many years the largest private barn in Iowa. After retirement from the farm, he became a bank president. John, my father, was next. He was a born educator. After graduation from high school he taught all classes in a country school house. One of his pupils was his youngest brother. Although his given name was Joseph he always was known as Jose (rhymes with the medical term "dose"). Later he became a famous lawyer. His most remarkable feat was to destroy the threat of Mc-Carthyism in the 1950s when he defended the Army in the hearings before a Congressional committee in Washington.[5] Frank was an excellent carpenter; he built many of the homes still standing in the town of Aurelia. The fifth, George, was a farmer.

Jose attended Grinnell College. One summer, now smoking a pipe, he came back to Primghar for a few days. Hiding inconspicuously in a corner, I still remember the tongue lashing given to him by Grandma. Use of tobacco and liquor ranked with playing cards as three of the cardinal sins.

The family spent much less time with Mother's parents. Historical details of their families are shrouded in mystery. Grandpa Daniel, an orphan adopted by the Phelan family, was born near Rutland, Vermont in 1849. Grandma was born Lophelia Goodrich in eastern Iowa in 1856. Both the Phelan and Goodrich families previously lived in northern Ireland. In the wave of emigration that followed the great potato famine in 1846 they became residents of Rutland, Vermont. When the rich earth of the West became available they moved to Waukon in eastern Iowa and later developed a prosperous farm near Cherokee in the western part of the state.

As a retired farmer in a spacious city home in Cherokee, Grandpa would entertain his grandchildren by hitching up the horse and buggy and driving us out to the farm, which he had given to his two sons. This exciting road crossed the Little Sioux river where the bank was so steep that the majority of the few automobiles we saw had to back up the precipice, because fuel pumps were then unknown.

From Grandpa Phelan's city home in the daytime we watched the black passenger coaches of the Illinois Central trains as they were en route to other hamlets with intriguing names—Larrabee, Cleghorn and LeMars as well as Primghar. The hot summer nights were brightened by millions of fireflies.

One December father was summoned to the deathbed of Grandpa Phelan. He had been taken ill a few days before and died of what was called diarrhea at the age of sixty-one. I went with my father on this trip but was too young to remember anything except the cheery glow of the coal fire in the stove in our bedroom. Whether Grandpa had perforated appendicitis or diverticulitis I do not know; at any rate doctors in 1910 usually were faced with a fatality in any such case.

The three Phelan daughters, Jennie, Lettie, and Ethel, were all highly intelligent. Jennie, who never married, became an osteopath and practiced in the city after graduation from the Osteopathic College in Kirkwood, Missouri. It is possible that, subconsciously, she also influenced my ultimate choice of vocation. At any rate, she was a very busy person but loved to give us boys treatments when she had time. They always ended with a snap of the cervical spine. What good that was supposed to do was never apparent, but at any rate, the sudden twist was followed by an appalling click. Fortunately, no one finished with a broken neck.

Lettie, my mother, was born in 1875. After graduating from high school, she was a schoolteacher in rural schools near Cherokee for a few years before she met my father. She was an extremely gifted, attractive person, always busy, always happy. Ethel never married, remained at home, and played caroms with her young nephews at every opportunity.

My father saved enough from teaching school in Cherokee to attend Wheaton College in Wheaton, Illinois. After graduation with a B.A. degree in 1903 he loved to read Latin and Greek and was ready to resume his chosen vocation as an educator. Prior to his first appointment in the high school in Crete, Nebraska he and Lettie were married in Cherokee. While in Crete, he became acquainted with Doane College, an institution that was to play an important part in my life. After two years in Crete he became superintendent of schools in Stanton, Nebraska.

This was the era in which life in America was being transformed by the invention of the automobile. The Ford Motor Company was founded in 1903 and Model Ts came soon afterward. Easy transportation and machines powered by gasoline were revolutionizing rural America. This is an appropriate time to comment on the problems faced by my forebears prior to my birth in 1906.

If there was any characteristic common to these pioneers it could be called a capacity for hard work from sunrise to sunset. Catastrophes were so common that they bred a sense of resignation and equanimity. Because farming was by far the chief industry, Nature was the chief opponent as well as the greatest friend. Prairie fires were a great hazard for my grandparents. They also all remembered the great blizzard of

1888. Other snow storms, spring floods, crop failures, tornadoes, cloudbursts, hailstorms, plagues of grasshoppers, drought and dust storms seemed to alternate in endless succession. Disease could destroy whole herds of animals or crops. In humans, a ruptured appendix or one of the multitude of problems that attend a birth usually were fatal. Nevertheless, periods of prosperity led to continued growth until, in the late 1920s and 1930s, a combination of the Great Depression, a severe drought and dust storms led to problems as serious as those faced by their parents in the previous century.

Life would seem very hard to any person living today if he or she were transplanted back to that time a little less than a century ago. Electric street lights did not appear in Stanton until 1903; even in towns kerosene lamps were common until 1910, and rural electricity came even later. Toilet facilities and water pumped from wells were nearly impossible to reach or use on many snowy winter days. Telephones hung on the wall; to get the operator, one turned a crank and "central" would ring the recipient after being told the proper number. She also was a mine of information and a source of help since she could listen in on all calls.

A strong physique was required to survive in those days. Medical care, compared with what we have today, essentially was non-existent. Life expectancy in 1900 was 49.3 years compared with 75.6 in 1990 and projected to 77.9 in 2010. Accustomed to illness, early mortality, and the destructive forces of Nature, our ancestors nevertheless maintained an underlying optimism, piety and faith that the future would be better than the past.

After Father became a banker in 1915, and our summer excursions to Iowa terminated because Father could not leave his bank for more than a week or two, Ronald and I would mow lawns. Throughout the year we carried milk from a farm on the outskirts of town to our neighbors. We were janitors for the New England Congregational Church and cleaned it thoroughly once a week. The standard charge for mowing a lawn was fifty cents, and for polishing pews and cleaning the church we received a dollar. We played in the band and had great fun with the trombone and trumpet. It was a rare treat to travel to Norfolk to see the Ringling Brothers' Circus. We found time to read most of the books in the small town library; they included the entire series about the Rover Boys. We saw ourselves as the heroes in Horatio Alger's novels, such as *From Rags to Riches*.

One time we heard that two women who lived in a house a block away from our home had left town in a great hurry. My brother and I rummaged through the building and found several whiskey bottles and some salacious literature. We were apprised of the significance of this finding by our butcher—a very bright man, who was said to be a socialist. He told us we had been looking through a whore-house. This new word led us to the dictionary for more information.

Revivalists would come to town about once a year. They would shake the rafters as they urged everyone to come forward for Jesus. I sang the revival hymns, such as "Beulah Land" but felt very uncomfortable. We did study the Bible a great deal, memorized many chapters in the Scriptures and, when asked to recite a single verse, made frequent use of the shortest one in the Bible—"Jesus wept".

We became experts at coaxing cars to run. A few years later, when I began working in the drug store and driving its truck, I often pushed it from the garage out on the street. There, on top of a hill, as the truck slowly began to move downhill, I would turn the crank a few times (it was situated on the front of the truck), jump out of the way, hop in, and manage to work up enough speed to start the engine. The radiator leaked badly but this was readily cured by putting in a generous amount of flaxseed meal. Gasoline was sixteen cents a gallon.

At age twelve I was hired to work in DeWitt and Drewelow's drug store. This pharmacy was by far the larger of two competitors in the town. The pay was not all that great—a dollar for a twelve-hour day—but the amount of candy and ice cream that I ate made a very satisfactory arrangement. The drug store had an impressive array of bottles containing liquids such as tincture of cannabis that lined the walls. I studied the pharmacopeia, sniffed all the drugs, and learned much later that cannabis is the source of marijuana and that the tincture was advised for the treatment of neurasthenia. So far as I know none of it was dispensed for the three years I was there.

At times I was the only person in the store and would put up prescriptions. Such orders were not very numerous since all the doctors in town kept large supplies of pills in their offices and dispensed them with great alacrity.

Father was intensely interested in public speaking. In the early nineteenth century many of the high schools in Nebraska participated in declamatory contests to establish state champions. Father had trained several winners who received first prizes, and when I reached the appropriate level in school, he decided that I should enter the state contest. Because of my obvious lack of ability to orate in the style of the noble Romans he chose a humorous subject entitled *Father's Talking Now*. He inserted many gestures and coached me vigorously. I won first place in the local school competition and thus was able to travel to Norfolk for the next level of the contests. I can still remember the dull gray clouds and the fiery sun in the western sky as we traveled by car. The dust in the air was the harbinger of the great drought and dust storms that nearly destroyed the land a few years later. For some reason I again was the winner, and went on to win in the third level, held some forty miles away. Because the travel was the most interesting part of the experience for me, I was delighted to know that now I could go to the state finals in some exotic spot. Much to my disgust—but I suspect because of state-wide respect for my father who probably had trained more winners than anyone else— the executive committee decided to hold the competition in Stanton. I won first prize.

I have often wondered what it was in these early years that made me choose medicine as a career. Obviously, the thrill of working in the drug store was very important. The respect with which all pharmacists held physicians imbued all persons who worked in pharmacies. Botany, the use of plants for drugs, the pharmacopeia, all were exciting. I also was stimulated by frequent trips I made with a veterinarian out into the country. On one visit all of the hundreds of pigs a farmer owned seemed about to die. The doctor killed one and found its intestines filled with writhing round worms each nearly a foot long and as thick as my little finger. The pigs were wormed and rapidly recovered. Such triumphs were impressive.

I graduated from high school at age fifteen, and spent the next year maturing and working in the drug store. Then it was time for the next step. I had been living at home; without any discussion about the matter, it was assumed that I was a permanent nonpaying guest of the family until the time came for departure to college. Now, for the first time I was ready for this adventure in the big, dangerous, unfriendly world. It was on to Crete, Nebraska and Doane College.

In retrospect it is obvious that nearly my entire future career was determined by my parents. They provided a deeply religious atmosphere and strict discipline, and taught the virtues of constant industry, financial stability without greed, and frugality. They instilled in me a love of teaching and of music, a desire to travel little known byways as well as highways, an ability to meet adversity, great curiosity for the unknown, and a sense that life is a grand adventure.

* * * * *

I shall move a little ahead of my story to tell about the later life of my parents because it illustrates the resilience with which they met adversity. In 1915, when I was nine years of age, father found that teaching, though rewarding in many ways, did not lead to a financial return sufficient to support his family. He resigned and became cashier and later president of the Elkhorn Valley State Bank. This institution was not large but it did have one unusual feature—that if a bank should fail, it would be supported by all of the other state banks in Nebraska. This form of insurance brought a large number of customers, but, unfortunately it was not infallible. The Great Depression was followed by a severe drought that lasted several years. Nearly all banks failed; even those that were once strong were weakened because they had to help the others. Few could weather the storm. With great difficulty, Father collected nearly all unpaid loans. When his bank failed only $100,000 finally appeared to be uncollectable. In a short time nearly three-quarters of this amount was recovered, so the loss for depositors was relatively small.

I was attending Harvard Medical School when, at age 50, Father found Nebraska in this sorry economic condition and his means of livelihood gone. It must have been a terrible blow for the family. For a short time he sold insurance. Then, through the efforts of his brother Jose, he was interviewed by the president of the bank in Winchendon, Massachusetts and shortly after became the chief executive officer of that institution. A few years later, by judicious investment of funds, he facilitated the establishment of the Clark Memorial Community Center in that city. During World War II, when I was in Italy, he made regular trips to Boston, where he helped Phyllis make necessary repairs to our house. He died in a nursing home after a stroke at age seventy-eight.

Mother accepted all of these changes with great composure and continued to be just as stalwart in the face of physical ailments until she died after a fracture of the femur at age ninety-two. But she did complain that she never liked New England as well as Nebraska; because of the mountains, she could not see far enough in Massachusetts.

2

College Years 1923–1928

In September 1922, after a year of full-time clerking in DeWitt and Drewelow's drug store, I was 16 years old and anxious to attend college. The choices available to me were Doane College in Crete, and the University of Nebraska in Lincoln, site of the state capitol. My limited finances restricted the options to the state of Nebraska. Only these two had sufficiently high academic credentials. I decided to go to Doane for at least the first two years, but at the end of that period I decided against moving and stayed there for the entire four years.[1]

My father approved of this decision. He thought I might be lost in a large school but have a good chance to develop in a small one. Other considerations that bulked high in the list of recommendations for Doane included a high ratio of qualified teachers to students and a close church affiliation that would protect an unsophisticated lad from worldly evils.

My mother hastened to make shirts for me to take away. And early on a September day, we collected my few belongings together with a laundry bag to mail dirty clothes back home every two weeks. In his old Model T Ford, my father drove us on dirt or gravel country roads through fields of ripening corn and stacks of freshly cut hay for about a hundred miles to Crete. This small city, twenty-five miles southwest of Lincoln, is located on the Big Blue River.

Thomas Doane, the surveyor of the Chicago, Burlington and Quincy railroad, located the college at what he considered to be the most beautiful site on the 500-mile section between Omaha and Denver. The buildings were situated atop a wooded hill just outside the city.

At present the size of the Doane student body is about 800. But in 1923 it was still small with less than 300 students even though the college had been in existence for about 50 years.

There were three large buildings, three small ones, and a music conservatory with an auditorium adequate to hold the entire student body. The freshman and sophomore classes were always relatively large. But many students transferred to other institutions at the end of two years and at the end of four only about thirty seniors were left in the class.

One of the small buildings on campus was a girls' dormitory; men lived in adjacent homes. The two sexes were present in nearly equal numbers. They were sons and daughters of Nebraska farmers, professionals and business-men. All were white, and, to my knowledge, all were Protestant. Many nationalities were represented. Typical of Nebraska at that time, parents or grandparents of the students often came from Czechoslovakia, Sweden, or Germany. No one was wealthy; many required small scholarships. At the very outset I secured a part time job in a drugstore. Income from this position, supplemented by my meager savings of approximately $200, provided for room, tuition and board that amounted to about $500 a year. I was responsible for all of my expenses.

In Doane we were isolated from the outside world. Even Lindbergh's flight across the Atlantic in 1927 attracted little attention. The demands of our instructors required us to work many hours in the evenings and on week ends. Immersed in our studies and extracurricular activities centered in the college, we rarely left Crete.

Doane had many fine teachers. Professor Taylor, a great scholar, taught history. Professor Carlson was a biologist of repute. Professor Wing, a chemist, persuaded me to take many of his courses and, in my senior year, procured a postgraduate fellowship for me in chemistry in the University of Missouri. Another teacher, Wesley Spink, who was an All-American football player at Carleton, later became a classmate and my dissecting partner in anatomy in Harvard Medical School. Professor Buell Gallagher, after a few years at Doane, became the president of the City College in New York.

There were some deficiencies in the college. The library was small, with less than 25,000 volumes. This was one of the reasons there was not a chapter of Phi Beta Kappa on the campus. These criticisms were relatively unimportant, and, because of my great satisfaction with the college, my younger brother, Ronald, entered Doane in the class after mine. He also worked with me in the drugstore and we roomed together for three years. After graduation with honors he obtained a Ph.D. in economics from Yale.

I took as many courses as possible while at Doane. One was in astronomy. A large telescope was available for our use. One night we carefully set the scope to determine the transit time of a certain star. We saw nothing. We tried another star. We saw nothing. We went outdoors and saw hundreds of bright stars glittering in the sky. We learned an important lesson—if you wish to see the universe, take the cap off the telescope.

One of my first year courses in English emphasized composition. A few years later I reviewed some of the daily theses that we were obliged to write. I found mine were unbelievably crude and dull. I usually divided the required two hundred words into three paragraphs. The first identified the problem, the second contained the message and the third paragraph summarized the first two in essentially the same words. It took several weeks for me to appreciate the fact that repetition can be intensely boring and ridiculous.

This training proved to be invaluable two years later. One of the prized positions in the school was the editorship of the weekly student paper, the Doane *Owl*. The editor was chosen yearly by vote of the entire student assembly. The contest introduced me to politics because my fraternity nominated me to run against another person from a rival frat. We managed to convert one of the sororities to my cause, and so I was elected by a narrow margin—one vote. At any rate, the editorship of the *Owl* proved to be a very interesting assignment. I had to write many editorials. Most important, a weekly deadline could not be missed. Headlines became my specialty. On the occasion of a victory over a rival school in football, the huge headline running across the entire top of the paper read "DOANE WALLOPS COTNER 9–6". (I was not averse to expanding Webster's definition of "wallop", particularly because the word exactly filled the allotted space).

Music, athletics and debating were other favorite nonacademic activities. I joined the glee club. Even though I had no musical ear, my love of music atoned for this defect. I became the business manager of the club and was allowed to schedule the tours that we made around the state during the springtime. Our musicians brought concerts and news of Doane to various congregations scattered throughout the eastern half of Nebraska. Transportation at that time had to be by train because there were no busses and not enough private cars to carry the group. The itinerary provided a great opportunity for me to fulfill one of my childhood desires—to ride on a freight train. It must have been somewhat surprising for a conductor to find thirty young men crowding into his caboose at the rather unusual hours of 11 P.M. or 5 A.M. However, this activity furnished great excitement for the business manager, even though there were rumbles of discontent by other members of the club about the hours of travel and the means of transportation.

The campus was always full of music: hymns were sung in chapel, pianists kept a dozen instruments busy in the conservatory and a "Pep Band" in which I played a trombone blasted away at all athletic events. In addition, I was a sixth class private in an Army band that practiced one evening a week and encamped with other reservists for a week during the summer. I am not sure that the practicing that I did on my noisy instrument pleased my neighbors.

School spirit was exceptionally high. Nothing was so important as winning our football games. During college I was a physical midget and never did qualify for anything important on the athletic field. Nevertheless, one of my greatest ambitions was to earn an "Honor D"—a huge capital letter that was placed on sweaters of athletes who earned positions on various teams.

These Doane athletic teams were highly competitive and excellent. One of my roommates, Ray Alf, ran the hundred-yard dash in a time just short of the world's record. Many others were close rivals. My first opportunity to join this group of athletes came in my senior year when I decided to go out for cross-country running. This was a deadly experience. Running for several miles on the country roads in the late afternoon was intensely boring. Finally I decided the sport did not interest me. Two weeks later, however, Olympic trials were announced and Doane had to send a team to Lincoln. Five people were required but only four runners were left. I was chosen to be the one to be rehabilitated for the event of the next day. I can still remember the horror with which I got out on that gravel road on the following morning. A great group of contestants started running for an invisible goal some four and a half miles away. Very soon some runners dropped out with various visceral disturbances and disappeared under roadside culverts. With the final post in sight, someone from another school was even with me. We put on one of the only close races of the day, coming in seventeenth and eighteenth. We were given silver medals; the University of Nebraska won the gold. Three teams had raced.

Then spring came, and with it another opportunity. I went out for track. The half-mile run offered another chance to attain fame. I entered one race with another school but barely managed to finish far behind the winner. I saw no hope if I continued, but did feel I still had a chance in tennis. I won enough matches to reach the semifinals in the state college tournament; this was sufficient to win an honor D just a few weeks before graduation.

In retrospect, I know that my college debating experience was very important. In my senior year, we argued the pros and cons of the McNary-Haugen farm bill with other college teams as we took alternating affirmative and negative sides in the debates. We won all but one of our encounters. From our loss we learned that it is desirable to save a few important arguments for the final statement, after the opposing team has had its last opportunity for rebuttal.

I recall a few occasions when I disturbed the even tenor of the college. For example, to break the winter's tedium I once placed some Limburger cheese on the radiator in the main dining room. A rather remarkable reduction in the appetite of the diners followed. On another occasion, I found in the drugstore a bottle of the most odoriferous compound in the entire pharmacopeia—ammonium valerate. I burned a teaspoonful of it in the entrance of the main lecture hall; this produced an evacuation of the entire building. Another time, having misinterpreted the intent of the directions in a chemistry manual, I placed some sodium in sulfuric acid; this produced a remarkable reaction with the sodium whizzing on top of the liquid until suddenly the whole mess exploded with a roar that practically brought down the entire chemistry laboratory.

Occasionally we would break away from the inbred life at Doane and go to Lincoln for some important affair. I remember one winter night when we drove there in an ancient model T Ford for a distance of 25 miles to hear Souza's band. It was bitter; the temperature must have been 25 degrees below zero. In those days there were no full sidewalls on the cars. There were isinglass windows that could be buttoned in place but they did not keep out the cold and of course there was no heater in the car. As we came home over the country road our lights burned out, and with no moon it was black as pitch. Finally when we were about two miles from home the engine died, apparently completely frozen. We tried to build a fire under the carburetor to see if function would return. Fortunately the fire refused to burn and we plodded home on foot, arriving shortly before dawn.

The Big Blue river was lovely in the springtime. Prior to that season, when the snows were melting, there often would be a terrific flood and we would be called out to place sandbags on the banks of the stream to prevent the adjacent mills from being flooded. The river also provided an excellent opportunity for boating. Nearly everyone had an opportunity to own at least a share in a canoe in order to reach the swimming holes.

Doane was known nationally as a church school, and received some support from the Congregational Church. During week days all students and faculty were required to attend chapel, which was held in the college conservatory. During a twenty-minute period we sang two hymns, and listened to a short prayer and a brief talk by one of the faculty. On Sunday most of the teachers and many students attended the Congregational church in the city. There was continuous pressure on the Doane students to teach classes in Sunday school. This assignment was far from appealing. After being conned into assuming the task, I decided to effect a social revolution. Dancing was not allowed in the college at that time. I dug out a text in the Bible that recommended this form of relaxation—the demand in Psalm 150 is to "Praise him (the Lord) with timbrel and dance". As I expanded week by week on that theme, the Sunday school class suddenly swelled to unbelievable proportions. Fortunately the academic year came to an end before the rumors that I might be expelled from the school became fact. Two or three years later Doane first allowed dancing.

My major concentration at Doane had been in chemistry. Two months before graduation from Doane I decided that I would prefer to enter the field of medicine rather than spend my life in a chemistry laboratory. Relying heavily on the advice of my uncle, Joseph Welch (who had graduated from Harvard Law School with high honors), I decided that Harvard Medical School would be my choice. The Dean at Harvard requested a summary of courses I had taken and my grades. I sent him this transcript, and a return letter came immediately saying I was accepted but, because I had not taken any premedical courses, it would be helpful for me to take them before entering medical school.

On a balmy summer's day in 1927, beneath azure skies and fleecy clouds, our graduating class marched into the chapel to the strains of "Pomp and Circumstance". We felt that life could never be sweeter or could we ever be happier. I was president of the senior class and was graduating summa cum laude, the first time this honor had been given for many years. The next steps in life were clear—summer courses at Columbia University in New York City to fulfill the premedical requirements, to be followed by an instructorship in chemistry at the University of Missouri where I hoped to obtain a Master of Arts degree in a year and a summer rather than the standard two years, and then the final goal—Harvard Medical School.

In accord with the suggestions made by the Dean of Harvard Medical School I made rapid preparations for the appropriate premedical studies. Three other Doane students also wished to take summer courses. The four of us decided to attend Columbia University in New York City and see an important part of the world during our travels.

My friends, Allen Burkhart and Clarence Noyce bought a decrepit model T Ford that appeared viable enough to last through the 3000-mile round trip. Harold Burdick and I completed the quartet. Prior to departure we calibrated the maximum speed of the vehicle by driving down the Nebraska roads. It was found to be twenty-five miles per hour. We concluded that the trip would take a week each way. That pace would certainly give us adequate opportunity to see the countryside.

The roads usually were made of dirt or covered with gravel; paving was unusual. They snaked in long curves over hills. However, they were superior to the function of our car. One day we had seventeen blowouts. We would stop every few minutes, remove the defective tire, patch the inner tube, replace the tire, and travel a few more miles; we finally conceded that we had to buy a new tire although that purchase nearly exhausted the exchequer. Eventually we came to the broad Hudson River and were ferried across. (There were no bridges or tunnels in those days.) We had arrived in New York City.

Columbia University, located in a lovely area not far from the Hudson and Riverside Drive, seemed isolated. Chimes rang every quarter hour from the campus belfry. In addition to the academic courses, numerous excellent concerts were available. Every weekend we explored the city or the surrounding countryside. New York City was completely safe at that time; it was even a pleasure to ride on the subway. On the hot summer evenings we sat high on the banks of the Hudson and watched the constant stream of brilliantly lit ferry boats criss-crossing the river.

I needed courses in botany and zoology. I loved botany, having collected flowers for many years; consequently I was impressed by the encyclopedic textbook. Much to my disappointment we covered only about 100 pages in six weeks. Despite this shortcoming, it was one of the most valuable courses I ever took. Every day we were quizzed on the contents of the assigned page and a half. This task required the utmost concentration. I learned a lesson for the future: it is possible to put many facts into a very few paragraphs, provided no words are wasted.

The sessions in zoology were not nearly as interesting. They were taught by a visiting professor from South Dakota. who had an accent that made his lectures almost unintelligible. Nevertheless, dissections of lobsters opened exciting new anatomic vistas.

To meet my financial obligations I worked daily in the cafeteria. My main job was washing dishes; I cleaned enough of them there to last me for the rest of my life.

We reserved one weekend for a trip to New England. It greeted us with a steady drizzle which soon became a downpour. The nights were wet and uncomfortable because we only had leaky tents for sleeping. My first trip to Boston was memorable. Seeing Joseph Welch (Uncle Jose) in his fine office at 60 State Street in the firm of Hale and Dorr was an impressive experience. When we turned right on a red light we had an equally impressive confrontation with a policeman. Later a fine gentleman—we never learned his name—stopped us because he saw our Nebraska license plate; he sent us to lunch at the Harvard Club as his guests. Boston clearly promised to be a stimulating community.

Our return trip to New York City was far from routine. While descending a long hill in Danbury, Connecticut, we burned out our brakes. One night as we slept beside a river a car dashed across the bridge over the stream and smashed full tilt into the cliff on the other side. Most of the occupants were killed. We picked up one person and carted him to a hospital but he died on the way. Driving through such cities as Worcester and Hartford was difficult because there were essentially no signs to direct travelers in the proper direction. As a result, we were somewhat benumbed as we drove through a small Connecticut town. Again we were apprehended by a policeman on a motorcycle. He maintained that we had been traveling forty-five miles an hour on a posted highway. Although we knew full well that our car was totally incapable of such speed even when going down hill, we had to follow him to the police station and pay a fine. As we were leaving, Burkhart was behind the wheel. He was not a particularly good driver and proceeded to prove it by driving over the policeman's motorcycle. We heard a lot of crunching, but luckily our car was intact and we sped away at our maximum speed—twenty-five miles per hour.

It was fortunate that the trip back to Nebraska was uneventful because our funds were nearly exhausted. I recall that I had only $2.50 left for food during that last week. On the other hand a stack of pancakes cost only fifteen to twenty-five cents; eating pancakes for every meal was monotonous but filling.

In the fall of 1927 I entered the University of Missouri as an instructor in chemistry planning to obtain a master's degree. This year was one of enormous excitement. Dr. Schlundt, the head of the department, was extremely interested in radioactivity. Although we carried out many experiments, about all that we did to protect ourselves from radiation damage was to have a weekly white blood cell count. One of the instructors was engaged in concentration of thorium. We put on rubber gloves and stirred his mixture. At night the liquid gave off an eerie glow that became progressively brighter as the material became more concentrated.

During the second semester I acquired two large laboratories. I carried out several experiments simultaneously, and produced several new compounds. To prove their structure I had to analyze them under a steady stream of hydrogen. Not unexpectedly, from time to time, the whole apparatus would blow up. This particular laboratory, with considerable foresight, had been placed in the basement. Miraculously none of us were hurt by the showers of glass.

I learned another of life's valuable lessons from a course in physical chemistry. The professor in charge gave us a list of fourteen problems to be solved in the laboratory during the semester. I remember the first one very well; it was to determine the specific gravity of a substance by the falling-drop method. I scoured the entire university library again and again and could find no leads. Of course, I was too proud to ask the professor for any help. Finally, when twelve of the fourteen weeks had been exhausted, I finally hit upon the relatively simple solution. Thereafter the other problems were easily finished before the end of the term.

Initially I found it difficult to accept this method of teaching— problem solving—because it was unique in my experience. But I soon found reasons to consider this approach was valuable because it excited imagination and initiative. It was an unusual variation from essentially all of my previous courses in which success was measured frequently by an ability to regurgitate the words of the professor rather than by the power to analyze, synthesize, or probe the unknown.

My next assignment in learning—a course in anatomy in Harvard Medical School—was to prove a reversion to memorization of an entirely new vocabulary and innumerable facts. The same pattern was to be followed throughout the coming four years.

It is interesting to observe that pedagogical methods change and today problem solving has become a favorite method of teaching in medical schools. Thus our professor in Missouri appears to have been far ahead of his time. There is one caveat—medicine has so many problems that attempting to solve a few may leave glaring deficiencies in knowledge that is essential to understand the vast vista that is opened for the young medical student. Unless one's career is certain to be in a limited field in medical science the student must acquire many facts.

In the University of Missouri, my schedule was so engrossing that I found I was spending day after day in the laboratory from 6 A.M. until midnight. Many of these hours were spent in isolation with test tubes and Bunsen burners as I carried out many simultaneous experiments. Finally, I confirmed my previous decision that I would prefer to spend my life with more human contacts, such as that provided by the practice of medicine.

By the end of the summer of 1928 I had completed my experiments and had written a thesis about the new diketopiperazine compounds that I had discovered. The work was accepted and I received a master's degree. Whether any of my new compounds have had any practical use or not I do not know. A few years later I examined the copy of my thesis in the university library; well thumbed, it obviously had been used frequently by other students.

It was somewhat difficult to leave such engrossing prospects as probing the unknown and teaching, but medicine appeared to offer the same opportunities—and even more. I never have regretted the change of vocation.

3

Harvard Medical School, 1928-1932

I arrived in Boston in September 1928 with practically no knowledge of the history of Harvard Medical School, of the University, or of my prospective classmates. I did know that Harvard and Johns Hopkins were the leading medical schools in America and that I was heeding Emerson, who had advised many years before to hitch your wagon to a star.

I came to Boston again by car, one that brother Ronald had driven as far as New York City while on his way to New Haven to work on a doctorate in economics. Because he had no further use for it, the ailing hulk was given to me for its last adventure. Being a Model T Ford, it was supposed to be indestructible. But my first inspection of it raised many doubts about its immortality. Almost all the floor boards in the front seat were absent; this deficit provided a good view of the pavement as one sped over it at the car's maximum speed of thirty miles per hour.

There was another vagary of the nameless wreck. When the steering wheel was turned too far to the left, the car reversed direction and started to go right. Having mastered this idiosyncrasy, Don Quixote sped down the Boston Post Road through the gathering gloom. The headlights on the front of the car shined dimly, and only when the engine was in motion. It was reassuring, however, to look down through the holes in the floor and see the red hot exhaust pipe; this metal conduit, which led back to the muffler, gave a cheery glow that at midnight on a particularly lonely stretch in rural Rhode Island was most agreeable. This good fortune did not last as far as Boston, however, for suddenly the two sections of the exhaust pipe fell apart, completely disconnecting the muffler. The car rapidly filled with fumes and to avoid asphyxiation it was necessary for me to stop the engine and attempt repairs. Needless to say, restoration of the connection was a problem since there now were no lights, the pipes were red hot, and the wrenches were hidden somewhere in the back of the car. A flashlight would have been a godsend. At any rate, with bare hands I finally managed to screw the contraption together. Getting through Providence took two hours in those days, but finally Boston appeared in the early dawn. It was time to start the new career.

The dormitory for Harvard medical students, Vanderbilt Hall, was a very deluxe establishment. Upperclassmen, dressed meticulously, came down to the dining room, and scanned a printed menu which showed a suitable variety of choices. The meals were served by a few impecunious freshmen who were lucky enough to get free board in this manner. Fortunately I was one of them.

It was not overly reassuring to glimpse the other hundred fifty-nine members of HMS, Class of 1932. All were males, and nearly half of them dangled Phi Beta Kappa keys conspicuously on watch chains crossing their vests. Later I learned that that many of them had spent several months at prestigious medical establishments abroad, chiefly in Vienna and Munich. Obviously the competition for academic prizes, gained chiefly on the basis of grades, was going to be fierce.

We assembled for the first time in the lecture hall in Building B to be greeted by Dr. Robert (Bobby) Green, Professor of Gross Anatomy, impressive in his starched white laboratory coat. Everyone looked on this course with some dread because it entailed a large amount of pure memorization. As our professors said, one must have a few wall pegs on which to hang facts as well as coats. Bobby Green was a master lecturer, a Greek scholar, an obstetrician who had delivered all of his own numerous children, and a total inspiration to the class. He immediately became our first role model; in 1932 our class dedicated its yearbook to him.

The class was divided into groups of four; each group had one cadaver to dissect. This dissection was done with extreme delicacy. In fact, it took one of our classmates all afternoon to enter the abdominal cavity as he meticulously divided the peritoneum into seven separate layers.

It was not long before we were introduced to other professors, many of them world famous. Walter Cannon, the great physiologist, was the first person to use a barium meal to study the actions of the gastrointestinal tract. Hans Zinsser, eminent bacteriologist and author, strode continuously about the demonstration table in the front of the room as he lectured. Bert Wolbach, a fine pathologist, sported an ever-present flower in the button hole of his coat. Otto Folin, an excellent biochemist, conversed with us as we carried out laboratory experiments. They were examples of the scientists to whom we were exposed day after day.

On Saturday mornings we attended clinical conferences at the Peter Bent Brigham Hospital. Here Dr. Harvey Cushing often lectured to us, illustrating his talk with artistic anatomical sketches that he drew rapidly on the blackboard. On the same board he also kept a running tally of the number of brain operations he had done, and of his astonishingly low mortality figures.

We were taught by example the skill of one-upmanship in these conferences. One day the leaders were Professors Henry Christian (whose chief contribution was what we called Christian's disease but now is known as calcific aortic stenosis), S. Bert Wolbach (who had just performed an autopsy on a patient who had succumbed after medical therapy for that disease) and Merrill Sosman (the radiologist-in-chief who had his office walls lined with stethoscopes he had collected from internists who failed to make proper diagnoses of chest diseases). Professor Wolbach, who had done the autopsy, showed the calcific valve that had led to death. Then, as he held up a long surgical needle, with considerable harrumphing said in a loud voice, "And now, Dr. Sosman, you took an X-ray of the abdomen, but failed miserably when you did not find this needle in the pancreas." Dr. Sosman examined the X-ray film of the abdomen very carefully, and retorted "You are right, Dr. Wolbach, but on the film I see two needles in the pancreas."

Very close friendships were formed during that year. My dissecting partners were Wesley Spink, Jim Sterner and Jack Thro. Ultimately, Wes became the world expert in brucellosis, Jim rose to be an authority in occupational medicine as chief medical officer of the Kodak empire and Jack worked himself to death running a small proprietary hospital in Hamilton, NY.

During the summer of the first year in medical school, I lived in the lovely seaside town of Nonquitt, a few miles south of New Bedford. In this community of wealthy families, I was an attendant for a gentleman who had multiple sclerosis. We swam in Buzzards Bay daily and often drove along the shore in the afternoons. The sparkling wavelets and the deep blue sky introduced me for the first time to the joys of living near the ocean with its ever changing views.

The second year opened with a semester course in pathology. The professors—Bert Wolbach, Frank Mallory and Shields Warren—were outstanding. The diagnosis of diseases by means of the microscope elevated the importance of this specialty to an Olympian level. Pathologists provided final decisions in the great majority of fatal illnesses after autopsies.

We had two examinations in pathology during the year; they involved diagnosis by study of microscopic specimens. In the mid-semester test we were given two slides. One of them appeared to be a benign adenofibroma of the breast. However, I managed to find six mitoses after a careful search of many microscopic fields; therefore I called the specimen a cancer of the breast. Unfortunately, such diligence led to an erroneous decision and a grade of 50% on the examination with a corresponding deflation of my ego. For the final examination we again had two slides. One of them was a lymph node with obvious inflammation. I thought I detected sufficient evidence to say the infection was due to typhoid fever. Such a rare diagnosis was not even considered by the pathologists in the Harvard hospital from which the specimen had been obtained a few days earlier. It was very comforting to have the diagnosis of typhoid fever made six weeks after our examination by further blood tests. Rumors became extant at that moment that the only grades of A in the class were given to Dr. Robert Fienberg, who later became a professor of pathology, and to me.

However, the most exciting part of the year was our introduction to patients. At the start of the second semester we were told to buy equipment in preparation for examination of patients. Stethoscopes became badges of distinction and, dangling from the neck, replaced Phi Beta Kappa keys. Some of my colleagues found that the nubile young women in Wellesley College were greatly impressed by this method of extra-curricular physical examination.

Students were divided into groups of eight and assigned to one of the three major hospitals for instruction in medicine and surgery. The Boston City Hospital, the Peter Bent Brigham Hospital and the Massachusetts General Hospital were available for this purpose. My group went first for introduction to surgery in the Boston City Hospital.[1]

The BCH at that time was an impressive hospital. It was located in a safe and stable neighborhood. We could park our car anywhere with complete trust that no damage would be done to it while we were in the hospital. In contrast, I can recall one day sixty years later when I planned to walk from the New England Medical Center to the BCH. I was told it was dangerous to go alone for those few blocks, even in the daytime. The descent of this section of the city into barbarism in 1990 was due chiefly to drugs and guns. Rejuvenation of the BCH by extensive rebuilding, now under consideration, hopefully will help to restore its past glory.

Three medical schools—Boston University, Harvard and Tufts—staffed the hospital in 1930 and used it for the teaching of medical students. House officers and medical students were treated very well in the BCH. There was a fine residence for the house officers with a squash court and excellent meals. In the course of my years in medical school I learned a great deal about the strengths and weaknesses of this institution. The Boston City Hospital then was a marvelous site for teaching medical students.

For example, one day we were given a clinic in surgery by a young professor, Edward Churchill. We were tremendously impressed by his demonstration of a patient who had been cured of staphylococcal pericarditis by surgery—a feat almost unheard of in those days. There were great physicians as well. Professor Soma Weiss soon left for the Peter Bent Brigham Hospital to succeed Henry Christian, just as Professor Churchill later went to the MGH as the John Homans Professor of Surgery.

Soma Weiss once was faced on ward rounds with a difficult diagnostic problem. A man had obstruction at the lower end of the esophagus that could have been due either to spasm or cancer. We all trooped into the fluoroscopy room with the radiologist. Barium, given by mouth, would not pass into the stomach. Because atropine would relieve spasm, in his Hungarian accent Dr. Weiss said "Gif him some atropine." The barium did not move. Again, "Gif him some atropine!" A double dose was given. "GIF HIM SOME ATROPINE!" was followed by an intravenous shot of atropine that would have been sufficient to supply an elephant. The barium was stationary; the diagnosis of cancer became obvious.

Another famous professor was Chester Keefer. He was an excellent bedside teacher. Once, in such a discussion of basal rales in the lungs, he referred us to a recent article on the subject in the *South African Medical Journal*. (At that time South Africa was essentially unknown in America.) He was an omniverous reader; his encyclopedic knowledge of medical literature and immediate application were very impressive. Some years later, during World War II, he was in complete charge of dispensing the minute amounts of the new drug penicillin to a relatively few of the hundreds of patients who could have benefited from it.

The BCH was the first hospital that I saw as a student. Perhaps that is one reason that it deeply impressed me. My classmates and I were astonished by the complexity of the institution, by the mixture of order and disorder, by the unusual illnesses, .the profusion of patients, pathological specimens, and autopsies. All of the house officers were working night and day trying to care for the hordes of the ill.

As students, we worked up patients and did physical examinations. Even though some patients had been in the hospital before, their records almost never could be found because of the disarray in that department. We had long rounds on the wards with such physicians as Soma Weiss, Chester Keefer, Edwin Locke or Henry Jackson. We heard the word "Thorndike" uttered with great respect.[2]

Many of the wards at the BCH were primitive in their accommodations. A large open room held nearly forty patients, separated only by curtains or movable screens. Examinations at night had to be done with the aid of flashlights.

I once was asked to examine a ward patient with pneumonia. I was escorted through a locked door into large rooms presided over by a genuine Amazon and her brawny male attendants. The ward was filled with alcoholic male patients who either were stark naked or nearly so. Some were ambling or staggering aimlessly around the beds; others were in restraints. Corners in alcoves were mistaken for bathrooms. Barred windows prevented escape. The sight was not a pretty one, but these patients, often homeless, were given shelter and food by a society that in some ways was more beneficent than ours is today.

Another ward of nearly 40 patients was filled with girls or young women, many of whom were quite attractive. They all were suffering from pelvic inflammatory disease due to gonorrhea. Nearly all of them either had had a complete removal of uterus, tubes and ovaries or were scheduled for the same operation in a few days. Today, of course, gonorrhea can be cured by penicillin but, then, it was one way that Nature provided a crude form of birth control for these unfortunate girls who soon would suffer from the severe effects of a surgical menopause.

Surgical wards contained many chronically ill patients. Chronic osteomyelitis was common. These open infected wounds were treated with maggots which, applied to the open ulcers, would live on necrotic tissues. Burns were covered by a mixture of three brilliantly colored dyes that would form a crust on the surface of the burn. This mixture of red, green and purple dyes did seem to reduce the amount of infection, but early skin grafting was far in the future.

Many memories stand out from that year. One urologist was trying to pass filiform catheters through a urethral stricture in a man whose bladder was the size of a six month pregnancy; the stream of oaths from the surgeon failed to help. I departed, wondering why he did not do a cystostomy. The same surgeon, showing us how to do a cystoscopy on a strapping young man while his entourage included a woman from a neighboring school, commanded her to keep her eyes focused on the cystoscope. One of our group was asked for the diagnosis of a large tumor of the lip. After some cogitation he pronounced it to be a "lip-o'-ma".

In our first semester in the BCH one group of students would examine patients on a given ward. On the following day the same patients would be examined by another set of students. Once, a man with a rare anomaly—his heart was in the right rather than the left side of the chest—was examined by the first group; none of the students made the diagnosis but they carefully remembered the location of the bed. That evening this information was relayed to the second group. So on the following day one of the medical students identified the bed and made the brilliant diagnosis of a right-sided heart. He was wrong, of course, because the resident in charge of the ward had cagily moved the patient's bed during the night.

In June 1930, at the end of my second year in HMS, I moved to the Huntington Hospital, where I served as resident for one year. Immediately after, I left for Ray Brook Sanatorium in New York. Dr. Churchill had arranged for me to spend the summer there. This institution, located near Saranac, had 500 beds for patients with early pulmonary tuberculosis. Six students from various medical schools gathered there during the summer months to learn about the disease; they possessed the only intact lungs in the sanatorium. On the night after our arrival a student from Cornell asked me to examine his chest. I heard apical rales—the only time I have found this sign of tuberculosis in my life. The student was Lauren Ackerman, and he changed his status from student to patient. This setback did not prevent him from beating me on the golf course day after day or from spending half of the night listening to classical music—or, for that matter, going on to have a remarkable career as a pathologist.

Medical school was expensive, even in those days. Inasmuch as I was paying my own way, I was fortunate to receive several scholarships. Work in the Huntington Hospital and the Boston City Hospital as well as summer employment paid for room and board during the last three years. Tuition was expensive but did not begin to compare with today's charges. Although I had to borrow some money from the school during my third and fourth years, I was able to pay all of this back before the end of my surgical residency. We had no huge charge for professional liability insurance which young doctors must pay today as they start practice. I have always felt that Harvard Medical School was very generous in that time of need and gave me far more than I have been able to return to it during my professional years.

During our third year in medical school my fellow students and I were educated in obstetrics. This course involved a series of lectures, observation of one or more deliveries, and then deliveries of a minimum of twelve patients by each student. These deliveries were made at home in certain specified geographical areas, or districts. The center to which I was assigned was mainly in South Boston, with its base of operations on Columbia Road.

The preliminary observation of a birth in the Boston Lying-In Hospital, adjacent to HMS, was not a trivial matter, in contradistinction to today, when it seems that nearly every grade-school boy knows all the details of female anatomy and physiology. For many males, activities such as a birth were carried out in terra incognita. During their first observation of such a hair-raising event most students usually either turned green, had to be assisted from the room by a nurse, or fainted.

Thereafter we were sent to the district in which we were to serve. Cooped up in an old house that served as headquarters, we disguised our nervousness by playing penny ante and waiting for a phone call, which could come any hour of the day or night informing us that another patient was about to give birth. Four students answered these calls in rotation. Patients had already been screened in the Lying-In outpatient clinic. Only those known to have had one or more pregnancies and presumed to be good risks were assigned to students. In theory, a Lying-In resident was to be either with us or available for any emergency; in practice we never saw him.

These deliveries furnished some of the most memorable and frightening scenes in my life. The blithe pronouncement by some unintelligent individuals that birth is always a natural and safe procedure was little comfort to me given the possibilities of a placenta previa, a ruptured uterus, an abnormal presentation of the fetus, life-threatening hemorrhage, or other unmentionable complications. Nor did the agony of the patient, and a husband frightened as much as the doctor (who was trying to maintain a professional mien despite his total lack of experience and his knowledge that the nearest telephone was at least a block or two away in the darkness), contribute to total composure on the part of any of the participants. Fortunately, despite these worries, most of these births proceeded relatively smoothly. We soon learned, however, that babies do not just drop out, but sometimes require several days to arrive and repeated trips by the medical student. Waiting spawns the necessary equanimity that is demanded of a doctor, even though he is shivering in his boots.

One night an emergency distress call came from another student. The baby was stuck; he needed help; the supervising resident could not be found; would I come in a hurry? Our professor had taught us that "in case of fire use the nearest exit" (which translated, meant to do a Caesarian if an emergency occurs.) This lesson might have been of value in a hospital but not in a home. Quickly starting up the Model T Ford kept for such emergencies, I dashed off into the night, found the proper street and house, and encountered a monstrously large woman weeping and yelling, the head of the baby visible but not moving, and the student doctor wringing his hands. I speedily jumped on top of the bed above the woman. Despite worries about rupturing the uterus, I pushed and pushed; she did her best to strain, and the other student did some manipulation. There was a sudden cry of relief as the baby popped out, still viable, and the mother was found to be intact as well. We were congratulating ourselves when the resident belatedly arrived and gave us quite a lecture. The other student and I were crestfallen but that oration must have made the resident feel better.

It is apparent that delivering babies as we did at that time has nothing in common with delivery in a hospital where there is a team of experts available to lend advice or help whenever it is needed. We were taught independence and innovation and learned the importance of the doctor-patient relationship.

During my fourth year in the medical school I lived in the BCH, where I had the title of assistant on the pneumonia service.[3] This

unusual appointment requires an explanation. At that time pneumonia
was a frequent and fatal disease. A great deal of clinical and laboratory
research was carried out on methods of control as well as treatment of
established cases. These duties were assumed by an outstanding group
of investigators in the Thorndike laboratories, among them Max Finland, Tinsley Harrison and William Castle. Infections were studied
by Dr. Finland; he delegated the responsibility of studies on the
pneumococcus to Dr. W. D. Sutliffe, who in turn appointed a resident
to serve during daytime and on alternate nights. I covered on the
nights he was not on duty. Any patient who came into the hospital
and was suspected of having pneumonia was seen by one of us. When
on call I obtained a sputum sample, and injected it into the peritoneal
cavity of a mouse. I killed the mouse four hours later, and examined
the peritoneal exudate under the microscope. If I found pneumococci
they were typed and, if the type was treatable I administered the
intravenous medication immediately. Thus, many sleepless nights ensued as well as some important lessons, of which I shall mention only
two.

One night a young girl arrived by ambulance. The nurses called me
to the emergency ward. I did not have enough sense to realize that
the patient was close to death because of laryngeal diphtheria and that
I should do an immediate tracheostomy. I never will forget her blue
face and the straining muscles of chest and neck as she tried to breathe.
We put her back on the ambulance to be taken immediately to the
South Department, where such cases were treated. It was only a block
away, but she died before she got there. I learned I should not delay
life-saving therapy even though it lay outside my responsibility.

At another time an extremely sick black man in the prime of life,
too ill to turn over in bed, turned out to have Type 1 pneumonia. A
rapid sensitivity test was negative and I quickly administered the life-
saving serum. He dashed out of bed, opened a window and tried to
breathe enough air to keep alive despite this tremendous allergic
reaction. Fortunately I was sensible enough to give him an unusually
large dose of intravenous adrenaline immediately and he recovered.
The lesson I learned was to have adrenaline on hand whenever a
potentially allergenic substance is injected intravenously.

In the last three months of my fourth year and the succeeding three
after my graduation prior to starting the internship in the MGH I
was able to combine an elective course in pathology with a residency
in the pathology department in the Boston City Hospital. This was a

large department under the charge of the famous Frank Mallory. Of the large group of assistants in the laboratory at least a third of them later came down with tuberculosis. The building must have been permeated with tubercle bacilli.

Every day agar plates were smeared with sputum samples and with throat cultures. On one morning I found such a plate covered with numerous colonies of staphylococci except for one big blank spot. I asked the technician what was wrong. She said, "Oh, that is some mold that killed the staphylococci." The date was 1932. None of us were alert enough to realize the significance of that simple observation. The British scientist Alexander Fleming had made a similar observation in 1928 but many years passed before he and others turned the mold into a commercial product: in 1945 Fleming, Florey, and Chain received the Nobel prize for their discovery of penicillin.

Professor Mallory was an expert par excellence in gross and microscopic pathology. He was a model of equanimity. I can recall only one time when he was angry. One of the residents, during an autopsy, had discovered a liver that closely resembled a sea sponge. In an attempt to find out what was wrong, he hacked it into smaller and smaller pieces. He finally took one of the remnants to Dr. Mallory for advice. Dr. Mallory turned livid and growled, "Young man, you have just succeeded in destroying a very rare specimen of actinomycosis of the liver."

Another time a resident thought he would spice up the tedium of the laboratory, so he sliced an oyster, made microscopic slides of the sections and mixed the oyster slices in with the assorted specimens of the day. Dr. Mallory recognized the oyster at once and remarked that nobody had tried that trick on him for ten years.

The old pathology building was replaced a few years later by a fine new structure. It was dedicated by Mayor Curley. This unusual man had the distinction of being elected to office while in jail. On the other hand he was a one man Health, Education, and Welfare Department for the city of Boston. By one tactic or another he redistributed generous amounts of money from the wealthy to the poor and was a great friend of the BCH. He was scheduled to dedicate the building at 2 P.M. on a certain day. The amphitheater was packed. At the appointed hour the Mayor had not appeared. At 2:10 there was no Mayor Curley. At 2:20 no Mayor had arrived to still the restless crowd that was rapidly becoming bitter rather than enthusiastic. Finally, at 2:35 Curley dashed in. He either was, or appeared to be, flustered and out of breath. He gasped and slowly gained enough strength to say, "Ladies and gentlemen, I am so sorry to be late. I have been arguing with the City Council and I have just obtained a generous block of funds for the City Hospital." The angry crowd, now pacified, broke into cheers.

During my years as a student at HMS there were many small societies. Many of them were social clubs similar in form and function to college fraternities. They were not very active then; and since that time nearly all have disappeared. The Aesculapian Club over the years has changed its function from a group that formerly organized a yearly show to one that now furnishes many needed services to the medical school. The organization most deeply concerned with scientific pursuits, the Boylston Medical Society, has maintained its admirable goals ever since.

It was at one of these Boylston Society meetings that two persons who were destined to become pillars of American surgery decided to spice up the heavy decorum of the after-dinner speech. Bert Dunphy, who later became a Professor of Surgery at Harvard and at the University of California in San Francisco, invited a guest, a famous professor from mid-Africa, to the occasion. Suddenly, as the reader of the evening's lecture was droning on and many of the audience were napping comfortably, a cry arose. "The Guest Professor is ill!" The African had blossomed with a violent eruption that Dunphy immediately diagnosed as virulent smallpox. Pandemonium reigned, for no disease was more dreaded. Just as everyone was rushing for escape through doors or windows, someone discovered that the famous professor showed a very close—in fact identical—resemblance to a fellow medical student, George Crile, Jr.—familiarly called Barney.

The greatest scholastic honor at that time was to be elected to Alpha Omega Alpha. Five juniors were chosen by the faculty in their third year; they presumably had the highest grades in the class. I was one of them and was elected president for the following year. In our senior year these five students elected another eleven persons; in these final selections, grades furnished only one of several criteria.

The Alpha Omega Alpha Chapter in Harvard was dissolved when the stigma of elitism was placed upon such organizations during the years of student unrest in the late 1960s. Other individuals argued that overemphasis on grades also can lead to competition that is destructive of more important values such as compassion, devotion to a noble cause, or modesty, that cannot be assessed in such a simple way.

Perhaps another method could be chosen. For example, I recall that in our graduation book a dozen individuals were cited, with tongue in cheek, for nomination to the Hall of Fame. My name was there because of my ability as a poker player. From a pragmatic point of view, election to AOA did not guarantee future fame in the HMS Class of '32; in retrospect there appears to be little difference between the contributions of AOA members to the profession in comparison with other members of the class.

However, in my opinion, it is unfortunate that the AOA Chapter no longer exists at Harvard. It stimulated students to excel in scholastic pursuits. Today, when all or nearly all medical schools have such chapters, the implication is that it is more important to be a Harvard graduate than a member of AOA from another school. That attitude certainly does not apply to selection of residents in surgery in many large hospitals in the U.S.A. such as the MGH. Only a few residents can be chosen each year from hundreds of applicants from many schools throughout the country. These applicants always have sterling recommendations from deans and other physicians. Election to AOA is much more objective evidence that a student is likely to succeed in his chosen field.

By the time we were ready to graduate from Harvard Medical School our class recognized that we had received a superb education in the science of medicine. We did, however, have little concept of many of the other aspects of the discipline that makes medicine one of the so-called noble professions. Our knowledge, although we considered it broad, actually was shallow in certain important respects. We knew very little for example, concerning the history of medicine and surgery. Then, again, our relationships were bounded by the walls of HMS and we lacked a global view. Although we had learned the importance of the doctor-patient relationship, we had had very little chance to develop our skills because contacts usually were brief.

Judged by today's standards, our education had other defects as well. One was the minimal attention paid to ethics. Although all of us mouthed the Hippocratic Oath we recognized its defects and were happy to learn that most authorities, including Garrison, believed the oath was not written by the great physician. Nevertheless it served for centuries as the sole codification of ethical standards for physicians. Today a far different statement is appropriate.

One particular feature, not emphasized but underlying the conduct of nearly all physicians from the time of Hippocrates, was their dominance in all decisions concerning medicine. For example, we were taught in pharmacology that, whenever or wherever we wrote prescriptions, they had to be honored by pharmacists. Even a sheet of toilet paper could qualify, if it were signed by a physician. Today we must prescribe only on certain forms; some state departments of health require that duplicates or even triplicates of all prescriptions must be deposited in state offices. Physicians detest this ruling chiefly because they believe it to be an infringement on their privileges. Doctors of medicine in 1932 were almost entirely free of harassment by lawyers, the courts, the Federal Trade Commission, legislative bodies and the public. Voluntary examinations were given by the National Board of Medical Examiners and were accepted by State Boards of Medicine as qualifications for licensure.

At graduation, I gradually began to realize that I alone was responsible for my future. No longer were the coming years a clearly programmed progression from one class or teaching institution to another. I was on my own and it was up to me to expand the vistas of medicine and surgery. At that time, further education was required only for specialty qualification; life-long medical education as we know it today was far in the future. In essence, a student graduating from medical school in 1932 was guaranteed few external controls, adulation by a public blissfully ignorant of medical facts, and a reasonable living. It is no wonder that many doctors considered themselves to be at least minor gods in the pantheon.

In my case, it was obvious that a rude awakening was imminent. It occurred when my final oral examination for honors included a question asking me to name the most recent recipient of the Nobel prize in medicine. Of course, all of the examiners knew the answer and probably considered themselves to be putative candidates for the honor. I did come out with an answer "Landsteiner", which happened to be correct but it was a pure guess. I realized at that moment that the domain of medicine was far more extensive than the medical school quadrangle.

In retrospect it is obvious that our professors did their best to inoculate us with respect for many of these broader issues. But youth does not recognize, or tends to disregard history and lessons of the past. And it is difficult for the novitiate to grasp the magnitude of the interaction of medicine with other professions, the public, the government and individual patients.

Professor "Duffy" Lewis, our first-year professor in histology, indulged his interest in history by telling students about famous anatomists and histologists. For nearly half of every lecture in histology he turned out the lights and in the pitch-black room showed slide after slide of noted scientists. Our class napped comfortably. His colleague—Dr. Lewis Bremer—often sat in the back row during these lectures. One day, while the lights were extinguished, a mighty crash sounded from the rear of the room. Professor Bremer not only had fallen asleep but had tumbled out of his chair into the aisle. This episode diminished our respect for the history of medicine. It took many years for me to realize that Professor Lewis was right and that much pleasure and knowledge can be gained from a study of medical history.

Our professor of pharmacology, Reid Hunt, also emphasized how heavily his specialty relied on past experiences. He spent day after day, week after week, talking in class about the anesthetic ether. We learned in detail about the discovery of the drug, the first use of it by Dr. Crawford Long in Georgia, the first public demonstration in the MGH in 1846, and the great controversy concerning the precedence of discovery that later was waged in the press and even in the halls of Congress. He ended his long lecture with a story about the statue in the Boston Public Garden that commemorated the discovery. The great controversy concerning precedence was solved by dedicating the work to *ether* rather than to *either.*

When not discussing ether, he expounded on the value of rhubarb, with which he had cured Egyptian epidemics of diarrhea as a young man. It is true that very few drugs were available for the use of physicians at that time. Entries in the tiny booklet listing drugs available in the MGH were limited chiefly to aspirin, quinine, insulin, digitalis, nitroglycerine, morphine, codeine, terpin hydrate, sodium bicarbonate, and numerous laxatives. No wonder that half of our class opted to become surgeons rather than to be limited, as other medical practitioners were, to this meager supply of medicines.

But Professor Hunt had again emphasized to us the value of history. Most drugs were sanctified by long usage; insulin, introduced in 1922, was an exception. Though he did not say so, it seemed clear that new horizons should be set for pharmacologists, and some of the most dramatic advances in the remainder of the century would be in this field.

Another person who extended the horizons of medical students was Professor Milton Rosenau, a distinguished leader in the field of preventive medicine and public health. He demonstrated the methods by which a whole community or a nation could provide certain features of medical care and conquer epidemics. In his course every student was expected to carry out a sanitary survey of a single town, make numerous investigations, and submit a detailed written report. I chose the city of Norwood and investigated the water supply, sewage disposal, and other public health functions. Such an assignment was stimulating and informative. It was a vivid demonstration to every student that a great deal can be accomplished by measures directed to masses of people and that a one-to-one relationship of physician and patient is not always necessary to obtain beneficial results. Perhaps more important, Rosenau expanded our purely parochial interests into global concerns.

A retrospective view in 1990 indicates that, in addition to the satisfaction and honor gained by practicing physicians, many of our class have achieved fame in other ways. Mark Altschule, called by some the epitome of clinical investigators, author of many books, a brilliant teacher, an iconoclast and collector of art, spent much of his time in later years supporting the Countway Library. Henry Beecher, originally trained as a surgeon, became the first Professor of Anesthesia in the United States, with the Harvard title of the Henry Isaiah Dorr Professor of Research in Anesthesia, and made other contributions to medicine; he chaired the Harvard Commission that defined brain death, and, with Dr. Altschule, wrote a detailed history of HMS.[4] David Cogan devoted his professional life to research in ophthalmology; after he retired from his professorship in HMS he continued his work in Washington, D.C. Seebert Goldowsky, originally a surgeon, later became editor of the *Rhode Island Medical Journal* and the author of an extraordinarily fine biography of the Rhode Island surgeon Usher Parsons. Lester King has a detailed history of the American Medical Association (AMA) among his many scholarly publications. John Longacre became a well-known plastic surgeon and a collector of rare books, which he subsequently gave to the Countway Library. George Marcy, an orthopedic surgeon, was and is a very generous contributor to scholarship funds for HMS. Augustus Rose, a world-famous neurologist, built an exceedingly strong department at UCLA, and in his later years, served as a Distinguished Physician for the Veterans' Administration. Wesley Spink became one of the Distinguished Professors at the University of Minnesota. James "Bud" Stillman, by a very fine gift, provided nearly half of the funds required to build the Center for Medical Education at HMS. Carl Walter, surgeon, inventor and philanthropist, was extraordinarily successful in his multiple vocations and has donated most generously to the medical school both in time and money. His ability to solve problems was manifest early in his period of training in the Peter Bent Brigham Hospital.[5] There is no doubt but that he is the individual in our class who has done the most for HMS. His portrait hangs in the auditorium of the Center for Medical Education.

This list of contributions to the science and practice of medicine and surgery is respectable. In addition, very few of our members deserted the practice of medicine except when disease forced early retirement. One is still in active practice—Edward Budnitz is a cardiologist in Worcester, MA. Members of the class also have been very generous contributors to HMS. We have felt extreme loyalty to the school, and believe that we received the best education in the best medical school in the world.

These results probably would not have been expected in 1932. We graduated in the midst of the Great Depression. At that time it would have seemed likely that the great majority of students, faced with straitened finances, would have turned immediately to general practice as physicians and surgeons to provide a ready source of income. Perhaps the depression actually spurred us to greater accomplishments. It is possible that today's medical graduates who also face uncertain futures can gain some comfort from our experience.

4

A Brief Glance at Medicine and Surgery in the MGH and the United States Prior to 1932

It was 1932. I was about to join the staff of the Massachusetts General Hospital and to enter into the real world. Unfortunately I knew little about either one. I did not know that the institution where I was destined to spend the rest of my professional life already had a long and interesting history. What follows are some of the facts that I acquired over many years. For convenience sake in delineating the important and sometimes fascinating events I have chosen two dates as markers: 1900, the beginning of the present century, and 1932, when I became an intern.

The MGH prior to 1900

Hospitals that opened prior to the MGH in the United States include the Charity Hospital in New Orleans, which was founded in 1736 when Louisiana belonged to France, the Pennsylvania Hospital in Philadelphia (1751), and the New York Hospital (1771).[1]

The MGH received its charter from the State of Massachusetts on February 25, 1811; this date is accepted as that of the hospital's founding. However, not until 1821 were the central portion and east wing of the Bulfinch building opened for the care of indigent patients. The first patient had secondary syphilis; he therefore was a medical admission. There was no great rush of patients despite publicity put out by John C. Warren, first acting and then visiting surgeon from 1817 to 1853. The second patient arrived three weeks later; he was a sailor with a huge mass of prolapsed hemorrhoids.

In 1821 there were no true anesthetic agents; alcohol and opium merely served to dull the pain. But, as happened in this case, four strong men held the patient on his knees on his bed with his head down and the dirty operative field close to the surgeon's face. With a few quick strokes of the scalpel, the piles were removed. Convalescence required three weeks; and every day the patient had a rectal irrigation with a highly irritating copper sulfate solution. At the end of that period, he was discharged cured.

John C. Warren was the first of his family to be associated with the Massachusetts General Hospital and members of this famous family have had a close association with the hospital ever since. His portrait, along with that of his grandson, John Collins Warren, are among the six that presently hang in the Bigelow amphitheater.[2]

Dr. H. H. A. Beach, a visiting surgeon, described the horrors of operations before 1846. According to Washburn, Beach stated that these "gruesome procedures were a terrible experience for the patient and put a great strain upon the surgeon and his assistants. The patient's cries of suffering were heard in the corridors and wards, as well as in the operating room, until he became too weak to utter them."[3]

The most important event in the history of the MGH and, perhaps in any hospital in the world, according to Lipp, was the first public demonstration of ether anesthesia in 1846. He added, in 1990, "with the possible exception of Bellevue Hospital in New York, the MGH has probably been responsible for more medical breakthroughs and firsts than any other hospital. Certainly, the MGH is now the country's most prestigious hospital".[4]

It was in 1846 in the amphitheater on the top floor of the Bulfinch building in what later became known as the *Ether Dome*, John C. Warren removed a tumor composed of a venous malformation from the neck of Gilbert Abbott to whom William Thomas Morton, a dentist, was administering ether. It was then that Dr. Warren uttered the famous words "Gentlemen, this is no humbug." The word describing the procedure, *anaesthesia*, (now *anesthesia* according to Webster) was coined by Oliver Wendell Holmes, who was a visiting physician in the MGH from 1847 to 1849. Publicity of this event is attributable particularly to Henry Jacob Bigelow, who published the first report of the proceedings. In the famous portrayal of the first public demonstration of ether by Robert Hinckley, Dr. Bigelow is shown in the back of the picture, standing against the ballustrade. It was this report that first established the MGH as a world-famous institution.

In addition to anesthesia, the second important development affecting surgery in the remainder of the nineteenth century was the giant stride made in the conquest of sepsis. Koch and Pasteur discovered bacteria, and Lister proved that carbolic acid spray could practically eliminate infection in the operating room. Surgeons were sharply divided concerning Listerism, as this new practice was called. J. Collins Warren embraced it at once but Bigelow accepted it only after great delay; indeed, he may never have been convinced that it was of value.[5]

In 1888 the first ward to care for patients requiring abdominal surgery was built in the MGH. This action signified that the trustees felt the problems of sepsis had been solved. Prior to 1884 what little abdominal surgery that had been done was performed in homes or small private hospitals. The story of Arthur Tracy Cabot and the first abdominal operation done in the MGH was recounted by Frederick Shattuck.[6] He said:

In 1874 to 1875 he assisted his father in the first two successful abdominal operations connected with the Massachusetts General Hospital. They were on hospital patients, but the operations were done in a neighboring house on Allen Street. It appears that Dr. Arthur Cabot did the first successful abdominal operation within the hospital walls in 1884, on a case of large strangulated umbilical hernia. The patient had been admitted to Dr. Hodges' service. He, however, being ill, Dr. Bigelow was taking his place, and Dr. Cabot, then Surgeon to Outpatients, was assisting the latter. Dr. Cabot was called in the evening. Dr. Hodges had recently published a paper on cases of this nature, concluding that operation was always fatal, recovery occasional without operation. Dr. Cabot therefore sought Dr. Bigelow, whom he found at Dr. Hodges' house. He stated the case. Dr. Bigelow; "What do you want to do?" Dr. Cabot: "Operate." Dr. Bigelow: "Whether or not you operate he will die, therefore do as you like. Is that not so, Dr. Hodges?" Dr. Hodges: "No, if you operate he will die; if you don't he may get well." After some discussion Dr. Bigelow agreed that Dr. Cabot should do as he liked, so he returned to the hospital, operated, and in a few weeks the patient was well. In 1886, Dr. Cabot had three successful cases of laparotomy in rapid succession, one for ovarian cyst, two for fibroids.

The most famous persons associated with surgery in the last half of the nineteenth century and the MGH were Henry J. Bigelow, Reginald Fitz, and J. Collins Warren.

Just as John C. Warren was the most important surgeon in the MGH from 1821 to 1850, Henry Jacob Bigelow towered over all of his surgical contemporaries in the latter half of the century until his death in 1890. He was particularly adept in orthopedic and urologic surgery, invented many new instruments, including one to crush bladder stones, and he described the Y-ligament of Bigelow. He also was a powerful professor in the medical school who sometimes tangled with President Eliot. In 1921, when the American Medical Association met in Boston, Bigelow still was proclaimed to be the "Deity of the MGH."[7] The Bigelow Medal and lectures, named for him, were initiated in that year by William Mayo of the famous clinic. He gave a generous salute both to Dr. Bigelow and to Boston surgery.

Reginald Fitz was a pathologist in the MGH, who in 1880 bore the resounding title of *Microscopist and Curator of the Pathological Cabinet.* In 1886 he earned the everlasting gratitude of surgeons when he was the first person to describe appendicitis; shortly thereafter he also was the first person to describe pancreatitis.

J. Collins Warren, who bridged the last portion of the nineteenth and the first part of the twentieth century, not only was an excellent surgeon and a president of the American Surgical Association, but was responsible for the erection of the imposing Harvard Medical School in 1906. At a later date he also raised funds to erect the Collis P. Huntington Memorial Hospital for cancer patients, and for Vanderbilt Hall, the dormitory for HMS students.

The MGH from 1900 to 1932

In the year 1900 the MGH and the Boston City Hospitals were the only two large hospitals in Boston. They catered entirely to charity patients. Most of the MGH patients paid nothing toward the weekly costs of $15.05. Some paid part of the expenses, and a very few paid all of the charges.

The century was ushered in by the erection of a modern operating suite named in honor of Henry J. Bigelow who had died in 1890. This suite, located in a separate building, served until 1937 when the new operating rooms in the White building came into service. The memorial building named for Bigelow then was razed. Dr. Bigelow's bronze bust survived, and was moved to the surgical lecture hall in the White building where it still stands. In addition, the Bigelow medal award, to which I have already referred, was established by the

Boston Surgical Society in 1921, providing future generations with a continuing stimulus from the past.

In 1900, the average daily census in the MGH was 261; nine and a half percent of the patients died in that year. The average length of stay was twenty days. Despite Billroth's opening of the field of abdominal surgery in 1881, the MGH lagged far behind. In 1900, only nine cancers of the stomach were operated on and only one gastric resection was done; this patient died. Six cancers of the rectum were excised by a posterior approach. Only six cholecystectomies were done (with two deaths) compared with twenty-nine cholecstostomies. Appendicitis was by far the most important abdominal surgical disease. There were 109 appendectomies for acute appendicitis with eleven deaths. General peritonitis due to a ruptured appendix was encountered in thirty-seven cases with twenty-seven deaths. These statistics proved that there was need for great improvement in surgery.

Several other very important changes had been made before 1932. The Phillips House, designed for wealthy patients, opened in 1917. Persons with moderate means finally were served by the erection of the Baker Memorial in 1929 and the agreement of the professional staff to moderate their charges for these individuals. Additional operating rooms became available in both of these buildings. Interns and residents were not allowed to participate in the care of Phillips House patients for many years, although they were welcome in the Baker.

During the period from 1900 to 1932 a few surgeons were outstanding. One who was not appreciated at the time, but whose contributions have been greatly appreciated at a later date, was E. Amory Codman. Maurice Richardson and Samuel Mixter were the most famous general surgeons. They (and Sam's sons, Jason and Charles, as well) lived through the era of peripatetic surgery performed on kitchen tables, and they truly were "general surgeons" in the full sense of the word. Both of them became presidents of the American Surgical Association, which had become the premier organization in the United States; at that time nearly all of its members were general surgeons.

Maurice Richardson was a man of enormous stature and strength as well as a famous teacher. He was a dynamic, enthusiastic teacher who could draw with both hands simultaneously on the blackboard during his lectures. He was an excellent technician and also as a typical itinerant surgeon, was called far and wide to operate in homes. He once walked from Fitchburg to the top of Mount Monadnock and back in one day, a distance of sixty miles. He was appointed as the first MGH chief of the surgical service in 1912, but died suddenly after a hard day's work in the operating room a few weeks later. The position of chief surgeon lapsed with his death.

But times were changing. In 1910 the medical service had sensed the need for clinical investigation. Science was burgeoning, largely due to the influence of Halsted and Welch in the Hopkins. David Edsall was called from Philadelphia to head the east medical service in 1912. This was a great break in tradition because nepotism was common; surgeons did not appreciate this transition. The MGH trustees took charge, established surgical laboratories, and placed Edward P. Richardson in charge in 1925. Unfortunately, illness soon led to his retirement. Edward Churchill, the next in line to fill the post of chief of the west surgical service, proved to be a fortunate choice.

Meanwhile the east surgical service continued to be dedicated to excellent clinical care, due to the support of such individuals as Daniel F. Jones—who also was president of the American Surgical Association—and his young assistants Leland McKittrick and Richard Sweet.

During this thirty-year period the MGH also could claim several other firsts. James Homer Wright, a pathologist, made important discoveries concerning the origin and function of blood platelets. He also stimulated laboratory investigation, particularly of staining techniques.

Robert Greenough, a surgeon, and George Holmes, a radiologist, established the first in-hospital cancer clinic in the MGH in the United States in 1925. This venture, which served as a successful prototype for other clinics throughout the country, is discussed in more detail in Chapter 10.

The first in-hospital social service was established in the MGH by Richard Cabot and Miss Ida Cannon in 1905. It soon became an essential department of all hospitals in the country. Richard Cabot also established his famous clinical-pathological conferences; these studies have been published in the *New England Journal of Medicine* since 1923.

Thus the MGH made many important changes between 1900 and 1932, and was moving forward with increasing momentum into the future.

American medicine and surgery in 1900

In 1900 American medicine lagged far behind that practiced in Europe or Great Britain. In the next thirty years it began to gather strength and proved capable to undertake the tremendous advances that were to follow the introduction of antibiotics and modern anesthesia in the thirties.

Life expectancy in the United States was 49.3 years in 1900, 10 years greater in 1930, and 75.6 in 1990. This increase can be ascribed chiefly to such social and public health factors as good nutrition, improved hygiene, pure water and control of pests. Physicians contributed in the early years of the century, particularly by treatment of infections and trauma.

In 1900 there were three or four doctors in the town of Stanton. This number may seem excessive, but house calls both in the town and the surrounding countryside by horse and buggy took a great deal of time. Each doctor had his own office, where he dispensed pills and carried out minor surgery. He delivered patients in their homes. There were no hospitals closer than Norfolk, which was twelve miles distant. I do not recall there were any professional midwives in the town though there must have been many knowledgable amateurs. A husband occasionally was enlisted to put a few drops of chloroform on a handkerchief for his wife to sniff to reduce labor pains. Unless deliveries were rapid, a physician could spend a day or two in some distant farm home. That situation changed rapidly with the advent of automobiles. By 1944 there were only two physicians and one chiropractor in the town.

Infections of many types were the scourge of childhood. My earliest memory of a physician occurred when, as a child of six, I became very ill with pneumonia. I was unconscious for several weeks, but finally began to realize the doctor was making daily visits to my sick room. In 1990, pneumococcal pneumonia is treated with penicillin and is cured within a few days.

At a later date I acquired one of the ubiquitous staphylococcal infections. This was a felon. The doctor froze the skin of my finger with ethyl chloride, made a swift incision down to the bone and released the pus that was under pressure. I retain the impression that many of those early physicians and surgeons were more resourceful and effective than many specialists are today.

The most serious infection of all was smallpox. It was the only one that could be prevented. Jenner's method of inoculating a person with cowpox vaccine had proved effective. Pockmarked faces were common results if non-vaccinated patients survived. When I was in medical school patients with smallpox were rare; they were isolated in the

South Department of the Boston City Hospital. In 1943 I saw cases of the disease in the pest house in Casablanca, Morocco. Due to strenuous efforts to isolate all cases with the disease, it seems certain that this dreadful disease was entirely eradicated from the earth in the nineteen eighties.

Children with other childhood diseases, such as measles, mumps, chickenpox, whooping cough, German measles, diphtheria and scarlet fever were quarantined for specified periods. There was no particular therapy, so sequelae that included cardiac damage, orchitis, rare cases of meningitis and rheumatic heart disease followed occasionally.

As we played about barnyards where horses and tetanus bacilli were common, we always were very careful to avoid stepping on a rusty nail. Today, tetanus as well as nearly all the childhood diseases listed above are routinely prevented by immunizations.

Another common childhood infection was otitis media. "Running ears" were usually due to staphylococcus infections; sinusitis and mastoiditis and deafness were sequelae. Any boil located on the face above the mouth was a potential cause of thrombosis of the internal jugular vein and death.

Frequently before 1900 and every few years thereafter, an epidemic of infantile paralysis terrified some community in the United States. One of the worst occurred in 1950 when there were over 33,000 cases. Paralysis often would follow and lead to lifelong crippling. In 1953 the last of these epidemics occurred. A full ward in the MGH was filled with "iron lungs" to provide respiratory aid for those individuals with paralyzed diaphragms. It was this epidemic that led to the first respiratory ward in the nation; it was run by Dr. Henning Pontoppidan and now are found in every major hospital. Shortly after this, Enders, Weller and Robbins discovered a method to grow the virus. Two methods of prevention of the disease were discovered soon afterward. Either an oral vaccine using an attenuated virus or an inactivated (Salk) virus may be used.

Tuberculosis was rampant throughout the United States from 1900 until mid-century when antibiotics and chemotherapy became available. I knew that I had had an infection at some time, because a tuberculin test produced an extensive reaction. Two of the surgical residents soon after my time—Gordon Donaldson and Gordon Scannell—had to spend a year in a sanatorium before the disease was arrested. Nearly a third of the residents in pathology in the Boston City Hospital when I was there had the disease.

Milk was an important vehicle to spread bovine tuberculosis. This agent often led to cervical lymphadenitis and calcified mesenteric lymph nodes—diseases that we never see today. Pasteurization of milk and elimination of infected cattle has solved the problems of tuberculosis and brucellosis.

Universal skin testing in the early part of the century would have shown that nearly ninety percent of the population had been infected with tuberculosis, either human or bovine. The treatment of this major chronic disease at that time was simply fresh air and rest. The Trudeau Sanatorium in Saranac Lake, New York, was founded in 1884 and furnished these amenities including frigid winter air. It became one of the most famous in the United States. In these institutions days lapsed timelessly into weeks, months, and years, as described by Thomas Mann in *Der Zauberberg (The Magic Mountain)*. Chemotherapy by isoniazide and the antibiotic streptomycin were not introduced as a specific treatment for nearly half a century; since then the disease has not been a major threat in the United States. However, it is a serious problem in many countries, and may reemerge as a major problem in certain areas because of the AIDS epidemic.

Typhoid fever was a public health menace. Discharge of raw sewage into the Merrimack River had produced frequent epidemics successively in down-stream cities; this story was in the grade school physiology texts in the years of World War I. No drug was effective in treatment until chloramphenicol was discovered and applied in 1947.

The sexually transmitted diseases—syphilis, gonorrhea and pelvic inflammatory disease (PID) were common. In 1900 mercury was the only available therapy for syphilis until neoarsphenamine was developed. There were no specific treatments for gonorrhea; prostatitis and female sterility were frequent sequels. As late as 1930 as many as 50 patients with gonorrheal prostatitis would appear in our clinic twice a week. We would obtain a urine sample. If it was cloudy on gross examination the patient would receive an especially vigorous prostatic massage. Whether or not the treatment did any good was questionable; it did make the patient wish he had never caught the disease. In common with many other infections the depredations of gonorrhea and PID continued until specific antibiotic therapy was available late in the nineteen thirties.

Streptococcus and staphylococcus infections were extremely frequent. Even in 1930, if a young woman entered the hospital because of a septic abortion, she was likely to die if a cervical culture demonstrated streptococci. In the same year one of my classmates had a streptococcus invade an area of epidermophytosis. He developed multiple abscesses of the lower extremity, spent six weeks in the hospital and had several operations before he was cured.

Obese diabetic patients were prone to develop carbuncles of the neck. Surgical treatment required either a large cruciate incision, or excision of the infected mass with secondary skin graft. The operation had to be carried out with the patient lying on his face. The anesthetist, with a can of ether in her hand would sit beneath a sheet breathing ether vapor along with the patient as she tried to maintain an airway.

Bad teeth were very common. Men were prone to fight with bare fists. As a result many knuckles were cut by jagged teeth. Infected knuckle joints resulted unless wide drainage of the joint and tendon sheaths was carried out. These peculiarly dangerous injuries are rare today, and are rendered less dangerous because of antibiotics.

At the beginning of the twentieth century, physicians were numerous but poorly educated. In 1900 there were 119,749 physicians in the United States or 137 per 100,000 inhabitants; in 1987 there were 612,000 physicians or one for 400 inhabitants. There were 162 medical schools with 5,200 graduates in 1900; schools were usually proprietary and of very poor quality. In contrast, in 1987 in the United States 142 medical schools graduated 17,500 students. In 1900, education in medical schools consisted of attendance at lectures. A brief apprenticeship to an established physician usually followed.

Despite the fact these doctors rapidly learned how to handle the usual medical and surgical problems which they encountered, some of them did suggest unusual methods of treatment. I recall trying to fill a prescription that was written for "Acetylsalicylic acid, vert." I could recognize the aspirin part but I couldn't understand the "vert." I had to run to our competing drug store for help. I returned with a bottle of green aspirin. I assume it was much more effective than the white.

Medical education by 1900 was designed only for medical students; the concept that it is a lifelong process for the physician was many decades in the future. Medical students in Harvard in the latter part of the nineteenth century had been notoriously fractious. Charles Eliot, President of Harvard University from 1869 to 1909, fought the Old Guard and eventually prevailed. Henry Jacob Bigelow, the powerful surgeon of the MGH, led the opposition to Eliot; he maintained (I hope in jest) that the majority of Harvard students could neither read nor write. Eliot imposed far higher standards on the students, thereby establishing Harvard as one of the major medical educational institutions in the world.

For centuries hospitals had been considered to be a combination of almshouses and sites for the care of the incurable or deathly sick. The patients often were chronically ill or had psychiatric problems. Acute care general hospitals evolved slowly. In the United States the earliest ones—the Pennsylvania Hospital in Philadelphia, the New York Hospital, and the Massachusetts General Hospital were supported by private funds.

In 1900 minor surgery was carried on in physicians' offices with minimal anesthesia. Patients with very serious disease, such as appendicitis, had to be transported to a hospital if one was available in the vicinity, although some operations still were being carried out on kitchen tables by peripatetic surgeons. However, many of the large hospitals were psychiatric institutions, and many of the smaller ones were converted homes. Thus hospitals, as we know them, did not exist at that time. Because of the great fear of hospital infections (also known as "hospitalitis") hospital wards often were completely isolated from one another. This pavilion design was used as late as 1913 in Boston when the Peter Bent Brigham Hospital opened its doors.

By 1900 there were 4359 hospitals in the United States; even though there were only 178 in 1872. By 1920 there were 4013 hospitals (including psychiatric), with an average of 78 beds; the 521 psychiatric institutions, however, had an average bed capacity of 5670. Thus most of the general hospitals were small, often proprietary, and had no standards of accreditation. There was no measure of control over them until the American College of Surgeons, which was organized in 1913, assumed this major responsibility. In 1986 the United States had 6,841 hospitals.

Medicines were abundant in 1900. Usually patent medicines, they were completely uncontrolled insofar as efficacy and safety were concerned. The Food and Drug Administration did not become active until 1937.

Hence drugstores sold a great number of proprietary preparations. Sloan's liniment came in family sizes; Lydia Pinkham's Compound was great for menstrual disorders (it contained about twenty-five percent alcohol); Father John's Medicine and Beef, Wine and Iron prepared by Rexall Drug Co. were both designed to put strength back into sagging frames. Snake oil was sold by hucksters at county fairs for internal or external ills. Various herbal medicines were deemed appropriate for many purposes; at times there would be calls in the drug store for substances presumed to be abortifacients. Homeopathy—the administration of minute quantities of drugs—still claimed many supporters.

Despite the major advances that had been made particularly in Europe, relatively few abdominal operations were done in major hospitals in the United States in 1900. Amputations, particularly of legs for vascular disease and diabetes, were major procedures. Cancer, except of the skin and possibly of the breast, was generally conceded to be incurable. Halsted had had some favorable results with his radical operations for breast cancer but followup periods were short. Chest, cardiac and vascular surgery, neurosurgery and microsurgery as they exist today had not been developed.

There are no available figures on the total costs of medical or health care in the United States in 1900. In 1953 health care consumed 3.6 percent of the gross national product so logically we can assume that the figure was far lower in 1900. This figure should be contrasted with thirteen percent in 1991.

Science began to displace empiricism. The history of this striking change from previous medical practices, which were based on empiricism or slavish repetition of former procedures rather than on scientifically proven principles, has been documented fully by Wangensteen and Wangensteen.[8] The influence of science accelerated in the latter portion of the nineteenth century but failed to gain speed in the next 30 years in the United States.

In summary, American medicine in 1900 appeared to be in the doldrums. It was almost totally dependent for progress upon Austria, Germany, France, Switzerland and Great Britain. However, America could offer such surgeons as candidates for immortality as McDowell, Sims, Gross, Halsted, the Warrens and Bigelow.

But perhaps the brightest beacon of all was lit when the Johns Hopkins School of Medicine opened in 1889, with its brilliant staff: Osler in medicine, Welch in pathology, Halsted in surgery, and Kelly in obstetrics and gynecology. For the first time in our country, a baccalaureate degree as well as courses in physics, chemistry and biology were required for entry; thus medicine became a postgraduate study. Women were admitted on the same basis as men. Great emphasis was placed on science as well as on critical clinical acumen.

Medicine and surgery from 1900 to 1932

This period was one in which the numerous major technical advances which had been made in abdominal surgery from 1880–1900, particularly in Germany, Austria and France, could not be equalled in America.

Nevertheless, the period between the turn of the century and the end of the Great Depression in the thirties was a time of great excitement in the medical and surgical professions in the United States. Initial advances on a broad front promised a bright future for American medicine. Methods of medical education changed completely, hospitals were regulated and upgraded, control of several major infectious diseases was secured, the initial signs of subspecialization appeared, abdominal operations literally exploded in frequency, laboratory and radiologic methods of investigation and foundations for basic and clinical research were laid in nearly every specialty. World War I also led to notable advances.

Despite evidence that America was preparing for a leadership role in medicine, in this period it still was very common for aspiring young students or scientists to spend a year in medical laboratories in Europe or Great Britain or visiting in famous clinics. This was the same pattern that had been followed in the nineteenth century, particularly by physicians on the eastern seaboard. It was followed by the Warrens before 1900, by Edward Churchill in 1926, and Henry Beecher in 1936. Visits to Europe became much less popular as the threat of Nazi domination increased.

Medical education   The education of medical students was in need of drastic reform in 1900. Johns Hopkins was leading the campaign with an emphasis on science. Harvard was not far behind, because practically all of its medical students had received an academic degree prior to admission to medical school. But at Harvard humanism was still emphasized more than science.

The American Medical Association also recognized the need for change. Under the leadership of Arthur Dean Bevan, a great Chicago surgeon, the American Medical Association organized the Council on Medical Education in 1904. This Council has played a supervisory role over education in medical schools ever since.

In 1910 Abraham Flexner, a graduate of Johns Hopkins and Harvard, published his devastating report on the state of medical education in the United States. Under the auspices of the Carnegie Foundation, he personally surveyed and graded all of the existing schools in the country. Many of them proved to be substandard, or grade C. He recommended closure of nearly half of them.[9] The lay press took up the cudgel and schools were identified by name. Nevertheless, after many sudden changes, the final stages progressed slowly. In 1943 the last of the grade C schools—Middlesex in Massachusetts—closed its doors. By that time, the 155 medical schools that had existed in 1901 were reduced to about 60.

Although there is no question about the importance of Flexner's work, he was criticized by Beecher and Altschule for his heavy emphasis on the importance of science to the detriment of humanism and for his insistence on the full-time system in which professors devoted all of their time to clinical work and investigation in a university hospital. Flexner's system differed from the Harvard system, which charged a cluster of hospitals and part-time instructors or professors with the education of medical students.[10] Needless to say, this controversy has raged for many years.[11]

The Mayo Clinic emerged in a spectacular burst of glory during this period. It shortly became a Mecca for the postgraduate education of surgeons and a world-famous refuge for patients. All this activity was going on in the relatively unknown city of Rochester, Minnesota.

As a result of the remarkable initiative of Will and Charles Mayo and their frequent travels, which brought them in contact with the leading surgeons of the world, their local practice grew rapidly as they pioneered an unprecedented development of abdominal surgery. Their paper on 105 operations on the gallbladder had been refused for publication in 1900 by the editor of the *American Journal of Medical Sciences* as unbelievable. It was followed by a second presentation of a thousand cases in 1905; Finney, of Baltimore, declared that "this report is unequalled in the annals of surgery." Crowds of surgeons thereafter flocked to the Clinic's surgical amphitheaters to observe the master surgeons at work.[12]

The most important advances in medicine in these years were the isolation of insulin by Banting and Best in 1921, the introduction of Salvarsan (neoarsphenamine) for the treatment of syphilis in 1909 by Ehrlich, the discovery by Minot, Murphy and Whipple that liver could cure pernicious anemia and the prevention of certain infectious diseases (typhoid fever, diphtheria, and tetanus) by vaccination.

Typhoid fever continued to be endemic in many countries. A vaccine had been produced by Wright in 1897 but its value was questioned in Great Britain until a special commission in 1913 ordered that it be given to all troops who were sent abroad. The result was the essential elimination of the disease in the expeditionary forces in World War I. Thus vaccination against typhoid joined smallpox as a second disease that could be prevented by vaccination.

Tetanus was a formidable disease in the past. No method of prevention had been established even by 1920. However, an antitoxin had been developed by von Behring and Kitasato between 1890 and 1893. The first World War provided the initial opportunity to employ this antitoxin on a large scale. It was given routinely to all wounded men and proved to be highly effective.

Diphtheria had been a highly communicable and extremely serious disease for untold years. Again von Behring and Kitasato had prepared an antitoxin in 1892 that was moderately effective in reducing mortality. However it was not until 1913 when Behring introduced a vaccine-antitoxin mixture that spectacular results were obtained. The disease was not controlled in America for many years; as noted previously, I saw a patient die of laryngeal diphtheria in 1932.

A huge pandemic swept through the world in 1918–1919. It was the so-called Spanish influenza. In Boston, the courtyards of the MGH were filled with beds trying to hold the overflow from the hospital wards. Army camps were especially vulnerable. Infection, followed by death in a few days, was a common occurrence. It is estimated that the astounding number of over fifteen million people died in the world from the pandemic. Knowledge that the disease was due to a virus and specific prevention of this disease was not available for many more years.

The foundations for abdominal operations were laid from 1880 to 1900 by such giants as Billroth, Czerny, Rydigier and Mikulicz. An important technical advance from 1900 to 1920 was the introduction of combined abdominoperineal resection for cancer of the rectum by Ernest Miles in 1908. He proved that incomplete dissections of nodes in the abdomen had led to many recurrences after simple proctectomy; as a corollary many deaths could be prevented by employing his more radical dissections.

Willy Kausch was a German surgeon, relatively unknown in the United States, who practiced in Berlin. He was the first person to use five or ten percent glucose solutions intravenously in the treatment of surgical patients and reported the method in 1910. He had obtained this idea from psychiatrists who had used it in their patients for no particular reason.[13]

Kausch also introduced another remarkable technique when he carried out the first successful pancreatoduodenectomy for cancer of the ampulla of Vater in 1909. His patient lived in good health for about nine months after operation. His encyclopedic collection of data and the minute detail in which he described his care of four patients with this disease led to a model paper.[14] This operation, rediscovered and redescribed nearly 30 years later by Allen Whipple and associates, is now known as the *Whipple operation.* [15]

One of the classical experiments on intestinal obstruction was performed by Hartwell and Hoguet in 1912. They proved that death from simple obstruction of the lower duodenum in dogs was due to dehydration brought on by vomiting of fluid. When water and a small amount of electrolyte were replaced by means of clysis, the animals survived.[16]

Abdominal surgery in the early part of the twentieth century was restricted chiefly to the attempted correction of major complications of underlying diseases which, in general, were considered to have too high a mortality to warrant prophylactic operation. Thus uncomplicated peptic ulcer, gallstones or cancer of the stomach or colon were difficult to diagnose in time to have potentially curative operations. After World War II a much more aggressive attitude was assumed by surgeons.

End results of operations were studied in detail by E. Amory Codman of the MGH. In the years 1900 to 1914 his mortality following abdominal operations was seven percent.[17]

Diagnoses of abdominal diseases amenable to surgical care were impeded by the limited methods available at that time—the touch of the surgeon's hands, his evaluation of the history and physical examination, the pulse, the blood pressure, the stethoscope, the blood smear and the urine examination were essentially all the tools at his command. Barium contrast studies of the gastrointestinal tract, although used and described by Cannon in studies on animals were not used widely. It is no wonder that diagnostic errors were common.

World War I led to certain surgical advances. For the first time, it was proved that early operative treatment of penetrating abdominal wounds led to far better results than delayed or nonoperative therapy.[18] Specialties such as reconstructive and neurosurgery attained greater importance. Soldiers who did survive their war wounds with severe disfigurement often required extensive reconstructive procedures. Thus a new specialty was born; Varasted Kazanjian of Boston, trained originally as a dentist, was one of the pioneers in this new craft. Sir Harold Gillies and many others shared in this development.

Harvey Cushing was developing neurological surgery in the Peter Bent Brigham Hospital which opened in 1913; he expanded his experience in World War I. He became the father of the specialty of neurosurgery, despite his reluctance to submit to army discipline and his slow meticulous technique which he continued to use even during the rigors of war.[19]

Other surgical specialties also were in their infancy. The discoveries of Alexis Carrel in vascular surgery and transplantation, for which he received the Nobel prize in 1912, were not to bear fruit for many more years. Matas, with his interests in vascular surgery and in intratracheal anesthesia attracted few disciples. Advances were made in solution of fundamental problems such as the treatment of shock and the use of intravenous fluids. In World War I a large commission, including Walter Cannon and George Crile, studied these problems. Adequate facilities for necessary blood transfusions simply were not available. Although Landsteiner had identified the four fundamental blood groups in 1901 he did not receive the Nobel prize for his discovery until 1930.

Shortly before World War I, the increase in the number of surgeons led to a proliferation of surgical societies. Two of the major ones—the American Surgical Association (founded in 1880) and the Southern Surgical Association (1888)—existed before 1900. The Boston Surgical Society was formed in 1912, the American College of Surgeons in 1913, and the New England Surgical Society in 1917. Comparable regional societies in other portions of the country developed either simultaneously or later.

Thus the period from 1900 to 1932 saw many changes in the field of medicine. Medical education was revitalized as a result of the influence of the Johns Hopkins Medical School, the AMA and Flexner. Hospitals expanded both in number and size. Some clinics became world famous. Medical advances included Salvarsan, insulin, liver for pernicious anemia, vaccines and antitoxins and the consequent control of a number of epidemic diseases. Surgeons became more numerous and vociferous; they formed organizations of their own and began to separate themselves from general practitioners. Surgical specialties appeared; orthopedics, urology, obstetrics and gynecology, neurosurgery, and plastic and reconstructive surgery were breaking away from general surgery. Laboratory investigation and experimental animal surgery continued to displace empiricism at an accelerated pace.

American medicine, despite numerous advances, still had not reached a position of leadership by 1932. But a strong spirit of optimism prevailed. One of these optimists was the Professor of Medicine in Johns Hopkins. Osler, famous as a scientist and master clinician, also had a phenomenal gift of prophecy. In his youth he studied medicine in Vienna. When he returned there in 1908, after an absence of 34 years, he paid tribute to Germany as one of the temples that harbored the spirit of Aesculapius. He wrote:[20]

Not until she (the Aesculapian center) saw in Johannes Muller and in Rudolph Virchow true and loyal disciples did she move to Germany, where she stays in spite of tempting offers from France, from Italy, from England and from Austria. I boldly suggested that it is time to think of crossing the Atlantic and setting up her temple in the new world for a generation or two. I spoke of the many advantages, of the absence of tradition—here she visibly weakened, as she has suffered so much from this poison—the greater freedom, the enthusiasm, and then I spoke of missionary work. At these words she turned on me sharply and said: "That is not for me. We gods have but one motto—those who honor us, we honor. Give me the temples, give me the priests, give me the true worship, the old Hippocratic service of the art and of the science of ministering to man, and I will come. By the eternal law under which we gods live I would have to come. I did not wish to leave Paris, where I was so happy and where I was served so faithfully by Bichat, by Laennec and by Louis"—and tears filled her eyes; her voice trembled with emotion—"but where the worshippers are the most devoted, not, mark you, where they are the most numerous; where the clouds of incense rise the highest, there must my chief temple be, and to it from all quarters will the faithful flock. As it was in Greece, in Alexandria, in Rome, in northern Italy, in France, so it is now in Germany, and so it *may be* in the new world I long to see." Doubtless she will come, but not until the present crude organization of our medical clinics is changed, not until there is a fuller realization of internal medicine as a science as well as an art.

A full half century was to pass before Osler's dream would be fulfilled.

5

The Student Becomes a Surgeon:
Life in the MGH 1932–1937

As medical students, we had spent several months in the Massachusetts General Hospital. Although I had no idea then that essentially the remainder of my life would be centered around the MGH, I quickly learned that my mission there was a very serious one. Three of us were walking down a corridor one day laughing about some trivial matter. Suddenly a hand was clapped upon a shoulder and the director of the hospital—Colonel Washburn—thundered "Young man, there shall be no levity in the Massachusetts General Hospital!"

The Colonel had gained his title from World War I when he was the officer in charge of Base Hospital 6—the MGH volunteer unit. He topped six feet and, stiff as a ramrod, never lost his military bearing nor his sense of essentially divine authority. Every Tuesday he inspected the entire hospital. Nurses quaked in terror when he, with his retinue, marched through their wards. Short girls were particularly at risk because some dust might be hiding on the top of a cabinet at the exact level of his eyes. House officers rarely saw him except to receive some dire warnings if they committed minor peccadillos. His gimlet eyes missed nothing, as he proved when he wrote a marvelously detailed history of the hospital.[1]

In 1932, in my last year of medical school, examinations for appointments as interns were held, as I recall, in late January. I was reasonably sure that I would obtain an appointment in either the Massachusetts General or the Boston City Hospital, so I applied only to those two institutions.

My oral examination was held before a group of visiting surgeons. These men bore a title hallowed by antiquity when visiting physicians or surgeons were given this distinction to indicate they were the most important doctors on the staff and to prove they were standing on the top rung of the clinical ladder. There was a day when their predecessors had been driven to the hospital by horse and carriage to make ward rounds or to operate. They sometimes were met by house officers bearing flowers for buttonholes. By 1932 this aura of divinity had diminished but still was impressive. The chiefs of the two surgical services—Edward D. Churchill and Arthur W. Allen—led the questioning. Dr. Daniel F. Jones, a past president of the American Surgical Association and a master surgeon, also was there. I remember being quizzed in great detail about nerves—their anatomy, distribution, and surgical operations in which they were involved. The examination lasted only half an hour but it seemed to me to be an entire day.

These very stressful examinations were designed to test the limits of a student's knowledge and composure under fire. Such exercises were considered by the candidates to represent remnants of barbarism. No doubt they were, for nearly all hospitals had abandoned them by 1980. But in 1990, they are still used by the MGH.

In March I learned that I had been chosen and that my duty in the MGH was to begin in September. I had already been told that during the summer months I could be a resident in pathology in the BCH, where I then was being instructed in that specialty prior to graduation from medical school. Those exciting summer months under Dr. Mallory are described in Chapter 3.

In September I arrived at the MGH as a victor in the struggle for an internship in the most prestigious hospital in the city. It was of little import to me that my title as an intern on the East Surgical Service did not convey a sense of importance: I was called either a house officer, a house pupil or—a name that was even less likely to inspire confidence—pup. Now it was to be my privilege to order students to carry out certain menial tasks and to criticize the histories and physicals that they wrote in the patients' records. Although I could not know it at the time, my appointment in the MGH would be extended later to include a residency.[2]

My colleague with a similar appointment on the West Surgical service, Dr. Henry Beecher, and I were issued ill-fitting white suits. These suits contained no pockets for Colonel Washburn had decided interns' hands should be busy elsewhere. It was not long before we learned a pup's routine: taking orders from everyone else on the staff, analyzing innumerable urine samples, giving clyses, drawing blood and matching samples for transfusions.

Reigning over all the residents, interns, and nurses were the visiting surgeons. To make it easy for them to determine which patients were in trouble, nurses made charts and hung them on the foot of the beds for everyone to see. These charts showed the vital signs—temperature, pulse rate, number of respirations per minute and blood pressure— every four hours. Every aberration required a detailed explanation. That simple method directed unerring attention immediately to nearly all serious problems. Today temperature elevations have been reduced by antibiotics. Blood chemistries and gases are essential and not only doctors, but medical students and nurses make frequent notes. The increased size of records makes it difficult to sort out salient facts.

Within a few weeks the new interns began to appreciate the history and traditions that had developed as the hospital matured. The Bulfinch building, the Ether Dome, the Phillips House, the Baker Memorial building, a few separate pavilion-type wards and the bronze bust of Henry Jacob Bigelow that stared down upon us whenever we entered the operating suite all acquired great significance.

In 1932 the chief features of the physical plant of the MGH consisted of the Bulfinch building in which half of our patients were housed and where conferences were held in the Ether Dome, a series of isolated wards that held the remainder of our patients, an operating theater (completed in 1901), the Phillips House (1917), the Baker Memorial (1930) and a combined pathology laboratory and mortuary known as Allen Street.[3]

The facilities for surgical operations have continued to change throughout the existence of the hospital. They were available in the Ether Dome until 1867 when two new rooms were added in a building that later was razed and replaced by the Bigelow amphitheater in 1901.

In 1901 anesthesia consisted of jamming a cone over a patient's nose and subduing him until he lapsed into unconsciousness. Occasionally the patient would jump off the table and have to be chased by the nurse until he could be forced into a corner. Then the surgeon and assistants would dash in to hold him down long enough for the ether to take effect.

All operating rooms had a relatively small array of instruments. Surgeons brought their own personal supplies into the Phillips House and often into the Baker operating rooms. In those facilities, scrubbing and induction of anesthesia were accomplished chiefly in the operating rooms which were small and poorly equipped. Air conditioning was provided by opening the windows.

As house officers in 1932, we quickly discovered that the visiting surgeons formed an elite group. Their staff room was fitted with leather chairs; ours had wooden benches. The visiting surgeons oozed Aesculapian authority. In the operating room—and everywhere else in the hospital—each one of them was a "captain of the ship." Interns and nurses who misread a gesture at the operating table were apt to get their knuckles rapped with an instrument. The lowly were supposed to anticipate every demand of the masters; we had to be gifted with extrasensory perception. "Don't give me what I ask for—give me what I need" was supposed to be understood, even by interns.

Many tales that emphasize the role of the surgeon as the master player on a stage could be told, but I will recount only two. Somewhat annoyed because a nurse was not on hand to grant his every wish, one of these men calmly crossed to the instrument table and pulled off the sheet. All of the instruments fell with a great clatter on the tiled floor. So great was the commotion that everyone in the operating suite ran to find out what catastrophe had occurred. To the multitude he said quietly, "May I have a mosquito snap, please?" (This is the tiniest instrument on the operating table).

The same surgeon was faced with a long, detailed consultation note from a physician that ended with the question, "What do you think about surgery?" The surgeon's complete written answer was "I like surgery." No wonder some of us later were a little abrupt and undiplomatic; as the saying goes "like father, like son."

Interns rapidly sorted the visiting surgeons into two groups, true role models and those who delicately might be termed nonmodels. Fortunately, two eminent model surgeons were head of the two surgical sections. Dr. Arthur Allen, chief of the East surgical service, was a dextrous technician. He had an unusual gift for making important decisions intuitively and correctly. He was adored by all of his patients and by his peers. Dr. Edward Churchill, chief of the West surgical service, was a pioneer in thoracic surgery and an intellectual giant. One of his most important innovations was to give residents a great deal of freedom; in this way he inspired initiative. Perhaps as a result of this delegation of responsibility, five of his residents and Dr. Churchill himself became presidents of the American Surgical Association.

For their important historical book *The Rise of Surgery*, Owen and Sally Wangensteen inserted the subtitle *From Empiric Craft to Scientific Research*. Empiricism in medicine has a double meaning. It is described both as learning from experience and as neglecting science. Dr. Allen never forgot his successes and errors, and he taught his pupils to follow his example. In this sense he was a master of empiricism. Dr. Churchill, however, was a true surgical scientist. Contact with these great teachers gave interns a phenomenal opportunity to amalgamate the values of both approaches to the science and art of surgery. Despite the ravages of disease, neither of these leaders ever lost enthusiasm or interest in his chosen profession and pupils.[4]

As interns, we had very little time to appreciate many of the activities in the hospital. In particular, we knew nothing about the newly organized surgical laboratories. For example, some of us knew that Dr. John Gibbon and his wife were working on some contraption in an attic room. None of us realized that in that spot they were producing the first heart-lung machine—a giant step in the development of cardiac surgery and worthy of a Nobel prize that was never awarded.

I helped the visiting surgeons in some unusual operative procedures such as two total gastrectomies and a hepatic lobectomy. (I found only 28 cases of excision of the left lobe of the liver in the literature at that time). In addition, a number of pericardiectomies and pulmonary lobectomies for bronchiectasis and failed pulmonary arteriotomies for pulmonary embolectomies constituted major intrusions into the open chest, an area essentially forbidden to earlier surgeons.

We were taught by Dr. Churchill to be flexible. Miss McCrae, a teacher in the nursing school, told her pupils to improvise. And, indeed, everyone had to do so. There were few machines. In the operating rooms, nurse etherizers made their own cones and monitored patients with blood pressure measurements. There were no intratracheal tubes or electrocardiograms. Harvey Cushing, the famous neurosurgeon, when a HMS student in the MGH in 1895 had inaugurated the use of an anesthesia chart (then called an ether chart) and later urged the routine recording of blood pressures and pulses throughout an operative procedure.

There was no source of wall suction on the wards; nasogastric suction was maintained by the cumbersome apparatus just popularized by Drs. Owen Wangensteen and John Paine. Usually there was a single toilet for men and another separate one for women on each ward; but there were dozens of bedpans. We were dependent on our hands and our wits, not on machines.

Nowhere in the hospital at the present time is the influx of machines into the practice of medicine more apparent than in the radiology department. Today it occupies a large floor that extends through much of the hospital and has experimental laboratories in the MGH East. In 1932 there was a single table devoted to contrast studies of the gastrointestinal tract. After a diagnostic enema it was not unusual to see a trail of barium running to the single toilet in the corridor.

Most medicines now available were not known at that time. Iodized salt was becoming common, and the frequency of surgical procedures on the thyroid was just beginning to decline in frequency. Radioactive iodine for treatment of hyperthyroidism, a vaccine against poliomyelitis, chemotherapy for tuberculosis, corticosteroids, effective diuretics, lidocaine for treatment of arhythmias, and essentially all cardiac medicines, except digitalis and nitroglycerine, and antibiotics were unknown in 1932.

Obviously, the diseases that occurred then were far different from those seen now. There were very few cases of cancer of the lung or of diverticulitis; trauma and parathyroid disease were rare. The main use of the endoscope was to observe the esophagus or the rectum (with a sigmoidoscope). All instruments were rigid; fiberoptic scopes were not invented until 1958.

Orthopedic wards were at times filled with iron lungs assisting young people paralyzed from poliomyelitis. Some patients recovered completely but many died or were left with permanent paralysis of some muscle groups. Orthopedic wards contained patients with fractures of the neck of the femur; they always were treated by traction and long periods in bed. Cancer of the stomach was extremely common. Peptic ulcers were far more virulent than they are today. In fact, at all times there usually was at least one young person dying of hemorrhage from a duodenal or gastric ulcer in the hospital. Surgical procedures for control of massive ulcer hemorrhage were extremely rare and certainly fatal. Peptic ulcers were still treated by gastroenterostomy. Cancers of the colon were less common than those of the rectum. Crohn's disease was first described in 1932, and surgeons attempted extensive resections in the hope of cure. Ulcerative colitis was a rare but horrible disease; it usually attacked young people, many of whom died from sepsis or hemorrhage. A few colectomies were undertaken but the mortality was high. Cancer of the breast, then as now, was a great scourge, but the cases arriving at the hospital in 1932 were far more advanced than those admitted today.

Errors in preoperative diagnosis were extremely common; today they are rare. Deaths also were frequent and were accepted with comparative equanimity. I recall one report that was given by one of our visiting surgeons. He had just replaced another surgeon as the head of the service and had to discuss all of the 17 deaths that had occurred in the previous two weeks. The wards had been seriously depleted by these tragedies. His macabre remark was "A new broom sweeps clean." Autopsies were done on nearly two thirds of the patient who died in the hospital.

Interns managed to fit into this kaleidoscope of activities without delay. They were given room, board, and uniforms. Their food cost the hospital twenty-eight cents a day. There was no salary for interns, but the two chief residents were given $65 a month. A tragedy occurred if an intern broke a syringe, because he had to pay for it. The tour of duty was 24 hours on one day and 12 hours on the next. Life was centered almost completely in the hospital. Few interns were married.

The life may have been Spartan, but nobody minded because it was exciting and everyone was participating. There was plenty of horseplay. One resident, after an exuberant graduation party, woke up in the morning with nothing wrong except a bad headache; however, his helpful colleagues had provided him with constant bladder drainage through a catheter, and a full-body plaster cast.

The nursing schools attracted many vivacious girls. They, by dictum, were not allowed to associate with soldiers, sailors, or house officers. That rule made both sexes mutually more desirable, of course, and many happy matches resulted.

Stories were bandied about concerning trysts in linen closets. Occasionally something happened. One nurse, who had a somewhat low neckline on her uniform, for some reason executed a deep bend in front of a medical resident who was interested in anatomy. Viewing the display, he said, "I'll take the one with the pink top." All he got was a slap on the cheek. One other nurse was told to peddle her virtues in New York City.

Rounds on surgical wards started immediately after a 6:00 A.M. breakfast. One of my early assignments was on the urology ward which could be detected many yards away even by insensitive olfactory nerves. The twenty to thirty charts hanging outside the door showed temperatures ranging up to 103 degrees Fahrenheit for nearly every patient, because of sepsis in the bladder or kidneys. Rounds consisted of complicated dressings and drainage of superficial abscesses. In one instance, a wandering fly managed to get too close and died as it sank in a puddle of pus on a patient's groin.

After rounds, all but the most recent interns dashed to the operating suite for a full day's work. The lowest of the pups went back to the wards to do further dressings, to give clyses (injections of normal saline into the subpectoral areas or the thighs, because intravenous administration was rare), and, later in the afternoon, to give transfusions. One intern would insert a large needle into an antecubital vein of the donor and in two minutes blood would fill a large paraffined receptor. The second intern meanwhile had isolated a saphenous vein in the recipient and was prepared to pump the blood into it. When all went well, 500 ml. of blood was transfused in less than five minutes. One time Henry Beecher and I established a negative world's record; it took us three and a half hours to transfuse two and a half milliliters of blood.

As soon as these tasks were completed it was back to the wards to take histories and perform physical examinations on the new admissions. Many women suffered from the ravages of multiple pregnancies—cystoceles, rectoceles, prolapses and huge hernias—and usually they had the associated enormous varicose veins. Hernias, gallstones and hemorrhoids were the common reasons for elective admissions among men. General surgery included gynecology, fractures, head and neck surgery and pediatric surgery—a selection of cases far wider than that now available to the general surgeon.

A typical evening on night call usually included one or more operations for acute appendicitis as well as other emergencies. A few fractures usually appeared; they were rotated respectively to the East surgical service, the West surgical service, and the orthopedic service. A statistically significant fact was discovered later: fractures of the long bones were much more common on the surgical wards and fractures of the bones of the toes on orthopedic wards. It should be noted that the emergency ward was run by surgeons. Then it was 6:00 A.M. and time to start another exciting day.

In retrospect, life in those days seems absurdly simple. Compared with interns today, those in 1932 led a monastic life, but they did not realize it, and it made little difference. Very few had a wife and family to take them away from surgery. All of them, physicians and surgeons alike, were strained financially, but so were all other young people. The country was in the throes of the Great Depression. Everyone was struggling for life, for a bed, and for food. Interns were buoyed by the satisfaction they obtained from caring for patients. Patients were most grateful for any crumbs of further life or happiness that they might be granted. Malpractice proceedings were unknown. Interns believed that their future careers would henceforth be solely a never-ending struggle against disease.

So it went on for two years until 1934 when our class of eight interns graduated. The twenty-four months of service had passed rapidly. Every senior intern had received an excellent training in general surgery and a smattering in several subspecialties. We were ready for the next step.

After internship, doctors next had to obtain a full license to practice. At that time the State of Massachusetts required a doctor to pass the examination of the National Board of Medical Examiners and to be accepted by the State Board of Registration in Medicine as a satisfactory candidate. The examination had already been taken and passed by all of the MGH interns during medical school, and the state Board's requirement usually was satisfied by a brief conversation with the Secretary of the Board. Every full license issued allowed (and still does) the applicant to *practice medicine and surgery* without regard for his previous training.

The graduating intern then had only three reasonable alternatives. The first required confidence on his part because if he chose it he assumed that he could hang up his shingle and patients would flock to his office. This choice often proved disappointing, especially when he planned to practice in a metropolitan community. One of my friends who later became a great leader of the profession tried this method. Six weeks after he opened his office the first customer walked in with a totally non-surgical problem; he had an acute case of gonorrhea.

Usually graduating interns went into practice as an assistant to or partner of an older practitioner—often a friend or a father. Such an arrangement provided a source of patients, especially during nights and holidays, as well as some further training by the senior partner. The beginner's practice initially consisted of medical and surgical patients; but as their number increased the junior doctor gradually shifted from general practice to surgery. In 1934 there were no group practices or clinics anxious to hire young surgeons.

The final choice was to take a further period of training. This alternative not only provided an opportunity for shoring up the many weak spots discovered in the previous two years but also was absolutely essential if one wished to obtain an academic post. It also was highly desirable if he hoped to receive one of the top clinical appointments with an established MGH surgeon. This choice was not open to all comers, however, for only one of the four interns on each service could be chosen for the one-year post of assistant resident followed by another one-year term as chief resident. Fortunately, I was appointed as the assistant resident on the East service to begin in 1935.

Seven months passed before I was able to move into the assistant residency position. I spent six of these months as a resident in the Pondville Cancer Hospital. This very interesting assignment is described in Chapter 10.

However, the first month after the completion of my internship was devoted to a somewhat unorthodox assignment. I was the physician in charge of the workers who were constructing the Quabbin reservoir, which within a few years provided the entire water supply of metropolitan Boston. I had some interesting experiences during that month. Caissons were sunk deep underground, so all of the sandhogs had to descend and return slowly by elevators. Pressure had to be high in the subterranean areas to prevent collapse of the excavations into which cement would be poured to form the bases of the huge dams. If workers came back to normal pressure at the surface too rapidly, that is, if they decompressed too fast, the excess nitrogen in their blood formed small bubbles that circulated throughout their bodies. Joints and the brain were the favorite resting places of these bubbles which then produced extreme local pain or mental aberrations. These dangerous symptoms of "the bends" meant that the victims had to be put into a pressure chamber and subjected to an increased amount of oxygen and decompressed more slowly so that oxygen could replace the nitrogen in the blood.

It was fortunate for me that I had to make very little use of the pressure chamber that was adjacent to my office. I soon found that my ear canals would not permit me to descend in the elevators or withstand high pressure. Unless the Eustachian tubes are wide or there is a perforation of the eardrum such pressure changes can cause perforation of the drum or more serious damage to the inner ear.

The day after I arrived, a pompous old gentleman—a general practitioner—puffing on a cigar stalked into my office, announced his name, and informed me that I could take care of the colds and the bends, but if there were any hernia repairs to be done he was the man. I was not about to do any operations myself but I was so disgusted by his attitude and appearance that I referred all of the patients who needed herniorrhaphy to a different surgeon. This episode was my introduction to the world of community medicine and surgery known in the profession as the "grass roots".

I spent many rather quiet hours in the office. A few newly-developed hernias came in, and there were several minor injuries and infections. But after payday the sandhogs were in a joyful mood. They loved the game of blackjack; I wanted to keep them happy so I looked up the rules and subsequently doubled my salary.

After this vacation in western Massachusetts I moved to Pondville. Six months later it was the summer of 1935 and time to come back to the MGH. The next two years were filled with operations and administrative duties. The pattern was not unlike that which had already been established during my internship, except that the number and type of operations were expanded greatly.[5]

The surgical residency a half century ago in the MGH was quite different from what it is now. The patient load at that time was heavily weighted toward abdominal, breast, thyroid, fracture, and gynecologic surgery. There was a smattering of other specialties for the interns, including urology and neurosurgery. Vascular surgery was restricted to varicose veins, postphlebitic ulcers, and amputations. Plastic surgery and endocrine surgery had not been separated from general surgery. There were few thoracic cases or endoscopies and no cardiac surgery or microsurgery.

From 1931 to 1948, there were two parallel surgical services in the MGH. Professor Churchill, on the West, allowed the residents to carry on in the operating room and call for help only if they needed it. On the East service, where Dr. Allen was chief, the major surgery was done by the visiting staff while the resident assisted and kept his comments to himself.

During the period in which this dichotomy persisted, good-natured competition between the services was the rule. From a pragmatic point of view and as far as the patients were concerned, the results appeared to be about the same.

I was on the East service, where there were several prima donna visiting surgeons. Some of the comments of residents who followed shortly after me captured the situation in prose. A typical resident's operation on a woman was described by Richard Thompson in 1937: an ether examination, D and C, amputation of the cervix, anterior and posterior colporrhaphy, exploratory laparotomy, bilateral salpingectomy, Olshausen suspension, appendectomy, and tooth extraction. The list of procedures at least was impressive. Howard Ulfelder was resident in 1940. He said:

The choice surgical plum for the resident during those years was a subtotal gastrectomy. To the best of my recollection Vernon Cantlon was the first resident (1938) to be handed down a subtotal and I well remember the scrumping and plotting that went on between the resident and the junior who made up the operating list deciding which visit could be shown which case, and in what order. On one occasion when Grantley Taylor was the visit of the day we scheduled two easy gastrectomies, one right after the other. I helped him on the first, thinking surely he would help me on the second, but he breezed through both of them without blinking an eye looking me straight in the face the whole time.

At the conclusion of my residency in August 1937, I had the distinct impression that I was a well-trained surgeon who had an excellent grasp of the entire field of surgery. Dr. Allen did his best over the coming years to prove to me that this egotistical attitude was not justified. And it has become painfully clear during the ensuing years that there actually were big holes in my knowledge and perception of the future. I will cite only three examples of these deficiencies.

First, I did not recognize genius even when it existed near me. The outstanding example of unappreciated talent is Dr. Ernest Amory Codman (known familiarly as Amory), whose reputation has grown throughout the years of this century.

He was a cantankerous genius. His active surgical career covered the period in which he was a member of the surgical staff of the MGH (1900–1914) and approximately twenty years afterward, when he either directed his own private hospital or returned to the MGH as a consulting surgeon. He died in 1945.

In 1900 surgeons were notoriously uninterested in the fate of patients after operations. This eccentric surgeon changed this attitude. His insistence on outcome and analysis of end results has set the pattern for cancer registries—such as the bone sarcoma registry of the American College of Surgeons—and for morbidity and mortality conferences that are almost universal in all surgical departments of teaching hospitals. It took him a decade to destroy the concept of promotion on the basis of seniority rather than of ability. He has not received the honor he is due in the standard histories of the MGH.

Another major contribution was his demand for special assignments to particular individuals, in order to provide adequate clinical information about certain diseases and thereby lead to advances in care. This system persisted until approximately 1940. In essence, it was a preview of the subspecialization and fragmentation of surgery that appeared a half century later. Dr. Codman himself received a special assignment for the treatment of shoulder injuries, and he wrote his classic book *The Shoulder* on the basis of his extensive experience.

I have very few personal memories of Dr. Codman. While I was an intern, he occasionally operated upon a shoulder. His meticulous, time-consuming procedures and acerbic comments to his assistants led most of us to shun his operations. In one case, in which a reluctant bowel failed to function after a resection and anastomosis of the colon, one of his progress notes suggested that an anal injection of air might be used to open the anastomosis. Even geniuses may deviate so far from orthodoxy that they can err.

The second example of my early shortsightedness was my failure to recognize the development of major trends in surgery, even though they were happening close to the walls of the MGH. I did not appreciate the relatively short period of surgical training given to many surgeons in those days, or wonder why it was allowed. Recall that in 1937 any practitioner could carry out surgical operations as soon as he obtained his medical license from the state of Massachusetts. The public was unconcerned about the length of training because most surgical operations were done by general practitioners. Nevertheless the situation was appalling to many surgeons who were at the head of their profession. The winds of discontent were blowing strongly in the discussions of the American Surgical Association, the most important group in surgical education in the country.

Led primarily by giants such as President Archibald from Montreal and Dr. Evarts Graham from St. Louis, a group of surgeons made a major decision at a meeting of the ASA held in one of the amphitheaters of Harvard Medical School in June 1937. They persuaded the Association to establish a Board of Surgery. The years of training were to be lengthened and the process upgraded; thereafter written and oral examinations would have to be taken and passed with a satisfactory grade. The Association believed that ultimately the practice of surgery should revert to properly trained individuals and should be wrested from the hands of others.

This challenging reform not only had a very important influence on our future careers but also improved the quality of American surgery. However, faced with strong opposition from the old guard, which at that time controlled the American College of Surgeons, a bitter struggle developed between the ACS and the ASA, which was composed chiefly of younger academic surgeons. The battle did not end until 1974 when, for the first time, the ACS adopted certification by the American Board of Surgery as a requirement for membership in the ACS.[6]

This agenda took many decades to complete. Probably the major influence that finally made general practitioners withdraw from surgery was the tremendous increase in malpractice premiums for surgeons that came in the mid-1980s; family practitioners could no longer afford to do an occasional hernia repair or appendectomy.

Thus the American Board of Surgery came into existence and gave its first examinations in 1937. My certificate, granted in 1939, was number 101. There now (in 1990) are about 1,000 certificates granted each year in surgery and many more in surgical specialties.

A third mistake was my failure to foresee the enormous expansion of the field of surgery that would occur in the next fifty years and the simultaneous transition of the MGH from a small parochial hospital to a large international institution. Dr. Churchill did foresee the former development and remained adamant in his battle to prevent the division of general surgery into numerous subspecialties. Dr. Allen clearly recognized the importance of maintaining quality care in hospitals as they expanded. Later he became one of the architects of the Joint Commission on Accreditation of Hospitals. But very few individuals can anticipate major changes in the domain of surgery or influence their direction.

During my residency, Dr. Allen asked me to join him as an assistant as soon as my in-hospital service was over. This chance to be his associate for nearly five years was to be one of the most exciting opportunities in my life. These details will be recorded in chapter six.

At this juncture I must add an intensely personal note. Many believe that a surgeon is a cold-blooded individual with an icy heart, trained to do what he conceives to be his duty with little regard for the patient. Quite to the contrary, I have found that caring for a sick person is the most important qualification of a surgeon. Much of what I have learned about this virtue, as well as many others, is due to the influence of my wife.

It was 1933 when I first saw Phyllis Paton. She was hurrying down one of the corridors in the MGH. Queerly enough, I cannot recall whether she was walking toward or away from me. I was a surgical house officer and she was a young student nurse. She had just graduated from Northfield School. Instead of accepting a scholarship she had been offered in Smith College, she decided, because of her father's severe illness, to earn a degree in nursing prior to entering medical school.

She was born in Montreal. The Paton family, true Scots, came from the Hebrides. One relative became a missionary in the New Hebrides. Her father, after fighting in the Boer War for Great Britain, came to Canada where he became a high official in the Canadian Pacific Railway system. Her mother's ancestors arrived in America from England on the Speedwell in 1620, the second boatload of Puritans to come to American shores. Her great grandfather, Henry M. Moore, was a close friend of the famous evangelist, Dwight L. Moody, and was the first president of the Board of Trustees of Northfield School. Phyllis was a member of the fourth generation of the family to attend the school.

We both felt that the prohibition on dating between student nurses and house officers or residents was unfair and discriminatory. Our occasional visits to a movie or a party fortunately brought Phyllis only one simple reprimand from Miss Sally Johnson, the understanding director of the school of nursing. By the end of the third year Phyllis had graduated, returned to Montreal, and matriculated in McGill to complete requirements for an academic degree that was to be followed by enrollment in McGill University Medical School.

But I had other plans. After a year punctuated by several brief trips to Montreal over Vermont country roads, which varied, depending on the season, from extremely hazardous to picturesque, a wedding date was set for August 14, 1937, shortly after the completion of my surgical residency. I was ready to conquer the world with the exciting prospect of a position as assistant to Dr. Allen that would begin two weeks later.

Phyllis tells me the wedding was a great affair. For me, it was a blur. I have a hazy memory of one of the delightful features of the marriage laws of the province of Quebec, namely that wives promise to henceforth obey their husbands.

Our honeymoon trip around the Gaspe Peninsula and in the Maine woods with an ascent of Mount Katahdin was the first of many travels that we have taken together. The pattern thereafter always has been the same—delight in the discovery of new geographic areas and wonderful friends everywhere.

So I came back to Boston to begin a great adventure in surgery at 6:30 P.M. on the last day of August 1937. But I was no longer alone; I had with me a lovely wife, a dependable second-hand car christened *The Embolus*, and $37 in cash.

Above: Lettie Phelan and John Hayes Welch at the time of their marriage in 1904. Below: John and Lettie's forty-fifth wedding anniversary in 1949. Left to right in second row: Claude (CEW), Ronald, Dorothy, Harold.

Above: Ronald Burton Welch and (CEW) at about ages two and four (left); Joseph (Jose) Nye Welch as portrayed on the cover of *Life* magazine July 25, 1954 (right). Below: Drought in Nebraska, 1938. Note the deserted house, broken windmill, dead trees, and stunted corn.

Above: The Harvard Medical School (upper right) in 1932. Aerial view taken from over the Peter Bent Brigham Hospital. Below: Classmates Henry K. Beecher (left) and Carl W. Walter (right), pictured in later life.

Above: John Collins Warren, surgeon (1778–1856), one of the founders of the Massachusetts General Hospital and one of the greatest American surgeons in his time (left); Henry Jacob Bigelow (1818–1890), the most important surgeon of the MGH in the second half of the nineteenth century (right). Below: the Bulfinch building of the Massachusetts General Hospital (left) and the Massachusetts Medical College (Harvard Medical School) (right) on the bank of the Charles River photographed about 1850.

Robert C. Hinckley's recreation (1882–1894) of the first public demonstration of ether anesthesia at the Massachusetts General Hospital on October 16, 1846. John C. Warren is shown operating; anesthetist William T. G. Morton is holding his ether inhalator; Henry J. Bigelow is the tall erect figure by the railing in the background (third from right).

Above: Visiting surgeons to the Massachusetts General Hospital during the years 1885–1892. Sitting (left to right), John Collins Warren the younger, Charles B. Porter, and John Homans; standing (left to right), Maurice H. Richardson, Henry H. A. Beach, and Arthur Tracy Cabot. Below: Reginald H. Fitz (1842–1913), pathologist (left), and Ernest Amory Codman (1869–1940), assistant visiting surgeon of the MGH 1907–1914 (right).

Richard Clark Cabot, founder of the Clinical Pathological Conference at the MGH, 1905, and medical social service, with Ida Cannon, head of the Social Service Department of the MGH for many years.

Above: The Mayo Brothers: Dr. Charlie, sitting; Dr. Will, standing. Below: The Mayo Clinic, as CEW saw it in the 1930s. Courtesy of the University of Minnesota Press and Helen Clapesattle.

Above: CEW as house officer, with young boy who had survived a left hepatic lobectomy for cancer (left); Phyllis Paton at time of graduation from the MGH Training School for Nurses, 1936 (right). Below: Phyllis and CEW after their wedding in Montreal, 1937.

Arthur W. Allen, a master surgeon of the MGH. This was one of his favorite photographs.

6

Learning From a Master Surgeon, Arthur W. Allen 1937–1942

The next five years, from 1937 to 1942, proved to be the most exciting of my life. I was thrown immediately into the busy practice pattern of Dr. Allen. I made preliminary rounds in the MGH at 6 A.M., speaking to each of his numerous patients; later we again visited each person, provided there was time. Visits were followed by operations, office appointments, and evening rounds. This schedule was taxing, but became even more demanding when I acquired other duties. Nevertheless, every moment was a delight because I learned how to become not only a better surgeon but a humane physician.

Dr. Allen became one of my two true role models; Dr. Edward Churchill, the other, will be discussed in a later chapter. Both of them personified the MGH throughout the nation. In brief, Dr. Allen was a master surgeon, and a true friend of all of his patients. He was a born teacher, both in action and by word. He assumed innumerable duties that spread the reputation of the MGH throughout the state and the nation. His loyalties were strong, to his family, to the hospital, and to the other organizations that he supported. He never spared himself; recurrent bouts of illness were followed by bursts of feverish activity. Without question he was one of the great surgeons of the twentieth century.

Arthur Wilburn Allen was born in Somerset, Kentucky in 1887, and later graduated from Georgetown University and the Johns Hopkins Medical School in 1913, having been a bookseller and a carrier of trays to pay some of the tuition. (His work as a waiter reminded me of my own experience as a dish-washer in Columbia University, and a waiter in HMS.)

When I first met Dr. Allen he was a heavy set man, with a full head of black hair, a face that could be laughing at a slightly salacious joke or stern when he was correcting an error made by one of his interns. He usually dressed meticulously in a dark blue three-piece suit. His portrait in the operating suite of the MGH showed him in a two-piece suit with an expanse of white shirt. The artist has made this change to draw more attention to his face; Mrs. Allen never forgave the artist for this departure from reality.

At the time Dr. Allen began his surgical career, surgery was still dominated by the mechanistic approach. Surgery was learned largely by the apprentice system; the operation was all important. Fortunately for all, he became a pioneer in the development of a new concept of surgery and its teaching. However, he brought to the new that which was good in the old practice of medicine—in distinction to a common characteristic of surgeons—namely, a devotion to his patients, each of whom was to him a human being with peculiar reactions that he stored in his memory. This trait naturally, made him adored by his patients.

Dr. Allen's scientific interests and contributions were many, ranging from all aspects of trauma to all organs and lesions in the abdomen to peripheral vascular disease, and from preoperative preparation to postoperative care and complications. He shed clear and logical light on every problem he discussed. His last work, a book entitled *Operative Surgery in the Abdomen*, was published after his death. In it he maintained his customary standards of excellence.

He was a lecturer in surgery in the Harvard Medical School during the same years he was Chief of the East Surgical Service from 1936–1948. The Medical School appointment carried a title but involved no particular duties. It was totally inconsiderate of his contributions to surgery; Harvard atoned when it gave him an honorary degree near the end of his career.

However, his most important and effective teaching occurred at the graduate level with interns, residents and assistants. His assistants had opportunities offered to very few persons in their formative years. I followed Richard Wallace as his assistant and worked at his side from 1937 to 1942, and was followed, in turn, by Dr. Gordon Donaldson. I have a rich stock of memories from those years. There was no other period in my life in which I learned more and none that molded my life more firmly. I worked every day and every night except for a two-week vacation during each summer. But it was exciting and thrilling and made very easy by the knowledge that the chief subjected himself to the same stern discipline.

And, indeed, Dr. Allen was *The Chief.* He not only was the chief of the East surgical service from 1936 to 1948, but also was dominant wherever he happened to be. His extremely quick responses, his intimate knowledge of all the surgical literature, and his rapid intuitive analysis of a person's character and ability were hard to match. In many respects he was the personification of the Old Testament Jehovah. His underlings viewed him with awe, respect, admiration, and, to a certain extent, fear. He also was a jealous god; anyone who attempted to take away one of his patients incurred his everlasting wrath.

Dr. Allen first and foremost was concerned with patient care. He often said that the surgeon who did not wake up at 2 A.M. and worry about his patients did not deserve to be a surgeon. He practiced what he preached, for he thought of his own patients day and night. For example, one day he returned from an operation in an outlying hospital, where the local surgeon had acted as his assistant. He sat down to recount the whole story of the difficult procedure to me, but as he progressed in the tale, it became apparent that he had made a technical error in the operation. He immediately jumped out of his chair, rushed back to the operating room, had the patient reanesthetized, and corrected the error. The patient made an uneventful recovery.

Every morning after I had finished rounds, he arrived at 8:30 for the first operation. His opening sentence always was "What is the BN?" BN, of course, stood for bad news, and that often was a long story. In those days, major abdominal operations were followed by serious complications in nearly thirty percent of the cases and by postoperative mortality in nearly ten percent. Many of the problems at that time were due to anesthesia, but the introduction of antibiotics, and replacement of fluids, electrolytes and blood have since made a tremendous difference in the outcomes.

We operated nearly every morning but occasionally there would be a momentary lull. On those days Dr. Allen would have more time to spend with patients. Generally, rounds were so hurried that one patient complained that all the people on the floor would catch pneumonia as a result of the speed with which Dr. Allen and his entourage swept through the room, leaving swirling air currents in their wake. On those rare days when he had additional time, however, he would spend an hour and a half or two hours talking with patients. Patients were enchanted by these rare, intimate conversations.

He reveled in the niceties of operative procedures. Every step was considered very carefully in advance, and then all was supposed to go exactly as planned, just as a symphony orchestra might replay its favorite repertoire. Dr. Allen's exacting approach led to some of the finest technical accomplishments ever seen in the MGH—and in those days technical accomplishments were absolutely necessary to avoid the ills arising from our lack of knowledge in many other areas.

Such a colorful person was certain to engender many tales. Gordon Scannell still remembers the patient who had just entered the hospital with acute pancreatitis. After discussion, Dr. Allen said the man would die in twenty-eight days from hemorrhage. Death from massive bleeding actually occurred on the twenty-ninth day.

He was a master technician and loved to have an admiring crowd of young residents observing his operations. He also happened to be an avid fisherman, a hobby of one of the spectators who was watching Dr. Allen do a hysterectomy. The technique was perfect, but the specimen was far from impressive. When Dr. Allen turned to the audience and said, "How did you like that?", the fisherman in the audience responded, "Dr. Allen, where we come from, we throw one that size back in." Not surprisingly, this fellow located his practice a thousand miles from Boston. At another time Dr. Allen was doing an unusual procedure, but speaking meanwhile about the fine details of technique, indicating that they were learned from many such operations. At the conclusion he again turned to the audience with the usual query, "How did you like that?" In a somewhat disparaging tone, a resident said, "And how many of those have you *really* done, Dr. Allen?" Dr. Allen's immediate retort was, "Young man, you don't need to see a garden to appreciate a rose."

He kept a very firm hand on the service. We trembled whenever he found something amiss. Once he operated on a very poor risk patient for a cancer of the colon. He sewed him up with every stout suture he could find. The resident, Gordon Donaldson, in a burst of optimism, broke the rules and took out all of the sutures on the twelfth postoperative day. Everything promptly fell apart. The patient was whisked back to the operating room and rapidly sewed up again; Gordon meanwhile was volubly thanking the Deity that the Chief was in Chicago. Just as the last suture was being tied, Dr. Allen, who had caught an earlier train, walked into the operating room. The result was predictable, and thereafter Gordon never removed stay sutures in less than three weeks.

Dr. Allen firmly believed that the papers he wrote should be based on actual experience in clinical fields. When the operating schedule happened to be a little slack, he gathered his material together and prepared another paper. His most important writings dealt with the subjects of digestive tract or peripheral vascular surgery. In addition, he wrote long review articles for the *New England Journal of Medicine* on the state of the art of abdominal surgery. Because he attended all major surgical meetings, knew all leaders in surgery, and read all major American surgical publications, he could compose these reviews over a weekend.

Dr. Allen served as a trustee of the MGH from 1953 to 1958. He also served on the general executive committee of the hospital when it was still a small, select group that conducted its business rapidly and effectively. He would probably have very little sympathy with the large committee that now exists. As a matter of fact, he was very jealous of any diminution in his authority. There was the usual competition between him and the other members of the staff in an era when it seemed more important to gain ascendancy in one's own hospital than to promote a unified spirit.

For the last seventeen years of his life, he remained under the shadow of a fatal disease. I can never forget the day he asked me to palpate his abdomen; I felt a huge tumor. A very private operation was performed by Dr. Leland McKittrick. Dr. Allen had asked me to administer the spinal anesthetic. For month after month, he required radiation therapy, that being the only treatment then available for lymphoma. He did remarkably well, but in the periods when he was incapacitated, his patients were operated on by his assistants. When he improved, he would return to his usual difficult schedule.

He never ceased working. He frequently asked me to tell him if he was becoming incompetent so that he would know when to stop operating. I never had to warn him, because he always was superb in the operating room.

Every task that he undertook was pursued with the utmost energy. As chairman of the Board of Regents of the American College of Surgeons, he broke the stranglehold some of the regents had held on the organization. Some of them had held their positions for over twenty years. They were ousted and a younger group elected. The organization later called The Joint Commission for Accreditation of Hospitals had been founded and run solely by the College for many years. It had become an enormous and expensive undertaking. He engineered the transfer to a new Commission, which included the AMA and, later, other organizations. His parting accomplishment was to persuade General Hawley to become Director of the ACS, and to head the battle against fee-splitting, which was rampant at that time. After Dr. Allen's stint as president of the ACS, the College was a much stronger organization than it had been when he first was elected regent.[1]

When he was persuaded to become president of the Massachusetts Medical Society, a minor complication arose. He had never been a councillor and the president has to be elected from that body. Rules were changed; he was elected immediately and spent two busy years directing the course of the organization. He also was president of the Boston Medical Library and raised a very large sum that assured the continuity of this institution as it joined Harvard to build the Countway Library. His portraits hang in the Allen Room of the Countway as well as in the MGH operating suite.

He had many honors in his later years. They included the Bigelow Medal of the Boston Surgical Society. In addition, he was rewarded with honorary degrees by Harvard and Georgetown. He also was an honorary member of the Royal Colleges of England and of Edinburgh and delivered a Hunterian lecture in 1950. His name will be remembered in the MGH for two other important reasons: the operating suite that is named in his honor, and for a permanent Residents' Training Fund established in 1965, due chiefly to Dr. Grant Rodkey.

His example inspired his many pupils so that several of them followed in his footsteps. He also stimulated a strong sense of loyalty to the Chief, because he was revered by all who were fortunate enough to be his assistants. Drs. Henry Faxon, Richard Wallace, Gordon Donaldson, W. Philip Giddings, Grant Rodkey, Glenn Behringer, James M. Shannon, George Richardson and John Burke as well as myself have been imbued with one or more qualities of this many-faceted giant and have tried in some way to emulate what he did so well.

On March 15, 1958, I operated on Dr. Allen for the final time. He asked, and I told him the findings. He said "That is that." As far as I know, they were the last words he spoke. He died quietly three days later.[2]

When I reminisce about all that Dr. Allen taught me, one of the most outstanding was the way in which he immediately made friends with his patients and treated each one as an individual. He sensed the questions they wanted to ask, and gave them truthful answers. If prospects for cure were poor, he still provided some glimmer of hope and the promise of continuing support.

He emphasized that I had acquired from my residency the technical ability to care for patients but still had a great deal to learn. Fortunately, if a doctor really *cares* for each person as an individual rather than as an example of a disease, the foundation is secure. Then it is possible for the physician to consider each person as a unique individual, anticipate his or her needs, and help answer the questions that he or she wants to ask but is afraid to put into words.

My busy schedule required a minimum of a hundred patient contacts had to be made during each day. Some method had to be developed that would permit an economical use of time. Meanwhile the patient had to be given something to remember—advice, sympathy, or perhaps some witticism—so that the doctor's visit would remain a pleasant experience.

A few lessons are learned rapidly. For example, when the physician is really in a desperate hurry and the patient wishes to engage in a long conversation, it saves time to pull up a chair by the bedside, assume a relaxed posture, and get to the point of his most important query as soon as possible.

As soon as a patient enters a hospital, he becomes apprehensive about what may happen. Not many persons today resemble the old surgeon who, when asked if he wished to discuss his own upcoming operation, said "Do what you need to do. I am only the passenger on the ship."

A sense of loneliness commonly pervades all patients in this foreign hospital environment. When the patient is placed on a stretcher and wheeled into the operating room, he has an overwhelming sense that his ship of life is being guided into uncharted seas, where rocks and reefs may lead to immediate disaster. The patient is buoyed by faith in his doctors and by the activities of nurses and others who are preparing him for the operating room. Unexpressed fear of the unknown often is more real and apparent within the patient's family. Fear often is stronger in relatives as minutes stretch into hours. The surgeon must never forget that they are waiting anxiously for word from him.[3]

Thus the early words given by a physician to a family after an operation never are forgotten. Also, the patient, waking from anesthesia, never forgets the first statements made by the surgeon.

In the early days after an operation, patients often are depressed and feel deserted by doctors and friends. At every visit the doctor must touch the patient and give the physical contact that is extremely reassuring. This always must be done before the physician leaves the bedside.

This matter of touching reminds me of a story. Many years ago a patient who was very ill lived in the hospital for nearly three years. During the course of her illness, she was confined to bed and required a high thigh amputation. She recovered from this experience but felt so unhappy about her loss that she always wore an artificial leg, even in bed. On one particular morning, a substitute surgeon, who knew nothing of the operation, had to make rounds. Recognizing the necessity of personal contact, he slipped his hand under the bedclothes and encountered a frigid lower extremity that felt like, and actually was, polished wood. Immediately he said to the patient, "My, but your leg is cold." "GET OUT OF HERE! NOW!", she snapped.

It is not necessary to spend a long time with a patient if matters are going well. Actually, if a protracted examination is made, the ill person will suspect that something is really wrong. On the other hand a few questions may show the patient is quite unhappy. Then, if no cause can be found, it is necessary to discover something that is going well. Perhaps a question reveals that the patient has just had a very satisfactory bowel movement. It is well for the physician to expatiate on the significance for improvement that has been demonstrated by this providential occurrence, and meanwhile get out of the door on the upbeat before another symptom is raised for discussion.

Obviously, there are times when the patient is deathly ill and all that can be expressed is compassion. Dying patients need a friend—someone who will listen in a sympathetic manner, even if little else can be provided. The fear of being alone is one of the most unhappy experiences individual patients can have, particularly when they are facing the great unknown.

One of my early lessons occurred when one of Dr. Allen's patients, a young man in his early twenties, was found to have disseminated melanoma. He was contemplating suicide. I was present when Dr. Allen spent nearly an hour with him, pointing out the fact that the young fellow was living for his family as well as for himself, and that his suicide would live in their memories as an ignoble gesture and destroy all memory of a man strong enough to face his fate.

During my first year with the Chief, my wife and I decided it would be very appropriate to give each of his and my hospital patients a small token during the visit on Christmas morning. Phyllis and I trudged through the snow on a stormy Christmas eve and bought fifty little

Santas for about a quarter apiece. On the following morning I distributed them. For years afterward, the Santas would be recalled as these patients came back. One woman kept hers by her bedside until she died several years later. Every year thereafter, I brought in small gifts for all of Dr. Allen's and my patients; my wife and I collected many of them during trips abroad.

Fifty years ago it was expected that major operations would be followed many times by an untoward event. To treat complications successfully it was necessary to be alert to trivial danger signs and to correct the problem whenever possible. It was particularly necessary during evening visits to discover these telltale symptoms that boded ill. Blood banks, antibiotics, respiratory therapy and diuretics were not available; each of them has made an enormous difference in the care of the usual postoperative patient.

The question is often asked concerning how much a patient should be told after an operation, particularly when malignant disease is found. In my opinion, he or she should always be told the truth unless the family absolutely refuses to have this done. Usually it will be found that the patient, even if dying from hopeless cancer, has more fortitude and resilience than the remainder of the family. It also is comforting for such sufferers to know that they have something truly wrong that accounts for their complaints. Finally, most patients can tell from the demeanor of the physician whether or not something serious is afoot, regardless of what is said.[4]

In certain instances the physician may find that his empathy with a patient is excessive and leads to disaster. When he identifies too closely, he may lose the necessary objectivity that can allow him to make correct decisions. Such a problem arises most commonly with patients who have chronic diseases. Consultation with other physicians should be obtained, and, if possible, the original doctor should share the responsibility of care with another colleague.

There are certain patients for whom death, at the present time, is ordained. Disseminated cancer, AIDS, and Alzheimer's disease are three major examples. Against them, we physicians are, at least for the present, ultimately powerless. For patients with these diseases, our feeble efforts must be buttressed by compassion as we see their lives slip slowly away.[5]

Thus there are many sources that can aid the physician in his important duty—the care of the patient. He may read about it, as, for example, in a classic essay by Dr. Francis Peabody, who believed it was far more important to understand the patient by interviewing him first in his home or in the doctor's office rather than in the hospital.[6] One may read the poignant address by Professor J. Engelbert Dunphy as he described the care of a dying patient; it was essentially a postscript to his own life when he suffered from terminal prostate cancer.[7] In it he quoted the words of another great physician, Professor Hans Zinsser, who knew he was dying from leukemia.[8] Zinsser said:

Now is Death merciful. He calls me hence
Gently, with friendly soothing of my fears
Of ugly age and feeble impotence
And cruel disintegration of slow years.
Nor does he leap upon me unaware
Like some wild beast that hungers for its prey,
But gives me kindly warning to prepare
Before I go, to kiss the tears away.

How sweet the summer! And the autumn shone
Late warmth within our hearts as in the sky,
Ripening rich harvests that our love had sown.
How good that ere the winter comes, I die!
Then, ageless in your heart I'll come to rest
Serene and proud, as when you loved me best.

As has been illustrated in previous paragraphs, the physician may learn from the experience and advice of others. But most of all he must learn from his own contacts with patients who, unfortunately, rarely can face death with such composure and equanimity.

Empathy in some respects is easiest with hospital patients. Those who have operations follow relatively similar paths. In office practice there often is a sudden transition from one person who revels in unusual symptoms and incurable diseases (for whom any attempt to lighten the conversation by a witticism is equivalent to negligence) to others who demand a sense of humor. There are patients who require authoritative statements from the physician; others insist on detailed conversations concerning every aspect of the suspected disease so that they can become partners in any medical decisions. The successful physician will be able to discern very rapidly which tactic is proper; to repeat, it cannot be taught, it must be learned. Once acquired, the rewards are great; respect, love, and adulation are certain to follow.

My personal narrative as a Boston surgeon ended in the previous chapter when Phyllis and I returned from our honeymoon. The first five years after our marriage in 1937 provided little opportunity for details other than attention to surgery. In the daytime Phyllis often waited for me in our car during the long hours in which I made rounds. In addition to my duties with Dr. Allen from 1937 to 1942, several other activities filled any spare time. Phyllis and I had a first son, Claude Jr. I served as a surgeon for the Harvard University Health Service where I had an enormous experience with minor surgery. The appointment also entailed many emergency visits to Stillman Infirmary, the hospital for University students. Once I had to go there five times in one night for separate admissions.

Dr. Allen and I wrote several papers together on clinical subjects. Elsewhere I recounted our experimental work on thrombophlebitis with leeches that provided heparin. The work was stopped suddenly when Phyllis found the leeches were escaping from our home refrigerator and were found in our bed.

The most important surgical triumph in the MGH in this period was the introduction of antibiotics. The introduction of effective antibiotics was almost too spectacular to be true. This occurred in 1937, several years after Prontosil, the first of these major antibiotics had been prepared by Domagh in 1932. One morning, at grand rounds, Champ Lyons showed us a woman who had had a mastectomy three weeks previously. For two weeks she had run a daily temperature of 104 degrees. Careful search was made but no obvious sepsis was located. She was given the experimental drug. The next day her temperature reverted to normal and remained there. Every one, except for the patriarchs in the front row, believed we had seen a miracle; the conservative oldsters believed it was due to chance.

For two years I was engaged with Champ Lyons in a clinical study of traumatic injuries to determine whether or not the introduction of sulfanilamide powder into wounds provided protection against sepsis. This compound would be distributed to all combat soldiers to be inserted into any such wounds immediately after the injury. Ultimately, it was not helpful; it tended to cake if put in deep wounds. My work in the project was terminated by the outbreak of war. Our lives changed abruptly on December 7, 1942, when the Japanese attacked Pearl Harbor. World War II had begun.

7

World War II: The 6th General Hospital—1942–1945

By 1935 a flood of refugees from Germany began to reach the United States. It soon became apparent that the United States could not tolerate this threat to civilization and humanity by the Nazis. Fortunately, the MGH already had a model that told us how to prepare. In World War I the director of the hospital, Frederick Washburn, organized Base Hospital #6. The professional staff, composed of physicians and nurses, was drawn from the staff of the MGH. During their time of service in France of about fifteen months they cared for large numbers of patients; over four thousand were counted at one time.

Nearly hidden in his history of the MGH, Colonel Washburn's summary of the results of the war deserves quotation. He said, in part:

> Horrible as war is, there are by-products of value. Lifetime friendships are formed. Men who have campaigned together know one another thoroughly. Fine traits of character are brought out, and in contrast the less admirable ones fail of concealment. Men learn the relative importance of things. A man who has parted from his home and risked his life has learned the comparative unimportance of social position and riches. He values accomplishment, service to others, his home life, his chance to raise a family in comfort and security.[1]

The history of the 6th General Hospital—the MGH unit in which many of us served in World War II—actually can be traced back to that Base Hospital #6 of World War I. When that war ended, a reserve unit was established. This unit, however, was essentially inactive until 1940. At that time, when Britain was being threatened with destruction by the Luftwaffe it was clear that it would be only a matter of time before the United States would be involved in the conflict.

The War Department asked many academic institutions to prepare a list of individuals and set up potential professional staffs for active duty. The MGH unit was assigned the title of the 6th General Hospital. It was organized under the leadership of Colonel Thomas Goethals. In civilian life he was a distinguished obstetrician and had been a member of the MGH staff for thirty years. His father, Major General G. W. Goethals, an American Army officer and engineer, was responsible for the completion of the Panama Canal.

A skeleton staff of physicians and surgeons was identified. As a member of the group, I can recall many visits we made to Camp Devens in Ayer, Massachusetts for training in military medicine. Eventually 123 members of the MGH active staff of 312 entered the armed services. This contribution to the armed services included forty percent of its active staff of physicians, forty-eight percent of its physician graduates, and thirty-three percent of the nursing staff. The 6th General was activated on May 15, 1942 in Camp Blanding, Florida.

Colonel Goethals became a strict disciplinarian as soon as he put on his army uniform. He did not spare himself. He became jaundiced following one of the injections we were given to prevent yellow fever; he did not miss a day on duty. He was an inveterate cigar smoker and kept one alight even in his daily shower. Typically, he marched at the head of our grueling biweekly hikes through the steamy Florida piney woods. He was one of the few people who knew what was going on in the hospital. His sprightly account in the Faxon history of the MGH accurately reflects the activities of our unit throughout the war.[2]

The trip to Florida took nearly three days, because we spent long periods on railroad sidings. Finally, we emerged one morning in Starke, Florida, in our heavy wool uniforms and were almost incapacitated by the heat. The high temperatures, intense beyond our prior experience, remained with us for the next six months. Our encampment, once a plantation, was labeled *Camp Blanding*. An artificial lake had been scooped out to provide some relief from the heat and the ubiquitous sand. Of the nearly 400 soldiers in the camp, forty-five were male physician officers, 120 were female nurse officers, and the rest were enlisted men. The officers were placed in cabins, each of which held four bunks. Air-conditioning was provided by screens all around and by the heavy downpours that occurred nearly every day during the summer months. We awoke in the morning dripping wet from sweat. The temperature in the cabins rose to nearly 116 degrees at times and the showers all were warm; there was simply no way to cool off.

Our major activity consisted of hardening our muscles, learning to obey orders, and awaiting our move to the next assignment. Meanwhile, we attended "troop school" every day to learn some of the essentials of military life. The officers taught the enlisted men the principles of asepsis, anatomy, and other subjects that would be of importance to them when we set up our hospital. On Tuesday and Friday afternoons, we put on our packs and went for an eight mile hike through the woods. These hikes in the sand proved to be rather galling because of the heat. Some times we were followed by an ambulance which picked up the men who fell out during the march. I recall the day Major Thorndike, who was somewhat corpulent, collapsed with a pulse of approximately 160. His blue face showed that he was in a state of acute cardiac decompensation. He recovered rapidly, however, and we had no casualties in the camp.

We spent hours on the obstacle course and a great deal of time on the drill field. Actually we had very little use for this accomplishment later, but it taught us to work together and instilled in us the idea that we had to submit to authority. One officer, Stanley Wyman, was commissioned to drill the nurses. He complained that when he ordered them to dress right he never knew which part of their anatomy to use for alignment. First he tried noses, but certain other physical adornments protruded irregularly. He finally decided to keep the backs in line and not worry about the irregular view from the front. Within a period of several months, our entire detachment could march very satisfactorily; for a visiting posse of officers we put on a good show.

Many amusing incidents occurred as well. One of our officers was troubled with nocturia; but instead of walking about fifty steps to the latrine, he put a large can under his bed. This practice did not impress his roommates, so one day they punched a number of holes in the side of the can. That night, when the water level rose in the can, loud oaths followed. Grantley Taylor, a gifted artist, painted a large number of scenes with his water colors and enlivened the whole course of our adventures with his pictures. Unfortunately, most of them now have been lost and we were forbidden to take photographs.

There was little opportunity for professional work at Blanding. Occasionally we carried out a few tasks in the Station Hospital. We were always more or less on alert, so practically everybody was kept in camp without leave. One fairly large group was split off to form the 160th Station Hospital and sent to England in June, 1942, but most of us stayed on. Fall came with a profusion of flowers in the piney woods and the hikes became more of a pleasure than a chore. It even turned quite cold at night. Finally, in January 1943 we received orders to move. We had no word where we were going. In November, however, there had been landings by the U.S. forces in North Africa so we assumed that was our probable destination.

We went north by train to Camp Kilmer in New Jersey, a staging point for embarkation. Deep snow covered the ground and the wind blew a gale. We purchased rubber overshoes, which lasted for over 40 years. And we were subjected to a large number of inoculations. Most of them were not very bothersome, but everyone who had been through the entire set warned us about the typhus shot. Eventually I got it. Absolutely nothing happened—that is, for thirty seconds. Just as I was walking out the door I suddenly thought my arm was going to fall off. It was several hours before the arm seemed to be reattached. I think the disease might have been less painful than the inoculation.

After approximately a week, we were loaded on another train. Each of us had a barracks bag which contained all of our transportable possessions. It is interesting to recall which items really were valuable and which turned out to be useless. Besides the appropriate clothes, materials for shaving, tooth brush and paste, the most valuable item I had was an air mattress. It served me well many times, particularly when I was forced to sleep on bare ground and stones.

Several hundred troops and most of our hospital personnel embarked on a reasonably large transport—the *Brazil*. Before the war it had plied the South American route as a passenger ship. Some members of our unit were loaded on two smaller sister ships—the *Uruguay* and the *Argentina*. We were maneuvered into a convoy of about thirty ships. We were guarded by a large battleship—the *Texas*—a cruiser and ten destroyers. We zig-zagged our way across the Atlantic. All ships would tack in unison for several hundred yards, and then change direction. One night, when the only light was furnished by the stars, one ship zigged when it should have zagged and collided with the *Uruguay;* it had to drop out to Bermuda for repairs.

The first few hours on board were very pleasant. We had a fine dinner and thought we would enjoy the voyage. But soon it became obvious that we were at sea. The ship tossed, turned, shivered, and quivered. I was not really happy again until I stepped out on dry land about ten days later.

Except for this one misadventure, during the pitch-black night it was very comforting to step out on deck and hear the ships swishing through the waves, and in the morning to see the entire convoy intact executing its maneuvers in perfect unison. Twenty-four hours out of port, I was appointed as one of the sanitary officers on the ship. Consequently with a few others, I made daily inspections of the entire ship. It was not particularly enjoyable to go through the decks housing the troops. There were three tiers of bodies, one above the other. When a person was sick above there was quite a commotion down below. Many were seasick. Sanitary arrangements necessarily were crude. So far as I was concerned, loss of appetite was followed by nausea and finally a fever. I was put in sick bay where I remained until the ship reached Casablanca several days later.

In the harbor there were half-sunken boats, including French warships. The *Jean Bart*, one of their largest, was under water. Somehow, though, space was found for our vessels. The city itself was white and gleaming, but underneath its lovely surface there ran undercurrents of tension—fear of the possibility of invasion by the Germans, and Arab hostility toward the French. The temperature was cool in Casablanca, but hot as a volcano during the day in the interior. It has been said that Morocco is a cold country where the sun is hot. It certainly was true that during the daytime, except near the sea, it was very hot during the cloudless days but very cool at night. The Atlantic ocean beat on the rocky shore with extraordinary force. The so-called bathing beaches were extremely dangerous. Even though there were ropes slung out for soldiers to catch if necessary, no one dared to venture out over his neck. Despite the precautions, several persons drowned in the surging waves that criss-crossed in every direction. Eventually we discovered Lingley's beach which was relatively peaceful and even allowed us to swim from time to time.

We were ensconced in the *École des Jeunes Filles*, a former school for girls. There we were introduced to the mysteries of bidets, an invention that seemed to be pretty useless so far as males could determine. One dormitory housed the male officers. We hurried to convert the other buildings into a hospital. This required a lot of work by the Arab laborers. It progressed rapidly and we began to accept patients in only one week. Soon we were inundated with casualties from the battle for the Kasserine Pass and other engagements. Despite the fact that we were nearly 1,500 miles from the front, we knew Rommel had almost broken the American line and we felt far from secure.

For several months the forty male captains and lieutenants were quartered in one large dormitory with no privacy and one busy latrine at the end. The traffic to the latrine was unbelievable and sleep impossible, particularly after prophylactic doses of Atabrine were given to all of the troops. The armed forces radio played music continuously, repeating the usual jingles (including the *Little Brown Jug)* over and over. Arabs ran up and down the street early in the morning selling their wares, and shouting "huitres et vieux habits" ("oysters and old clothes").

Late in the fall Fortune smiled on us for we were moved into tents in a city park. But shortly thereafter, Captains Hamilton, Aufranc and I were promoted to the rank of major, and that promotion enabled us to live with the other majors in the Hotel Majestic. We moved there with great fanfare, because the winter rains had begun. Inasmuch as Major Hamilton had received his promotion a day ahead of Otto Aufranc and me, he decided to take the one single room that was vacant; Otto and I had to be content with the large double bed in the other room. During our first night there, however, after Otto and I fell into a sound sleep, Major Hamilton suddenly appeared in our room in his pajamas. His face was about twice normal size, and his nose was far more imposing than that of Jimmy Durante. It was clear he had sustained numerous bites. The diagnosis was cimicosis, or what is familiarly known as bedbug bites. In keeping with their location, the welts had attained a majestic size.

The Red Cross put on nightly movies. We would emerge from these excellent shows into a complete blackout and try to find our way back to our quarters unharmed. Inasmuch as there were many horses in Casablanca at that time, a walk down the streets during a blackout was accompanied by considerable hazards.

The Arab workmen proved to be very efficient with bricks and mortar. In only a few days the medical facility in the girls' school, which had been previously occupied by the Eighth Evacuation Hospital, was expanded by converting a huge adjacent storage building into large wards. The operating rooms, which were very similar to those in the Phillips House, were functional almost immediately. Major Langdon Parsons performed the first operation in them—an appendectomy done on one of the privates in the detachment.

Only a short time later the first hospital train arrived directly from the Kasserine Pass where American troops had been repulsed by a strong German force. The sudden deluge of several hundred patients quickly taught us many lessons. The first one was that when a ward suddenly fills with wounded men, a leisurely workup is wrong. The whole group must be examined rapidly, and those patients who needed immediate treatment identified quickly. The medical officers rapidly became adept at this practice of triage.

The next lesson was to forget some of the principles carried over from previous conflicts. For example, from 1936 to 1939 in the Spanish Civil War, a new method of therapy for fractures had been developed that appeared to offer definite advantages. A cast was placed on the fractured extremity and left in place for a week, or even more, before being replaced. We found that this method simply did not work in the presence of severe vascular injury or infection. In our early cases, all casts were removed and, if amputation was necessary, it was done expeditiously, frequently with closure of the amputation stump. Later, in our hospital, we became even more impressed with the use of thorough debridement of compound fractures and early stabilization, if necessary, by internal fixation, combined with delayed primary closure.

We believed this was an enormous advance in the treatment of injuries that involved many extremities. However, not long thereafter a directive appeared from Washington stating that no amputation stumps should be closed. The innovative methods that were being developed by Major Aufranc were immediately stopped.

A lesson taught from World War I was that abdominal injuries should be treated by emergency laparotomy. General Ogilvie, in charge of the British Armed Forces based in the eastern desert of North Africa, found that his wounded patients had to be transported by ambulance or truck for long distances after emergency operations. Under those conditions, wounds of the colon that had been closed by suture did very poorly. Colostomies were ordered for all colon wounds. This practice proved to be a very important advance, although we now know that wounds in civilian life can be treated far differently.

Later in the war we learned much more about the treatment of abdominal wounds—such as provision for adequate blood replacement, placement of colostomies away from the laparotomy incision, and closure of abdominal incisions with sturdy sutures placed through all layers of the abdominal wall to prevent dehiscence.

Early repair of vascular injuries was not done until the time of the Korean War, which began in 1950. (Incidentally, I did the first vein graft in the MGH in 1945; a damaged popliteal artery was replaced with a femoral vein with excellent results.) Amputations were nearly always necessary for damage to the femoral arteries in the groin in World War II.

Combined injury of a contiguous artery and vein often led to an arteriovenous fistula. The usual method of repair early in World War II was considered to be ligation of both the artery and vein just above and below the fistula. Today both artery and vein almost always can be reconstructed. In Casablanca I was able to successfully repair such a fistula between the internal carotid artery and internal jugular vein.

We had many medical adventures in Casablanca, but I will mention only a few. General Patton came into the hospital one day to have several blotches removed from his face. He was blustering about, so our head nurse, Miss Coughlin, said to him, "You lie down on that table. There aren't any generals here; there are only privates". He immediately did as he was told. She maintained discipline in the operating room very well.

Many of our Kasserine Pass casualties seemed to have serious nerve damage associated with penetrating missile fragments. We expected that we would have to do frequent surgical repairs. However, much to our amazement nearly all of the soldiers staged a remarkable improvement spontaneously within a few weeks. We had not realized that nerves, apparently interrupted, could recover completely. This discovery diminished our enthusiasm for exploring presumed nerve injuries at an early date after wounding.

We were able to evacuate patients reasonably rapidly, and it soon became clear that it would be better to transfer many of the patients rather than keep them in our hospital. For example, we felt a great urge to operate on bad backs early in the campaign as the hospital preceding us in Casablanca had done very frequently. We removed a few disks but it soon became clear that the disks were not as abnormal as we had expected and the patients were not returning to duty. We decided that back injuries required evacuation to the States unless the soldiers improved rapidly. Many soldiers with psychiatric problems also needed to be evacuated. (It was at this time that the famous episode occurred when General Patton slapped a soldier ill with a psychiatric disease; this disciplinary action was not received kindly by physicians or soldiers.)

We treated many major injuries prior to the patient's return to the United States. We did many amputations but no chest injuries appeared in Casablanca. The bulk of the operations were for closures of wounds of soft tissues or closure of colostomies. Gunshot wounds, shell fragments from artillery fire and mine fragments were the common causes.

In the spring of 1943 the campaign in Italy was well under way and we were transferred to that site. We left Casablanca with some regret, but, sensing the excitement that was ahead, we were eager to go. On the train trip across northern Morocco and into Algeria, we were served contaminated food that caused a number of us to become ill with a *Salmonella* infection. We set up our tents, blew up the air mattresses, and slept on the stones on Goat Hill near Oran awaiting the arrival of the hospital ship. However, I was victimized by diarrhea and had to go into the Seventh station hospital. I did not realize how sick I was until I saw another of our fellow officers. He was a red-head but his whole face and hair seemed to have turned purple from the same disease. We were given one of the sulfanilamides, staged a recovery in the course of a few days, and were able to join the hospital ship to make our way across the placid, beautiful deep blue Mediterranean. It was hard to believe we were sailing into a war zone. Our ship docked in the harbor at Naples, and we were transported to a staging area some thirty miles north of the city. The encampment was surrounded by a wire fence to keep the paesanos out. They had no food and were eagerly awaiting any garbage that we might throw out. Naples itself was terribly dirty, heavily damaged, and essentially devoid of toilet facilities. The streets appeared to be the only spot for the disposal of body wastes.

Fortunately I did not have to stay long in the staging area because I was quickly assigned to one of the general hospitals close to the actual front. It was there that I learned one of the most important lessons of the war—the efficacy of decortication of the lungs.

This hospital was inundated with soldiers who had wounds of the chest caused by shell fragments or bullets. Major William Tuttle was in charge and spent most of his time directing the younger surgeons. This arrangement gave us a lot of experience and opened a new vista on the treatment of thoracic injuries.

I remember how surprised I was to find that a soldier with a chest full of clotted blood and pus, a collapsed lung and high fever could almost miraculously be cured by removal of the thick peel around the lung, clearing all foreign material from the pleural cavity, and then expanding the lung to fill the chest. I later operated on many such patients when we arrived in Rome with excellent results.

After a few weeks on detached leave near the front, I rejoined the MGH unit; we embarked on a landing craft infantry (LCI) near Naples. That overnight trip was an absolute nightmare for most of the troops. The ship rolled from side to side and nearly everyone was seasick. In the morning we landed in Anzio, which had been taken the day before from the Germans. Before the war it had been a lovely seaside town; but when we saw it, it was essentially destroyed. The countryside was extensively pockmarked with huge holes caused by the artillery bombardment. Nevertheless, the vistas toward the Alban hills were beautiful. We were immediately put in trucks to go on to Rome.

When we arrived on the outskirts of Rome—an open city—we were surrounded by cheering crowds that lined every road. The Italians were extremely happy to see the Americans on this, the first day after the Germans had evacuated.

We made our way to the *Buon Pastore* (a home for wayward girls), which, incidentally, was the second largest building in Rome. It accommodated 1,000 people without much difficulty, but, it was rumored, there were only two toilets in the whole building. There was a lovely chapel because the school had been run by the church. A lot of renovation was needed to turn the building into a decent hospital, even though the Germans had used it previously for that purpose. They obviously departed in great haste just before we arrived, leaving uneaten breakfasts on the table and a few dead bodies lying around.

Soon everything was cleaned, many more toilets were installed, and the building was transformed into an excellent hospital. Meanwhile, we had an opportunity to discover the wonders of Rome. We made our way down to the Forum and explored the old buildings, many of which were familiar. We had seen pictures of them in grade school and now felt as though we had been there before.

Rome had been declared an open city so there was no destruction. The streets were empty, and the terrible smog that hangs over it in 1990 was entirely absent. Our hospital was located about a mile beyond the Vatican in what then was open country. Today the huge building still stands, but it is surrounded by apartment buildings.

The officers were quartered in tents near the hospital. We were quite comfortable during the hot summer nights, but during the winter it was almost impossible to keep warm in bed even with numerous blankets and newspapers stuffed between them. And we were so busy with the large wards and patients that there was little time except for occasional excursions into the city.

One memory of Rome centers on Christmas eve. We went to hear the Pope celebrate Mass in St. Peter's. It has been estimated that 50,000 people crowded into the building that night. The scene was a nightmare, because the guards had opened only one door. An enormous crowd was milling about trying to get in, while others were trying desperately to get out. Some people were sick in a corner of the rotunda. If a bomb had come our way then, the carnage would have been unbelievable. The flow of the huge crowd simulated water flowing down a river; the main current went forward, but along the margin a countercurrent formed that went backward. We finally were pushed out by the crowd behind us.

We were extremely busy during our first six months in Rome. At one time the hospital had nearly 3,000 patients. One huge operating room contained ten tables. In addition, smaller rooms were used for more difficult procedures. The operating list often ran to over 150 cases a day. The commonest operations by far were wound closures. Soldiers had been treated near the front with thorough debridement and removal of all foreign bodies from their battle wounds; we repaired the defects in the soft tissues that had been excised and closed the wounds. This was one of the great advances developed in the Italian theater; essentially it eliminated sepsis in wounds. Colonel Churchill was responsible for introduction of the method.

There were so many surgical cases that I had to enlist two of our able physicians on my service. Drs. Alfred Kranes and Daniel Ellis became interested in sewing up wounds, but they balked at more complicated procedures like skin grafts. These physicians were glad to return to their specialty as soon as possible. We also acquired some presumably well trained surgeons from other allied countries.

As the fighting moved up to the northern end of the Italian peninsula our hospital moved to Bologna. When the number of patients began to diminish I was placed on detached service and had a very interesting time in northern Italy during the winter months. First I was assigned to a station hospital (#7) in Leghorn. It was a very busy spot, on the shores of the Mediterranean, and close to the front lines. Many fresh casualties were brought there. Russell Best of Omaha was in charge of the surgical service. My main memory of this assignment is the penetrating cold and the heavy daily rain. It was difficult to keep our tents warm because the temperature was in the low thirties. But we ate welcome Christmas fruitcake after fruitcake from home.

This assignment only lasted about three weeks and then I was transferred to the Eighth Evacuation Hospital. It was located in the Apennine mountains, halfway between Florence and Bologna, only a few miles behind the front—or, as it was called, the Gothic Line.

Mussolini had had a ski lodge in the near vicinity. During the off-duty hours, we were able to tramp around the woods and up some mountain trails. Later the snow fell heavily, rising almost to our hips. We had a small coal stove in our tent and heated water for shaving in our helmets.

Occasionally we would drive down to Florence, about thirty miles south. This absolutely beautiful city was warm and like a breath of spring. Although our visits were very short, we were able to see some of the famous spots and many of the lovely views in the valleys and mountains of that wonderful country.

The work in the hospital was taxing. At times the operating rooms were in continual use; surgeons worked in three shifts of eight hours each. I did not mind the daytime shifts but at night it was very, very difficult to maintain an effective level of performance. I remember, for example, one unfortunate GI who came in with such terrible wounds on his anterior abdomen that I started at once to repair them. As soon as I turned him over, I found that almost his entire backside was nearly destroyed. The time spent repairing this soldier's anterior wounds was totally wasted and would have been saved by a more adequate preoperative examination.

There were many hours spent in removal of foreign bodies and debridement of wounds throughout the body. Most patients survived but some had severe disabilities. For example, one poor fellow had one entire carotid destroyed up to the base of the skull. There was no way to effect a repair. Not unexpectedly, he developed a hemiparesis.

Despite the fact that we were close to the front lines we had only one real scare. One night while I was watching a movie, a bomb went off a short distance away. I found that all of the GIs on both sides of me were well under their seats before I even knew it was time to move. At times we would get up very close to the front where surgical teams from the Second Auxiliary Surgical Group were at work. Undying friendships sprang up between members of the two groups. I shall always cherish my acquaintance with Robert Wintersmith Robertson (Red Robby) of Paducah, Kentucky; he was a very modest man who received an O.B.E. (Officer of the Order of the British Empire) for bravery in action.

Other episodes stand out in my memory. Lang Parsons and one of his compatriots formed a surgical team that was sent up close to the front. They arrived late one night and had to stay in the tent that received casualties. At midnight a nurse came around to give everyone a shot of penicillin. The dose was 25,000 units; today, when penicillin is plentiful, the dose is ten times greater. However, even that small dose was uncomfortable. The doctors wanted to sleep; they could not persuade the nurse to stop; the needle sank in. She came back three hours later; they were sleepy and despite a long argument they could not stop her from giving another shot. Three hours later she was back again; this time they did not even argue as they turned over on their left sides and awaited the needle.

A healthy-looking G.I. came into the emergency tent one day and told me that he had drunk a can of Sterno. I did not see anything wrong with him and did not believe his tale. About an hour later he said "I cannot see". Two hours later he was dead. Such is the power of wood alcohol. I should have washed out his stomach, but I doubt that it would have made any difference.

In Bologna we took care of a large number of Americans and several hundred German prisoners. Fred Kranes, to his amazement, drained an enormous echinococcus cyst of the liver in a prisoner. He also cured a German officer's frozen right shoulder by commanding the whole ward of prisoners to stand at attention and then suddenly shouting "Heil Hitler!" The supposedly immobile right arm shot up into the air. All of the other Germans laughed heartily.

The armistice was signed in the Italian theater on May 2, 1945. The Americans were assigned to take charge of German prisoners who were patients in the German hospitals. Many of these hospitals were located in Merano—a lovely city in northern Italy on the south slopes of the Alps. It was a famous health spa and contained thousands of wounded Germans. I was sent, with a few other officers, to inspect these hospitals and determine the number of prisoners who would be transported to Bologna.

We drove up the valley of the Adige River. Farmers in Alpine dress were driving their horse-drawn carts along country roads beneath showers of apple blossoms. The snow-covered Dolomites rose thousands of feet above us. The remnants of a freight train, destroyed by an aerial bomb lay as a memento in green fields in the valley. Peace was about to return and remnants of the war were disappearing.

When our hospital was nearly ready to close, we began to organize our impressions concerning the lessons we had learned during the war.

At the end of the Italian campaign, I considered the chief contributions made by surgeons in the Mediterranean Theater to be:

1. The principle of complete debridement of wounds of the skin and underlying tissues shortly after injury, followed by delayed primary suture in an evacuation, general, or station hospital four days later. This method was used by an unnamed surgeon in an unnamed station hospital in Tunisia. It was observed by Colonel Churchill, and quickly instituted by him as a part of the s.o.p. (standard operating procedure).

2. The use of whole blood rather than plasma for the treatment of wound shock. Blood banks were established in large hospitals, and adequate amounts were supplied to various other stations. At the outset of the war, plasma was available in large quantities from the United States but was found to be inadequate for treatment of serious injuries accompanied by hemorrhage.

3. The use of colostomies for wounds of the colorectum. This procedure had been established in the British Eighth Army. General Ogilvie was keenly interested and ordered all surgeons to use this routine. It was especially important when evacuation routes for the wounded were long and rough.

4. Early decortication for chest wounds. About a month after the initial injury, many soldiers with such wounds had developed a pyo-thorax with partial collapse of the lung. By this time, a thick peel had formed about the lung, preventing expansion. Decortication—excision of this fibrin coat—and removal of other debris from the chest, allowed complete reexpansion of the lung and almost miraculous improvement in the patient.

5. Restricted use of morphine early after wounding. On the Anzio beachhead, Dr. Henry Beecher had found that many soldiers had been given large doses of morphine early after wounding. He noted that as they were resuscitated the morphine was absorbed and intoxication followed.

6. *Auxiliary Surgical Groups* consisted of several teams of two persons: a surgeon and an anesthetist. They could be mobilized rapidly and sent to any forward installation that found itself suddenly in need of more surgical manpower. By this action, well trained surgeons were placed close to the front. The Second Auxiliary Surgical Group was the most active in the Mediterranean Theater. The members of this unit formed a tightly cohesive group that maintained yearly meetings until dissolution in 1988.

7. Antibiotics were used as soon as they were developed. At the outset of the war, sulfanilamide was available and was given to all stations. Penicillin arrived a few months later; it was employed in

doses of 25,000 units. This very small amount was sufficient to demonstrate its great value.

8. Colonel Churchill was responsible for moving the halls of academe to the battlefields. In Italy there were numerous hospitals that were staffed by university surgeons. Meetings and exchange of information continued throughout the war just as it had at home.

9. Strong bonds of fellowship were created between the surgeons who worked in this Theater. The *Excelsior Surgical Society* was formed in the closing days of the war to cement these friendships.

As the time to leave Italy drew closer, memories of frustrations and horrors of the war gradually became displaced by happier recollections and even by a sense of nostalgia. Throughout our stay in Italy we had used our recreational leaves to see many of the beautiful and historical spots in this phenomenal country. We had seen a nation that had survived invasions and wars. A civilization in many respects unique had survived another potential catastrophe. Meanwhile we had been able to observe many areas that even enthusiastic tourists would find it difficult to locate. Many of them are indelible in memory.

The breath-taking vistas from the Amalfi drive, the beguiling shores of Sorrento (where the haunting strains of *Lili Marlene*—the theme song of the German Army—were still being sung when we were there), the lost opulence of Pompeii, the lovely harbor of Naples, the mountains and grottoes of Capri, the forbidding mountains of the Apennine chain, the cold days in Volterra where the natives warmed their fingers with charcoal braziers as they carved their mementoes of alabaster, the flowers and kaleidoscopic beauty of Lago Maggiore, the faded but still effulgent charm of the Last Supper on the church wall in Milan, the apple blossoms and snows on the Dolomites in Cortina and along the Adige River, the leaning tower of Pisa, the charm of Venice, the doors of the Baptistry in Florence, and above all the historical monuments and famous edifices in Rome—all of these sights were ours to savor in all their glory in our hours of leisure. They were made even more spectacular by the momentary horrors of World War II that were defacing but not destroying the heart of Italy. It is a wonderful country endowed with a vigorous people who have outlasted war and famine for centuries—the true test of a civilization. All honor to Italy and the Italians.

The 6th General Hospital continued to operate in Bologna until July, and finally was deactivated on September 15, 1945.[3] I received

Above: Camp Blanding, Florida, staging area for the 6th General Hospital (the MGH unit), 1942 to early 1943. Below: Colonel Thomas Goethals, Commanding Officer. Courtesy of Dr. John McKittrick for both pictures.

Above: Review of the 6th General troops. Below: Completing an eight-mile hike every Tuesday and Friday. Courtesy of Dr. John McKittrick for both pictures.

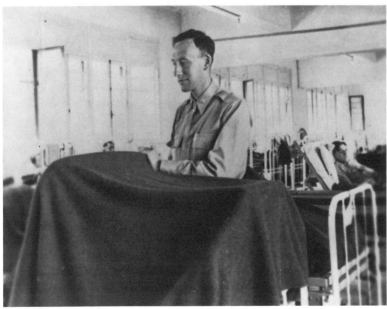

Above: John McKittrick, Daniel Ellis, and CEW on hill overlooking Casablanca harbor, 1943. Below: CEW making ward rounds at the 6th General Hospital in Casablanca, 1943.

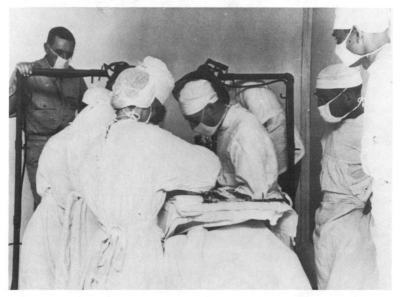

Above: The 6th General Hospital, Rome, 1944. Below: CEW operating at the hospital in Rome, being observed by the chiefs of the surgical service, Horatio Rogers and Marshall Bartlett.

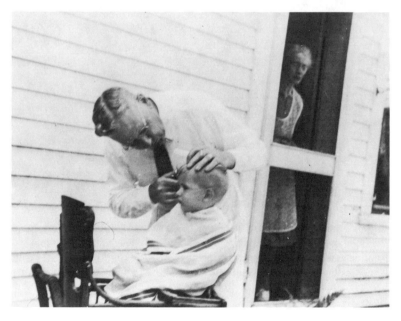

Keeping the home fires burning. Above: Phyllis shoveling the driveway, 1944 (left); Phyllis with our cocker spaniel Suzie, John Paton Welch, and Claude E. Welch, Jr., 1943 (right). Below: Grandpa Welch cutting Claude Jr.'s hair with Grandma observing, 1944.

Edward Delos Churchill: as Colonel in Casablanca, 1943 (upper left); awarding the Bigelow medal to Clarence Crafoord, 1961 (upper right); shown in an oil painting at a conference with residents (below, left to right) Edward Salzman. Henry Edmunds, Ronald Malt, Anthony Monaco, John Constable, Harold Urschel, unidentified visitors, 1962. Courtesy of the Massachusetts General Hospital.

an elevation in rank to lieutenant colonel and was given an Army Commendation Ribbon. The assignment in Italy ended. We embarked at Leghorn on the Joel Chandler Harris, a Liberty boat that cruised at a maximum speed of twelve knots. It took us three weeks to reach Newport News; we arrived in October 1945. And then there was the deep emotion of the first telephone call home and Phyllis's voice!

8

Edward D. Churchill
and MGH Surgery 1942–1950

By 1950 all of the physicians and surgeons who had been in the 6th General Hospital in World War II had resumed their familiar civilian routines. Those of us who returned from abroad had wondered whether there actually was a place for us in this city already crowded with eminent physicians and surgeons. As it turned out, there was no problem. The surgeons who had been left behind were overworked and tired. They were glad to see new blood appear. Patients agreed. The fraternal affection that officers had formed in the 6th General Hospital strengthened rather than diminished. This tie led to mutual respect and patient referrals. I became deeply immersed in surgery in the MGH as soon as I returned and would be for nearly four decades more.

However, some major differences were apparent in the MGH between 1942, when I left for war, and 1950. An enlarged surgical staff and increased popularity of the hospital led to a severe shortage of beds for patients. Some surgeons had to shift their loyalties to other hospitals. In addition, in a major change, Dr. Churchill had been appointed in 1948 chief of both the East and the West surgical services. For the first time in the history of the MGH, except for a few weeks when Maurice Richardson had the title, there was one chief of both surgical services.

A major loss for the MGH was Leland McKittrick. He was a wise, thoughtful surgeon whose advice always was welcome. In addition he was a strong supporter of organized medicine and had a particular interest in the AMA where he served for many years as the chairman of the council on medical education. He had confidently expected to rise to the position of chief of the East surgical service until the trustees abolished that position. Reginald Smithwick had been appointed chairman of the department of surgery in the University Hospital during the war; Langdon Parsons later followed him to become chief of the gynecologic service. Otto Aufranc took his patients to the New England Baptist Hospital. Francis Moore became the surgeon-in-chief in the Peter Bent Brigham Hospital and Moseley Professor of Surgery in the Harvard Medical School in 1948.

These major changes demonstrate that the MGH has been a fertile institution to allow young surgeons to mature and assume important positions in surgery in Boston as well as elsewhere.

By 1950 Dr. Churchill was firmly in charge of the surgical services in the MGH. During the remainder of his career, among other accomplishments, he would perfect the MGH surgical residency into one of the most important and popular in the United States, establish the Surgical Associates, and supplement his emphasis on teaching by writing his masterpiece, *To Work in the Vineyard of Surgery.*

Our mutual experiences during the war as well as in the hospital increased my great respect for Dr. Churchill. He became a true role model, my only one other than Dr. Allen. This is an appropriate time to consider the reasons for this statement and why he personified the MGH for many years.

In brief, he was appointed as Chief of the West surgical service in the MGH and Professor of Surgery in the HMS in 1931. He was healthy until 1952, when he had a small stroke and developed diabetes. He did well until 1962 when his health deteriorated, and he resigned his positions in the MGH and the HMS.

I have already mentioned that our medical school group met him first when he demonstrated his patient—one of the first persons ever to survive an operation for staphylococcal pericarditis—in an afternoon teaching session in the Boston City Hospital. I met him next when he returned to the MGH in 1931 as professor and chief of the West surgical service. Later we learned that he had graduated from HMS in 1920, had been a surgical house officer in the MGH for four years, had held a research fellowship in Cecil Drinker's laboratory, and had had a *Wanderjahr* as a Moseley traveling fellow. Fortunately he kept meticulous notes of all of his visits to foreign clinics; they have been recently edited and published by Gordon Scannell.[1]

He was an excellent bedside teacher. I recall the first patient I presented to him—a young woman with an abrupt onset of abdominal pain—and my diagnosis of ectopic pregnancy. He agreed and operation shortly afterward confirmed the diagnosis. At a later date, I brought down a patient from the medical wards for him to discuss with the third-year surgical class. The patient was being treated for ascites. He percussed the greatly distended abdomen and within three minutes had made the diagnosis of a huge ovarian cyst. Today nearly every resident would require ultrasound to make a diagnosis that required only Dr. Churchill's fingers and brain.

His interests and techniques changed as dramatically as those of Picasso. Having paid minimal tribute to laboratory investigations in the 1920s, in the 1930s he shifted to operative surgery. He developed the proper operation for constrictive pericarditis. Although Sam Robinson removed a lobe of a lung for bronchiectasis in the MGH in 1909, and was the first surgeon to work in the open chest in the MGH,[2] Churchill followed with many such procedures for bronchiectasis, tuberculosis, and cancer. He was also a pioneer in the surgery of the parathyroid glands.

Many of these operations were done with little aid from assistants or anesthetists. I remember watching him briefly one afternoon when he was struggling to do a lobectomy for an obstructing carcinoid tumor of the bronchus. The pleural cavity had been obliterated by a previous infection. His only assistant was a student nurse. The air was blue from his comments. He finally removed the lobe and closed the bronchus and sutured the chest incision. He opened the specimen; there was no tumor in it. A few minutes later the patient coughed up the tumor, which had been dislodged by his dissection and was lying free in the trachea.

He handled tissues with the utmost delicacy and his technique was meticulous. He was particularly proud of his thyroidectomies. Three days after operation, an observer could barely see the operative incision. On the other hand, there were times when he proceeded with the utmost boldness and speed. Deaths from massive pulmonary emboli were quite common in those days. When a massive embolus was diagnosed, the patient was brought immediately to the operating room. As soon as it was certain the patient could not recover (in other words, when the patient essentially was dead), Dr. Churchill would rapidly open the chest and the pulmonary artery and, in the midst of spouting blood, attempt to withdraw the embolus. In the first case he opened the aorta by mistake. Several other attempts at salvage were made later, but none were successful.

In the 1930s he did no laboratory work himself, but he gave strong support to others, in spite of lack of research funds. Jack Gibbon, after working for years with his heart-lung machine, later became Professor Gibbon in Jefferson Medical School in Philadelphia and, in 1953, used an extracorporeal pump during heart surgery for the first time.

In 1935 all departments of anesthesiology were part of the surgical services. Professor Churchill recognized the weakness of the system that chiefly relied on nurses as etherizers. He picked Henry Beecher, who was a very able man just out of his surgical internship and who had excellent clinical and laboratory training for research. He sent Dr. Beecher to study with August Krogh in Denmark with the promise that he would return as head of the department of anesthesia.

The decade of the forties and World War II provided the happiest years of the newly appointed Colonel Churchill's professional life. He enjoyed tremendously the innumerable professional contacts he had with officers as well as patients. His official title was *Consultant to the Mediterranean Theater.* Although his office was based in the Army Headquarters in Caserta for much of the Italian campaign, he was continuously on the move. He visited all of the hospitals, made certain officers were content in their assignments, observed patients closely, learned from errors and successes, and instituted important programs that saved innumerable lives.

One of his important tactical moves was to place highly trained surgeons and anesthesiologists as surgical teams in hospitals close to the front lines.

Early in the war he visited a small station hospital where a surgeon was treating a number of battle casualties that had occurred in the same area. He saw, in particular, the highly successful treatment of such wounds by primary debridement; primary suture was delayed and done four or five days later. He recommended this method by communications to all hospitals very soon afterward. It reduced the number of septic wounds to nearly zero, provided bones or viscera were not involved.[3]

He brought a highly skilled group of consultants with him. They included Champ Lyons, Fiorindo Simeone, and Henry Beecher. Beecher served as an anesthesiologist amid falling shells on Anzio Beach and found that many soldiers were dying from shock due in part to over zealous administration of morphine to wounded men. One of Churchill's greatest contributions was to set up blood banks and to prove that whole blood was more efficacious under battle conditions than saline solutions or plasma.

Chest wounds were common. Pulmonary decortication was found

to be an extraordinarily effective method to save many soldiers dying from pulmonary sepsis. (It should be recalled that there were no antibiotics available in most of these cases; when penicillin did arrive, the maximum dose was 25,000 units, a trivial amount by 1990 standards.)

Many of the general hospitals in the Mediterranean Theater had been formed in academic centers. So the medical officers were highly trained and became colleagues with the Colonel. He turned the battlefield into a clinical laboratory. Friendships deepened. Details for the future Surgical Associates of the MGH were discussed in our tents in Rome and Bologna. He kept detailed notes of his activities and several years later published the diary he had kept during these years.[4]

At the conclusion of the war, a group of officers from various medical centers organized the Excelsior Surgical Society. Eldridge Campbell (professor of neurosurgery and chief of the department in Albany), Oscar Hampton (orthopedic surgeon from Washington University and later associate director of the American College of Surgeons), Lyman Brewer (eminent chest surgeon from Los Angeles), Carl Mathewson and Frank Gerbode from San Francisco, and Howard Snyder (Army consultant and owner of a large surgical clinic in Winfield, Kansas) were among the founders. Dr. Churchill was made the single honorary member. Every year thereafter, as long as health permitted, he and his charming wife, Mary, attended every meeting. The organization was finally dissolved in 1988.

The early years of the Excelsior were among the most pleasant that any group could offer. We were all young, ambitious, and on the crest of the wave. A famous surgeon would be invited each year as a lecturer. The common experiences we had from the war and the wonderful social events that included our wives never can be erased from memory. The Excelsior included surgeons from every section of the country, and blurred all differences between the East and the West and all traces of the Mason-and-Dixon's line.

During the war, Dr. Churchill was elected president of the American Surgical Association. His brilliant philosophical address on Humanism was in sharp contrast to the highly technical paper that he had given earlier to the same organization in 1944. This 1944 paper was described by General Rankin as "one of the finest dissertations on management of wounds which has been submitted through the Office of the Surgeon General of the U.S. Army." The title also demonstrated Churchill's flair for the dramatic—The *Surgical Management of the Wounded in the Mediterranean Theater at the Time of the Fall of Rome.*[5]

In 1945, after the war ended, he had nearly two decades of professional life ahead. Again he made an important change of direction. After 1950, probably because of his diabetes and, in 1952, because of the small stroke, he began to abandon his private practice and concentrate on teaching and writing. He completed his remarkable history, *To Work In The Vineyard of Surgery,* in 1958, only four years before his retirement. Ostensibly it was a biography of John Collins Warren. In reality it was a platform from which he could express his views on medical education and many aspects of surgery. It was here that his opinions about Henry Jacob Bigelow were developed in considerable detail.[6]

Throughout most of his life, he fought for the unity of surgery and strongly opposed its fragmentation into specialties. He also became deeply interested in the historical aspects of the treatment of wounds.[7]

Unfortunately, his discussions of these subjects did not attract a large audience so they did not produce great acclaim. But scattered in them he made many statements that deserve further quotation should a full biography ever be published.[8] Some of them were included in a tribute to Evarts Graham, one of the men he greatly admired.[9]

Probably Dr. Churchill's greatest contribution to surgery was to establish a residency system that guaranteed that all residents could obtain the necessary qualifications for Board examinations. His residency system combined excellent clinical education and responsibility for the care of patients. He gave his residents great responsibility, particularly in the operating room. In his opinion the visiting surgeons should serve as consultants and called by residents only at the residents' option. Many visiting surgeons at that time believed that residents learned best by watching well-trained older surgeons at work and assisting them. Today, Churchill has been proved correct; his point of view was rendered tenable in large part by improvements in anesthesia. Many of us believe the MGH surgical residency program is the best in the country.

He promoted anesthesia to academic status with the appointment of Dr. Henry Beecher as the Dorr Professor of Research in Anesthesia in HMS in 1941, and Chief Anesthesiologist in the MGH. In 1955 he led to the establishment of the first respiratory care unit in the country under the direction of Dr. Henning Pontoppidan. He delegated the surgical care of parathyroid disease to Dr. Oliver Cope, of burns to Drs. Cope and Francis Moore, of plastic and reconstructive surgery to Drs. Bradford Cannon and John Constable, and of esophageal and pulmonary disease to Dr. Richard Sweet. His own special interests in wound healing were promoted by his activities in World War II and his later historical research. Half of his residents later became members of the American Surgical Association, one of the highest honors that can be obtained by American surgeons.

Many professors of surgery and chairmen of departments were his former residents. Some of them excelled in developing specialties that Dr. Churchill to some extent had neglected in his later years. Dr. Moore, for example, was able to forge ahead in the Peter Bent Brigham Hospital with his early work on metabolism in surgical patients, as well as supporting organ transplantation and cardiac surgery. Dr. Churchill has been criticized because of his lack of early support of these two specialties. In retrospect, one feels he should have foreseen the importance of these developments. However, he may have been waiting for dynamic persons schooled in general surgery with a sound training in research. The appointments of his successors, Drs. Paul Russell in transplantation and W. Gerald Austen in cardiac surgery, both world leaders, more than atoned for this delay.

He also has been criticized for his neglect of basic research, particularly at the resident level. Here I believe he had a fundamental disagreement with those surgical departments that require such introductions to the laboratory. He believed education in clinical surgery was so intensive that only certain individuals should delve into laboratory investigations, and only at the expense of a separate year or more. He also was a strong advocate of humanism in surgery and believed that it should not be replaced completely by science.

Considering all of the contributions of Dr. Churchill to surgery and particularly to the education of residents, it seems entirely appropriate to speak of the Churchill School of Surgery as one of the most important in the twentieth century.

In retrospect, he reached the zenith of his power and satisfaction with life when he was in the army, surrounded by young, vigorous surgeons. It was only fitting that, in the year of his retirement from his appointment as chief of surgery in the MGH and from the position as the John Homans Professor of Surgery at the Harvard Medical School, a major celebration of his accomplishments was hosted by the Excelsior Surgical Society. This meeting in the Bigelow Amphitheater in the MGH in 1962 was opened by Oliver Cope, who replaced Dr. Churchill as the chief during the war years. It was followed by numerous papers from his colleagues and all were later published as a Festschrift.[10]

While suffering from diabetes and at least one small stroke, Churchill kept up his habit of smoking cigarettes. He believed that there was no solid evidence linking smoking with cancer of the lung. As time passed, he became involved more deeply with writing and historical research concerned with wound healing. Gradually he became more isolated from the numerous personal contacts he had maintained during the war and began to spend more time with his family on their Vermont farm. One afternoon in 1972 he went for his usual walk— and did not return. He died in the woods presumably of a coronary thrombosis.

Edward Churchill was an extremely proud, reserved person. He believed firmly, for example, that it was the duty of the hospital administration and the community to provide funds for support of hospitals. He never asked anyone for financial help. Once when I gave him enough to support one of our residents abroad for a year, he thanked me; I said more would be available any time he wanted it, but he never made such a request. He was quite jealous of many men on the clinical ladder. Eminent surgeons such as Robert Linton and Grantley Taylor never obtained an academic appointment above that of assistant professor of surgery. Even some of his closer associates were not awarded titles that many would have considered appropriate.

I would not wish to imply that he was wrong. Instead I am certain he believed that the title of professor of surgery was a mark deserving the highest respect and that there were very few persons who could qualify. His intellectual powers were enormous; they were on a level entirely above that of most persons, including nearly all of his confreres as well as deans and contemporary professors in other disciplines.

His attitude did conspire to produce a sort of loneliness of power. But his influence has not diminished. It lives on in the American College of Surgeons by means of a special lectureship, funded by the Excelsior Surgical Society, that is given once a year in the spring meeting. I hope future generations will continue to honor him, and that his portrait will hang on a wall in the MGH as long as the institution lasts. Harvard now has a chair named in his honor: the Edward D. Churchill Professor of Surgery is W. Gerald Austen.

In addition to Dr. Churchill's contributions to surgery, other MGH surgeons were important in the era of 1937 to 1950. Dr. Richard Sweet was an outstanding thoracic surgeon. He concentrated on the esophagus and lungs but also ligated the ductus arteriosus in several patients.

Dr. Linton developed his splenorenal shunts for portal hypertension, resected aortic aneurysms, and did innumerable arterial bypasses. Dr. Allen was particularly interested in gastric and colon resections. Leland McKittrick, Marshall Bartlett, and Claude Welch also were involved particularly in abdominal surgery. Grantley Taylor was a typical surgical oncologist prior to the time the title had been invented; he was followed by Claude Welch, John Raker, William Wood and Alfred Cohen. The eminent gynecologists Joe Meigs and Howard Ulfelder were on the surgical service at that time.

Blood banks and antibiotics made major operations much safer. Anesthesia changed dramatically as the MGH and HMS were the first in the United States to establish anesthesiology as a department separate from surgery. Ether essentially was discarded. Intratracheal tubes, first used by Meltzer in 1909, and muscle relaxants—curare was used by Griffith and Johnson in 1942—and intravenous barbiturates such as pentathol added to the safety of anesthesia as well as comfort for the patient.

In 1942, at the time of the Cocoanut Grove fire, a large number of patients with severe burns were treated in the Massachusetts General Hospital. Important studies on these patients were made, particularly by Drs. Cope and Moore.

Another first for the MGH was recorded when Saul Hertz used radioactive iodine to treat hyperthyroidism in 1941. Since that time it has become the accepted therapy for the great majority of patients with this disease.

Many other important discoveries were made in institutions other than the MGH during the brief period from 1942 to midcentury. Heparin and warfarin became available for treatment of thrombophlebitis and arterial surgery. The first clinical trials of penicillin were carried out. Gross ligated the ductus arteriosus in 1939, initiating cardiac surgery; Dwight Harken removed shell fragments from the hearts of 300 soldiers during World War II. Vagotomy was rediscovered by Dragstedt and applied widely. Streptomycin and chemotherapy proved successful against tuberculosis. Synthetic penicillin was produced. Magnetic resonance imaging was invented. The coronary sinus was catheterized. Cortisone was discovered. Extensive abdominal operations increased; for example, total proctocolectomy for ulcerative colitis was introduced by Gavin Miller in 1949.

This brief summary barely describes the sense of excitement and discovery that pervaded the medical community near the end of the forties. Progress was made on a broad front in both medicine and surgery; certainly this was one of the most productive periods in medical history. It appeared that science, physicians, insurance companies, and the government were united in this great adventure. Hospitals were expanding. The benefits of medicine and surgery were becoming available not only for citizens who could pay but also for the indigent in major cities where the needy could receive care in large municipal hospitals and in rural areas where Hill-Burton hospitals were being constructed. The future for American medicine and surgery appeared to be very bright. And, finally, in 1953, only three and a half per cent of the gross national product was used for health care contrasted with the twelve per cent that is spent today.

9

Academic Pursuits

Thus far, each chapter of this book has been identified with a certain period in my life, starting with my early years in Nebraska, my education, early medical practice, military service in World War II, and the reestablishment of my surgical career at the Massachusetts General Hospital. When I returned to the General in November, 1945 I was nearly forty years old and ready to commence the second phase of my medical career in the MGH at a more senior level than before. Beginning with this chapter, I will desert chronology and instead discuss individual institutions, organizations, and specific topics that have occupied my attention simultaneously for many decades.

The major institution affecting my professional life obviously has been the MGH. A runner-up is Harvard Medical School, which also has influenced my career in many ways. In addition to patient care, most surgeons who practice in an academic center do so because they wish to engage in teaching and in some type of research. The teaching is carried out at several levels—from the teaching of medical students to that of practicing physicians. Research, either in the laboratory or clinical, is documented by publications. Ascent of the academic ladder usually depends on their content, quality, and number. And, of course, certain assignments are given to every individual to promote the welfare of the institutions with which he is associated.

A favorite method to teach clinical medicine, based on long experience, is to study individual cases of illness to determine whether or not correct diagnoses have been made and the proper therapeutic measures applied. Students would study a difficult case, make their own diagnoses, and then listen to a discussion by an expert physician, who would make his own diagnosis. Finally they learned what actually had been found by operation or autopsy. This method provided a medical detective story, intriguing to students of all ages.

I recall a humorous incident relating to one of these clinical studies. One day in the late 1940s, I brought home a case report that I had to discuss on the following day at a clinico-pathological conference. Richard Cabot had initiated these exercises in the MGH about 1905. In 1923 *New England Journal of Medicine* began to publish one case every week. The *Case Records of the Massachusetts General Hospital* continue to be published weekly, nearly seventy years later. This particular report described a teenager who was jaundiced and had a palpable mass in the right upper quadrant of the abdomen. My son, then ten years of age, was excited by puzzles. He read the report. I asked him to make a diagnosis. Based on his monthly perusal of the *Reader's Digest,* he said the mass was a cyst of the bile duct. I had to make my diagnosis before a critical audience on the following day. I agreed with my son. The surgeon who operated on the boy had made the preoperative diagnosis of a liver tumor. What did he find? A cyst of the bile duct.

My academic activities throughout my professional life were concentrated at the MGH and at Harvard Medical School and involved me in teaching at all levels. Harvard Medical School concentrates on teaching candidates for the degree of doctor of medicine; teaching of interns and residents is done by the associated hospitals. HMS also serves as an umbrella organization for continuing medical education and as a coordinator of such activities in various hospitals that belong to the Harvard network. Medical education in the MGH, however, is offered for a wide range of participants, including medical students, interns and residents, and practicing physicians as well as nurses and other health care practitioners.

The three levels in medical education are usually specified as (1) medical education for undergraduates, over which the Liaison Committee on Medical Education (LCME) presides and which ends with the granting of the degree of Doctor of Medicine; (2) graduate medical education for interns and residents, with a comparable Accreditation Council for Graduate Medical Education (ACGME) in charge; and (3) continuing medical education for physicians who have completed internship and residency programs and which is overseen by the Accrediting Council for Continuing Medical Education (ACCME). I have been involved in the activities of all three of these organizations, not only as a participant in teaching, but also in a regulatory capacity as a member of the Residency Review Committee of the ACGME (which inspects and identifies the institutions that should be approved for surgical residencies), and in the ACCME (on the Committee which specifies organizations qualified to engage in continuing medical education). (See Chapter 13, Notes 2 and 3.)

The Liaison Committee on Medical Education conducts an investigation of each medical school roughly once every eight years. Prior to the committee's appraisal of Harvard in 1978 Dean Daniel Tosteson organized an elaborate survey to investigate all of the educational activities of HMS. Sixteen committees were appointed to review various aspects of education, and five others were named to review and coordinate the report. The mission was completed with a final report that was submitted to the Dean on January 3, 1978.

I was the chairman of the committee devoted to an examination of continuing medical education. Harvard has played an outstanding role in this field, beginning post graduate medical education well over a hundred years ago. Much of the CME has been carried on by departments in individual hospitals. Coordination of these activities was difficult until Stephen Goldfinger was appointed the director of the Harvard Medical CME program in the early 1970s. He eliminated conflicts and strengthened the CME program.

In accord with President Bok's appeal to make education a life-long adventure, our committee recommended even further expansion of continuing medical education in the medical school. We recognized the increasing need and demand for continuing medical education, but also warned that it would be essential to monitor such activities to be certain undergraduate education was not slighted if medical education for practicing physicians continued to expand.

Harvard passed this review as well as the subsequent one in the eighties with approbation. It has continued to be one of the premier medical schools in the United States.

While I was interested in the education of individuals at all levels, I was particularly concerned with the teaching of interns and residents, and in continuing medical education. I instituted postgraduate courses in the MGH in cancer and in gastrointestinal surgery in collaboration with Ronald Malt. Thus teaching and patient care have been closely associated. The same relationship of patient care with clinical research has led me to prepare a long succession of papers dealing with such diverse problems as life expectancy in patients with cancer, and operative techniques.

Some of the surgical techniques I initiated and papers I have written have led directly to improvements in patient care. The promotion of catheter duodenostomy in certain operations for difficult duodenal ulcers has been the most important. Although the method was tried and discarded many years before by other surgeons, I developed and popularized a safe technique that has led to the salvage of large numbers of difficult cases. The promotion of more radical operations for combined intestinal obstruction and peritonitis and for intestinal fistulas also have saved many lives. I also performed the first replacement of an artery with a vein graft in the history of the MGH; this procedure now is very common.[1]

Today, laboratory research has become almost essential for an academic surgeon. I shall not enter into a discussion of the values and disadvantages of this approach, except to say that a surgeon who is deeply involved with patient care finds it extremely difficult to arrange a schedule to permit laboratory research unless the major portion of the labor can be done by technicians. I have regretted that I have had no time for such activities.

Administrative details at the medical school continued to take up part of my spare time and energy. In the 1960's, vandalism was rampant about the campus. I was appointed chairman of a committee to promote fire control of the Countway Library, which seemed particularly vulnerable. We decided that carbon dioxide or some gas rather than water would be the best form of fire control. Smoke detectors and alarms to a police station were installed. Some money was raised. Later, however, our drive was merged with another one led by Richard Warren, to provide funds for general use by the library. Fortunately no problems from fire have occurred at any time.

During the 1970s a governance committee was appointed by Dean Robert Ebert to handle many difficult problems. As I was one of the members, I contributed to the resolution of some matters. For example, it had been the custom for many years for the Dean to appoint a small group of faculty members to serve as an advisory council. There was a strong feeling among many of the faculty that this method did not provide adequate representation from all of the institutions under the medical school aegis. Then, one evening in my Belmont home, Professor Elizabeth Hay and I devised a plan for a type of faculty senate. We were following the advice of my son, Claude Jr., who had worked with such a system when he was chairman of the faculty senate in the State University of New York in Buffalo. This recommendation later went through appropriate channels and was adopted.

Dean Ebert also was pressed by many members of the younger faculty who desired promotion but, in the opinion of others, were deemed unworthy. He set up a buffer committee, with me as the chairman, to investigate all such complaints. This was a sticky business, (especially when members of my committee told me that if I would investigate a candidate for a professorship and give a yes or no answer, they would agree with my decision.) However, we found that this delaying action tended to tire applicants and the few persons we had to investigate gave up before they hit the next hurdle.

By 1970, when the federal government decided to support a universal program to pay for treatment of end-stage renal disease, two Harvard Medical School faculty members perceived gold at the end of the rainbow. They—Dr. Constantine Hampers (Assistant Professor of Medicine) and Dr. Edward Hager (Clinical Instructor in Medicine)—started a commercial firm for dialysis of such very ill patients, called National Medical Care. They also built the Babcock Artificial Kidney Center. This building was a short distance from the Peter Bent Brigham Hospital, where they held their academic appointments. Charges for dialysis were higher in the Brigham than in the Babcock. Their venture immediately became highly successful. Stock in National Medical Care rose spectacularly, and the firm built similar centers throughout the United States. Soon, adverse criticisms began to come from within the walls of Harvard Medical School as well as from elsewhere in the country.

On December 17, 1971 the HMS Department of Medicine appointed me chairman of a committee to investigate the activities of the renal dialysis program in the Peter Bent Brigham Hospital and its relationship with the Babcock Artificial Kidney Center. The committee was strengthened immeasurably by the appointment of a special legal counsel, William Waldron.

It became evident that both Hampers and Hager were major stockholders in National Medical Care. Many of the Babcock patients were drawn from the Brigham pool. The quality of care in both institutions was excellent. Nevertheless, intricate questions involving ethics, economics, and legal matters were raised. The major question was whether or not faculty members should profit collectively or individually from a procedure that had been developed either by themselves or by other members of the faculty. We decided that if the Department of Medicine did not approve of such actions, the only measure HMS legally could take would be to relieve the two individuals of their faculty appointments.

We made our report to the Department of Medicine on March 15, 1972, after seven meetings. Our final report contained a set of questions the Department had to answer. The report was considered by the Department and by the entire faculty. After due process, the two individuals were dismissed from their faculty appointments.[2]

The Harvard Medical School Alumni Council is a self-perpetuating body that meets several times a year. Members and officers are elected by ballots cast by all HMS alumni. It oversees the *Harvard Medical Alumni Bulletin*, a quarterly publication that has had a succession of fine editors. This magazine has grown remarkably in its literary content over the past years and now, under Gordon Scannell's direction, is a superb publication. The Council also serves in an advisory capacity to the Dean, to the Director of Alumni Relations, and to fund-raising activities. I was a member of the Council for three years and thereafter its president from 1972–74. During this period Dr. Carl Walter was in charge of the drives for funds. His administrative ability and personal generosity have had a remarkable effect on the school.

Nineteen eighty-two was an important date because it was the bicentennial of the founding of Harvard Medical School. John Warren deserves the credit for this important step; he was appointed the first professor of Anatomy and Surgery on November 22, 1782. But 1982 was notable for another reason. It was the fiftieth anniversary of the graduation of my class from HMS. The year was filled with a series of lectures and publications that paid homage to the great persons of Harvard's past and stressed the frontiers of medical education and research.

The contrast between 1932 and 1982 was astonishing. The method of education had changed radically. When I attended HMS we had a series of lectures that ran nearly continuously throughout the first two years and somewhat less frequently during the last two. Didactic lectures have since become a minor method of transmission of medical knowledge. To memorize all of the facts pertinent to medicine had become a hopeless endeavor. Computers now are the storehouses of knowledge. Recent discoveries and publications now are available to everyone.

After Daniel Tosteson's appointment as Dean in 1977, he made plans to alter the whole system of medical education. His *"New Pathway Program"* would stress the inculcation of lifetime learning, problem solving, and the use of computer techniques not only for retrieval of facts and medical literature, but also as a necessary aid in understanding biostatistics. Although a common instruction in core subjects (which would include biostatistics as well as the common specialties) would continue to be essential, other objectives for general medical education would need to be included. Small groups of students would be identified to work together under specified leaders to further these ends.[3]

Viewed from the perspective of 1990, this method has been a great success. In addition, spurred by the Dean, a drive for $185 million for the school reached a successful end in December 1991. Medical research has attained new heights as well; the annual expenditures for this purpose in the school and associated hospitals is nearly $200 million in 1990.

During the Bicentennial celebration, our class of 1932 was designated to provide a program covering the history of surgery in HMS. We thought it appropriate to concoct a dialogue between the major figures in the history of Harvard surgery. Four of our special deities appeared, coming from the shrines of Valhalla.

Focus, the News sheet published by HMS, reported:

> Claude Welch HMS '32, was moderator and narrator for a very special historical retrospective organized by members of his class, who were celebrating their fiftieth reunion during the School's Bicentennial. Fellow alumni stepped into the roles, the words and the garments of former HMS heroes for a lively exchange of philosophy, irony, and wit.

John C. Warren (played by Richard Warren), entered the auditorium with Oliver Wendell Holmes (Lamar Soutter), the illustrious professor of anatomy. Holmes carefully placed his kid gloves and stovepipe hat on the table. Henry Jacob Bigelow (Howard Ulfelder) was nearly invisible behind his bushy beard. Edward Churchill (Francis Moore) was resplendent in his typical red vest. A vigorous discussion of this past century and a half of surgery indicated a surprising degree of egotism on the part of all of the participants. Finally Bigelow eclipsed the others. When I asked him his opinion on the importance of role models for students, he growled "Balderdash" and brought down the house.

In the mid 1970s, a committee based in the Countway Library developed a program designed to honor persons whom they designated *"Leaders in American Medicine."* Each designee conversed informally with one of his peers, and the hour's interview was recorded on video tape. Several months thereafter, the tape was played at an afternoon meeting and the honoree was discussed by two persons. A festive dinner followed.

Four or five persons were honored each year. Nearly every one was well past the prime of life, and in certain instances, this record has been one of the last and most intimate of the individual's life. Thus each tape is a memorable recital of the life and times of each of the participants. Occasionally a surgeon was chosen for this honor. Dr. Oliver Cope preceded me; Drs. Francis Moore, Joseph Murray, and Bradford Cannon followed. When I received the award in 1985, about twenty-five persons had already prepared and presented their recollections.

Undoubtedly the success of such a venture depends on the ability of the interlocutor to dig out and elicit innumerable facts and comments in this brief period. I was particularly lucky to have George Richardson carrying out this task. We had worked together in the past and had an enjoyable time with this project. The film was discussed at the public viewing by Paul Russell and Arnold Relman.

This venture has been very successful. It provides future generations with many recollections of great historical interest that otherwise might be lost. It is very similar to the series that continues to be prepared under the auspices of Alpha Omega Alpha. Perhaps there is a separate Harvard series because, in the spirit of egalitarianism that swept universities in the decade of the 1960s, the Harvard chapter of AOA was discontinued.

The Committee on the *Leaders* series continued for fifteen years.

As a result of many initiatives, the reputation of Harvard Medical School has continued to grow. A peer review of medical schools in the United States by the *U.S. News and World Report* in 1990 and in 1991 rated Harvard Medical School number one in the nation.[4] The other top 14, listed in order, are Johns Hopkins (Baltimore), Duke (Durham), University of California (San Francisco), Yale (New Haven), Washington University (St. Louis), Cornell University (New York),

Columbia University College of Physicians and Surgeons (New York), University of Washington (Seattle), University of Pennsylvania (Philadelphia), University of California (Los Angeles), Stanford University (Palo Alto), University of Michigan (Ann Arbor), Baylor (Houston), and the University of Chicago Pritzker School of Medicine). The five most often named as "up and comers" are University of Alabama (Birmingham), University of California (San Diego), University of Iowa (Iowa City), University of Pittsburg, and the University of Texas Southwestern Medical Center (Dallas).

This article lists several reasons why applicants for admission to medical school are decreasing. The profession of medicine is not nearly as attractive to students because of the high cost of tuition, the staggering costs of malpractice insurance faced by a doctor when he goes into practice, the overwhelming amount of paper work especially for medicare patients, the financial attractions of competing career choices, and the declining status of medicine as an elite profession.

Harvard is preeminent for many reasons but one of the most important is the novel approach to medical education. When introducing the New Pathway eight years ago, Dean Tosteson said "We are trying to cultivate attitudes and skills that would sustain a lifetime of learning in medicine".

The average MCAT score of applicants for the 124 medical schools in the USA now is 9.2; in Harvard it is 11.2. There are an average of 1.6 applicants for medical schools in the country; for Harvard it is 15 applicants for each of the 165 acceptances for the first year class.

I would like to end this chapter by quoting several paragraphs from *Medicine at Harvard*, a book written by Henry Beecher and completed by Mark Altschule after Henry's death.[5] In these paragraphs, Drs. Beecher and Altschule define and emphasize the importance of scholarship in surgery:

> There are, of course, many types of surgeons. Some can be distinguished by the limited fields in which they work, others by their breadth or by their research, teaching, or academic preferment. There is yet another category, the scholar-surgeon. Such individuals have scant or no interest in academic preferment. They do have a profound interest in all aspects of information concerning their special field of activity. Such individuals may have titles, generally that of Clinical Professor but often of lower rank. They are characterized by the breadth of their profound knowledge, as well as by their great skills. Although they may be con-

sidered to hold secondary status, below that of full-time men, the contributions that some of them make to teaching, clinical research, and
improvements in patient care may far outlast those of many academicians.
They are important for another reason: they represent the persistence of
a way of life that was the only one in the not-too-distant past of the
Harvard Medical School and has been the traditional mode since the
beginning of modern medicine. One should never forget that even An-
dreas Vesalius, today revered as the founder of modern anatomy, spent
far more of his time practicing surgery than he did investigating and
teaching anatomy. The same was true of all the pioneers whose advances
created modern medicine—they were all practitioners of clinical medicine, whatever else they did within the confines of their specialty. The
same was true of all the men who held the endowed chairs in medicine
at Harvard during the nineteenth and, in a few cases, into the twentieth
century.

The persistence of this mode in surgery is remarkable. It persists in
medicine, as the large number of clinical professors of medicine attests,
but for men who make no house calls and very few night visits, and
whose practice in the main is either in an intern-served hospital or else
in an office that has ready access to laboratory, roentgenologic, and
consultant services, developing a scholarly status in one's medical specialty does not present overwhelming difficulties. This is not true of
those who live on a surgical practice, for its demands in time in the
operating room and in the handling of unexpected postoperative complications not only keep scheduled hours occupied but make the free
ones unpredictable. That some of these men become medical scholars
is worthy not merely of recognition but of the highest praise.

There is no small number of such men in the Harvard Medical Faculty
and teaching staff. Mention will be made here of two.[6] One individual
who stands out is Dr. Claude E. Welch. Everyone who knows him will
easily understand what is meant by the term "scholar-surgeon". He is
Clinical Professor of Surgery, Emeritus, at the Harvard Medical School
and Senior Consulting Surgeon at the Massachusetts General
Hospital. . . .

As President of Harvard Medical Alumni, Welch tried to increase
loyalties to the Medical School, . . . and also to promote the cause of
continuing education in medicine as a life-long activity. In short, here
was a man whose record as a student, a house officer, and subsequently
must have afforded him a dozen opportunities to enter and pursue an
academic career. He chose otherwise.

10

Cancer—The Formidable Enemy

In 1900, cancer—defined loosely as a synonym for all types of malignant diseases—except for a few superficial lesions generally was considered to be incurable. However, one very hopeful report by William S. Halsted from Johns Hopkins in 1894 had cast some rays of hope in the gloom. He had developed his radical mastectomy for cancer of the breast and had better results than those reported previously. But even Halsted, whose operation had offered optimism concerning control of breast cancer, found, in 1907, that only forty-two percent of 210 patients had survived three years; they were said to be "cured" although it was recognized many recurrences could occur after that time.[1]

Cancer was far less common in 1900 than it is today. Aging of the population undoubtedly is the most important reason for the increase. In 1895 Coley stated that cancer led to only half as many deaths in the United States as were caused by accidents and injuries.[2] Ravitch noted the contrast in 1976, when the ratio was 3.7 cancer deaths to 1 from accidents.[3] In the MGH in 1900 there were only nine operations for cancer of the stomach, of which a gastric resection was possible in only one. There were six resections of a cancer of the rectum in that year.

Despite the fact that all surgeons had some contact with cancer patients, there were no organized activities in Boston until 1899. In that year Harvard University was given a sizable sum by Caroline Brewer Croft to study cancer. A Cancer Commission was formed with nine members. The chairman was the eminent MGH surgeon J. Collins Warren. Progress was slow but steady in Boston as elsewhere.

The main contributions made by the MGH between 1900 and 1930 included the development of radiation therapy as an alternative treatment to surgery for some types of malignant disease; the provision of professional personnel to staff two future nearby cancer hospitals; the emphasis by A. E. Codman on end-results and careful follow-up of patients; and the development of the first in-hospital cancer clinic by Robert Greenough and George Holmes. Laboratory research was centered from 1912 until 1942 in the Huntington Hospital and then was transferred to the MGH.

In the early decades of the twentieth century only three hospitals in the United States cared exclusively for cancer patients: the New York Cancer Hospital, the Roswell Park Institute in Buffalo, and the Collis P. Huntington Hospital in Boston.[4] These institutions were unique at the time of their founding in great contrast to the multiple cancer centers that exist today. The New York Cancer Hospital in New York City was the first cancer hospital in America. It was completed in 1887; but because a few years later many of its beds were empty, in 1899 its name was changed to the General Memorial Hospital for Cancer and Allied Diseases. In 1939 the hospital moved to form the Memorial Sloan-Kettering Cancer Center. It now is the largest and is generally recognized as the most prestigious cancer hospital and cancer research center in the country. The Roswell Park Institute, the first facility dedicated to cancer research, opened in 1899.

The Collis P. Huntington Memorial Hospital in Boston, the third institution for research and treatment of cancer, admitted its first patient on the site now occupied by the Countway Library and the Harvard School of Public Health in 1912.[5] Because of financial difficulties, it closed in 1942 and its laboratories and patients were transferred to the MGH. It was made possible by Mrs. Huntington, who gave a large sum to Harvard to build a cancer hospital in honor of her late husband, a railroad tycoon. Approximately two-thirds of the three-story building were devoted to patient care and a third to laboratories. The equipment for radiation therapy was ultra-modern, but feeble by modern standards. Ernest E. Tyzzer, the original director, was interested in research and had shown that some types of cancer were hereditary in mice. The new laboratories were dedicated to Dr. J. Collins Warren.

Originally designed for the care of terminally ill patients, the facility had two large clinical wards, each containing about 20 beds. It was not long, however, before potentially curable patients filled the wards.

A large outpatient department provided treatment for many patients with cancers of the skin; two operating rooms were used chiefly for patients with cancer of the breast, gynecologic procedures, and head and neck operations. Staff members came from the MGH. Dr. Channing Simmons, chief surgeon for many years, also was an able pathologist. Much of his work was carried out in the head and neck where the elementary lessons of asepsis (sometimes irrelevant to a pathologist) were less important than in other parts of the body.

I spent a year in the Huntington as a house officer (1929 to 1930) and then five years (1937 to 1942) as a staff surgeon. Dr. Shields Warren was the pathologist; I spent many hours examining microscopic slides with him. Dr. Joseph Aub was in charge of research, having succeeded Dr. George Minot. Radiation therapy was given chiefly by X-ray machines under the direction of Dr. Milford Schulz. Superficial lesions also could be treated by radon; this gas was provided by an outside laboratory in tiny hollow globules ("seeds") or needles. Radon has a relatively short half-life. Alfred Duncombe, my fellow house officer, and I measured the strength of these applicators each morning and prepared proper combinations to use on superficial cancers or cancers of the uterus. Somewhat similar methods of providing radiation therapy are still used today but more powerful machines such as linear accelerators have replaced many of the older methods.

House officers also did physical examinations, drew blood through incredibly dull, resharpened needles, and helped in operations. One day as I was administering anesthesia, Dr. George Leland wandered into the operating room. He taught me an invaluable lesson when he looked at the blue patient and said to me, "Young man, we anesthetize the patient with ether, not with carbon dioxide."

About once a month we received an emergency call at night. A dash to the wards ended at a trail of blood on the floor. Usually the site of bleeding was the jaw, where a cancer had been destroyed by electrocoagulation a few hours previously. Because the bleeding arterioles were located in bone, local ligation was impossible. Staunching the flow required minutes to hours of pressure with adrenaline-soaked sponges. None of the patients ever required carotid ligation, although that would have been more effective.

Except for J. Collins Warren, a history of organized activities directed toward the control of cancer in the MGH must properly begin with Amory Codman.

By the year 1900 Dr. Codman had developed his plans to evaluate both surgeons and methods of treatment of diseases by comparisons of end results. He crystallized his program by 1910, but despite his abrasive advocacy of this principle, further progress was difficult. Nevertheless, he soon found a willing ally in the newly formed American College of Surgeons. The College, organized in 1913, was devoted to the improvement of surgical care, and at that time the treatment of cancer patients rested almost entirely in the hands of surgeons.

Dr. Codman established a Registry for Bone Sarcomas; he asked all members of the College in 1920 to voluntarily report all patients with this rare disease so that the methods of therapy could be compared. The College eagerly assumed the task in 1921. Dr. Ernest Daland also played a key role in the development of the end results study in the College.[6] The Registry for Bone Sarcoma was transferred to the Armed Forces Institute of Pathology in 1953, but the important emphasis on end results for all types of malignant disease remained. Ever since, the prime method for evaluating therapy has depended on end results. Like many innovators, Codman was several decades ahead of his colleagues.

The first cancer clinic in a general hospital in America was organized in the MGH in 1925 under the direction of Dr. Robert Greenough, as surgeon, and Dr. George Holmes, as radiotherapist. By 1931, sixty-two clinics patterned after the cancer clinic at the Massachusetts General Hospital were operating in the United States and 120 others were beginning to organize. This great advance led to the election of Dr. Greenough as President of the American College of Surgeons in 1934, two years after his retirement from the active staff in the MGH. The Commission on Cancer of the American College of Surgeons gradually assumed the mantle of approval of cancer clinics which now exist throughout the country; there were 1204 ACS-approved programs in 1988.

The principles of organization of cancer clinics have remained essentially unchanged since their conception in 1925. The purpose is to provide voluntary consultation to other physicians and surgeons concerning treatment of individual cases. There is no requirement that all cases of malignant disease must be under control of the clinic. The number of physicians in the clinic—at first only a radiologist and a surgeon—was rapidly expanded to include all specialists who deal with malignant disease. In recent years the advent of chemotherapy has greatly augmented the number of medical oncologists; surgical oncologists—defined as surgeons who treat malignant disease—have dignified their specialty in the same fashion.

One of the duties assumed by the early clinics was to schedule protracted follow-up visits for all patients with cancer after their discharge from the hospital. This practice proved to be impractical and was discontinued.

The MGH Tumor Clinic has continued to be active since its founding. After Dr. Greenough, successive chiefs were Drs. Channing Simmons, Ernest Daland, Grantley Taylor, Claude Welch, John Raker, William Wood and his associate Alfred Cohen, and Herbert Hoover. For many years, the MGH also provided nearly all staff members to the succeeding cancer hospitals, including the Huntington Memorial and the Pondville Hospitals.

My introduction to the Pondville Hospital occurred during the year I was at the Huntington. The pathologist on duty at the Huntington, Dr. Ralph Irwin, also performed autopsies in Pondville and occasionally I accompanied him. I can remember the first visit I made there. I was met by a powerful odor as we opened the door to the institution. Decaying, infected cancers on living patients have distinctive, sickly sweet, nauseating odors that make it easy to diagnose cancer of the cervix on that basis alone. Some of the horribly large tumors on dying patients surpassed anything I had seen before or have seen since.

The Pondville Hospital was the first cancer hospital in the United States to be established and supported by a state. It opened its doors in 1927, when a cluster of buildings formerly belonging to the Foxborough State Hospital were renovated as a facility for the treatment of cancer. Seventy beds were available at the outset, but the daily census increased to a maximum of about 135 a decade later. A new operating room had been included in the renovation, and facilities for radiation therapy, by both X-ray and radium, were available.

Initially, the hospital was filled with patients suffering from terminal cancer. But later, approximately a third of the beds were devoted to early cancer, a third to cases of intermediate grade, and a third to terminal care. A large outpatient clinic also was established. The maximum number of admissions to the hospital in a single year was 1,567. Two or more surgical residents were always available to operate and assist various consultants. Many young surgeons viewed a six-month residency in this hospital, where up to 2,000 operations were performed annually, as a highly desirable post.

In 1935, along with Ira Nathanson, I spent six months at Pondville. At that time it was an exceptionally good cancer hospital with two surgical residents and a staff of MGH surgeons. The most active surgeons were Ernest Daland, Grantley Taylor and Joe Meigs. The surgical service was very active, providing operative treatment and radiation therapy for many cases of breast, head and neck, and gynecologic cancer.

Although there was no chemotherapy in 1955, Ira Nathanson, the other surgical resident, later gained fame as the first person to prove clinically that estrogens could produce regression of cancer of the breast in some postmenopausal women. He carried out valuable experiments on the same problem in mice in the Huntington Hospital and later in the MGH.

During my term at Pondville, an epidemic of streptococcal infections in the hospital led to several deaths. Although I had absolutely no symptoms, I was identified as a carrier. Consequently, I had a tonsillectomy and was given a month's leave of absence.

During that month, Ira Nathanson and I spent much of our time reviewing all of the records in the Pondville and Huntington hospitals to determine the life expectancy of patients with various types of malignant diseases. Fortunately we were able to use comparable studies of life expectancy in untreated individuals with cancer of the breast and colorectum. The series of papers, published by the Commission on Cancer of Harvard University, showed, for example, that the best treatment available at that time for cancer of the breast increased the length of life after symptoms first were noted from 1.5 years in untreated patients to 2.5 years in those with treatment.[7]

The hospital continued to expand its services, and in 1969 a major building program was completed. Soon afterward, the patient load declined rapidly—chiefly due to Medicare—and the hospital soon was converted into a community institution serving the surrounding area as a general hospital.[8]

As the years roll on, cancer statistics do not show the continued improvement in results that we hoped for or expected. For example, in 1985 the death rate in females from cancer of the breast was just what it was in 1930.[9] The five-year survival after gastric resections for apparently curable cancer of the stomach was the same in 1985 as it was in 1930; however, the incidence of this disease has gone down so remarkably (for unknown reasons) that far fewer patients develop that disease or are dying from it.

It was clear that we were fighting against a redoubtable enemy. The only course for a surgeon was to fight an individual battle in every single case—to remove premalignant lesions, to provide safe operations and resections of cancers, to follow patients, to teach established concepts of therapy, including radiation and chemotherapy, and perhaps to innovate. Such an opportunity was offered to me in 1957 when I was asked to assume the post of Chief of the Tumor Clinic in the MGH.

I followed Ernest Daland, who had been chief from 1942 to 1946 and Grantley Taylor, chief from 1946 to 1957. Dr. Daland also was chief of staff at the Pondville Hospital and continued for the entire life of that institution when it functioned as a cancer hospital. When the Huntington Hospital closed in 1942, Dr. Daland also assumed the duties of the Chief of the MGH Tumor Clinic. He was greatly interested in cancer of the head and neck, breast and rectum.

Dr. Taylor was a colorful person who was as well known for his quotably acerbic and off-color commentary as for the elegance of his radical dissections. He drew most of the Tumor Clinic staff from clinical associates whose contacts with the hospital were essentially only those with the Tumor Clinic.

I was introduced into that situation as the new chief in 1957. As just noted, the staff of the Tumor Clinic appeared to be divorced from the remainder of the visiting and house staff, and the house staff saw nothing of the patients in the clinic. We had a single office for the secretaries and three examining rooms. Waiting patients sat in the corridor; physicians stood. Facilities for radiation were just as limited and had no resemblance whatsoever to the present luxurious facilities in the Cox Building.

After my appointment as Chief of the Tumor Clinic, Dr. Churchill suggested that Dr. John Raker be invited back from a rather unhappy assignment as Chief of Surgery at the Philadelphia General Hospital to serve as Associate Chief of the Clinic. Doctor Raker and I had worked together very closely and amicably in the old Huntington Hospital, and we had common goals for the Tumor Clinic and for cancer surgery in the MGH. He accepted the offer and arrived a few months after I did.

Our first task was to amalgamate the Tumor Clinic into the mainstream of the hospital. Soon the house staff was rotating through the Clinic. Gradually the associates in surgery were replaced by fulltime members of the MGH staff. Dr. William Rogers, who had joined Dr. Grantley Taylor after training at the Memorial Hospital for Cancer and Allied Diseases in New York City, also enjoyed teaching resident surgeons. Students were involved in the clinic; some were outstanding, such as Charles Huggins, son of the Nobel prize recipient, and later head of the MGH blood bank.

The next task was to establish a cancer registry to gain approval by the American College of Surgeons, the organization that investigated and accredited all cancer clinics.[10] A registry is a list of all patients with malignant disease seen in an institution, the diagnosis, and a description of the type of treatment. The most difficult requirement is following all patients at yearly intervals until death, with notes on their status and further treatment. Because we were caring for about 3,000 new cases of cancer a year in the MGH—a quarter of all those seen in Massachusetts—this proved to be an essentially impossible task. We were plagued by a shortage of personnel and funds, but some aid was received from the State Department of Health and we gained approval. Then, at a later date, approval by the American College of Surgeons was lost again. More recent computerization led to reapproval.

We continued the very popular weekly rounds in the Bigelow amphitheater and soon established an annual postgraduate course in cancer. The course was multidisciplinary and attracted many practitioners, who nearly filled the Shriners auditorium for the three days of presentation. The proceeds were far from exorbitant but were kept entirely in the Department of Surgery—a feature not entirely appreciated by the other disciplines involved. More recently, Drs. Wood and Cohen, as co-chiefs of Surgical Oncology, oriented the course to surgeons, with similar success.

The patient load in the Clinic was reasonably heavy, although it did not increase significantly during my entire tenure of office. Approximately 10,000 patient visits a year were made to the Clinic, and approximately 130,000 treatments a year were given by the radiation therapists. Equipment, particularly for radiotherapy, was extremely restricted, and it was very difficult for Dr. Milford Schulz and Dr. C. C. Wang to maintain their treatment schedule.

Fundamental research in cancer was carried on by Dr. Paul Zamecnik and others; many of these activities had been transferred from the Huntington Hospital. The papers from the Clinic published in the 1950s and 1960s were chiefly due to individual efforts. They were almost entirely clinical in nature and retrospective in view.

There was no attempt then to develop what now are termed surgical oncologists. Some individuals such as Dr. Raker were extremely knowledgeable in the entire field of malignant disease. In general, however, clinical care of malignant disease in separate areas of the body was given by only those surgeons interested in that particular area of the anatomy. Neurosurgeons, thyroid surgeons, breast surgeons, thoracic surgeons, abdominal surgeons, and orthopedic surgeons functioned comfortably under the umbrella of the clinic. During my entire tenure, the Eye and Ear Infirmary was represented regularly in all of the teaching exercises. These surgeons also carried out a large portion of their outpatient work in the Tumor Clinic itself. Relationships with the Departments of Radiation Therapy and Surgery also were extremely close because clinics and individuals were contiguous.

I transferred direction of the clinic in 1966 to Dr. Raker, who continued the same policies. He was followed by Drs. William Wood and Alfred Cohen as Chiefs of Surgical Oncology in 1975. That year saw not only a shift in the title of the clinic but also a major change in the activities of the department. A period of study in the National Institutes of Health had become a desirable prerequisite for appointment.

In 1968 Dr. Howard Ulfelder and others began to draw plans for a Cancer Center that would fill an entire new Cox Building. Under their supervision, the construction of fine new facilities for radiation therapy, and clinical care were completed in 1975.[11]

Under the direction of the Chief of Surgical Oncology, William Wood, participation in prospective studies following protocols and involving many institutions have become common. Additional teaching clinics have been established. The Cancer Registry is on a firm footing, and has produced some interesting data under the direction of William Gallagher and Herbert Hoover. The most recent development has been the opening of a very large center located in MGH East (in Chelsea) under the direction of Kurt Isselbacher; it is devoted to basic research in malignant disease.[12]

My own chief assaults against cancer continued throughout my career as surgical measures succeeded in gaining cures in a large number of individual cases. In addition to the contributions noted above in the battle against cancer, I should include the educational papers, chapters, and books I have written particularly on cancer of the colorectum and stomach. My book *Polypoid Lesions of the Gastrointestinal Tract*, and the second edition written in collaboration with Dr. Stephen Hedberg, were authoritative volumes. I was happy to urge my associate, Dr. Hedberg, to become interested in the development of fiberoptic colonoscopy and watch him became one of the outstanding endoscopists of the world before his untimely death. The instrument, invented in 1957, make possible the early detection and treatment of cancer and polyps.

In 1969 I was elected President of the New England Cancer Society; and in 1983 I was called to New York City to receive a special award from the Sloan-Kettering Cancer Center, where the New England Cancer Society was meeting. I was told that I had to be present. Phyllis and I drove to Hartford and, joined by our children John and Marylouise, went on to New York City for the meeting.

During the late hours of the morning, Professor Jerome DeCosse, head of the surgical service, took the podium and made the announcement that a special award would be given to me. It was true, I had devoted a great deal of my life to the control of cancer. I had made several presentations to the New York Academy of Medicine. Our son John had been the Recorder of the New England Cancer Society for many years. For these reasons, the complimentary introduction and the plaque given to me was engraved and presented to "a giant in the fight against cancer and especially for his renowned surgical expertise directed toward curing patients."

In my ad hoc remarks of acceptance, I recalled the old days of the Huntington and Pondville hospitals in Massachusetts and their friendly rivalry with the Memorial Hospital as it began in a brownstone mansion converted from a dwelling near Central Park. Since that time the Sloan-Kettering has received many large donations and as a result has outstripped its Boston competitors. Nevertheless, Boston has continued to produce important fundamental research and excellent clinical care for patients even though the old names are gone. The Huntington and the Pondville hospitals no longer exist, but the Dana-Farber Center and the Cox Cancer Center in the MGH have replaced and enormously extended these old facilities.

The Dana-Farber Cancer Institute in Boston is closely allied with the hospitals in the Longwood Avenue area adjacent to HMS. Opened in 1947 for the treatment of childhood cancer and lymphoma, it was named for a pathologist who was one of the favorite teachers of many classes in Harvard Medical School, Dr. Sidney Farber. Later the name of its major benefactor was added. It is an exceptionally fine research center; their physicians obtained the first complete remissions in childhood lymphoma and leukemia.

In the past half century many cancer clinics have been accredited by the American College of Surgeons. Several major institutions have established true cancer centers that have been characterized by clinical and fundamental research in malignant disease. Two of the most important, the M. D. Anderson and the National Cancer Institute, opened soon after World War II. In 1945 the American Cancer Society—a potent source of funds—was activated. Many state health departments collect statistics on cancer patients and exercise some control over the activities of hospitals. The Federal Government has given grants to many other institutions that are designated as cancer centers.[13]

The Massachusetts General Hospital has played a very active role throughout the century in the clinical treatment of patients with cancer. Important surgeons included Daniel Jones, for his strong advocacy of the Miles combined abdominoperineal resection for cancer of the rectum, Arthur Allen and Leland McKittrick for cancer of the colorectum, Edward Churchill and Richard Sweet for cancer of the lung, Richard Sweet, Earle Wilkins, and John Burke for cancer of the esophagus and stomach, Grantley Taylor for cancer of the breast, Henry Mankin for excision of bone sarcomas with preservation of extremities, Ernest Daland for cancer of the face and plastic repair, Joe Meigs and Howard Ulfelder for surgical therapy of cancer of the cervix and other tumors of the female genitourinary tract, Ronald Malt for cancer of the liver, Andrew Warshaw for cancer of the pancreas, and Wyland Leadbetter for cancers of the genitourinary tract. Radiation therapy has been aided greatly by cobalt and linear accelerators in the Cox building, by intraoperative radiation, and by Drs. Schulz, C. C. Wang, and Suit. Medical oncology has been expanded and centralized in the Cox building by Drs. Kelley, Carey and Kaufman.

Today, investigations into chromosomal abnormalities and the basic nature of the human genome, are generating the hope that molecular biology will unlock the key to the mechanism of cancer. Viruses have been implicated as the cause of nearly twenty forms of malignant disease, most of them various types of lymphoma. Angiogenesis also appears to be a characteristic of cancer cells, and Professor Judah Folkman has identified the particular protein that is responsible. As a result of these enormous efforts throughout the country, the secrets of this dread disease may finally be discovered. Furthermore, some of the dreams excited by the Regional Medical Programs in 1965 have come to pass, although the public has played a larger role, and the Federal Government a smaller one, than the designers expected.

The New England Cancer Society is one of the organizations that has gained a great deal of strength in recent years. Credit for the formation of the Society in 1939 belongs to Dr. Milford Schulz. By that time many cancer clinics had been founded in major hospitals

Above: Robert H. Ebert, Dean of the Harvard Medical School, 1965–1977 (left); Daniel C. Tosteson, current Dean, with Daniel D. Federman, Dean for Students and Alumni (right) at the time of celebration of the School's bicentennial, 1982. Below: Today's surgeons portraying Harvard Medical giants of the past during the 1982 bicentennial ceremonies: (left to right) Richard Warren as John C. Warren; Howard Ulfelder as Henry J. Bigelow; Francis D. Moore as Edward D. Churchill; Lamar Soutter as Oliver Wendell Holmes; CEW, moderator.

Above: The Collis P. Huntington Memorial Hospital, Boston. Below: The position of Chief of the MGH Tumor Clinic passes from Grantley Taylor (right) to CEW (left), 1957.

Above: Recent distinguished Presidents of the Massachusetts Medical Society: Grant V. Rodkey, 1979–1980, Visiting Surgeon MGH, Associate Clinical Professor of Surgery HMS, (left); Barry M. Manuel, 1990–1991, Associate Dean, Boston University Medical School (right). Below: Three world-famous Editors of the New England Journal of Medicine: (left) Joseph Garland, 1947–1967; (center), Franz J. Ingelfinger, 1968–1977; (right) Arnold S. Relman, 1977–1991.

Presidents of the Massachusetts Medical Society, pictured together in 1991. All are Past Presidents except for Philip McCarthy, who is the present incumbent. Seated (left to right) Thomas Ballantine, John Norcross, CEW, Barry Manuel, John Ayers; standing, Louis Alfano, Joseph O'Connor, Grant Rodkey, Philip McCarthy, Barbara Rockett, Percy Wadman, Goodwill Stewart, Nason Burden. Below: The new Headquarters of the Massachusetts Medical Society and the New England Journal of Medicine, opened at Waltham in 1982.

Above: Homes of the Boston Medical Library in this century: At 8 The Fenway, 1905–1965 (left); in the Francis A. Countway Library of Medicine, together with the Harvard Medical Library (right). The Countway Library opened in June, 1965. Below: Two major supporters of the Boston Medical Library: Arthur W. Allen, for whom the Allen Room in the Countway Library is named (left), and Frank H. Lahey whose clinic provided funds for the Lahey Room (right).

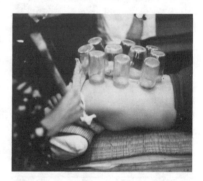

Pictures taken during the trip of AMA officials to China, 1974: Above: Eppie Lederer (Ann Landers) before the statue of Mao Tse-Tung in Shenyang, 1974 (left); two workers, each holding his medical record in a replanted hand in Beijing, 1974 (right). Below: moxibustion for neck pain, in Shenyang, 1974 (left); cupping for chest pain, in Shenyang, 1974 (right).

throughout the state. He extended this concept to a state-wide organization where physicians, surgeons and radiologists could discuss their common problems. This multi-disciplinary group brought together members from all branches of medicine or surgery who were interested in malignant disease.

Milford Schulz and I had worked together for several years in the Huntington Hospital where he was a young radiation therapist. When the Huntington closed, he moved to the MGH and for many years presided over an enormously busy clinic in unbelievably restricted quarters. He developed great judgment and skill in his specialty through long experience and became recognized as a leading radiotherapist throughout the country. He had essentially reached the time of retirement when the Cox Cancer Center was opened and Dr. Herman Suit became the chief of the department.

It was an honor for me to be president of the Society in 1969. I presided over the two yearly one-day meetings of the society. Though no spectacular triumphs can be recorded for the year, each group of physicians interested in cancer became increasingly aware of the contributions of other disciplines. Instead of treatment solely by surgeons or radiologists, the value of combined therapy by surgeons, physicians and radiotherapists was becoming increasingly apparent. Basic scientists, public health physicians, biologists, pathologists, and medical specialists such as pediatricians, gynecologists, urologists, otolaryngologists, and neurosurgeons now are members.

The Society has grown in the past decade to include many new members and now conducts a three-day annual meeting. The meetings are interesting and discussion stimulating. Credit for this vigorous expansion is due chiefly to Paul Kuehn of Hartford and to the present secretary, Robert Carey.

11

Some of My Unusual Operations

A surgeon must be able do many things, but first and foremost he must be able to operate. I started in 1932; by the time I decided to leave the operating room for good in 1981, at age seventy-five, I estimated that I had done between 15,000 and 20,000 procedures. Not only would a complete list be difficult to obtain because of the large number of operations done during training and in war time, but it also would be of little significance. Such data are mainly important to establish the reputation of a surgeon.

During an informal session when I was the visiting professor in another medical school, a resident asked me to tell them about some of my most interesting operations. I was taken aback and said that as one grows older he remembers his mistakes rather than the victories; finally I managed to recount a few. Afterward, when recalling the discussion, Phyllis immediately reminded me of many that I had forgotten; thereupon I talked for at least two hours, recalling others. A few of the most interesting are recounted here.

In the late 1930s, a severely bleeding duodenal ulcer was a deadly disease. Frequently when one visited a medical ward in the MGH some comparatively young man could be found lying on a bed in the corner, curtains drawn about him, as pale as the sheet. The diagnosis of a bleeding ulcer was never in doubt, but physicians were loath to call in surgeons because the results of operations were so bad. Arthur Allen approved of operation in such cases and presented a paper describing six patients on whom Dr. Allen had operated; they were all in extremis at the time of the operation and all died. Nevertheless this paper, which was given at the annual meeting of the American

Surgical Association, evoked a great deal of interest and convinced us that if we could get the patients earlier we might save a few. In those days there were no blood banks, and a single transfusion of 500 ml. of blood was a major event.

Incidentally, I remembered one of those operations done by Dr. Allen. Everyone in the operating room was extremely jittery since a life was about to reach its end. The technical problems were severe. Dr. Allen was sweating like a galley slave, and a great wave of perspiration suddenly fell from his face onto the bib of his gown. There was no time to waste. A towel must be placed over the front of his chest. Dr. Rolf Lium, the second assistant, seized two towel clips to fasten the towel to the gown. The second clip, because of Rolf's shaking hands, penetrated towel, gown, and Dr. Allen almost to his sternum. The resulting yell must have echoed throughout the entire hospital. The patient died almost at once.

Now the scenario was to be played out again. This time I was the young surgeon called to the medical wards. We transferred the patient to the surgical floor and then our knees began to weaken. We gave him a single transfusion—no mean job in those days. He pinked up appreciably and actually improved for a few days. With a somewhat supercilious smirk we transferred him back to the medical wards. A few hours later an emergency phone call revealed he had had another massive bleed. This time there was no escaping the verdict—he must be operated on. And so he was. In those days the standard operation was a Billroth II resection. It was assumed that bleeding from his duodenal ulcer would stop thereafter. John Stewart had suggested putting some Gelofoam plugs in the duodenum, and perhaps I did that as well. At any rate he did well after operation; that is, he did well for seven days and then had another major hemorrhage.

Again there was no question—it was back to the operating room. By this time the poor patient was in a dreadful state of nutrition and obviously dying from blood loss. It was easy to open the abdomen—the wound fell apart as soon as the sutures were removed. The duodenal stump was identified and opened. There was a great gush of arterial blood that rose three feet above the table. A finger in the duodenum quickly compressed the gastroduodenal artery and stopped the bleeding. Then, what should be done? There was a large open posterior ulcer. The head of the pancreas was swollen to the size of a baseball. It seemed almost certain that any sutures placed in the ulcer would not hold. Because it was impossible to recognize any normal anatomy, an old-fashioned Reverdin needle—a murderous curved piece of steel about four inches in length—was passed through the head of the pancreas and a heavy ligature tied around the tissue that contained the main artery. It was then necessary to pass a second ligature through the head of the pancreas to occlude the distal end of the vessel, for there still was brisk bleeding. Despite the size and strength of the needle, the huge thing broke and, buried in the pancreas, was never to be seen again. When a second needle successfully traversed the pancreas and a heavy ligature tied, all bleeding stopped.

But what had to be done about the duodenal stump? It was almost certain that no sutures would hold in it considering the bad nutrition of the patient. Again I resorted to a method never used previously in our hospital. With great trepidation a catheter was placed in the open end of the duodenum and the duodenum closed about it. It drained for about 12 days, and then was withdrawn. The patient left the hospital, a well man, twenty-one days after the last operation.

*   *   *   *   *

At almost the same time in the late 1930s, I was called out to a neighboring city to operate upon the leading undertaker of the community. It is always a great responsibility to operate upon a mortician, because if anything goes wrong, the news travels rapidly throughout the community. Furthermore, adding to the technical problems, this person's practice had been very profitable so that he was more than moderately obese.

He had had an ulcer of the duodenum for many years, and now he had so much pain and vomiting that an operation was necessary. At that time we were taught that a two-stage gastrectomy was the proper procedure for bad ulcers. The theory was that when a duodenal ulcer appeared to be too difficult to remove, one could divide the stomach horizontally between the upper and middle thirds, do a Billroth II anastomosis, and six weeks later remove the lower two-thirds of the stomach. We had been taught that after the first operation, inflammation about the duodenum would subside. We also were taught that when six weeks elapsed the operation would be so simple it could be done by a resident. (Only visiting surgeons operated on stomachs in those days.)

The patient did very well after the first operation. But the second one was a horror. The duodenum, previously believed to be too difficult to remove, now was even worse than before. It was mired down in adhesions and acutely inflamed. The only option was to complete the removal of the lower two-thirds of the stomach because my dissection already had made anything as simple as a gastroenterostomy impossible. Any attempt to close the duodenal stump in the customary manner was bound to be both difficult and dangerous. Here was another opportunity to place a catheter in the duodenum.

This patient also had an entirely normal convalescence. These two successes led me to question a number of surgeons in an effort to find out how often the procedure had been used. The first reference to the method had been published about 1930 by a German surgeon. But, unfortunately, his death rate had been 100 percent. I concluded that he had used so large a drainage tube that an enormous duodenal fistula resulted through the tube and the patients died of electrolyte imbalance. However, Reginald Smithwick, a brilliant but modest surgeon, who often found himself in tight places when he operated in local hospitals, had used such a catheter with success. I also found that John Waugh, one of the famous surgeons in the Mayo clinic in that era, also had had success with it. The method certainly needed a recommendation. I reported it in the *JAMA* in 1949. Thereafter in the next few years many other papers on this procedure appeared and it now is an accepted method of therapy that has saved innumerable patients when they have been confronted with a difficult duodenal stump.

*   *   *   *   *

By 1960 surgeons had the benefits of antibiotics, blood banks, respiratory care, and better anesthesia. Nevertheless, very serious problems still occurred, requiring emergency surgery if a patient was to survive. About this time I encountered a 45-year-old man who, a few days before, had had a vagotomy and gastric resection in another hospital for a duodenal ulcer. He did not do well; his sister knew Miss MacDonald, the nursing chief at the MGH, who asked me to see him. I immediately went to the nearby city and found an extremely ill man with a high fever, and a tender abdomen. The key to the diagnosis was an X-ray film. A swallow of barium showed a huge hole at the lower end of the esophagus. Undoubtedly, there had been an accident at the time of the vagotomy. Later, when I looked for the film, it had mysteriously disappeared.

A short time later he arrived in the MGH. He was in respiratory failure and in coma, almost dead. His left subdiaphragmatic abscess had ruptured into his chest. He was placed quickly on a respirator with an intratracheal tube, and drainage tubes were inserted into his chest. Thereafter it was touch and go for several weeks. At first he bled severely from disseminated intravascular coagulation; this bleeding required two laparotomies and packing of the abdomen, because he was bleeding from innumerable areas. He also had a pressure suit applied; this helped stop the bleeding, but also resulted in a cessation of renal function, although it was possible with the respirator to maintain oxygenation. Later he had resections of the splenic flexure of the colon because of perforations, a temporary colostomy, and removal of parts of several ribs damaged by osteomyelitis. He developed spontaneous drainage of empyema just lateral to the sternum at the level of the left fifth rib. During all of this time, he was comatose.

Two months later he miraculously came out of his coma. His main complaints at that time were that he could not see or hear. Examination of his eyes showed the intraocular balls of cotton, typical of *Candida* abscesses. The deafness was due to the effects of the aminoglycosides—the antibiotics given to help control his infection.

This story had a happy ending. Now, nearly twenty years later, he sees very well, and his hearing is almost normal. He has an appetite like a horse, and has no intraabdominal complaints. He is a professional photographer and travels around the world. His mind is very keen, and except for his abdomen, which appears on the surface like the remnants of a battlefield, he shows no other physical signs of his harrowing experiences, nearly all of which he cannot remember. He has had no more trouble with his ulcer.

*   *   *   *   *

A teen-age girl came into the office with an enchondroma of the left middle metacarpal bone about 1955. Athough these tumors are benign, they are hard to eradicate. In this case, the accepted therapy of removal of the entire marrow cavity by curettage was only temporarily successful; the tumor recurred and involved the entire metacarpal. The usual procedure was amputation of the entire metacarpal and the finger. However, considering her tender age I thought it might be desirable to attempt a bone transplant. Accordingly, a section of rib was removed, rongeured to appear like the metacarpal which was excised in toto. The finger was replaced at the end of the new metacarpal.

The girl did very well. Her finger, now forty years later, appears normal. She has used it ever since the operation. She types, plays the piano and in all respects has a normal finger.

*   *   *   *   *

One of the most serious football injuries is a dislocation of the knee. The popliteal artery often is injured or torn, and gangrene of the leg follows shortly. In the days before vascular surgery and repair of arterial injuries became commonplace, amputation of the leg was an inevitable consequence.

During World War II one of the patients that I treated had a gunshot wound of the groin in which the femoral vessels had been divided. At that time (1944) the only acceptable therapy was ligation of the severed artery, supplemented by the hope that there would be enough collateral circulation to avoid gangrene. Such an optimistic outcome rarely occurred nor did it happen in this case. An above-the-knee amputation was done a few days later. I concluded that something else must be done if I ever encountered this situation again.

The opportunity occurred in 1946 when a young man was brought into the MGH with a dislocated knee. The orthopedic surgeon and I reduced the dislocation. I then took a piece of the popliteal vein, excised the traumatized section of the artery, and did an arterial reconstruction. The lifeless leg immediately regained viability. Clement Darling replaced the graft with a Dacron prosthesis twenty-five years later; it is working well in 1990.

It was nearly fifteen years after that episode when, during the Korean war, the necessity of early vascular reconstruction came to be appreciated. Since that time, an enormous number of such operations have been done, and today vascular anastomoses are done by residents at all levels of their training. However my 1946 repair was the first one done in the Massachusetts General Hospital.

*   *   *   *   *

A good assistant is invaluable in every difficult operation. In the 1950s I was called to resect a cancer of the splenic flexure in an old patient hospitalized in one of our neighboring cities. The first assistant was to be the chief of surgery. He was a distinguished, capable man of impeccable demeanor. He was a devout Protestant; the hospital was run by Catholic nuns. One day he entered the operating room, and, surrounded by a flock of nuns, exposed the abdomen, supposedly ready for the knife. Unfortunately it was still covered with a mass of long hair. "Holy Jesus, Mary, and Joseph," bellowed the surgeon. "Who prepped this patient?" The nuns adored him.

But that was another case. In this instance, my assistant apparently was in fine fettle. It should be noted, however, that ever since a right colectomy for cancer some years before, he had had sudden uncontrollable attacks of diarrhea. So this morning we lined up. This doctor was supplemented by a fourth year medical student. I had brought my own nurse. The anesthetist gave a pontocaine spinal; he guaranteed that the anesthetic would last an hour. Just as I put the knife to the skin my first assistant collapsed on the floor. They quickly wheeled him out on a stretcher to have an electrocardiogram; that was his last appearance of the day.

I struggled on with the medical student, and just as I was beginning to close the abdomen, it was apparent that the patient's anesthetic was wearing off. Hurrying along with no time to lose, I heard the circulating nurse ask if I would like to dictate the operation. This I did as the closure progressed; I finished with the words "Sponge count reported correct," just as we always did in the MGH. But the recording secretary said "Doctor, we do not have sponge counts in this hospital."

I decided it would be unwise to give another anesthetic, so I finished the closure. On the way home my nurse and I recounted every sponge we had used in the abdomen. I had told her on the way up that the operation might be a little sticky, that we were to use no small sponges; only handkerchiefs would be put in the abdomen and every one of them would have a Kelley clamp attached so that they could not be lost. Fortunately, this method had worked perfectly.

*   *   *   *   *

Itinerant surgery was necessarily a way of life until nearly 1975. From the days of Maurice Richardson and the Mixters it was actually the only way that good surgeons could be brought from the MGH to smaller communities. But it was not always satisfactory. Every such procedure was an adventure and was always subject to stresses exactly like those accompanying an athletic contest in an opponent's field.

At one time the chief surgeon in a major hospital in a neighboring state called me to operate on two seriously ill patients. I found the first one to be a reasonably spry 70-year-old woman with a cancer of the rectum, for whom a combined abdominoperineal excision was necessary. The chief surgeon stood on the side lines; I, of course, had brought my invaluable nurse.

In such cases there was no extra time to be spent in dilly-dallying. The anesthetist—in this case a general practitioner, whose virtues and defects had not been made clear to me—administered the ether by cone. I moved along without delay and, an hour later, as I was completing the perineal dissection, the last part of the operation, I asked the anesthetist how much blood he had given the patient. His answer was explicit but somewhat unnerving: "I haven't got the intravenous started yet." The result was a smooth convalescence.

*   *   *   *   *

Of all the patients on whom I operated during World War II, the most spectacular were the soldiers with chest wounds which produced a combination of contused or collapsed lung, pneumothorax, and empyema. All were ill, with high temperatures and X-rays that demonstrated serious changes, usually confined to one chest cavity. The operation of decortication had been developed in the Italian theatre and I had acted as an assistant in many of these cases in a General Hospital in Caserta, Italy that was staffed chiefly by physicians from Detroit. Major Tuttle taught me in 1943 how to clean out the chest, excise a heavy peel from the lung, and reinflate the lung to fill the chest cavity. I brought this method back to our hospital. The medical chief of pulmonary disease shook his head and decried the temerity of surgeons who operated on such ill patients. Later he shook his head in another direction when he observed how well the patients had done after decortication. Dr. Claude McGahey and I did many of these operations in the 6th General Hospital.

*   *   *   *   *

One of my earliest so-called triumphs occurred when I was a surgical intern. I was visiting my parents in Winchendon, Massachusetts for a few days at Christmas. The local physician-surgeon was anxious for me to see what went on in the local hospital. As was usual at that time in about 1934 Winchendon, like most other small towns, had converted a large house into a hospital with several beds and an operating room. A second physician gave an ether anesthesia, dropping ether in front of the patient's nose to the accompaniment of sneezing, wheezing, and coughing.

On this winter's evening, I was called by my friend, who asked me to come up to the hospital to help with a strangulated hernia. I was not loath to see what was going on, so I scrubbed up to act as an assistant. At that moment, the patient, who obviously had a large irreducible inguinal hernia, gave a sepulchral cough, just as the ether cone was about to be clamped over his nose. The ensuing hemming and hawing by the doctors was finally settled by my offer to provide local anesthesia. This technique was a novelty; no one had ever used local anesthesia for a hernia repair before in that hospital. Swayed by my oratory and more effectively by the patient's continued coughs, the others agreed it was worth trying.

Another problem developed, however. Even though some novocaine eventually was found, a long search revealed that there were no needles for a syringe in the hospital. Finally the surgeon broke his scrub, went back to his office and returned with a needle. Thereafter everything proceeded without a hitch.

*   *   *   *   *

One of the most difficult cases that I ever had to manage was a young fellow in his late teens who came to me in 1965 after he had had a gastric resection and probably a vagotomy as well in an outside hospital. He complained of severe abdominal pain and repeated vomiting. I spent the next decade or a little more trying to improve his status. He developed severe problems with pancreatitis and gallstones as well as vomiting after eating solid food. In separate operations I removed his gallbladder, did a higher resection of his stomach, then a Tanner-19 resection of the stomach, and intestinal anastomoses, all without relief.

Then I was relieved to learn that he was going back to Hawaii. Our relationship was not ended, however. Every few years he showed up with the same problems and the last time he came he was in terrible shape. He had seen many surgeons on the west coast. He had not had any solid foods for three years. He had had a Hickman catheter inserted for total parental nutrition three months previously and had taken nothing by mouth during that time. Altogether, he had had over a dozen abdominal operations. He was over six feet tall and weighed 100 pounds. A drink of barium would pass easily through the stomach and intestine, but if he took any food he vomited.

We decided that his stomach remnant (only about a quarter of it still remained) was acting as an atonic viscus, and that he had a type of unrelenting motility disorder that could be helped only by a total gastrectomy and esophagojejunostomy. After considerable soul-searching, this was done; the convalescence was very difficult with a leaking anastomosis, left subdiaphragmatic abscesses, splenic abscesses, and empyema. But finally he began to improve and then rapidly gained weight. When I last saw him about 5 years after operation he was so obese that he needed a weight-reduction diet, and had had no further trouble with his digestive tract.

*   *   *   *   *

Severe bleeding that follows an attack of acute pancreatitis is very difficult to treat. In 1947 I was called by the chief of surgery to one of our satellite hospitals to operate on a sixty-year-old man with acute pancreatitis. It had progressed to the stage of massive necrosis. I scooped out a large portion of his necrotic pancreas. He recovered, and for several years I congratulated myself because of his almost miraculous recovery. Then he turned up again, this time with massive upper gastrointestinal bleeding. This episode occurred before the days of flexible endoscopy or of angiography. The only diagnostic method available was an upper gastrointestinal barium study which did not reveal any abnormalities. He did well for several days, then bled again. Treated conservatively, he recovered nicely. But on the day of discharge from the hospital he bled profusely.

There was nothing to do but operate. I quickly opened the stomach and found a hole posteriorly in the antrum. Blood was pouring from it. Rapidly dividing the stomach to gain adequate access, I found the hole from which the torrent of blood was escaping. I stuck my finger in the hole and shortly decided that it was an opening in the portal vein the size of the ball of my thumb. In the midst of all that inflammation, there was no hope of a delicate closure. Using a number 0 catgut that was large enough to gain purchase on the wall of the vein, I closed the large hole with a running suture. The bleeding stopped. I sewed the stomach back together. The convalescence was uneventful, and he had no further difficulties. I have wondered ever since how long that hole existed and whether extra pressure in the stomach ever sent the contents directly into the portal vein. At any rate he was fond of his wine, and the hole, if present, provided a rapid method of absorption.

*   *   *   *   *

In 1948 a woman came up from New York City where she had had her sixteenth operation for intestinal obstruction. Now she was obstructed again, conservative methods of therapy had failed, and she had to be explored. I found that the last operation had consisted of a

Noble plication in which the loops of small bowel had been sutured together in a fashion that was supposed to prevent further obstruction. I never was fond of that procedure prior to this operation and have been less than fond ever since. It took hours to take down the adhesions, eliminate all the points of obstruction from adhesions, and thread a splinting tube down the intestine. By that time, we were using Baker tubes; I kept a supply in the office for the use of the residents.

Her convalescence was uneventful. I followed her for over twenty years after the operation. She never had any more problems from intestinal obstruction.

*   *   *   *   *

One of the most unusual cases of obstruction had to do with a young geologist who was referred to me about 1950 for relief of multiple episodes of partial obstruction. X-rays had been taken and suggested a rare form of intestinal malrotation, namely, a reversed rotation. This diagnosis indeed was confirmed at operation. It was found that the right colon was greatly dilated and it passed behind rather than in front of the superior mesenteric vessels. At that point the colon was constricted between the artery and the spine so that its diameter was no larger than that of my index finger. The smaller arteries arising from the superior mesenteric were very short and very difficult to expose. But, eventually we removed the whole right colon and appendix and made an anastomosis between the terminal ileum and the sigmoid. The patient did very well and recovered uneventfully. A search of the literature revealed that only a few cases of this particular anomaly in adults had been reported and there were very few recoveries. This finding prompted Dr. Chin-an Wang, who was working with me at that time, to report all the congenital anomalies that had led to operation in adults at the MGH from 1938 to 1962. This paper, presented at the New England Surgical Society, is one of the very few that have appeared on this subject.

But that is not the end of the story. Several years later, I received a telephone call from Houston. NASA informed me that a certain person was being considered as the first scientist to walk on the moon. It so happened that that scientist was this same person. The authorities had looked at his generous abdominal scar and had wondered whether anyone with what must have been so horrible a background would be capable of such a journey. I assured them that my patient was even safer than the so-called normal man. Not only was he devoid of an appendix, but also he contained only a small amount of colon, so that altitude changes and distension of the colon would not bother him nearly as much as it could others. He was accepted, walked on the moon, and later became a United States Senator.

*   *   *   *   *

Just as small acorns can lead to mighty oaks, what starts as a simple procedure may become very complicated. One of my close physician friends developed trouble with an axillary bursa. In 1978, after a period of conservative treatment, he still had a great deal of swelling. Consequently I opened it, evacuated a lot of fluid, and put in a drain. Much to our surprise, a few days later he had a brisk hemorrhage from the drain site. This bleeding was repeated two or three times in the next few days, so it was necessary to reexplore. We found that the bursa was enormous, running high up into the axilla and around the axillary vessels and the major nerve trunks. The whole lining of the bursa looked like red velvet as blood seeped from innumerable capillaries. By this time, the number of observers had increased dramatically in number. Numerous suggestions were made, none of which worked. Finally it seemed that the only way to stop the bleeding was to take out the whole bursa. This was done as expeditiously as possible, but still during that period of twenty minutes or so he lost 2000 cc. of blood. After the excision, however, bleeding was completely controlled and he did very well, with no further trouble from his bursa. Later I learned that he had taken large quantities of aspirin prior to the time of the operation. I have had a very healthy respect for aspirin ever since.

*   *   *   *   *

In 1962 a local physician wanted me to operate on an enormously fat young man because he could not lose weight. I agreed to do so, but I am sure when you read this tale you will understand why I never operated on any others. This fellow—about 25—must have weighed about 350 pounds. Through a yard-long transverse incision, I did what was considered proper in those days; this was to defunction the great portion of the small bowel, leaving only a short section of proximal jejunum and distal ileum in continuity. The operative procedure went extremely well. The following morning, as we were making rounds, we found the patient in severe respiratory failure. He was intubated within a matter of minutes. After several days on the respirator, he recovered and was discharged.

Thereafter I saw him in the office from time to time. He did very well and his weight came down to about 200 pounds. Then one day a *Harvard Bulletin* appeared. On the cover was a resplendent general decked out in full regalia and riding a horse. "My God," I said, "that's my patient." And so it was. And he looked considerably more portly than before.

I called him in for an explanation. It was some time later when he finally appeared. It turned out that he, a Harvard graduate, had been picked to replay a historic march of General Knox who, during the Revolutionary War, brought 300 cannon hauled by oxen from Fort Ticonderoga to Boston in the dead of winter. It was a long journey. I was told the story by my young patient, who, by the time I finally saw him, was back to his original 350 pounds. His explanation was rather lame. He said they could not march very far every day, and the inns they stayed in treated them royally. He also said he never rode a horse before and that he had to be lifted into the saddle. At any rate, he was indeed impressive. (I have looked in the history books and there is no reference that General Knox weighed 350 pounds.)

I was very annoyed with this manifest demonstration of the lack of success of my operation, so I gave him quite a scolding and tried to put him out of my mind. However, several years later gastric bypass became an effective operation. I finally managed to get in touch with him and have him come back to the office to consider the possibility of another operation. Wonder of wonders, here he was, weighing about 175 pounds. My ego rapidly inflated, but, just as I was patting myself on the back, he gave me the story. I had told him to see a psychiatrist. He finally found a hypnotist who believed in group therapy. Very rapidly my patient became his star performer and the model for a galaxy of fatties who gathered about him and found out what hypnosis could do. Again, *sic transit gloria*.

*   *   *   *   *

Because of lack of space I have omitted a large number of stories. These interesting summaries are enough to prove that a general surgeon, at least in the time period that I was active, was faced with a great variety of cases and had to improvise in many instances. He often had to make a diagnosis without delay, select an operation fitted to the patient's condition, and persevere under conditions that now would be judged primitive and hazardous. Today, superior diagnoses mainly due to new radiologic techniques, excellent anesthesia, antibiotics, blood banks, respiratory care, and support of nutrition by central venous lines now provide enormous benefits for surgeons. However, I regret that a major virtue of surgeons—to rapidly choose a correct course of action and act upon it—has diminished in importance.

12

The Massachusetts Medical Society and the New England Journal of Medicine

I. *The Massachusetts Medical Society*

For approximately twenty years after World War II, my life was occupied nearly exclusively with the practice of surgery in the MGH. In 1964 a competing interest arose and eventually blossomed into an avocation that was to become increasingly important. This new interest was the world of medical politics and the relationship of the government, and other organizations with practicing physicians. It was then that I was persuaded to accept the post of president of the Massachusetts Medical Society (MMS).[1]

The relationships between the MMS and the MGH in general have been cordial. Two of the Warrens were early presidents of the MMS, John Warren (1804–1815), and John Collins Warren (1832–1836). Since 1900 seven surgeons from the MGH—Arthur Tracy Cabot (1904–1906), Robert Greenough (1929–1931, Arthur W. Allen (1949–1950), Leland S. McKittrick (1951–1952, Claude E. Welch (1965–1966), H. Thomas Ballantine, Jr. (1971–1972), and Grant V. Rodkey (1979–1980)—have held the chair. One MGH physician, Roger I. Lee (1943–1944) and one radiologist, Stanley M. Wyman (1981–1982) also have been presidents of the MMS.

Examples furnished by Drs. Allen and McKittrick were instrumental in establishing my interest in the position. Both of them were extremely loyal to the Society and free of egocentricity.

The seeds that developed into this new activity for me actually had been sown in 1950 when, for some reason that I cannot remember, I became a councillor of the Middlesex South Medical Society. A few words of explanation are necessary for those persons who do not recognize the intricacies of organized medicine in Massachusetts. For many years the state medical society had been divided into slightly over twenty geographical districts. Physicians in each district had the privilege of appointing members of the Council in accordance with the number of practicing physicians who were members of the Society and lived in the district. The Council is the supreme ruler of the Massachusetts Medical Society. It meets three times a year.

Prior to each Council meeting the councillors from each district meet in their respective locations to consider the various changes in bylaws, the resolutions to be submitted to the Council, and all of the other business of the Society. These meetings of the district councillors usually were scheduled to begin at 8 P.M., but were always delayed, poorly attended, and boring. Beginning at the hour of my usual attempted bedtime, the meeting enhanced my torpor by consisting of a discussion of minor details. For several years the meetings were enlightened by the presence of Dr. Charles Hayden, the director of Blue Shield, who spent uncounted hours trying to convince the conservative audience that Blue Shield had a role in their future.

Most of the Blue Cross and Blue Shield plans had begun in the late 1930s amid a sea of resentment from the profession. The same antipathy was rampant in Boston, and was directed against the strongest supporters of the plan—Dr. Edward Young, chief surgeon of the Faulkner Hospital, and Dr. Channing Frothingham, a physician. This distrust was due solely to the fact it was a new concept; rancor persisted despite the fact that in the early years of the rise of these prepaid insurance plans in this state, the MMS had a controlling interest on their boards of directors. Now it is far different; physician members are in the minority.

I pursued a totally undistinguished career as a councillor. I rarely opened my mouth in the meetings of the Council but listened with interest to the tirades of some unhappy souls and marveled at the final decisions that usually were made in a very democratic way, and with obvious justification and fairness.

In 1964 the nominating committee urged me to accept the post of President-elect of the society; this position was automatically followed by the Presidency in the following year. Matters were far different then than they are now. At that time, the president was expected to carry on an active professional life while performing the duties of the office. A few hundred dollars were paid for expenses, but there was no salary.

At that time the Society's headquarters were located at 22 The

Fenway in an old converted brownstone residence. Three stories were sufficient to house a combined office for the President and the Secretary of the Society, another for the Executive Secretary, two rooms for general secretaries, and a number of larger rooms that could be used for committee meetings. There was space for parking six cars in a back alley. The building was immediately adjacent to the Boston Medical Library and the offices of the *New England Journal of Medicine*. The library had a large room that would accommodate the meetings of the Council. These compressed quarters seem ludicrous today, but they were sufficient to support the activities of the society at that time. Expenses were minimal. For example, five of us on the Committee on Ethics and Discipline met regularly at least once a month under the chairmanship of Dr. John Spellman. After we had completed our morning's work, we would adjourn to a neighborhood eatery. The total bill for the entire committee's sandwiches and glasses of milk amounted to about five dollars.

Dr. Robert Buck, the secretary of the MMS was a cultured gentleman. He usually brought his morning newspaper (in German) to the office every day. Everett Spencer, the Executive Secretary, and later Executive Vice-president, was extraordinarily efficient.

The President's main duty was to preside as the parliamentarian in charge of the three yearly Council meetings. This duty was not to be shouldered lightly, for there was always some amateur in the audience who was anxious to point out mistakes made by the President as he tried to follow *Robert's Rules of Order*. The President knew he had done well if Dr. Robert Holland had not risen to the floor on a "point of order" at least a dozen times during each session. Fortunately Allen Johnson, as President, who had presided over the meetings two years before me had produced an excellent summary of the *Rules* that were to be followed religiously by his successor, Dr. James Baty, and by me. I was greatly pleased, after my term as President had expired, to receive a congratulatory letter from Dr. Holland.

The President attended as many committee meetings as possible. Because he had carried out the same routine during his apprentice year as president-elect, he became very conversant with all of the affairs of the society.

The two most active committees in the Massachusetts Medical Society in 1964 were the Ethics and Discipline Committee and one that considered complaints by patients or physicians against other physicians. Because many of these complaints dealt with charges for medical services, that committee, in particular, raised a great deal of commotion. We did not recognize that we were in conflict with constraints about to be laid down by the Federal Trade Commission and our committee was very rough on doctors who appeared to be gouging their patients with excessive bills. I am sure that we saved many individuals large amounts of money. It was about one decade later that the Federal Trade Commission called this activity a restraint of trade, and ruled that no attempt could be made by an organization of doctors to either maintain a higher or a lower price for specific services. Most physicians find it hard to recognize the wisdom of such a ruling. At any rate, the committee finally was eliminated about 1977.

But in 1964 physicians had a great deal of independence, and the medical profession was riding high with comparatively little external or internecine warfare. The public adored physicians at that time. However, the first rumbles of increased federal and state control were being heard from Washington.

In 1964, at the instigation of Mary Lasker, Congress appointed the Regional Medical Programs Commission. This action was one of the first of many decisions from Washington that were to effect enormous changes in the practice of medicine for at least several decades. The commission, under the chairmanship of Dr. Michael DeBakey, reached the logical conclusion that the care of patients with heart disease, cancer, and stroke—the three major killers of that era—could be provided far more effectively in large regional centers than in community hospitals. But patients rebelled against being transported away from their own communities for procedures such as breast biopsies. And physicians were equally adamant as they saw their patients being siphoned over into metropolitan centers.

After Dr. DeBakey delivered the report of the Commission, funds were allotted to Regional Medical Programs throughout the country. In Massachusetts a group of directors was appointed. The chairman was Dr. Leona Baumgartner, and I was a member. Unfortunately the original main purpose of the Commission—to establish centers for treatment of heart disease, cancer and stroke—gradually was modified. The purpose became to provide access for treatment of all citizens in existing hospitals. The whole program gradually deteriorated.

Some of the problems that were settled in meetings of the Council were of great importance at that time, although they seem trivial today. One was concerned with operations in which interns and residents participated; was it ethical for the surgeon-in-charge to allow the resident to assume major responsibility in the operating room and for the surgeon-in-charge to collect fees for such operations?

I was president and in the chair as parlimentarian in this acrimonious discussion. Today, in 1990, everyone realizes that a team approach is necessary in nearly all major operations to avoid protracted delay. I recalled an operation I had witnessed in a teaching hospital in another city. The resident was allowed to hold a retractor. The professor clamped every blood vessel, tied every knot, and cut every suture. The operation dragged on interminably. Surgeons in the Council debate agreed that an operating team is essential to perform difficult operations. The idea of a team approach had been instituted by Dr. George Dunlop, a Worcester surgeon who later became president of the American College of Surgeons. He informed his patients prior to operations that the procedure would be done by a group of surgeons under his direction. Patients accepted this method, and it was deemed ethical by our Council after long and heated discussion.

During my presidential year, the Council for the first time in many years moved away from its cramped area in the Boston Medical Library and held meetings in various hotels. I presided over the last meeting of the Council for the year in the Hotel Statler. The Council made some trivial changes in bylaws. The Council meeting was followed immediately by the annual meeting of the members of the Society. All actions of the Council during the year had to be approved by the fellows of the Society at that time. This always was a rubber-stamp procedure, and took me only a few moments.

In the following year Warren Babson was president. He was in the chair for the annual meeting when members of the MMS, who rarely attended meetings, suddenly filled the room. Under the leadership of a notorious trouble-maker they voted a change in the bylaws whereby the deans of the Massachusetts medical schools and the editor of the *New England Journal of Medicine* were excluded from membership in the Council, appointments they had had for many years. This retreat to isolation by practicing physicians was a black mark in the history of the Massachusetts Medical Society. It took many years before the bylaws again were changed and the sage advice of these persons could be heard again on the Council floor.

At one time Urban Eversole (chief of anesthesia at the Lahey clinic and past president of the MMS) and I, at the request of the American Medical Association, went to Washington to "show the flag." We were not entirely certain what we were supposed to do there, but we did meet with our representatives in Congress and gave evidence that the AMA was speaking for the state medical societies of the country.

A very important development occurred during my term as president. Actually, I had little to do with it, because all of the planning and fund-raising had been done before 1965. This achievement was the erection of the Countway Library—a joint undertaking of the BML and the Harvard Medical School Libraries.

Historical details of the formation of the Countway, the largest medical library in the country with the exception of the National Medical Library in Washington, can be found in *The Centennial History of the Boston Medical Library*. This account was written by Joseph E. Garland, son of the former editor of the *New England* Journal *of Medicine*.[2] Records showed that the first BML was founded in 1805 and ceded to the Boston Athenaeum in 1826. The second BML was organized formally in 1875; Oliver Wendell Holmes was the President. From 1901 to 1965 the Library was located at 8 The Fenway; it became affiliated with the MMS in 1947.

Construction of the Countway Library at HMS began in 1964. In 1960 President Howard Sprague of the BML and President Nathan Pusey of Harvard University agreed that the two libraries should be united. So the books from the Fenway site were transferred in 1965, the year after the cornerstone of the new building had been laid.

The Countway contains many visible mementos of the BML. Rooms dedicated to Drs. Allen and Lahey—both strong fund-raisers for the institution—and numerous portraits of former presidents of the MMS and of the BML are on the walls. The Rare Books Collection, under the supervision of Richard Wolfe, is another particular contribution of the BML to the union; this special collection had been started by Oliver Wendell Holmes. The partnership has proved to be felicitous and highly beneficial to both organizations.

There were no other important developments during the year of my presidency. It was a year in which storm clouds were just beginning to appear on the horizon. Malpractice was not a threat. The country seemed able to support guns, butter, and medicine. None of us could discern with enough clarity the trouble spots that would emerge in the future or do anything that would prevent deterioration of the favorable condition in which medicine then existed. The office of President, however, was for me an important introduction to the House of Delegates of the AMA, where momentous issues would need to be met head-on.

Ex-Presidents of the MMS can be appointed *ex officio* to the Council, if members in their districts agree. Hence I have continued to attend these meetings and to be conversant with activities of the Society. It is apparent that the MMS is now very much stronger than it was a quarter century ago. In fact, there are great differences between these two eras. The differences are illustrated by the variations in size between the small building at 22 The Fenway and the present huge headquarters of the *New England Journal of Medicine* and the MMS in Waltham. Differences between the MMS in 1965 and in 1990 and important events that occurred in the intervening years can be summarized as follows:

1. Physicians were far more independent in 1965 than they are today. Then they controlled fees, had a voting majority in Blue Shield, were more highly regarded by patients, and had very few problems with professional liability.

2. The MMS has erected new headquarters for the MMS and the *New England Journal of Medicine*, increased services for members and the number of employees. There has been a corresponding rise in the costs of running the Society.

3. The Postgraduate Medical Institute has developed strong programs, because continuing medical education is a requirement for licensure in the state. This regulation had been established in 1976 by the Board of Registration in Medicine, of which I was chairman.

4. There has been a great increase in members. Student members have been admitted and are assuming an active role in the Society.

5. It has been possible to exert increasing influence in the House of Delegates of the AMA. Two of our powerful members in 1965— Norman Welch, as speaker of the House of Delegates and president of the AMA, and Leland McKittrick, as chairman of the Council on Medical Education—engendered great interest in the AMA. Their examples have led to a succession of highly qualified delegates, appointees to important councils, and candidates for high office.

6. The MMS lost a bitter legal contest with Blue Shield over the issue of whether or not MMS members who were not members of Blue Shield plans should be recompensed for services rendered to Blue Shield subscribers. The MMS said "yes"; the Blue Shield said "no."

7. Closer relationships with legislative bodies and the public are being fostered.

8. Most important of all, the great success of the *New England Journal of Medicine* has led to a great increase in income of the MMS and the expansion of services it now can afford.

9. Annual dues were five dollars in 1900, twenty-five in 1950, thirty-five in 1965, two hundred in 1970, and three hundred dollars in 1990.

During this same period two particularly strong leaders emerged as presidents. Dr. Grant Rodkey was instrumental in obtaining consent of the Council to erect the new headquarters building. He was a tireless worker in drives for new members of the AMA. He has been very active for nearly a decade as a delegate to the AMA. He served on the Council on Medical Services for six years, a portion of which he was the chairman.

Dr. Barry Manuel, immediate past president at this writing, furnishes an example of what a president can accomplish when he is a respected surgeon, an educator, and devotes full time to his presidential duties. Personal contacts with many individuals in important positions in the state, and the development of his personal no-fault professional liability program have earned him a nation-wide platform.

II. *The New England Journal of Medicine*

The *New England Journal of Medicine* (NEJM) is the oldest medical journal in continuous production in the world and one of the most successful enterprises in America in the twentieth century. This name was bestowed in 1928 on a combination of previous journals that were founded during 1812 and 1813. The annual circulation has risen from about 6,000 in 1928 to over 232,000 in 1990. In the same period the *NEJM* emerged from penury into prosperity.

The progenitor of the *NEJM* was the *New England Journal of Medicine and Surgery and the Collateral Branches of Science;* it began as a quarterly in 1812. In 1828 it purchased the *Boston Medical Intelligencer,* the first medical weekly in America, which began publication in 1823. The new combination was entitled the *Boston Medical and Surgical Journal (BMSJ).* This journal continued the weekly format and its independent existence until 1921 when it was purchased by the Massachusetts Medical Society (MMS) for the astonishing sum of one dollar. In 1928 the *BMSJ* indicated the broadening of its interests by changing its name to the present *New England Journal of Medicine.* Little did the supporters of this purchase (or the many opponents) realize that in less than a half-century the *NEJM* would become the pearl of the MMS, or, to use another metaphor, the purveyor of its life's blood.[3]

I was deeply involved with the *NEJM* for over forty years, first with its conduct and later with business matters and policy. Dr. Allen began to write a yearly survey of abdominal surgery in 1939. (He told me later that he undertook this arduous job with the understanding that he could appoint his successor.) When he became ill, the duty devolved on me. We collaborated on several articles: thereafter for nearly thirty years, I carried on with the series. Eventually the interval between reports stretched to two and then to three years, for although Dr. Allen could write his survey during one weekend, the task soon became much more difficult for me. In fact, for many years I used most of my spare time in the summers to produce the review. About 1980 Ronald Malt became a coauthor and thereby lightened the load. In 1986 the *Journal's* editors decided to eliminate these rather long encyclopedic articles.

In addition to these reviews, I contributed many other articles. They were devoted chiefly to abdominal or cancer surgery. Important socioeconomic issues such as "Professional Standards Review Organizations" and "Medical Malpractice" were considered in review articles. I also wrote some editorials and book reviews and was the discussant in numerous cases described in the Cabot Case Records, a feature of the *NEJM* ever since they first were printed in 1923.

My second contribution to the *NEJM* was made as a member of the Committee on Publications of the MMS. I was appointed to the committee in 1962, became chairman in 1969, served in that capacity until 1980, and then acted as consultant for another year. This long tenure was the maximum allowed by the by-laws of the Society and covered a period of dramatic development.

During my tenure, the committee led the drive that finally resulted in the authorization of a new building which eventually housed both the *NEJM* and the MMS, selected one editor, Arnold Relman, appointed annual Shattuck lecturers, and presided over the great expansion in circulation and prestige of the *Journal*.

Appointments to the Committee on Publications are made by the president of the Society. For the many years, while I was chairman, they were balanced fairly well between practicing physicians and members with academic appointments. Because this committee has been one of the most exciting in the MMS, and because immediate past presidents have the privilege of joining any one committee, in some years nearly half of the members of the committee are past presidents.

By far the most unusual event during my tenure as chairman was the erection of a new building, initially planned to house subscription and production facilities for the *Journal*. At the start of my term, this work was carried on in a renovated warehouse in Allston. We dreamed of a new building that would be modern and capacious; editorial offices were to remain in the Countway Library. However, it took many years to convince the MMS Council. Our first major request was made in a meeting of the Council held in Worcester in 1975. The proposal caught fire with the officers of MMS, and John Byrne, the incoming President, provided enough spark to get a potential site chosen in 1977. But it was promptly turned down by the Council. When Grant Rodkey became president in 1979, he pushed the project strongly, and finally the Council allotted four million dollars for a new building.

This cost seemed exorbitant to some members of the publications committee. William Sweet had succeeded me as chairman, and strongly supported a move into the Harvard Community Health Plan building close to Kenmore Square. James McDonough (a member, and later chairman of the committee) and I together opposed this plan, and in a somewhat heated exchange of views, urged an entirely new building. Finally a site was chosen near the Polaroid complex in Waltham. A magnificent, spacious building was erected, and not long after, to nobody's surprise, the executive offices of the MMS on the Fenway were sold, and headquarters of the MMS were moved in with the *NEJM*. The editorial offices of the *Journal* continue to be centered in the Countway Library. Of course, the new building doubled in value within a few years. In retrospect, it seems impossible to believe that it was so difficult to convince the Council that the structure should be built.

Choosing the editor of the NEJM is the most important duty of the Publications Committee. The second is to free him from the encumbrance of printing what the MMS wants him to print. This policy has continued throughout the past twenty-five years.

Selection of the three editors who served during my tenure was inaugurated by small subcommittees of the Committee on Publications. Joseph Garland, Franz Ingelfinger, and Arnold Relman have been very different from one another but each has been spectacular as authors and editors. Their abilities have lifted the *NEJM* to its present prestigious level.[4]

One of Ingelfinger's great contributions was to appoint an editorial board in which members had limited tenure. He also maintained meticulous supervision of all the *Journal's* activities. When he became ill and his retirement was only a few months away, I asked him to provide our committee with advice concerning a prospective editor. His answer typified Franz exactly—thoughtful and thorough. He listed the following attributes and expanded on their substance and importance:[5]

1. Status in American medicine "recognized and respected as an expert or leader"; one "who enjoys high academic status"
2. clinical interest and "considerable clinical experience"
3. breadth of interest: "interest . . . should encompass aspects of medicine that extend beyond strictly scientific or clinical topics", including "all aspects of the interface between medicine and society"
4. flexibility and tolerance: a "catholic approach to controversial issues"
5. leadership and personality: "should . . . insist on . . . standards" but "should exhibit . . . appreciation, humor, and flexible response" to the opinion of his associates
6. literary ability: writes with "elegance, imagination, or forcefulness"
7. editorial experience: should have "served as a reviewer"
8. ideation and devotion to detail: "ready to experiment" and "obsessive about trivial details"
9. general: should have "intelligence, motivation, industry, overall personality, and adherence to high standards."

Using this advice our subcommittee of two, namely, Samuel Proger and myself, proposed to the full Committee that Arnold Relman should be the next editor. (Dr. Proger was a wonderful man of great vision, modest but firm, extremely knowledgeable, and the architect of the expanded New England Medical Center.) It did not take long, once Franz became extremely ill for the Committee to decide that Arnold Relman was our man.

As the *NEJM* continued to gain prestige, the number of readers, subscribers, and advertisers increased. For many years after it was founded, the Massachusetts Medical Society had to subsidize the publication. Gradually, however, the *NEJM* became profitable. But prosperity brought other problems. Because the Society owned the *Journal*, it was necessary to keep salaries in both the MMS and *NEJM* offices equivalent, so the MMS became highly dependent on the *NEJM* for funds. Meanwhile, the *NEJM* became dependent on advertisers to support its financial needs.

In the early sixties the Internal Revenue Service decided to tax the advertising revenue of many magazines such as the *NEJM* and the *National Geographic*. The MMS was fortunate to win one suit against the Internal Revenue Service in 1964, but thereafter a large slice of our annual profits disappeared as taxes.

In years before my tenure, the *NEJM* offered a lifetime subscription for $500. But subscription rates began to rise rapidly and a huge loss became a possibility. Fortunately, we were able to halt this venture before much harm had been done. Dr. Relman has succeeded in persuading the Publications Committee to raise subscription rates so that any decline in advertising could be borne by the *NEJM*. However, because the MMS is dependent on the *Journal* for a large part of its income, it must watch its expenses.

The *NEJM* has reached the greatest heights in history under the guidance of Dr. Relman. He served as editor-in-chief from 1977 to 1991. His final report, written in April 1991, included a summary of changes that had occurred during his tenure.[6]

The period from 1977 to 1991 was one of enormous expansion. Total annual subscriptions increased from 166,909 in 1976 to 232,805; total text pages per year from 3,159 to 4,319; total advertising pages per year from 2,469 to 4,044; and total annual revenues from $5,983,000 to $37,886,000. This great increase in revenues has allowed the Massachusetts Medical Society ample funds to supply increased services to itself and to the public. The paid, nonmember worldwide circulation for 1990 was 215,503, and, according to Dr. Relman, "by far the largest and widest such circulation of any medical journal in the world."

Peer review of *NEJM* articles is called by Dr. Relman "probably the most painstaking of any medical journal." Only eleven percent of submitted manuscripts were published in 1990. The editorial content of published articles has shifted toward social, economic and ethical issues. He described the textual content of the *NEJM* as follows:

In recent years the *Journal* has become a major forum for discussion of health policy issues. While the general format of the *Journal* has changed but little, the scientific content of its articles has changed considerably— a reflection of the rapid transformation of modern medical research. Fourteen years ago most original articles were descriptive clinical studies. Since then, clinical description has been largely replaced by complicated studies of the molecular and genetic mechanisms of disease, and by carefully designed and controlled randomized clinical trials. The statistical analysis of clinical results has become much more sophisticated. Growing public interest in medical research has attracted unprecedented attention from the media. Many of our articles generate national debate. The *Journal* has become a public institution, widely quoted, carefully scrutinized, and sometimes stringently criticized.

In 1976 I received the Distinguished Service Award of the AMA and became the subject of an editorial published by the editor Franz Ingelfinger in the *Journal*. The article was entitled "The Distinguished Services of Claude E. Welch, M.D.[7] Franz wrote:

The Distinguished Service Award of the American Medical Association, the Association's highest honor, is given for meritorious service in the science and art of medicine. The list of past awardees includes such outstanding physician exponents of this art and practice as James B. Herrick, Elliott Joslin, George Minot, Evarts Graham, Paul Dudley White, Alfred Blalock, Michael DeBakey, Lester Dragstedt, Irvine Page, Tinsley Harrison and George Whipple. Once it was given to a non-physician, Anton J. Carlson, (a distinguished physiologist.) The recipient of the Award this year was Claude Emerson Welch, M.D.

The presentation of the Award to Claude Welch made *The New England Medical Journal of Medicine* understandably proud, for Claude is the head of the Journal's family. Since 1969 he has been chairman of the Massachusetts Medical Society's Committee on Publications, a post to which he has just been reappointed this year. The Committee acts like a board of trustees. Major decisions concerning the *Journal's* personnel, the *Journal's* general activities during a given year and the *Journal's* financial status are among its principal concerns. The Committee could also influence the Journal's contents, but it is to the everlasting credit of the Committee, and of the Society on whose behalf it acts, that it does not interfere in the selection of items to be printed in the *Journal*. Indeed, in over nine years, only once did a member of the Committee try to influence the editor's decision, and that member was not Claude Welch.

It is characteristic of Claude that he would not interfere, for among his other virtues he is a scrupulous observer of procedure that he believes to be fair and proper. Furthermore, not everything he submits to the *Journal* is automatically accepted, and he complies with requests for revision with gentlemanly grace. Not that he has always been pleased with what the editor has printed. He was, for example, quite annoyed to discover that Che Guevara was the subject of a Doctors Afield article. Yet he rigorously insists, and his fellow Committee members agree, that decision about the *Journal's* contents, nature and makeup is the privilege of the editor. Not that the Committee is without power: should it not care for the totality of an editor's performance, the Committee could dismiss that person forthwith.

Dr. Welch's Distinguished Service Award and the many other honors he has received reflect the numerous contributions he has made in the practice of surgery, the offices he has held in various national societies, and his membership in high level advisory and administrative bodies, both public and private. Few physicians, if any, can rival him in the long list of organizations he has led as president: Massachusetts Medical Society, American College of Surgeons, Boston Surgical Society, Society for Surgery of the Alimentary Tract, New England Cancer Society, American Surgical Association, Excelsior Surgical Club, Daland Society, International Surgical Group and Harvard Medical Alumni Association.

Being president of a medical organization, or belonging to influential committees, sometimes reflect political adroitness and manipulation, but the reasons why Claude Welch has held so many offices are to be found in his character, his experience and his performance. His pre-eminence among surgical specialists is attested to not only by his many patients but also by his multiple contributions to the surgical literature, including, of course, his Medical Progress reports on abdominal surgery of which he has contributed 13 (the first two with Dr. Arthur Allen) since 1949.

During the meetings of the Committee on Publications, Claude Welch's advice, whether on matter of principle or of procedure, is invariably sagacious and designed to achieve an equitable solution. His conduct is that of a man seeking an appropriate course of action rather than that of a partisan determined to have his own way. His tenure as chairman of the Committee, moreover, has been marked by ever helpful and reassuring support of the editor—even when times were trying and issues potentially inflammatory. I could not have had a more dependable and sympathetic chief to whom I had to report. Hence this editorial, which, with gratitude and admiration, seeks to add my own private distinguished award to the larger and more formal honor that he has so appropriately been given by the AMA.

Never have I received an accolade that I have appreciated more than these words from my great friend, Franz Ingelfinger. He also received the AMA Distinguished Service Award a few years later—a great tribute to his own superlative editorial work.

In 1985, I was selected as the Orator for the Massachusetts Medical Society. In order to maintain the continuity of the narrative, this occasion is described in the notes rather than in the text.[8]

13

American Medical Association

My first direct contact with the activities of the American Medical Association (AMA) on a national level occurred in Miami in 1964. I had been appointed as an alternate to the House of Delegates from Massachusetts. Since all of the delegates from our state were present, I had an opportunity to wander and observe the activities of the House. For those persons who do not know the intricacies of the AMA, the House of Delegates is the policy making body, and the Trustees form the executive branch carrying out the will of the House.

For several hours I sat in the audience before a reference committee that was considering the recommendations of the Council on Medical Education. The chairman of this Council was Leland McKittrick, one of the great surgeons of Boston and particularly of the MGH. As a neophyte I had always been impressed by the wisdom he had shown in solving clinical problems. Now he was being treated with similar deference by the reference committee.[1] All of his comments were obviously wise, and the conclusions of the Council were adopted and approved without modification by the committee. Not only did Dr. McKittrick sustain his fine reputation, but the American Medical Association rose in my opinion because they adopted his recommendations.[2]

Actually, I had received one important appointment from the AMA the year before to the Residency Review Committee for Surgery. This committee was established in 1950 to judge and accredit institutions for education and training of interns and residents in general surgery. The Committee for Surgery included three members each from the American Medical Association, the American Board of Surgery, and the American College of Surgeons. I was asked by Dr. McKittrick to join the Committee in 1963 as a representative of the AMA and served for two 3-year terms.

These committees have a very important role to play because they can disqualify an institution if proper academic standards are not maintained or if enough surgical experience as independent surgeons is not given to their graduates. When I was a member, there was a great attempt to expand teaching programs to satellite community centers. Today, sharp restrictions have become the rule, even in academic centers. Thus, in many ways Residency Review Committees are as important as Boards in matters of qualification.[3]

I sat in the House as a delegate for a decade. I recall many incidents that occurred during that time. Once one of the high AMA officials introduced Dr. Wilbur Cohen, secretary of the Department of Health, Education and Welfare, with the tongue-in-cheek statement that he would never want to appear in the dark with Dr. Cohen. That year the meeting was held in New York City and the sidewalk in front of the convention hotel was covered with demonstrators bearing signs reading "AMA—American Murder Association." Such remarks and placards have become rare in recent years. Both delegates and the public today are more cognizant of the gravity of the decisions of the AMA.

I also recall a stormy session in San Francisco in 1968. The problem we confronted was racial equality, which existed in name but not in fact in the AMA. Indeed, for almost 100 years the problem of racism had bedeviled the AMA. Despite many years of controversy and the introduction of many resolutions before the House of Delegates, the AMA had continued to affirm its well-established position—that the AMA is a federation of state societies, and each component society has the right to establish its own rules for membership. There were no blacks in the AMA in many states; instead they joined the National Medical Association, an organization of black physicians.

In 1968 Massachusetts decided to enter the fray. As Everett Spencer said in his dramatic, detailed description of the whole process, "The Massachusetts (delegates) brought to the controversy planning and persistence, direction and doggedness."[4] Early in that year, Spencer wrote a ringing editorial that was published in the *NEJM*. The Massachusetts delegation, of which I was chairman, prepared a resolution to be submitted to a reference committee. The resolution called attention to the fact that the AMA had already declared that membership should not be denied on the basis of color and added the following radical proposal—that, after due process, any state association found guilty of such discrimination would be expelled from the AMA. Because we were unable to secure support from the entire New England delegation, Massachusetts was standing alone.

I assigned Urban Eversole to speak in favor of our resolution before the reference committee. The two of us spent long hours in our hotel rooms, drafting statements and discussing tactics. Eventually Urban made an excellent presentation before the Reference Committee which appeared to be favorably impressed. But much to our amazement, when we were finally given the committee report just before it was to be presented to the House of Delegates, we found that they had refused to endorse our resolution. Under such circumstances, when a delegate does not approve of a report, the politic and usual method to obtain further consideration is to move referral of the report to the Board of Trustees. But this method was certain to guarantee a quiet burial, and we had already decided that such a course would mire the AMA in its familiar conservative stance. Furthermore, we had decided that we would fight on the floor of the House to overturn the committee report.

Urban Eversole rose and spoke before the entire House. He succinctly outlined the issues involved, called attention to the fact that at that time we were in a highly charged situation, with cries for equality rampant, and that the AMA must take definitive action. His words were quoted later in the press who called him "a mild-mannered anesthetist."[5] Little did they know that he, a stalwart deacon of his church, had an overwhelming sense of right and wrong that was matched only by the persistence of a bulldog.

I rose immediately thereafter to add further fuel to the fire. I said:

Amendments to the Constitution of the United States declare that the privileges of a citizen shall not be denied on the basis of creed or color. All of us, as members of the AMA, are therefore committed to active support of this principle, while any action in opposition to this amendment is indefensible. There remains only the question of enforcement. Should we offer only token support and leave decisions to the courts? Should enforcement be the duty of constituent societies or should it be the function of the AMA as a whole?

This resolution, for the first time in the history of the AMA, calls for the exercise of disciplinary measures that may be exerted on the constituent societies, primarily by the Judicial Council, and ultimately by the House of Delegates. It is our contention that this Council and House must have such power whenever any action is so fundamental that it involves guarantees extended by the Constitution of the United States.

Further debate followed. The temper of the House began to favor our resolution, but approval was not certain until Howard Nelson, a delegate from Mississippi, spoke in our favor. This speech by a member from the Deep South was enough to swing the opposition. The resolution was adopted in place of the report of the reference committee and appropriate changes in the by-laws were approved at the following session of the AMA.

In retrospect, a quarter of a century later, our action had very little effect insofar as the composition of membership in the AMA is concerned. I believe the option we established never has been utilized. Meanwhile the American Medical and the National Medical Societies have continued to follow independent courses. Such an outcome is one that we had hoped to correct.

A second very important conflict in which I was involved arose in the early 1970s when the AMA was required to take a stance concerning support of Professional Standards Review Organizations. These organizations were to be composed of physicians who would, in their geographic areas, review treatment and length of stay in hospitals of patients whose hospital expenses were paid by the government; thus the care of all Medicare and Medicaid patients would be reviewed. Norms of diagnosis and care would need to be established and profiles then could be drawn for each doctor. Senator Bennett of Utah introduced the bill in Congress, and fought vigorously for it. The President signed the bill into law in 1972.

Such a project obviously needed the cooperation of physicians throughout the country. Many of us believed that the law would lead to better quality of medical care of hospital patients. Alan Nelson, a delegate from Utah and later president of the AMA, supported cooperation with the government. On the other hand, many delegates felt this was an unwarranted intrusion of the government into physicians' affairs, leading to cookbook medicine, and actions against individual physicians who did not follow specified standards.

On the day the House was scheduled to vote on approval or disapproval of cooperation of the AMA with the government, a bitter conflict was expected. Dr. Thomas Ballantine, a neurosurgeon on the staff of the Massachusetts General Hospital, distributed reprints of an article I had published in the *NEJM* which strongly supported the concept.[6] After many speeches, approval finally was won on the floor of the House by the strong intercession of the Board of Trustees, and particularly by Dr. Robert Hunter who delivered an impassioned speech. He convinced the members of the House that cooperation was essential.

Following approval of the resolution supporting Professional Standards Review Organizations, I was appointed chairman of an interspecialty group to draw up model criteria by which the quality of care of patients in short-stay general hospitals could be judged. This very large committee also contained one or more representatives from the Department of Health, Education, and Welfare because the grant and funds for this project had been provided to the AMA by the government. I did not look forward with great pleasure to chairing meetings in which all major specialties were represented because turf battles could easily arise. Remarkably, except for minor disagreements that were quickly settled, we succeeded in producing the prototype of a method to judge whether or not care in individual cases had been satisfactory. The printed book took two years to produce and was published in 1976. It was a large volume covering approximately 75 percent of admissions to short-stay hospitals in the country. These volumes were distributed throughout America. Literally thousands of criteria sets have been developed since then; but our effort was the original one. In retrospect it appears that the criteria were quite loose, but they furnished a framework that has been imitated widely.[7]

When trustees of the AMA were invited as guests of the Chinese Medical Association to visit the People's Republic of China for three weeks in 1974, the trustees appointed half of the group and told me that I could appoint the remainder. Rejecting all modesty, I counted myself in. We had a wonderful red-carpet trip. These years were near the last of the Mao regime, and it was easy to see the seeds of discontent sprouting under the iron rule of the cadres. Nevertheless, despite the terrible depredations that ensued during the cultural revolution, there were many matters of which the Chinese could justly be proud. (A detailed description of that visit is given in Chapter 17.)

In another interesting assignment I served as chairman of a committee to set up an AMA long-range planning council. In addition, I had a great opportunity to revitalize the composition of the House of Delegates when I served as a chairman of a committee to consider the growing influence of specialists in the practice of medicine. Since the time of its origin, the AMA has been primarily an association of state medical societies. Our committee set up a mechanism by which major specialty societies could be represented in the House. This change meant a great addition to the number of members in the House who represented their individual specialty societies. This shift in the balance of power from state medical societies toward national specialty organizations has made an important change in the complexion of the House of Delegates of the AMA. State delegates are more likely to entertain parochial views than those who represent national organizations, and in the House, every vote can be important when critical issues are considered. Unfortunately, the ACS has never cooperated closely with the AMA: this matter will be discussed in the next chapter.

In 1975 I was persuaded by the New England delegation to run for the presidency of the AMA. However it was impossible for me to criticize my rival because he—Carl Hoffman—was a fine man, a good friend, a professor of urology, and a member of the ACS. Certainly the ideologies of most members are not very different, but most of the delegates greatly fear the liberalism that exists east of Dedham, Massachusetts and it is not easy for a Massachusetts man to break this barrier. Norman Welch had done so a few years before, but he had been an exceptionally fine speaker of the House of Delegates. Unfortunately he died from a severe stroke shortly after he began his term of office.

I thought that competition for the office of president would be a good thing for the AMA and that past activities could count in the balance. However, those concepts were completely eclipsed by political facts. Any member of the Aces and Deuces (delegates from states with only one or two delegates) becomes favored by his comrades and automatically garners at least forty votes. Carl was not only from the small state of West Virginia but had served as secretary of the Board of Trustees. At any rate my political campaign was a flop and Carl won in a landslide. I was not greatly disappointed to be left out in the cold.

I formed many strong friendships during these years. Mutual respect and a desire to do the best for medicine and the public were the hallmarks of the actions of the AMA. Critics have stated that the AMA is only interested in the welfare of physicians but I feel strongly that this is not true.

In 1977, after ten years in the House, much to my surprise I found that I was one of two nominees to receive the Distinguished Service Award of the AMA. This annual award is the highest honor conferred by the organization. Nominations are made by the Board of Trustees; they submit the slate to the House of Delegates, who, by secret vote, elect one person. The names of the nominees are kept secret until the day of the election. Hence I was astonished when I learned at the time of the annual meeting a few hours before the vote was taken in 1977 that I was one of two contenders. The other nominee, Dwight Wilbur, was a previous president of the AMA, and a distinguished physician and statesman.

As soon as I saw the statement, I said to Richard Palmer, the chairman of the board of trustees, that I should withdraw in favor of Dr. Wilbur. He said I should not, and a few hours later, I learned that I had been elected.

Obviously I was very proud of this award because very few surgeons had received it in the past. Alton Ochsner and Owen Wangensteen were among these few, and it was a pleasure to join them. Paul Dudley White had been the last person from Boston to gain the honor. Of all the accolades I received afterward, the greatest was that written by Franz Ingelfinger and published in the *New England Journal of Medicine*.[8]

14

The American College of Surgeons

The American College of Surgeons is the largest and the most influential of the national surgical colleges in the world. Franklin Martin of Chicago, a surgeon specializing in gynecology, founded the organization in 1913. Based on initial premises that there was a sharp dividing line between the disciplines of medicine and surgery, that a coterie of senior practitioners should dominate the society, and that splitting of fees was the greatest evil conspiring against the welfare of the patient, the organization survived through many rocky years. Thereafter it attained financial stability, became more democratic, fought off competitors, and continues to be an increasingly powerful force in promoting high quality surgical care.

The MGH has supported the College in many ways. The first president of the College (1913–1916) was John M. T. Finney who previously had been a house pupil in the MGH prior to his appointment as clinical professor of surgery in Johns Hopkins. Harvey Cushing, MGH house pupil in 1895 and later chief at the Brigham Hospital in Boston followed in 1922–1923. Succeeding presidents from the MGH were Robert Greenough (1934–1935), Arthur Allen (1947–1948), Claude Welch (1973–1974), and W. Gerald Austen, who was elected in 1991.

Other MGH surgeons who played important roles in the College were vice-presidents Lincoln Davis and Leland McKittrick; other vice-presidents from Boston included Thomas Lanman, Francis Moore, and Joseph Murray. Drs. Allen and Austen also were chairmen of the Board of Regents, an important post in the organization. Codman, Daland and Grantley Taylor played important roles in the society's cancer program. Today, all general surgeons in the MGH as well as a majority of surgeons in speciality societies are members of the College.

Martin's historical volume detailing the earlier years was followed by another, written by Loyal Davis. The issues in the years 1969 to 1987 when C. Rollins Hanlon was the director, were defined and analyzed with inimitable lucidity in his monthly editorials in the *Bulletin* and later collected in a printed volume. George Stephenson, a stalwart officer of the College for nearly half a century, prepared the last of these historical volumes, covering the years 1955 to 1990. These sources provide a detailed description of the problems faced and, in many instances, solved by the College.[1]

My introduction to the College occurred during the annual meeting in Boston in 1928; I was a medical student checking hats and coats as the eminent visitors filled the amphitheater in the Brigham Hospital. Harvey Cushing then was the president. We students did not appreciate the deep undercurrents that existed in the College until later when we heard that Martin dashed to the train for Chicago, exclaiming that he could not get out of Boston fast enough. However, Martin, in his position as the secretary-general of the College, later did send a very courteous letter to Cushing thanking him for the excellent program.

By 1934 or shortly thereafter, many of my classmates from medical school, nearly half of whom had opted to become surgeons, had to decide whether to join the ACS, the AMA, or both. At that time the Board of Surgery did not exist, and the College was the only group that was attempting to elevate the standards of surgery, of surgeons, and of hospitals. Meanwhile the ACS was suffering financial losses, in large part because of the cost of its hospital standardization program, which had been founded in 1919.

Dr. Arthur Allen, my revered chief, mentor, and councelor for many years, spent an enormous amount of time on the College's behalf, playing an important role in its governance. In the late 1940s Dr. Allen often went by train to Chicago to spend a three-day weekend with the regents or the director. He was President of the College in 1947 and 1948, and Chairman of the Board of Regents from 1949 to 1951. His great devotion to the organization was communicated to me, so I became a fellow of the College and life member in 1939 as soon as I was eligible.

Except for attending the annual meetings and presenting several papers, I took no active part in the affairs of the College until 1960. My first participation in a program was in a symposium held in Cleveland which focused on cancer of the stomach; the program was headed by Owen Wangensteen, a future president of the ACS. William Long-mire was championing total gastrectomy as the treatment of choice, while I defended subtotal resections, provided an adequate proximal margin could be obtained with this more limited operation. (I think the audience favored the Longmire approach, though subtotal gas-trectomy is preferred today.)

Speaking of Owen Wangensteen, another of my idols, I am re-minded of a story. One year, not long after World War II, the Surgeons' Travel Club, of which I was a member, met in Minneapolis. We hosted a small dinner for the local surgeons who presented papers. After the dinner, Phyllis (who as a student nurse knew all about the Wangensteen suction) asked me who the delightful man was who sat next to her and entertained her with such amusing anecdotes through-out the evening. I murmured, in awe, "Dr. Wangensteen." She nearly collapsed.

About four years later, when I thought he surely would recognize me, because of our various contacts, Phyllis and I were walking down a street in Los Angeles. A man suddenly appeared about two blocks away and began to wave his arms in greeting. I immediately recognized Dr. Wangensteen and felt greatly elated that he did indeed recognize me. But then came the bitter denouement as he shouted, "Hello, Mrs. Welch!" Again, for me, *sic transit gloria*.

During the seventy-five years the College has existed, there have been few organized challenges to its power. One contending group was the International College of Surgeons, which was organized as a competitor to the ACS. It did succeed in establishing a strong foreign contingent of members in the thirties, but the U.S. membership was enlarged by including members of specialties other than surgery. How-ever, the International College of Surgeons fell on hard times in the 1960s and is no longer a threat.

A second challenge to the power of the College never fully mater-ialized. The threat came from the Society of Abdominal Surgeons. This society, organized chiefly by Dr. Blaise Alfano of Medford, Mas-sachusetts, attracted a large number of members who were interested in abdominal surgery. Qualifications for membership were minimal, and the organizers attempted to promote a Board of Abdominal Sur-gery.

Meanwhile, the AMA Section on General Surgery met once a year to elect officers, who then could appoint members to the Surgical Residency Review Committee and assume other important positions.

The usual attendees at the annual AMA meeting were also members of the American College of Surgeons, but at one annual AMA meeting they found the room so packed they could not enter. It had been filled by other AMA members who also had joined the Society of Abdominal Surgeons: they proceeded to elect officers from their group and later founded a so-called Board of Abdominal Surgery. This board, however, was recognized neither by the ACS nor by the AMA.

The ACS, under the direction of the Chairman of the Board of Regents, I. S. Ravdin, reacted immediately. Fearing that the same tactics could be used by the Abdominal Surgeons at the time of the annual meeting of the ACS, the regents passed an emergency rule stating that any nominations for elective positions in the ACS would have to be made a minimum of forty-eight hours prior to elections. The threat that the Abdominal Surgeons could elect officers of the ACS evaporated at once.

When the House of Delegates of the AMA was reorganized, however, the Society of Abdominal Surgeons did obtain a seat, thereby increasing tensions between the ACS and the AMA. The ACS criticized the AMA for its failure to take strong action against this group, particularly because the Abdominal Surgeons had attempted to set up a spurious Board.

The ACS has developed very amicable relations with many other surgical societies. One of the most important is the International Society of Surgery, known also as the Société Internationale de Chirugie, or SIC. The ACS and the SIC cooperate closely and membership in the American chapter of the SIC requires membership in the ACS. The International Federation of Surgical Colleges, of which the ACS is a member, meets with the SIC.

The close relationships between many foreign colleges and the ACS have led to numerous sessions in areas such as England, Ireland, Scotland, Sweden, West Germany, Mexico, Panama, Argentina, and Australia. Biennial meetings of the SIC and frequent meetings by the ACS in foreign countries cement very important international relationships. The ACS also is increasing the number of scholarships given to surgeons from foreign countries.[2]

After three years as a governor I was elected to be a regent, and continued in that post for the maximum period—three, three-year terms. The last of these terms extended into the Hanlon era, a period in which our director maintained a very firm hand on the wheel and inaugurated many new projects. Dr. Hanlon is a man of strong character, with an ability to distinguish right from wrong as well as to phrase his decisions in words that although they may seem arcane, are chosen with superb precision.[3]

For four of these nine years as a regent I was chairman of the Program Committee. This duty involved planning and overseeing programs both in the fall and in the spring from 1968 through 1972. The annual meeting, held in the fall, at that time was attracting up to 15,000 participants. The spring meeting was considerably smaller and stressed postgraduate courses. These courses became so popular, and the number of participants in the fall meeting became so numerous that the postgraduate courses were expanded greatly in number both in the spring and fall. Preparation of the program was a delightful task that was made easy by the work of Edwin Gerrish, an assistant director of the College.

One of the problems in preparing the program was turf warfare between specialties. For example, three specialties each considered that they "owned" surgical thyroid disease (general surgeons, endocrine surgeons, and head and neck surgeons). The program committee decided that whenever a turf problem occurred, members of each involved group should be on the panel or symposium.

One of the most important parts of the program is the Forum on Fundamental Surgical Problems. Many papers are given during this session, all concerned with surgical research. This forum, first held in Boston, was inaugurated by Owen Wangensteen and has proved to be a very important vehicle for combining academic with clinical surgery and for acquainting young surgeons with the College.

During my long association with the College, the annual programs have changed greatly. In my earlier years clinical surgery held center stage; either lectures or panels presented the latest information. Then television became very popular. Dr. Ravdin was the surgeon in the first program presented in color; he made a great show out of the excision of a wen. Eventually the audience tired of television, because many operations moved too slowly. Consequently, previously prepared movies or Cine Clinics became more popular. In recent years the number of presentations on socioeconomic topics, particularly on professional liability, has increased.

Named memorial lectures (Martin, Ravdin, Churchill, Hanlon) also have increased in number. Postgraduate courses, in which special clinical problems are considered in depth, now attract large audiences. And, of course, scientific and commercial exhibits are outstanding.

Without question, the annual meeting is the greatest surgical show on earth.

Periodically, the officers of the ACS hold a retreat in which all programs of the College are reviewed. At one such event, held in Oak Brook in 1965 when Preston Wade was chairman of the board of regents, I was appointed as chairman of a new committee—Surgical Education in Medical Schools. The Regents felt strongly that surgery was being neglected at an important point in surgical education. Our yearly programs included items such as new methods of education and we particularly stressed issues such as malpractice and ethics. In succeeding years chapters were urged to send medical students to annual meetings of the ACS. These students were given financial support, and a special daily session brought them together for an exchange of views. These appointments have proved to be very popular. Scholarships have become more numerous and more generous, and several international scholars have their way paid to the college every year.

The regents tried to arrange formalized rotations between residents in other countries such as England and Ireland with those in similar positions in the United States and Canada. Because of the complexities involved, this project never could be organized. Fortunately, however, a somewhat similar plan was a resounding success when the James IV Association of Surgeons was formed by William Hinton in New York City, Ian Aird in London, and Sir John Bruce in Edinburgh. This society, largely through the efforts of Dr. Hinton, acquired sufficient funds to support many traveling fellows, who criss-crossed the Atlantic and later the world. American surgical scholars went abroad; those from the United Kingdom came here. At a later date, other countries also became involved in the James IV Society.

At the conclusion of my third term as regent, I was elected president of the College, a post giving me two more years in the governing body. This appointment required a great deal of traveling and personal appearances, particularly at chapter meetings throughout the country.

I followed William Longmire as president of the ACS. My term of office culminated in a very posh banquet given at the time of the annual meeting in Miami. The chief guest was Harrison Schmidt of NASA (later, Senator Schmidt) who was the first scientist to walk on the moon. I had operated on him many years before.

The *Study of Surgical Services of the United States* (SOSSUS) by the ACS and the American Surgical Association was formulated in the early 1970s. This extensive study—a unique self-examination by specialty organizations—engendered a great deal of intramural argument.

However, a very creditable and almost encyclopedic study finally emerged in 1975. The most important portion was an examination of surgical manpower, both present and projected, by Francis Moore. His conclusion—that we were training too many surgeons—was amply confirmed by later events. But initially it stirred up controversy, because the final recommendations implied there had been complete agreement between the College and the American Surgical Association. In fact, they had jointly supported the investigation, but the ACS (which was enrolling nearly 1,500 new members a year) was not prepared to agree that demands for well trained surgeons would diminish in the future.[4] Because this important project originated with the American Surgical Association it will be discussed in more detail in Chapter 15.

During the period when I was regent and then president, there was a great deal of friction between the ACS and the AMA at high levels. At the same time I was deeply involved with the AMA in many projects. I felt that there was some personal animosity between certain leaders in the two groups, although Dr. Hanlon adduced other facts.[5] In addition the regents felt the AMA was supporting primary care rather than recognizing the importance of medical and surgical specialties. The Council of Medical Specialty Societies was formed in 1965 to counteract this trend, with the ACS as one of the founding bodies.[6]

In the 1970s the ACS also began its long fight against itinerant surgery, a practice that left potentially unqualified persons in charge of postoperative patients as the responsible surgeon flitted from one locality to another, performing only the technical procedures of operations, but neglecting preoperative evaluation and postoperative care.

One of the main functions of the ACS is to promote education. My Presidential address dealt with the matter of lifetime education for surgeons and the relationship of the ACS to specialty boards.[7] The College is a strong supporter of the Boards; certification by one of them is necessary for membership in the College. The ACS also supports the American Board of Medical Specialties, which was formed in 1970 by an association of all existing Boards.[8] Many of the Residency Review Committees in surgical specialties have members nominated by the ACS. The ACS also in 1971 initiated the self assessment examinations known as Surgical Education and Self-Assessment Program (SESAP); six editions of the examinations had been published by 1990.

Other issues also surfaced during my term of office. The ACS

Commission on Trauma has had an enormous influence on the development of adequate patient care and the founding of Trauma Centers. Cancer clinics continue to be accredited by the ACS. The ACS strongly supports the Joint Commission on Accreditation of Health Care Organizations (JCAHO)—the successor of the Joint Commission on Accreditation of Hospitals (JCAH). In other words, the College has striven to support the care of the patient and to evidence its desire to promote the practice of surgery by highly qualified individuals.[9]

Whether or not the ACS should have an office in Washington was the subject of discussion for many years. After it became obvious that the increasing involvement of government in medical care would make this project indispensable, the office was established in 1979. Since then, presentations by members of the College have been made with increasing frequency to congressional committees.

Socio-economic Fact Books for Surgery were initiated in 1977 and have appeared yearly since that time; they are distributed to all fellows. They furnish a major source of information for all persons interested in the relationship of the ACS to other medical organizations and the national socioeconomic scene.

Another major activity of the College has been to discipline fellows for matters such as poor surgical care, breaches of ethical standards, or itinerant surgery. Such investigations and decisions are made with scrupulous care to protect the rights of any person involved. Some of these actions have been extremely expensive for the College. Fortunately, they have not been frequent.

Considerations of socio-economic affairs, and particularly that of professional liability have increased greatly in the annual programs. The ACS is attempting to provide or support some solution to the numerous unsolved problems that seem to proliferate every year.

This brief discussion shows the magnitude of the decisions that have been faced by the officers of the ACS in past years. Within the past two decades, the actions of the governors and chapters located in the various states have contributed significantly to the final decisions of the regents. The wisdom of all of the fellows as well as the officers will be required in the coming years as the revolution in our national health care system continues.

In 1986 the Hanlon era ended as Paul Ebert, an eminent cardiac surgeon, became his successor. Dr. Ebert's years in office have been devoted chiefly to the socioeconomic problems that are reshaping the whole practice of medicine. He and the chairman of the board of regents, W. Gerald Austen, have made many presentations before Congressional committees. The position of the ACS in 1990 on certain important issues is that universal medical insurance is necessary and certain to come, that reimbursement of physicians and surgeons must be made on different bases, and that medical liability costs must be reduced by transfer from physicians and surgeons to third-party payers or by some change in the present tort system.

During the long period I served as Governor, Regent and President, Phyllis and I made innumerable friends. Born of mutual respect, these relationships have made the duties a pleasure and have been rewarding. After all, as Charles Drake stated in his presidential address a few years ago, "this is what fellowship in the College is all about."

15

The American Surgical Associaiton

Samuel Gross, Professor of Surgery at Jefferson Medical College, founded the American Surgical Association in 1880. Mark Ravitch concluded that "the American Surgical Association by every account was the inspiration of Samuel D. Gross, unquestionably the greatest figure in American surgery at the time."[1]

Beginning humbly as an offshoot of the American Medical Association, its purpose was "to foster surgical art, science, education, and literature, to cultivate good feeling in the profession and to unite the prominent surgeons of the country in one harmonious body."[2] Starting inauspiciously, the first scientific meeting in 1881 attracted eleven of the original forty-four members, who listened to three papers. In the same year the name of the organization was changed from *American Surgical Society* to *American Surgical Association*. Boston surgeons began to join two years later. By 1885, it had become apparent that a paucity of papers did not lead to abbreviated sessions. In that year papers delivered at the scientific meeting were limited to one hour apiece. A published paper could fill over 130 pages.[3]

The Association has grown steadily in reputation and in membership since that time. It now is the most prestigious in America, and, combined with its honorary members, one of the most important in the world. The scientific sessions now usually last three days. The papers represent the cream of all recent surgical investigation from America and, often, abroad. Competition for a spot on the program is great. At present only about thirty-two papers are accepted. In sharp contrast to the early days, only ten minutes are allowed for presentation; each discussant is allotted three minutes and one slide.

Founding members in 1880 were mostly professors of surgery who had strong clinical interests. Later, at the time of the Mayos, clinics that were not linked to academic institutions developed, and the pendulum swung to include many other clinical surgeons. At present, nearly all of the 350 active members are chairmen of departments or are associated with medical school faculties. Qualifications for election include membership in the American College of Surgeons, certification by the Board of Surgery or other surgical boards, and membership in certain other organizations of which the Society of University Surgeons has become increasingly more important during the past forty years.

The presidency of the American Surgical Association is one of the greatest honors that is bestowed upon a surgeon in the United States or Canada; the list of Past Presidents and other past officers is published yearly in the *Transactions* of the Association. Boston surgeons who have held this office include David W. Cheever (1889), J. Collins Warren (1897), Maurice Howe Richardson (1903), Samuel Jason Mixter (1917), Harvey Cushing (1927), Fred B. Lund (1930), Daniel Fiske Jones (1934), David Cheever (1941), Edward Delos Churchill (1946), Elliott Carr Cutler (1947), John D. Stewart (1961), J. Engelbert Dunphy (1962), Oliver Cope (1963), Leland S. McKittrick (1966), Francis D. Moore (1972), Claude E. Welch (1977), W. Gerald Austen (1985), and John A. Mannick (1989). Nine of these men came from the MGH, namely Warren, Richardson, Mixter, Jones, Churchill, Cope, McKittrick, Welch, Austen; four had been trained or previously were on the staff of the MGH—Cutler, Stewart, Moore, Mannick; Cushing was a medical student at the MGH when he inaugurated written charts of every operation performed under anesthesia. These names furnish evidence that the Massachusetts General Hospital has contributed as much and possibly more than any other institution in the country to the ASA.

It is important to remember that some of the most famous individuals in the history of American surgery never have been presidents of this organization. William Halsted, Arthur Allen, and Frank Lahey are outstanding examples. Ravitch, in his history of the ASA, and many others have deplored this lack of recognition.[4]

Why I, who had never held an office in the ASA, should have been considered for the presidency is not entirely clear. Perhaps it was because I had contributed many papers to the programs, had been president of the American College of Surgeons and other surgical organizations, and had played an active role in teaching residents in the MGH and Harvard. Incidentally, a paper that I thought was one of my best—on intestinal obstruction in the presence of general peritonitis—was not mentioned by Ravitch in his history, probably because the *Annals of Surgery* did not include titles of published papers for several months in one yearly index.

Phyllis and I had planned to leave the New Orleans meeting of the ASA in 1976 prior to the election of officers in order to catch an early plane back to Boston. Just as we were ready to go, Francis Moore saw me and said, "You can't go!" I ran back to our room, overwhelmed, and told Phyllis what I thought would happen. And so it did. I heard the report of the nominating committee and my election as President. I was escorted down to the platform by Leo Eloesser and Marshall Bartlett. It occurred to me that I was one of the more elderly persons ever to hold the office of president and that it had taken me many years to accomplish what other persons had done in a much shorter time.

Fortunately the year in office does not entail a great number of duties. The most onerous, without any question, is the preparation of the annual address, which has to be given one year after election. Selection of a topic is not easy; appropriateness and acceptability are necessary qualities. In this field that had been well plowed by previous incumbents, I finally decided to speak on the future partnership of medicine and government that would soon be needed to maintain competence in the surgical profession. In view of the developments in the following years, this was a reasonable, although unpopular, objective. I illustrated the presentation with some events that had occurred in the Board of Registration and Discipline in Medicine of Massachusetts, of which I, at that time, was chairman. I am not certain that the point of the dissertation was as clear as it is today—that medicine, the public, and the government would become increasingly entangled—nor was the message particularly savory even to the writer.[5]

There were no spectacular events during my presidential year comparable to the heady days in which Edward Archibald and Evarts Graham established the American Board of Surgery or Owen Wangensteen fostered the Committee on Issues that later spawned the Study of Surgical Services of the United States. However, there were three important issues that required considerable attention.

The first problem was concerned with the Federal Trade Commission. At this time, the Federal Trade Commission was deeply involved with all professional activities that smacked of restraint of trade. As mentioned in a previous chapter, the same problem had led to changes in the Massachusetts Medical Society. Several national organizations had published suggested charges for procedures carried out by their members. This process was considered restraint of trade. Relative value studies, as developed by the California State Medical Society and adopted by many states, were considered illegal. An association of anesthesiologists had been taken to court and had to pay a large fine for similar actions. The American Surgical Association also received notice that it had to forward a large amount of material to the Federal Trade Commission so that it could determine whether we were guilty of any such errors. Fortunately, nothing of an incriminating nature was found and we did not have to face a protracted legal challenge.

The second problem was concerned with malpractice. Francis Moore, then chairman of the Committee on Issues, established a helpful relationship with Attorney Laurence R. Tancredi of New York City. Tancredi was a member of a special committee of the American Bar Association that was investigating the same problem.

One of the methods being explored by Attorney Tancredi was that of *designated compensable events*. Prior to an operation, a patient would sign an agreement that he would accept a given compensation for a certain surgical error, should it occur; in return there would be no compensation for pain or suffering and no further legal procedure for recovery of more than the specified amount.

I was asked to be chairman of a subcommittee that would produce such a list of compensable events for general surgery. I asked John Madden, a New York City surgeon, and Robert Coffey, Professor of Surgery at Georgetown University, to help. Our list of twenty-five errors included items such as unintentional retention of a foreign body in the abdomen, wound dehiscence, and postoperative hernia. We were confident that this method would reduce the burden on the courts by withdrawing a large number of cases that now must be processed through the tort system.

Unfortunately, when the procedure and list were presented to the American Bar Association, they refused to endorse it. We were not surprised, even though we felt that we had established one method that had promise as a variant of no-fault insurance.[6]

The Study on Surgical Services for the United States (SOSSUS) had been completed by the time I became president of the ASA. The summary report was published in 1975 and the entire report of 2,782 pages came out in 1976.[7] By that time a certain amount of acrimony had developed between the two sponsoring organizations and the editors of SOSSUS. The main issue appeared to be simple. The position of the American College of Surgeons was that the SOSSUS committees were empowered only to gather data and that the interpretation of the data was the duty of the ACS and the ASA. However, it proved to be almost impossible as well as undesirable for investigators to collect data and not draw some conclusions from them.

The major conclusion in the report that led to controversy was this:

> There will be a continuing need for an adequate cohort of highly qualified, highly trained and well-motivated young men and women entering the practice of surgery each year. Our current estimates suggest that this number should be in the neighborhood of 1600 to 2000 persons per year between 1976 and 2012. The number of surgical residency positions offered in this country, approximately 16,000, is excessive by any standard. The number of persons now entering and completing surgical residency each year (2500 to 3000) is larger than that required by population needs. A conservative manpower goal involves the reduction of residency output and board certification rates to 1600 to 2000 persons per year in the next decade.[8]

For my own benefit, I wrote a personal analysis of the original report. Mark Ravitch, while writing the history of the ASA, read this statement and wanted to publish it. It was his opinion that the arguments concerning the report had lost their acerbity and that my analysis should be printed; he felt that it would not stir up previous controversy. On that basis, I consented to have it published in his history. A portion of this analysis, written in 1978, is reprinted in the Notes.[9]

The effects of SOSSUS have been enormous. Unfortunately there may be a tendency to judge the success or failure of the entire study by a single criterion, namely, whether or not the total number of board-certified surgeons can be reduced to the figures suggested in the study. Another important recommendation, on the contrary, has been to continue the manpower studies and projections that need to be kept current at least for the next decade.

Since 1976 many other studies and prognoses of physician and surgical manpower have been made. Government-funded groups such as the Graduate Medical Education National Advisory Committee (GMENAC) have made reports.[10] As a result of these opinions, entry of foreign medical school graduates into the U. S. system has been severely curtailed, and the Residency Review Committee for Surgery has made sharp reductions in the number of surgical residents and many programs in community hospitals affiliated with medical schools have been reduced or eliminated.

No consensus has been reached concerning the appropriate surgical manpower needs for the future, perhaps because other important factors have entered into the equation. High malpractice premiums for surgeons have eliminated many general practitioners from the field. The impact of women in surgery has not yet been appraised; more women than men may turn out to be necessary to perform the same duties. The aging population has increased the demand for many types of surgery such as lens implants for cataracts, vascular lesions, and joint replacements. Any type of surgery is more apt to lead to complications in the aged than in the young and require more surgical care.

One of the most interesting recent comments has come from Francis Moore and Cedric Priebe. The massive data they have collected has led to conclusions different from those voiced earlier in SOSSUS by Dr. Moore. They have concluded that "the work force of physicians did not grow as rapidly in the 1980s as in the 1970s. This nonlinearity of growth and massive changes in the epidemiology and treatment of disease render predictions about the need for or the numbers of physicians a decade hence unreliable."[11]

I agree that conditions are so different in 1990 from what they were in 1976 that it is impossible to make any accurate forecast of medical manpower. The AIDS epidemic and the aggressive attitude of the government in controlling physicians' fees are two recent powerful forces that will tend to reduce the number of persons entering the profession.

Personal contacts made at the annual meetings are of great importance. A sumptuous banquet was inaugurated by President Gross in 1883 as a major method to promote this fellowship. For many years males gathered together and solved the problems of the world around port and cigars. Any wives who had been brave enough to accompany their husbands were left to fend for themselves. Eventually, when J. Engelbert Dunphy was president, matters came to a head. Many members thought wives should be invited to dinner and that they might even elevate the level of conversation. Other members believed, just as firmly, that dinner talk would descend from its Olympian level to chitchat.

The matter was solved rapidly. Usually dinner is followed by an address that is given by a person unknown to the audience until he is presented by the president. In 1963 the guest speaker—President Eisenhower—refused to utter a word until the wives were rounded up and brought into the banquet room. Ever since, they have been invited to dine in company with their husbands. Now there are women who are members of the ASA; their spouses also are welcome.

The meeting at which I presided in 1977 was held in the Boca Raton Hotel and Club. In this luxurious structure James Maloney (the secretary), Pat (his wife), Phyllis, and I shared an enormous suite that was more aptly fitted for the Godfather. Calvin Plimpton gave the after-dinner address. His scholarly paper drew upon the Bible, Emily Dickinson and President Kennedy for support; it later was printed privately.[12] Dr. Plimpton and I had been friends for many years; we played badminton on his farm when he was a boy. Later he became Dean of the Down State Medical Medical College of the New York State System, president of Amherst College and of the American University in Beirut. He persisted in the latter assignment until the civil war in Lebanon made it unwise for him to stay. He had tried to enlist me as professor of surgery in the American University in Beirut.

The president, after his term of office, becomes a member of the Council for the next three years. Thus he continues to have an important continuing influence on the selection of future officers as well as on policies of the organization. These policies have deviated very little from those enunciated by our first president, Samuel Gross. He wrote, in the constitution of the association that was adopted in 1882, "The objects of the Association shall be the cultivation and improvement of the art and science of surgery and the promotion of interests not only of its Fellows, but of the medical profession at large."[13] Today we must add as one of our objectives the duty of our profession to maintain the welfare of the public.

16

The Boston Surgical Society and the Bigelow Medal

The Boston Surgical Society was founded in 1911 and ever since then the society has been an important medium for disseminating knowledge among the members of the surgical fraternity of the city. When I was elected to membership in 1940, the very small elite group contained all the older MGH surgeons. We met several times a year in a small room in the Academy of Arts and Sciences. My first presentation to the society was a short paper extolling the virtues of a certain type of gastric resection for very difficult duodenal ulcers; Dr. Allen had done many of them and I had done a few, and all had proceeded smoothly. The method involved removal of the antral mucosa, retention of the antral muscle, and resection of the midportion of the stomach. (This operation was named for a New York surgeon, Dr. Frederic Bancroft). Frank Lahey, head of the Lahey Clinic, discussed the paper briefly; he said I would regret my statements. This opinion was quite a blow to a neophyte, especially because it was given by such a famous surgeon. Two years later, however, we had two successive patients who developed tiny leaks from the antrum and died of peritonitis. Then I recalled Dr. Lahey's wise advice and never used the procedure again. Instead I developed catheter duodenostomy which proved to be a safe alternative.

In 1949 I became secretary-treasurer of the Boston Surgical Society. During my term (1949 to 1953) the membership list expanded significantly and the usual meeting format changed to a dinner in the Harvard Club followed by the scientific program. Presidents of the society during my term of office included Reginald Smithwick and Richard Cattell—two of the most brilliant surgeons and fine gentlemen who ever graced the surgical profession. Dr. Smithwick already was famous for his operations of sympathectomy for hypertension, and later he introduced vagotomy and hemigastrectomy for the treatment of duodenal ulcer. Dr. Cattell was a marvelous technician, who was known internationally for surgery of the biliary tract. With Dr. Lahey, he spread the fame of the Lahey Clinic throughout the world.

The recipient of the Bigelow Medal in 1951 was Dr. Evarts Graham of St. Louis, one of the most important surgeons of the century. I remember that occasion with horror. Six years before, the medal had been given to Dr. Lahey. That ceremony had been held in a huge auditorium in the downtown building of a large insurance company and the room had been packed with friends and admirers of Dr. Lahey.

When Dr. Graham's turn came, however, we officers made a terrible mistake. We held the preceding dinner in the Harvard Club and then adjourned to the other building two blocks away for the ceremony. Sadly, the great bulk of the dinner audience went directly home. So Dr. Graham spoke to a sparse group of sleepy souls, who numbered no more than the potted palms on the stage. His topic had to do with the evils of smoking. But his message must have fallen on deaf ears, for, at the end of the lecture, many members of that tiny audience eagerly rushed outside for a cigarette. This fiasco was further compounded by the fact that my secretary failed to send him the expected travel expenses. I have never forgotten the lessons I learned that night: food for the stomach is more attractive than food for the mind.

It became my turn to be president of the society in 1966. While I was secretary, I had started the tradition that one of the meetings should be addressed by the president on a matter of his choice. So for my topic, I chose to discuss the surgical treatment of peptic ulcer disease. The speech never was published: it was devoted chiefly to technique and the state of the art. Since cimetidine had not yet been invented, I am sure the subject was of interest to the audience. Today, however, it makes rather dull reading.

The greatest honor awarded by the Society is the Bigelow Medal. It is given approximately once every three years to a distinguished surgeon. The Bigelow Medal award originated in the early days of the Boston Surgical Society. It memorialized Dr. Henry Jacob Bigelow, Professor of Surgery at Harvard and Surgeon at the Massachusetts General Hospital for many years, and one of the greatest surgeons of the nineteenth century. Funds for the award were furnished by the nephew of Dr. Bigelow. The award, a gold medal, was to be given to

persons who had contributed to the art and science of surgery. The
history of the medal has been recounted by Dr. Bradford Cannon in
his history of the Society.[1] The first medal was given to William J.
Mayo in 1921; by 1991, twenty-five persons had received it. During
this period it has become one of the most prestigious awards in American surgery.[2]

My mentors, Drs. Allen and Churchill, had been medalists and I
had always hoped that some day I might earn that honor. Imagine
then, my joy in July 1985 when the word came from the secretary, Dr
Leslie Ottinger, that I was to receive it in 1986.

Like all speakers in search of a topic, I scanned the previous addresses. I found that no recipient had considered the history of the
medalists and their influence on the course of surgery. So I chose that
topic and delivered the lecture in January 1986 in the Harvard Club.
Because many of the spouses who were present were not entirely
familiar with surgical history, I enlivened the text with numerous
slides.

A subsequent recipient of the medal was Dr. Thomas Starzl, the
famous transplant surgeon now in Pittsburgh. In 1990, when Dr.
Joseph Murray received the Nobel prize for the first renal transplant
and for the development of immunotherapy, he became a certain
prospect for the medal, which he received in January, 1992.

The medal itself is gold, large and heavy. It is too valuable to be
worn at any time, although I long to attend some formal function when
decorations are supposed to be pinned upon the breast. Then it will
occupy a central position, for there is no award that I treasure more
than this one. Meanwhile, the medal resides quietly in a safe deposit
box, awaiting an unknown destiny. My address follows.[3]

From Mayo to Kirklin: Riding on Bigelow's Coattails

At the outset I wish to thank the Society deeply for the signal honor
you have accorded me by the presentation of this medal. It is without
doubt one of the most important awards in the domain of surgery.
Conceived with a noble purpose and illumined thereafter by legendary
recipients, it is destined to have a continuing influence in the years
to come.

A sense of history and, as time passes, of tradition pervade the
entire ceremony. They combine to form one of the hallmarks of a
profession which has a long and honorable past. This respect for

historical details is neglected in the hectic days of the present, when computer searches of the literature rarely encompass more than ten years. Youth often does not appreciate the lessons history teaches until maturity supervenes and the individual himself merges imperceptibly into the past.

The theme that I will dwell on in this discussion is to reacquaint you with the previous recipients of the medal, some of whom you barely may recognize, and to assess their influence on the onward course of surgery. It is important to consider whether or not the Society has chosen wisely in accord with the direction in which surgery has progressed from the time of the first award in 1921. This assignment is a pleasant one, for I have had some personal contact with nearly two thirds of the recipients, and owe a tremendous amount to two of them, Drs. Allen and Churchill, for their influence on my career. I also am indebted to Bradford Cannon for his history of the Boston Surgical Society and Mark Ravitch for his *A Century of Surgery*, as well as to other friends.

The Boston Surgical Society had its origin in 1911, at nearly the same time as the New England Surgical Society and the American College of Surgeons. Just as today, it was a period of great ferment. The Flexner report was in preparation. Surgeons were disassociating themselves from general practitioners. The relatively few giants of the past were being jostled by a new army of recruits who threatened to undermine established priorities. Indeed, for many years it had been possible for one person to dominate the entire field of surgery in each country. Thus, in France, where many Boston physicians studied in the early days of the last century, the Baron Dupuytren turned the Hôpital de Dieu from a charnel house into the prototype of a modern hospital. His ability and power were so great that his era became known as the age of Dupuytren. Lister had proposed his theory of antisepsis but the importance of his method was not appreciated in Boston until long after its introduction in 1865.

Henry Jacob Bigelow cast just as important an influence over Boston surgery for many years as Dupuytren had done previously. Bigelow's bust still has a commanding place in the surgical amphitheater of the Massachusetts General Hospital where he glares down on fledgling surgeons, and where Churchill regards him with an admiring but critical air. Who could not be envious of a professor of surgery who had the time, ability and temerity to argue publicly with the president of Harvard?

When the Bigelow medal was first struck in 1921, it must have been the hope of the Society that it could pick candidates who would be worthy of the mantles of their great predecessors. Little could they realize that the field soon would expand so enormously that it would be impossible to find such paragons who would be able to exert so much power either here or abroad. But the Society's selections have signaled the paths by which surgery was destined to progress for the past 65 years.

Now is the time to introduce you briefly to the previous 22 recipients of the medal, together with their contributions that are most likely to be recognized by today's surgeons. Any attempt to analyze each of these great men in a few pages or to compare them rigorously would do to them great injustice. They have been complex characters, extraordinarily individualistic, all giants of their times. If one is chosen as an example in the following pages to the exclusion of others, it is only because of lack of space to record all of their achievements.

The medal has been given in nearly all cases because of established reputations, quite in contrast to the usual method of selection of chiefs of departments for whom youth and promise are prime recommendations. A few, such as Matas and Moore, professors and departmental chiefs at age 35, were destined for success in the days of their youth; most of them, however, were latecomers. The majority received the award in their 60s; only Cutler at 59 was younger, and four were over 70 years of age. Keen, a great Philadelphia surgeon, was honored at age 85 and lived to the age of 96, when his textbook of surgery was still in press.

All of them had received numerous honors previously, both in this country and abroad. Huggins is one of the two American surgeons who have earned a Nobel prize in medicine. Thirteen had been presidents of the American Surgical Association, 9 of the American College of Surgeons, and 7 of both organizations. Three had been presidents of the American Medical Association. The American Surgical Association award for scientific achievement was established 15 years ago; it has been given to ten persons, four of whom (Dragstedt, Gross, Moore, and Murray) have been Bigelow medalists.

To some observers it may appear that there has been an almost incestuous relationship between the medalists and Boston (seven recipients), Harvard Medical School (nine), the Brigham (three), and the Massachusetts General Hospital (two), whereas one recipient came from Canada (Archibald), one from Great Britain (Turner), and one from Sweden (Crafoord). Perhaps this emphasis on Boston should not be considered as evidence of myopia, but viewed in the much more kindly light of the Biblical observation that a prophet is not without honor save in his own country.

The enormous changes in surgery that have occurred in these 65 years can be sketched only briefly. Some of them were documented in the individual Bigelow lectures, because in the majority of their presentations, the recipients elaborated on their special interest. However, a short glance at the surgical scene in 1921 will make many of these changes apparent.

At that time, operations were performed widely by general practitioners. Fee splitting was rife. Itinerant surgery not only was common but necessary. Many patients still were operated on in their homes. Sophisticated diagnostic equipment was unknown; surgeons depended on histories, careful physical examinations, and frequent exploratory laparotomies. The resident system had not developed. The Board of Surgery was not established until 1937. Anesthesia had not essentially progressed from the days of 1846; etherizers used cones or masks to provide a mixture of ether and room air. Malpractice suits were infrequent.

Although Johns Hopkins had shown the way, academic practice and full-time staffs were rare. Surgical research had remained in its infancy since the days of John Hunter. Subspecialties had not declared their virtual independence from general surgery. Transfusions were rare, dangerous and difficult. Antibiotics had not been discovered. The value and significance of electrolytes and body fluids were unknown. As a result, postoperative complications were very common, and deaths from surgical diseases unbelievably frequent when judged by today's standards.

Graduate medical education and continuing medical education were unrecognized. In addition, women were not welcome in the Harvard Club as late as 1951, when Graham gave his lecture in the auditorium of the New England Life Insurance Company. Many other details could be added easily to this list. However it is important to dwell on the Bigelow medalists. For it is on the deeds of individuals that history is written, and it was these men, preeminent among many others, who recognized and corrected the deficiencies just mentioned. What were the characteristics of these physicians who thereby captured some claim to immortality in the history of surgery?

First, above all, these men were surgical pioneers. All of the medalists had a broad training in general surgery. Many of them were honored because they identified new fields of interest that later developed into important subspecialties. Matas, for example, was not only a pioneer in vascular surgery who had extraordinary success with the treatment of aneurysms; in addition, as early as 1899, he had experimented with intratracheal tubes for anesthesia that were not adopted widely by anesthetists for 40 years. Bronchoscopy and esophagoscopy, forerunners of today's endoscopy, were the forte of Chevalier Jackson by 1915, but it was not until about 20 years later that the first endoscopist was appointed at the Massachusetts General Hospital.

The heart was considered with awe for many years, since any cardiac procedures were extremely hazardous. Perhaps it was this respect that has led more cardiac surgeons to be selected as medalists than any other specialty. They include Cutler, the first American surgeon to operate on mitral stenosis; Blalock; Gross; and Kirklin. Turner was famous because of his interests in the esophagus. Other pioneers in previously undeveloped fields were Graham, Churchill, and Crafoord in thoracic surgery; Keen, who removed a meningioma in 1888, and Cushing in neurosurgery; Whipple, as a developer of surgery of the pancreas; and Huggins, primarily in urology. Thus, nearly all of the major subspecialties have been represented by recipients, orthopedics, gynecology, plastic surgery, and transplantation surgery being exceptions.

Nearly half the medalists began their professional careers and remained as general surgeons with interests in all parts of the body; they include Mayo, Finney, Cutler, Allen, Lahey, Dragstedt, Moore, and Dunphy. The most outstanding example of a general surgeon in recent times is Gross; not only did he have a thorough knowledge of the underlying principles of surgery (which is the definition of a true general surgeon, according to Churchill) but he was at home in operating on essentially every child's extremities, cavities, or viscera.

Despite their technical interests, it should not be inferred that all of these surgeons were technical virtuosos. In fact, only a few could qualify for that honor. Cushing and Allen were extremely meticulous and dextrous. Lahey spent many years practicing and teaching safe and effective methods of thyroidectomy. Kirklin has produced results unequaled by other surgeons in specific fields of cardiac surgery; he has used the computer to identify optimal methods of therapy in the operating and recovery rooms. Gross was as fastidious in the operating theater as he was in his personal attire.

Second, many identified problems peculiar to surgery and solved them. New concepts often influence surgery more than new techniques. Moore's studies on metabolic changes in surgical patients opened entirely new vistas of investigation and therapeusis. Huggins developed important relationships between the ductless glands and cancer of the breast and prostate. Dragstedt's impressive laboratory experiments reintroduced vagotomy as a useful adjunct in the treatment of duodenal ulcer. Archibald, one of the great Canadian surgeons, conceived the idea of the American Board of Surgery; it was Graham who immediately appreciated it and was able to push the dream to completion.

Third, all of the medalists were strong supporters of patient care, research, and education, the tripod on which medicine is based. Patient care has the most ancient roots, and it was in this respect that the early medalists excelled. Matas' infectious enthusiasm and love of people, one reason for his excessively verbose presentations, have been described beautifully by Cohn and Deutsch and by Schumacker. Cushing's detailed accounts of his patients remain as models. Allen was worshipped by hundreds of patients. Fortunately, this virtue is not completely lost at present, although much of the humanness of surgeons tends to disappear as personal contacts are replaced by machines. Dunphy's sensitive essay on the care of the cancer patient provides evidence of the persistent need for care and compassion that must be attributes of the surgeon.

The education of medical students, residents, and practicing surgeons has developed into an enormous and extremely expensive project. At present, financial considerations indicate fundamental changes in the whole process and challenge the profession to maintain its present level of excellence.

Surgical research originated in the observation of patients. This method has been denigrated by many observers, since empiricism readily leads to slavish imitation of the past. Without question, clinical studies still have great importance. Despite the fact that they have been replaced to a large degree by laboratory investigations, it was not until about 1930 that the pattern was established throughout the United States.

It is apparent that support of research and education can be managed most capably and effectively by academic surgeons who are chiefs of departments. This has been reflected in the selection of medalists, particularly in recent times. The trend points very strongly in that direction for the future. It is to be hoped that the time consuming essential item of compassionate patient care will not be neglected by these leaders.

Fourth, all medalists have been scholars. To cite all of the important publications they have authored would be a difficult task; instead, I have selected five that indicate the diversity of their interests. No precedence is implied in the order in which they are listed.

First is the extremely important text, *The Surgery of Infancy and Childhood*, written originally by Ladd but expanded by Gross into a superb collection of descriptions of diseases, operative techniques, and summaries of his own experience at the Children's Hospital in Boston. His impressive results were far better than any reported previously.

The next is Cushing's *Life of Sir William Osler*, an encylopedic and reverent account of the life of one of the four major founders of the Johns Hopkins School of Medicine. This book deservedly won a Pulitzer prize, an honor achieved by no other medalist.

Next is the three volume compendium *Surgery in the United States*. This detailed medical and socioeconomic work was the product of many surgeons and committees under the direction of the American Surgical Association and the American College of Surgeons. However, the backbone of the whole study was formed by the manpower studies conducted by Francis Moore. He obtained many details concerning surgical practice in the United States and predicted an oversupply of physicians and surgeons, a point of view that was hotly contested when it was first proposed but is now accepted as fact.

Fourth is Churchill's *To Work in the Vineyard of Surgery*, a masterful combination of history and philosophy. The text is ostensibly a biography of J. Collins Warren, an illustrious Boston surgeon of the last century; however, the footnotes are pure Churchill, with his searching comments on all aspects of surgery.

Finally, there is the smallest contribution of all, but for clinical surgeons of the past 40 years, the most important. It is Dragstedt and Owns' original two page description of two patients who had had truncal vagotomies and were followed for a minimum of 2 months. They observed that the patients' night secretion of gastric acid was decreased greatly by this procedure. From this trivial start, the whole world of ulcer surgery was changed immediately and completely. It must not be forgotten, however, that this paper had been preceded by innumerable careful experiments in the laboratory before the operation was attempted on human subjects.

Scholarly pursuits are difficult to maintain during the life of a busy surgeon. Cushing required 5 years to write his monumental work, and meanwhile carried on an extremely busy schedule. On the other hand, Churchill believed strongly in the necessity for withdrawal from mundane activities to gain inspiration or discover new challenges. He wrote,

> "Withdrawal gives opportunity for a man to develop powers within himself which otherwise may remain dormant in a life crowded with the pursuit of limited objectives. In accord with the scale of Toynbee's approach to history he chooses as examples the great mystics who on their return bend the courses of whole societies. But surely there can be echoes of this process in ordinary mortals".

Fifth, the recipients have developed relationships far beyond parochial interests. Without exception all of them received wide national and international acclaim in their particular fields. Many, such as Cushing, Finney, Archibald, Cutler, Churchill, Allen, Moore, and Dunphy, have been international statesmen. Many of them opened their laboratories to numerous foreign fellows and scholars. Whipple had a great interest in educational activities in the Middle East; for many years he was one of the guiding trustees of the American University in Beirut, and helped to establish there the most eminent medical school at that time in the entire area.

Sixth, many were founders of surgical schools. It is a fortunate person who can stimulate a body of pupils who owe their inspiration to him and follow the master's teachings but are not fettered by them. These leaders are the role models of the next generation. In this regard, a few of the medalists were outstanding. I shall return to Blalock and Churchill shortly. In addition, Cushing was the mentor of all the neurosurgeons of his era. Gross trained many of the pediatric surgical professors of his generation. Fellows from the Mayo and Lahey clinics have occupied key local positions in clinical surgery. Archibald established the Royal Victoria Hospital in Montreal as an important training center. Dragstedt's pupils carry on his teachings. Moore's fellowships have spread the fame of the Brigham across the academic world.

Seventh, let us consider the personal characteristics of the medalists. Generalizations are extremely difficult; however, a few qualities appear to be predominant. All were ambitious workaholics. Many pursued their goals despite physical adversity. For example, Cutler, dying from cancer of the prostate, received several transfusions to provide the strength to give his Bigelow lecture. Allen did much of his best work as he suffered for over 17 years with disseminated lymphoma, manifested by intermittent periods of activity and rest after radiotherapy. Dunphy's last years were active, although he was wracked by pain from prostatic cancer.

In addition to this evidence of personal bravery, a pervasive sense of loyalty to their own institutions was the rule. Thus, the last words spoken by Alfred Blalock to his dear friend David Sabiston were "There is little difference between loyalty and integrity".

One possible exception was Cushing. His medical roots included the Massachusetts General Hospital and Johns Hopkins, but his career flowered at the Brigham and Harvard. Just after retirement from the Brigham and a trip to Europe, he found his books and belongings stacked in a corridor and his successor in his former rooms. He took umbrage and immediately removed his office and library to New Haven. In defense of his action, it should be noted that Cushing, as an undergraduate, was a true Eli and a fine athlete. Nonetheless, never since the days of Bigelow had a professor of surgery dealt so unceremoniously with Harvard.

When the United States became involved in conflicts, a number of the medalists were prompt to answer the call of duty. Brigadier generals Mayo, Finney, and Cutler, Colonels Cushing and Churchill, and Major Graham were outstanding examples. Beside the routine duties incumbent on them, several made important discoveries. Graham proved that empyema often should be treated by closed rather than open drainage. Churchill demonstrated the advantage of whole blood transfusions rather than plasma for the care of the wounded. He promoted the concept of delayed primary closure of wounds, a method that essentially eliminated the problems of infection. He also found that pulmonary decortication was of great value in many soldiers with chest wounds.

Both Cushing and Churchill left memoirs concerning their army activities. *From A Soldier's Journal 1915–1918* by Cushing provided a relatively complete description of tactical as well as the medical problems in France in World War I. Churchill's *Surgeon to Soldiers* is essentially a diary of his happy productive days in the army when he served as surgical consultant in the Mediterranean theater in World War II.

Most of the medalists were forceful, articulate, and eager to express their opinions. Aesculapian authority, equated with dogmatism and the captain of the ship theory, was strong in early years but has waned in the recent past. There was a time when every subaltern in the operating room would quail as the chief marched in. Modesty was unknown to many of them. We still regard such prima donnas with some measure of admiration and envy. Fortunately, evidence of this trait is still exhibited. Thus, Gross often peremptorily cleared his operating room of spectators. In the early days of cardiac surgery, Kirklin had as many as 17 assistants and technicians in the operating room; he clearly remained completely in command as he barked orders to his army of helpers.

The great majority of medalists also were extroverts, reveling in the adulation of their pupils, and enjoying the companionship of their peers. On the other hand, a few have been loners. Some were true medical statesmen; they assessed the problems not only of the present but of the future and developed plans to cope with them. Archibald and Graham saw the need to elevate surgical standards and spawned the American Board of Surgery. Moore's investigations have prompted complete reevaluations of surgical manpower.

Finally, our medalists were men of strong principles. Such idealism often begets intolerance and vindictiveness. Hence, lest this discussion be considered to be unadulterated praise, let me add that many of these men were not immune to some of the meaner vices, such as jealousy of colleagues or connivance in academic appointments. Some of these disputes progressed to public vituperation, but fortunately, most were kept from public notice and usually were apparent only to close friends or colleagues.

The reputation of many will grow as time passes. Of the groups, history probably will deal most kindly with Cushing. He was a master technician, a scholar, a source of at least two eponyms (Cushing's disease and ulcer), a bibliophile, precise, dynamic, and egocentric. He could be overbearing and rude to his assistants. He barely avoided a court-marshal in World War I. His surgical treatises on diseases of the hypophysis and the superb biography of Osler established his reputation in both medical and literary circles. His greatest monument is the library in the Yale School of Medicine.

It also is tempting to consider the 18 deceased Bigelow medalists to decide who made the greatest imprints on American surgery, and to list the characteristics that led to their preeminence. Although a contemporary observer always is swayed by personal bias and cannot anticipate ultimate historic judgments, I would like to proffer a few names for consideration.

The first is that of William J. Mayo. Soon after they joined their father late in the last century, William J. and Charles Mayo were foremost in the history of American surgery for at least 30 years. Charles was a skillful surgeon who concentrated on the thyroid gland, whereas William J. preferred abdominal surgery. They were great travelers, gleaning knowledge here and abroad. They brought information back to Rochester, Minnesota, which soon became one of the temples of American medicine. Mayo-trained fellows thereafter practiced throughout the continent. The clinic, always open and exceedingly hospitable to visitors, served as a postgraduate institute for hundreds of other physicians and surgeons.

William J. epitomized one of the few builders in the terms of brick and mortar among the medalists, even though many others observed spectacular growth in their institutions during their lifetimes. Cushing provided the nucleus for the collection in the Historical Library of the Yale University School of Medicine. He intended it to hold 200,000 volumes; it soon doubled in size. Allen and Lahey devoted Herculean efforts to their support of the Boston Medical Library, which merged with the Countway Library at Harvard. On the other hand, Lahey, who perhaps intuitively foresaw some of the difficulties of modern hospitals, was never convinced that his clinic should own a hospital; the present ultramodern institution was built after his death. Hence, the name of William J. Mayo remains preeminent as the the builder of a great institution.

The second person is Evarts Graham. Ravitch has noted that he dominated American surgery for two decades. When he arrived in St. Louis as the new professor, there were only 97 patients (including 10 newborns) in the Barnes Hospital, and only 40 of them were surgical cases. During his tenure, he saw the evolution of the great modern hospital that exists today. Based broadly in clinical surgery and in the laboratory, he trained numerous men who soon occupied important professorships or other posts throughout the world. Graham himself was no shrinking violet. He gained positions of power in the American College of Surgeons and the American Surgical Association and used them wisely, as, for example, to father the American Board of Surgery. A reformed smoker, his tirades against cigarettes have finally borne fruit. Meanwhile, he became a martyr to a cause that he had espoused too late, for he died from lung cancer. Blunt, uncompromising, and authoritative, he was a true giant in American surgery.

The third medalist is less easy to single out. However, my vote is in favor of Alfred Blalock. He had a productive laboratory when he investigated shock at Vanderbilt. His later stunning success with the Blalock shunt gave an enormous impetus to cardiac surgery, which then was in its infancy. However, in my opinion, his greatest contribution rested in the progeny of residents that he trained. Just as Halsted had done before him, he scattered them to important posts throughout the country, and they in turn became teachers and leaders of the next generation. They were schooled by Blalock in his modest way that invited thoughtful application but, above all, cooperation. David Sabiston recalls that Blalock could never speak ill of any one. The harshest criticism Sabiston ever heard Blalock make about a person was "that fellow is not exactly one of my favorites". Thus, in contrast to some other training programs in which cutthroat competition is fostered, the graduates of his program became a cohesive whole. They became, in today's vernacular, the movers and shakers of American surgery from the time of his death until the present. It is well for us in these days when competition is stressed as an economic virtue to look carefully at this example of the fruits of cooperation and to study Sabiston's thoughtful analysis of this great man.

A close runner-up in this competition is Edward Churchill. His early years were distinguished by pioneer surgery of the pericardium, the lung, and the parathyroid glands. His investigative laboratory later included John Gibbon who, with his wife, developed the first heart-lung machine in the world. Churchill strongly supported his residents, preferring to leave them alone in the operating rooms to develop their own independence. His residency program became, in the opinion of many observers, the best in America. He also had an extraordinary opportunity to influence the lives of many surgeons when he became Surgical Consultant to the Fifth Army in the Mediterranean Theater in World War II. There he moved the principles of academia onto the battlefield. Aided by a galaxy of stars that included Beecher, Simeone, Lyons, and DeBakey, he developed the same spirit of trust and co-operation with surgeons and anesthesiologists as that which had been obtained both by him and by Blalock with their residents in civilian life.

These brief remarks, distilled from many sources, affirm that the Bigelow medalists have exemplified the onward march of surgery throughout the last 65 years. The recipients were men of genius even though they had weaknesses common to all persons. They combined originality with respect for their illustrious predecessors, and were buoyed by a sense of optimism, good cheer, and camaraderie. They

Past presidents of the American College of Surgeons, 1975 (above) and 1986 (below). Above: (Seated, left to right) Robert M. Zollinger, Frank Glenn, Warren H. Cole, Alton Ochsner, Owen H. Wangensteen, Loyal Davis; (standing) Charles W. McLaughlin, Jr., Jonathan E. Rhoads, Joel W. Baker, Walter C. MacKenzie, Claude E. Welch, William P. Longmire, Jr. Below: Past presidents, 1986. (Seated, left to right) Jonathan E. Rhoads, Charles W. McLaughlin, Jr., Robert M. Zollinger, Claude E. Welch; (standing) Henry T. Bahnson, H. William Scott, Jr., Charles G. Drake, George R. Dunlop, Paul A. Ebert (director), William H. Muller, Jr., James D. Hardy, David C. Sabiston, Jr., G. Thomas Shires.

Two key figures in the American College of Surgeons: C. Rollins Hanlon, Director, 1969–1986, President 1987–1988, (left); George Stephenson, alter ego to the Director, Historian of the College, recipient of the College's Distinguished Service Award, 1973 (right).

Important presidents of the American College of Surgeons: Above: Alton Ochsner, anti-smoking warrior, founder of the Ochsner Clinic, famed teacher who ran "The Bullpen" (left); Owen Wangensteen, founder of the Forum in annual meetings of the College (left) with William Longmire, Jr., one of the founders of the UCLA Medical Center (right). Below: J. Engelbert Dunphy, international teacher and diplomat, with his wife Nancy, (left); David Sabiston, who made Duke the Johns Hopkins of the South and wrote popular encyclopedic textbooks of surgery (right).

Patty and Jerry Austen in 1991 at the time of his induction as President of
the American College of Surgeons.

CEW in the Presidential robe of the College.

Four of the present ten recipients of the American Surgical Medallion for Scientific Achievement, the highest award of the American Surgical Association: Above: Robert E. Gross, pediatric surgeon, Harvard, who first ligated a ductus arteriosus (left); Francis D. Moore, Harvard and the Peter Bent Brigham Hospital, who brought the metabolic changes of surgery to the bedside, and supervised a laboratory where basic research on surgical metabolism and organ transplantation was carried out (right). Below: Richard L. Varco, a pioneer cardiac surgeon in the University of Minnesota Medical School enjoys a visit with Sir Andrew Kay in Glasgow in 1978 (left); Jonathan E. Rhoads, Professor of Surgery in the University of Pennsylvania, who proved with Stanley Dudrick, that puppies would grow normally when sustained only by intravenous alimentation (right).

Some recipients of the Bigelow Medal (center) of the Boston Surgical Society: Above: Evarts A. Graham (left); Allen O. Whipple, on the campus of the American University in Beirut (right). Below: Harvey W. Cushing (left); Alfred Blalock (right).

Scenes of travel: Above: Phyllis with koala during trip to Australia, 1960, (left); Phyllis with Cecil Watson and guide on the bridge over the River Jordan near the Dead Sea, 1954, (right) Below: Auschwitz camp in Poland, where four million Jews were killed (left); ghats (funeral pyres) on the banks of the Ganges River, Katmandu, Nepal, 1960.

More scenes of travel: Above: Ruins of the cathedral of Saint Simeon, Kalat Semen, northern Syria (left); Amphitheater dedicated to Aesculapius, Epidaurus, Greece (right). Below: Running the white water, New River, West Virginia (left); CEW with Professor Peter Morris, Nuffield Professor of Surgery, in Oxford, England,1987 (right).

Above: Professors Sir William Illingworth (Glasgow) and Walter MacKenzie (Edmonton) before the entrance to the Royal College of Surgeons of England, 1969 (left); Lord Smith of Marlow (Rodney Smith), the first to deliver a Samuel Jason Mixter Lecture, Bretton Woods, New Hampshire, 1985 (right). Below: Grace and Philip Sandblom, Sweden (left), 1981; Jerry Urban and Martin Allgöwer, Basle, Switzerland, 1985 (right).

have not only ridden on Bigelow's coattails, they have achieved heights he never could have anticipated.

All but four of the previous medalists are no longer alive. In their honor, it is appropriate to quote a few of the lines written by George Stewart that are carved over the fireplace in the Historical Library at the Yale University School of Medicine:

> "Here, silent, speak the great of other years, the story of their steep ascent from the unknown to the known, erring perchance in their best endeavor, succeeding often, where to their fellows they seemed most likely to fail; Unshared must be their genius; it was their own; but you, be you brave and diligent, may freely take and know the companionship of others' ordered thought."

These men will serve as beacons for the coming generations, for the irrepressible dynamism of surgeons will continue; they form the activists of the profession. Churchill, paying a tribute to Graham, quoted Bigelow:

> "Most eminent men are in a large degree self-made and have pursued their subject from the attraction before them, not from a stimulus behind. You cannot create this talent. You may indeed give it opportunity but you cannot force it".

Undoubtedly, such ability will continue to reemerge and will guide us into a more ordered future in these days of turmoil.

(This paper originally was published in the *American Journal of Surgery* 1986; 152: 245–251. Permission to reprint has been granted by the publisher. References may be found in the original publication. An up-dated list of Bigelow medalists is given in Note 2).

17

Travels

In my youthful days, when travel was a luxury and more difficult than it is today, it possessed an allure that has persisted throughout the remainder of my life. Fortunately, the pleasure of visiting new or exotic areas also has often been shared by the remainder of our family, and Phyllis has been able to join me in nearly all of the major adventures. But the reader would soon tire of a recitation of all of these activities which, in certain years, required nearly a third of my time. So I shall describe only a few of the most unusual trips that were associated with visiting professorships.

Like nearly all professors, I have had many calls to occupy temporary posts. During the course of my career, I have lectured in all but four of our fifty states, and in many of the large countries in the world except those that in past years were behind the Iron Curtain. The terms of duty ranged from a single lecture to visiting professorships that lasted a month. The vicissitudes encountered by visiting professors were described in a highly original, and amusing paper written by Ben Eiseman and James Thompson.[1] But as far as I am concerned, nearly all my visits were stimulating, exciting, and informative. Indeed, several were outstanding.

Professional trips to other cities, states or countries are exceedingly valuable for surgeons. Young surgeons will find relatively small groups more intimate and valuable than large congresses. Small groups not only exchange scientific knowledge but also stress personal contacts and professional support; spouses are just as important as members in scheduled meetings.

Early in my career I joined the Surgeons Travel Club. Organized by fellows in the Mayo Clinic at the time of World War II, other young surgeons scattered about the United States and Canada later joined to form a compact group that met every year in a different city. It has continued ever since, and, by adding young members regularly, it continues to play a vital role in the life of the members.

At the present time there are many professional societies available for individuals who wish to attend educational meetings either as guests or as members. Regional surgical organizations, such as the Southern Surgical Association which was founded in 1888, or the New England Surgical Society, founded in 1917, are important examples.[2] The American College of Surgeons, the most famous of all, has been described in Chapter 13.

I joined an International Surgical Group that now includes nearly 100 members. It was formed in 1958 and is composed chiefly of academic surgeons. Sir John Bruce of Edinburgh, Erling Dahl-Iverson and Eivan Hasner of Denmark, Philip Sandblom of Sweden, and Jonathan Rhoads of Philadelphia were the organizers. New members are added regularly; the yearly programs are exceptionally good.

Another compatible group was the Excelsior Surgical Society. It contained slightly over 100 young surgeons who had served in the Mediterranean Theater during World War II. Each yearly meeting included a special lecture by a famed surgeon; it was dedicated to Colonel Edward Churchill. When the Society finally dissolved in 1988, ample funds had been given to the American College of Surgeons and to the University of the Armed Forces of the United States to fund similar lectures on an annual basis.

The International Society of Surgery is the most outstanding and largest surgical organization that is organized on an international rather than a national basis. For many years Alton Ochsner and I were the guiding members of the United States chapter, which now has nearly 1000 members. Due to the strong leadership of Martin Allgöwer, and such stalwarts as Jonathan Rhoads, James Hardy and Lloyd Nyhus there now is an International Surgical Week held every second year in selected cities throughout the world. I am one of the eight honorary members; Linder from Germany, Mallet-Guy from France, Petrovsky from Russia, Sandblom from Sweden and Switzerland, Rhoads, Hardy, and Longmire from the United States are the others.

The James IV Association was organized by William Hinton, Ian Aird, and Sir John Bruce shortly after World War II. Aided by numerous bequests, its primary purpose was to send young surgical scholars to the British Isles or vice versa. It has continued to expand and extend its geographic confines so that every year approximately half a dozen surgeons can receive the necessary funds for a six week visit to medical teaching centers in one or more foreign countries. Meanwhile the members of the Association meet for a brief time yearly, alternating between the United States and abroad.

Turning from meetings to individual trips, I shall begin by recounting the first out-of-the-city presentation that I made as a young surgeon. It was before a meeting of a county medical society in the western part of Massachusetts. I was told that I should speak on peptic ulcer. So I armed myself with a large number of slides that contained all the important data. The lecture was to take place at 8 P.M. I arrived after dark and found much to my amazement and discomfiture that it was being held around a campfire. Soon recovering from my stage fright, however, I gave a long and impassioned discourse, with special emphasis on the incompatibility of smoking and ulcer disease. The message certainly was clear because I never smoked. The audience seemed impressed by the lecture, probably because they had had a few cocktails ahead of time. They gave me a gift—a cigarette lighter.

Beirut and the Near East

My first medical assembly abroad which I attended as a member of the faculty was combined with fascinating sidetrips. In 1954 I was invited to speak at the Middle East Annual Medical Conference. This yearly event was sponsored by the Medical School in the American University in Beirut. The chief of surgery, John Wilson, was a former MGH resident, and Professor Churchill had been the lecturer the year before. Participants came from all of the Arab countries, because the American University in Beirut was the outstanding educational forum in the whole area and its graduates were scattered widely throughout the Middle East.

The Assembly lasted only three days but we traveled in the area for nearly six weeks, thanks to a subsidy from the U. S. Department of State. From Beirut, John Wilson, the Professor of Surgery, took Phyllis and me to Biblos and to the Bakaa valley to visit Baalbeck. Others took us to Tripoli in the northern part of Lebanon to see the cedars of Lebanon. And we traveled by ourselves to Damascus, to Cairo, to Jerusalem, and to Baghdad. But the most intriguing of all—

and each site is worth a long chapter—was the trip to Amman, Damascus, Aleppo, and Kalat Semen.

We left Beirut on a fine spring morning in an army light truck. There were three of us—Cecil Watson, distinguished Professor of Medicine from Minnesota, Phyllis and myself. We had two drivers; they kept a loaded pistol in the glove compartment. The first stop was Amman, the capital of Jordan. At that time it looked like a nineteenth century city in Wyoming. (It has changed greatly since then.) During a conference with several native doctors, one of them, a surgeon, said he was to resect a stomach the following morning. When I told him I would like to see him operate, he paled, began to sweat, and practically went into shock. But I quickly withdrew my request and he recovered his composure.

We went down to breakfast in the hotel dining room. A mouse scampered across the table. Cecil gave one shriek, jumped out of his chair, and headed back to Beirut; Phyllis and I were left to take in the excitement of the rest of the trip on our own.

In Damascus we saw a fine hospital put up by the Ford Foundation. Unfortunately, it contained very few patients. We traveled nearly forty miles further north in Syria to Nebek, a little town in which there was a Danish mission hospital. During our visite there, we found about fifty patients, many of whom had had gastrectomies or cholecystectomies. Obviously the most difficult surgery in the country was being done in this mission hospital. We also saw other signs of their inventive skill—in the kitchen they were making aspirin and boiling down opium poppies to make morphine.

After Nebek we traveled on through the Fertile Crescent, crossing old Roman roads, and traversing verdant meadows full of migrating birds. Large tells that contained ancient cities were numerous. Many apparently were the sites of old towns or palaces and had not been excavated. Capacious yellow dwellings that resembled bee hives housed the northern rural Syrians. Homs, a large city, contained a very independent group of natives, who many years later were massacred by the ruler of the country. When we were there, however, the main attraction was a huge water wheel—a noria—that lifted water for irrigation from the Orontes River. It probably had been there since Roman times.

Aleppo, a city of about 600,000 people at that time, seemed to be full of swarthy men selling huge onions and building lovely dwellings out of the native stone. I well remember a meeting of physicians there. I gave a brief lecture which was discussed by a French physician. The discussion in French was far longer than my paper. A British doctor who lived there was disgusted by the length of his comments.

The next day was one of the most exciting of our lives. We went north of Aleppo through denuded hills—the site of the dead cities of Syria—to a high elevation. Here, at Kalat Semen, we found the ruined cathedral where St. Simeon the Stylite lived atop his high perch for some forty years. From there he dispensed wisdom to supplicants who included a Pope. The cathedral, originally larger than St. Peter's in Rome, was destroyed by earthquakes. The desolate scene was entirely devoid of visitors other than the four members of our party. The beautiful blue hills of southern Turkey to the north, the spring sky above, and the spectacular cloud formations were sad reminders that at one time this must have been a breathtaking scene. Now, in the twentieth century, long after the human destruction of the forests, little more than the hills and the clouds survive. Rocks and stones were everywhere and the landscape was devoid of vegetation.

On the return trip, we went back a thousand years in time and explored the immense Krak des Chevaliers. This fort was one of the last strongholds of the Crusaders. Its location on top of a hill and the enormous walls and great size made it essentially impregnable by direct attack. Eventually, however, after a long siege, the defenders were starved out.

One weekend we packed a little bag and went by plane to Cairo. To arrive in the large airport at 10:30 P.M. and to find it empty was rather scary. Finally we found a driver with a car, who seemed ready to take us into the city. But when we reached the in-town terminal, we found a little room full of men and no hotel accommodations. So the taxi driver offered to take us to one of the best hotels in the city. Because it was already midnight, we decided to accept his offer. Imagine our dismay when we drew up before a dark and forbidding building. (Later we found that many of the hotels are on the top floors to avoid the heat). We went into the lobby on the eighth floor; it also was full of men. But this time we were told there was a good room with a private bath available. We said we would look at it; someone else was using the bathroom, but at least it had western appliances. We took the room.

The next day we saw the pyramids. Phyllis rode Canada Dry, a mangy camel. And after forty-eight hours we flew back to Beirut, still bearing our tiny handbag. Obviously I have skipped over many of the unusual things that we saw, such as the City of the Dead, the shopping sections, and the museum.

Jerusalem was divided into two sectors. We stayed entirely on the Arab side. I doubt that it had changed very much in nearly 2,000 years. The road to Jericho was deserted. The Mount of Olives was indeed topped by an olive-colored grove. The Garden of Gethsemane contained some flowers. The Wailing Wall had a few mourners. We stayed in a lovely little hotel run by Americans; it was called the "American Colony" and was close to the barbed wire fence that divided the city. At night the stars were absolutely brilliant; there was neither smoke nor clouds to dim their brilliance. No wonder the natives in this country felt close to heaven and generated religions time and again.

Baghdad was a city of contrasts. The whole central area of the city had just been knocked down; it was the former red-light district. The wide Tigris river, dinner with the dean of the medical school, where we ate a native fish from the river, the suffocating heat in the Hotel Zaia, the doves cooing in the hot noon hours, the sight of an Englishman peeling an apple (he produced one continuous peel that eventually seemed to be yards long); the long lines of servants that followed us as we left the hotel begging us for coins—all furnished unforgetable moments. Incidentally, I did give a lecture in the medical school; the very large amphitheater was packed. I am not sure that I contributed to their knowledge of massive gastrointestinal hemorrhage, but the audience was enthusiastic.

Finally, back in Beirut, the assembly convened. Soon afterward we returned home in a DC-6. It took about two days and we had the same meal three times. It was a delightful trip because of our long conversations with professor Allen Whipple, one of the most remarkable men in the history of American surgery. He not only was the professor at Columbia-Presbyterian Hospital in New York City but was deeply involved with the American University in Beirut and the medical school in Shiraz, Iran.

People's Republic of China

In 1974 the American Medical Association was invited to send a delegation to the People's Republic of China in return for a tour of the United States that had been hosted by the AMA for the Chinese. The delegation included the president of the AMA (Malcolm Todd);

past presidents (Carl Hoffman and Russell Roth); chairman of the AMA board of trustees (Richard Palmer); executive vice-chairman of the board (James Sammons); deputy vice-president of the board (Joe Miller); member of the board (Kenneth Sawyer); past members of the board (John Chernault and Donald Wood); director of the AMA Department of International Relations (John Cowan); Ann Landers (Eppie Lederer, internationally known columnist); Mrs. Roth; Mrs. Hoffman; and members of the Interspecialty Council of the AMA (chairman pediatrician Jay Arena, anesthesiologist Marion Jenkins, and vice-chairman surgeon Claude Welch).

We represented one of the first American groups to visit the mainland of China under the Mao regime. We were treated with the utmost courtesy and respect. Our schedule was filled with visits to hospitals, clinics, and rural installations. In every hospital we were met by the medical staff and by the director of the hospital, a member of the Peoples' Revolutionary Committee. He did all of the talking. If there was any dissent among the physicians present, it was not voiced. Undoubtedly the comments we heard were biased but we were able to read between the lines. For example, acupuncture was said to be the analgesic of choice for 90 percent of operations in some hospitals; we found it was used in closer to 10 percent. We were told that legs and feet were transplanted freely; but we never could get the exact number. Because of the known lack of regeneration of the sciatic nerve, we believe that very few attempts at transplanting legs had been made and that the results were poor.

Soon after we returned from China, I published an article describing our findings and impressions. Excerpts from the article follow.[3]

The little creek that forms the border between Hong Kong and the People's Republic of China is wider than the Pacific Ocean. This was the conclusion of our American Medical Association delegation as its members recrossed the bridge after a three-week tour of the medical facilities of the major cities of the mainland. We visited China as guests of the Chinese Medical Association from July 9 to July 30, 1974.

As we first walked into the Chinese border town of Sumchun, we were greeted with free literature—the *Peking Review*, a slick periodical titled *China Reconstructs*, and the famed red-colored handbooks of Chairman Mao's statements—all of which are published in a dozen languages. It soon became clear that we were invited by the Chinese Medical Association to learn about China and not to bring messages from abroad.

But first some words about the Chinese. They are a justly proud people, with millennia of history behind them. They have seen it all before at some time in their variegated history: high civilizations and fratricidal wars, famine and plenty, monarchy and republicanism, bureaucracy and communism, freedom and slavery. There is a parallel in the nation's past for nearly every new direction of the Chinese ship of state.

The people of China are immensely courteous, punctual, clean, and apparently happy. They are fine artisans. They possess in addition the great advantage of an essentially homogeneous population; only five percent are included in minority groups. Furthermore, the symbols that comprise the written language are the same throughout the country and the literacy rate is high.

The Chinese are stoic, athletic, exceedingly kind to their children; and though they still are impoverished, there is no violence in the streets or crime. It is unnecessary to lock doors or to hide valuables. We heard no voices raised at any time, never saw a child reprimanded, and only saw one baby whimper slightly when he was "menaced" with several acupuncture needles. Indeed it is hard to speak about the Chinese people except in superlatives.

But what about their medicine? To answer this question, we must look at the background upon which the present system was founded. In 1949, the date of "The Liberation" there were estimated to be 10,000 doctors in the country who had been trained in Western medicine. They were located almost entirely in the coastal cities. Traditional medicine had been outlawed by the Kuomintang, which became Chiang Kai-Shek's Nationalist faction.

Therefore, medical care had been restricted chiefly to the well-to-do; large areas of the country were devoid of physicians. For example, in the northwestern province of Sinkiang, which covers a sixth of the area of China, there were only six doctors, all practicing in the capital of Urumchi.

Suddenly, all was changed by Mao's pronouncements in 1965 and cemented by the Cultural Revolution. Put into practice, these four simple statements have revolutionized Chinese medical care. They are (1) first serve the workers, peasants, and soldiers; (2) put prevention ahead of treatment; (3) unite the doctors of traditional and Western medicine; and (4) integrate health care with mass movements.

Since medicine must serve the masses, urban-based specialists return every few years for a period of six months to work in the countryside or in a factory. This is done not merely to spread the principles of advanced medicine to the rural areas and to educate barefoot doctors but chiefly to "elevate the political consciousness" of the doctors themselves.

The second Maoist principle has given preventive medicine a leading role in Chinese health care. Many scourges have been eliminated by the near abolition of flies (we saw about one in each city, and there were no screens on the windows), mosquitoes (there still were some in the coastal areas), rats and bedbugs.

Emphasis is placed upon the common diseases. Research, such as it is, is directed to such subjects as acupuncture, coronary disease, and bronchitis. Rare and exotic diseases receive little attention in the universities.

The third point has resurrected traditional medicine and placed it on a par with Western medicine. The important features of Chinese traditional medicine include the use of acupuncture, moxibustion, cupping, and the compounding of herbal or other mixtures as drugs, and the redevelopment of an old Chinese method of treatment of broken long bones by splints that allows free motion of both adjacent joints.

Finally, since everyone is working for the masses, it is thought selfish and inconsiderate to do anything for oneself. Financial incentives are entirely absent. Doctors become medical workers who no longer comprise an elite profession; nor can they exercise any degree of independence. Just as other workers, they are sent by the government to assigned posts.

The apparent and superficial result of the application of Chairman Mao's four points is that medical care of some type now is widely available everywhere, and nearly all infectious diseases have been eliminated. Obviously, we had to accept the sweeping claims on faith that were made by the officials of the Ministry of Public Health, though our limited observations were completely in accord. Furthermore, the populace now appears healthy and buoyant and is bending its talent and dexterity toward an industrial revolution that within a decade or two should make China a dynamic world power.

A list of the outstanding contributions of the new system to the nation's health must include the following:

1. A remarkable improvement of public health has occurred, with the elimination of the most serious infectious diseases. Neurosyphilis, which formerly filled ten percent of hospital beds in the nation, is

gone. Cholera and plague have disappeared. There is no evidence of trachoma. Malaria is rare. Poliomyelitis still remains, but free vaccination for it as well as for whooping cough, measles, smallpox, and diphtheria is available. Tuberculosis has decreased, perhaps due to BCG vaccination, yet the Chinese penchant for spitting (there are spitoons in most hotel corridors) would indicate that respiratory disease still is common. Schistosomiasis remains a serious scourge, but great efforts are being made to destroy the snail hosts.

Personal health has improved. Beggars, drug addicts, and prostitutes have disappeared along with the bureaucrats and wealthy landlords. One wonders why and how this could have been done so rapidly. We never learned, but Harvard sinologist John K. Fairbank has suggested it was done at the cost of one to eight million lives. At any rate, now the people appear completely regimented and adequately fed. Babies and children are all well nourished.

2. The science of replantation of amputated extremities has been developed to an astonishing degree. The results are the best in the world. Over 400 replantations have been accomplished, including more than a hundred in the Sixth Hospital of Shanghai, where the first one in China was done in 1963. They include replacements of arms, hands, fingers, feet, and legs. (We doubted legs had ever been successfully replanted.)

The success rate of replantation is now about eighty percent except for fingers, where it remains somewhat lower. About sixty percent of those with salvaged extremities return to full work. This success is due not only to the skill of the surgeons but to the techniques that they have developed.

3. Much attention in the West has been given to the development of acupuncture as a means of analgesia. After a great deal of exposure to its use on the scene in the People's Republic, we were convinced that it cannot be explained simply as hypnotism in a stoic race.

We visited one of the Shanghai hospitals where the Chinese surgeons promised to perform a number of operations under acupuncture anesthesia. They put on a fine show, carrying out a gastrectomy, a removal of an ovarian tumor, an excision of a semilunar cartilage from the knee, and a thyroidectomy. Except for minimum muscle relaxation in the patient undergoing gastrectomy, the operations proceeded without difficulty.

But the most interesting observations were made by Professor M. T. Jenkins, a member of our group and the chief of anesthesia in a

Dallas hospital. He wandered into a room where a lung was being removed under acupuncture. He found the patient cyanotic, blue as the summer sky. Her chest was open, and two surgeons were busily removing one of the lobes of her lung. She was gasping, breathing room air with no added oxygen, using all her accessory muscles of respiration. He felt certain the woman was about to die but was powerless to do anything about it. He left about two in the afternoon when the surgeons were ready to close the chest.

About three hours later he went back to the woman's ward where he expected to find she had expired, or if she fortunately had survived, comatose and on oxygen. Instead he found her sitting up beside the bed, eating supper.

The preceding evaluation was written in 1974. Now, fifteen years later, it is highly exciting to learn how rapidly the Chinese have succeeded in resuming its common contacts with the Western world. Instead of the monotony of Mao clothes, women have resumed a wide variety of colors and styles. Professor Wei Kai Wu has become a world-famous surgeon with a remarkable series of successes in treatment of esophageal cancer. The Capitol Hospital has renewed its ties with the West. A few scholars are coming to the United States for study. Modern anesthesia has displaced acupuncture in the operating room. Other famous surgeons in Hong Kong, such as G. B. Ong, promise to leave a legacy that will carry over into the People's Republic when the territory is ceded by Great Britain to mainland China in another decade. Human rights and individualism have a long way to go but are far better than they were.

Melbourne, Australia

In 1960 St. Vincent's Hospital in Melbourne Australia invited Phyllis and me to spend a month with their staff. The whole month was an unforgetable experience. Every day I was presented with a long operating list, some of which I farmed out to others. They had saved up their difficult cases for months. I had the help of the senior resident, Peter Morris. Of course Peter and his wife Jocelyn became our lifelong friends; we were immensely pleased when he later became the Nuffield Professor in Oxford. The professional work was stimulating but the social evenings were man-killers. Never had we seen such cordiality. There were lots of speeches and even a day on the Royal

Melbourne golf course with Peter. That game was a complete disaster for me, especially when I visited the traps with completely vertical walls. Phyllis' low point was the day she was taken to see the lyrebirds. Her tour included a champagne lunch that was obviously designed to make a single lyrebird look double. She saw no birds and had a rather rough evening.

One weekend we were taken out to Targoora, a lovely estate in the outback. This was our great opportunity to see the green countryside. Considering the size of the country the amount of fertile land is very small. On the way home, we detoured through dense woods, where one eucalyptus tree was burning like a huge candle. We managed to keep the director of the hospital, Mother Dorothea, out past her permitted time. I am not sure she ever explained it satisfactorily to the other sisters.

The hospital was very modern and efficient, and morale of the staff was excellent. Some of their ways were different from ours. For example the early postoperative care was not in the hands of the surgeons but was under the charge of the anesthetists, known as "resuscitators", who also were in charge of all transfusions.

We were privileged to meet many of the staff, including Mother Dorothea and Bernard O'Brien, a world famous plastic surgeon.

South Africa

In 1979 I was invited by professor Johannes (Bert) Myburg to participate in a postgraduate assembly and to take a trip through the remainder of South Africa. In Johannesburg we stayed with Bert and his devoted wife, Teddy, in their home. While I was visiting the hospital just outside of Soweto, Phyllis had a tour in the township itself. She saw the degradation of the town from which blacks could not escape, heard about the damage inflicted on them by other blacks, and felt the despair they must have experienced as prisoners in their restricted area. Meanwhile I saw an unbelievable amount of pathology in the hospitals.

The postgraduate course was interesting. A large group of surgeons attended. Edwin Wylie was the other visiting professor; his authoritative lectures on vascular disease were very well received. We saw Bert's remarkable transplants in baboons; his "patients" required no cortisone, azathioprine or other immunosuppression. There was no color bar as far as doctors on the wards were concerned, but when everyone went in for tea, the blacks and the colored went to their own separate spot.

We traveled to Bloemfontein, in the midst of the Afrikaans country. Cornelius Nel, a very fine young man, was the professor in the medical school there. He had a special interest in carotid body tumors and had treated about two dozen of them. He took us out to his farm. As we were walking through the pastures, he picked up a shell casing—a remnant of the Boer war. Phyllis remarked that his grandfather and her father probably were on opposite sides during that war.

We went to Capetown and were greeted by Professor Luow, who was essentially retired at that time. The Grote Schur hospital was impressive. But even more so, was the huge building a few miles away that was divided into two symmetrical halves—one for the whites and one for the others. What a waste of money and space! (This division was eliminated several years later.) There was some excellent experimental work on baboons being done there too, particularly by a young fellow who later spent a year or so with Peter Morris in Oxford.

From there we flew to Durban. The most impressive medical sight there was the hospital for the natives. The turnover was unbelievable. We were told that the emergency ward provided about 130 patients every day for the surgical service. Most of the emergency patients had knife wounds; the common point of attack was the neck. There was also a new hospital for the whites; it was nearly empty at the time. Professor Lynn Baker took us out to his home on the shore, where he and I went swimming in the very active surf. I nearly lost my bathing suit in the melee. But we felt very secure because we knew there were shark nets protecting the beach; it was not until later that we learned that all of the sharks which had been caught were trying to get out rather than trying to come in.

We went by air from Durban to the Kruger National Park. There we had a few days of relaxation. We saw many animals, including a white lion, but the excitement and the number of animals were not as impressive as our memories of upper East Africa. From there it was back to Johannesburg. We had a nice dinner as guests of professor Daniel DuPlessis who is an honorary member of the American College of Surgeons and the principal of the University of Witwatersrand. The last night we were there the police picked up his son. The young man, a journalist, had failed to give the police a copy of one of his news dispatches to a London paper so he was put in jail. It took his father years and nearly all the family fortune to gain the son's release.

This episode was a final commentary on that country—geographically beautiful, but as comfortable a spot to live in as the rim of a volcano.

The trip back to New York was long and tedious; the only stop was on the tiny Sal Island, well out in the Atlantic. The planes land there for refueling because nearly all of the African countries refuse landing rights to South African airlines.

McLaughlin-Gallie Visiting Professorship

In 1978 I was called by Walter MacKenzie, our good friend and chairman of the department of surgery in Edmonton, Canada with an invitation to be the McLaughlin-Gallie Visiting Professor in Canada. My duties were to travel for a month or so throughout Canada, visit medical schools, converse, hold rounds, and lecture. The month was to be concluded with the annual meeting of the Royal College of Physicians and Surgeons in Montreal, where I would be presented with an honorary degree and membership in the College.

At the outset I felt that I did not have the qualifications to carry out such an arduous task, but Phyllis and Walter had an opposite point of view, and finally I agreed. So, in the dead of winter we visited half of the sixteen medical schools in the country. They were in Hamilton (McMaster), London, Vancouver, Calgary, Quebec, and in Montreal (two, The University of Montreal and McGill). We finally made it to St. John's Newfoundland on the third attempt; twice we were stopped by severe snow storms after reaching Halifax and had to return home, to set out again at a later date.

Needless to say, this was an enjoyable month for both of us. We saw and made numerous friends. We were greatly impressed by some of the schools, particularly those in Calgary and in St. John's, Newfoundland. We were somewhat ambivalent about the architecture and the method of teaching in McMaster. We found that Canadian doctors were very troubled about political problems, especially the matter of balance billing.

In our last days in Montreal it was even colder than usual. We rented a car and drove through the city and up to St. Adolphe and the ski country but not as far north as Mont Tremblant. It was a wonderful trip that brought back many poignant memories, for Phyllis had spent her childhood summers in that very spot.

At the conclusion of the visit I was awarded an honorary fellowship in the Royal College of Physicians and Surgeons of Canada. It was a fitting climax to a visit that has been experienced by very few surgeons.

In many other locations as well, the joys of visiting new countries or continents have been augmented by the bonds of world wide friendships. Such personal relationships have been so rewarding that they will be considered in a later chapter of this book. But before I leave the topic of our travels, I must add brief descriptions of two other exciting trips that Phyllis and I made in association with lectures that I gave. We experienced high drama when we innocently accepted an invitation to be flown by private plane from Caracas, Venezuela to view the spectacular Angel Falls. That flight resembled a ride in a Mixmaster as the pilot made passes at the highest falls in the world, diving down and bringing us back up for another look. Our hosts, devout Catholics, had their eyes shut tightly, their lips moving silently, and their hands making the sign of the Cross. A few minutes later, we made a landing on a short crushed-rock runway near another massive falls. The pilot got out and walked under and around the Lear jet to see whether there had been any damage from flying rocks and pebbles. He told us that as far as he knew, no jets had ever landed there before. We learned later from our friend Kennedy Gilchrist that he had made the same trip in a propeller-driven plane, which had crashed in the jungle and came to rest in the tree tops. Fortunately, their party was able to make their way back to civilization after many days, with bruises and minor fractures.

A more sobering event occurred in the spring of 1983 when we ran the white water of the New River in West Virginia. As our rubber raft went over Tatlow's Folly, we passed too close to a hydraulic where the black waters were pouring into a dark hole. Before we could even take a deep breath, we were catapulted into the water. Phyllis was trapped beneath the raft, but finally was able to extricate herself. She found herself being carried swiftly downstream toward the next rapids, only a short distance below. Ropes were thrown in her direction and, with great effort she was able to swim to them, catch one, and be hauled to shore. As for me, I found the dim light getting rapidly darker as I was pushed down toward the depths. I had about exhausted my ability to keep from breathing when the light began to increase and I popped to the surface with nothing worse than a bleeding nose. I understood why I had signed a paper prior to the adventure declaring that the company in charge was free of any liability if an accident occurred. Our guides told us this was the first such disaster in seventeen years; we either were very unlucky or exceedingly fortunate to have had an experience we will never forget, even if we try.

We left nearly all of our lecture or professorial visits with some interesting memory and some token. This could range from a small memento to an honorary degree such as the *Doctor Honoris Causa* granted to me by the University of Montevideo in Uruguay in 1982. Most important of all, however, were the many friendships that we established throughout the world.

In conclusion, Phyllis and I often are asked to identify the most outstanding spots that we have seen in our travels. Such a decision is difficult. However, we have identified twenty-five that were particularly impressive. They are listed and described briefly in Note 4 in this chapter.

18

Board of Registration
in Medicine 1975–1981

In the late 1960s commercial insurance companies warned Massachusetts physicians that they would either have to raise insurance premiums significantly or withdraw from doing business in the state. The main reasons appeared to be an increased number of lawsuits against physicians, inflation, numerous large awards by juries, and the need to fill the coffers of the insurance companies. However, as Charlotte Cloutier showed in her analysis of this problem, malpractice crises are repetitive and in many respects are similar to a disease that strikes once every decade.[1]

The financial problem was so severe, however, that it was apparent to both physicians and the public that a catastrophe was imminent. Affairs came to a climax in 1975, when the legislature passed a bill that contained four important provisions and Governor Dukakis signed Chapter 372 into law. Tribunals were established to review all medical malpractice cases. Each tribunal included a judge, a lawyer, and a medical expert. If the tribunal decided there was no merit in the complaint, it was dismissed and did not enter the tort system unless the plaintiff paid a fee of $2,000. It was believed that this measure would reduce the number of cases that went to trial.

The second provision was the formation of a new insurance consortium that would insure all physicians in the state. The Joint Underwriting Association, or JUA, as it was called, shortly was followed by a second major insurance company known as CRICO that was set up by the medical institutions associated with Harvard. CRICO insured the physicians and hospitals at lower rates than the JUA.

The third provision was to strengthen the Board of Registration in Medicine by changing its name to the Board of Registration and

Discipline in Medicine with the expectation that it then would be more effective in removing incompetent or criminal physicians from practice. The final provision was to form a Commission on Malpractice, which had to report annually to the legislature.

The previous Board of Registration in Medicine had taken very few disciplinary actions. It was expected that the new Board of Registration and Discipline in Medicine would be considerably more active in its investigations of erring doctors. Consequently, members of the new Board were screened very carefully. I was asked to serve and subsequently was elected chairman—a post that I held for five years. Other members who served for several years included George Annas, J.D. (a professor at Boston University and a distinguished contributor to numerous publications on legal matters and ethics relating to medicine); Carl Cassidy M.D., (internist and professor at the New England Medical Center); Charlotte Cloutier (who had made a detailed study of the former Board and later became a professor at Northeastern University); and Kathleen Mogul, M.D. (a psychiatrist in private practice). A brilliant young attorney, Garrick Cole—an Assistant Attorney General and intensely interested in medicolegal problems—was assigned to us from the attorney general's office; he was invaluable.

At the outset each new Board writes its own rules and regulations. But prior to writing regulations, it is necessary to hold a public hearing. Because the rules and regulations written by each new Board are essentially equivalent to statutes, we wrote them with great care.

We defined the "practice of medicine" on the basis of the doctor-patient relationship rather than on the basis of a laundry list of actions a physician is allowed to take that others in the health care system cannot. This definition proved satisfactory to lawyers and judges as well. We wrote regulations concerning the treatment of Medicaid patients, stating that any physician refusing to care for a Medicaid patient solely on the basis that the patient was on Medicaid, would be subject to disciplinary action.

Judging from the complaints that occasionally appeared in the newspapers, we expected an important public outcry from indigent patients on Medicaid, saying doctors refused to treat them. In fact we had only one such case, and after a hearing, we decided the physician was not guilty. The problem undoubtedly was there, but we did not see it because the Welfare Department also had listened to the complaints of the physicians about low, delayed payments and had raised the compensation for physicians' services.

We wrote regulations concerning the duties of a physician treating a patient with cancer of the breast. This is part of the much more universal problem of informed consent prior to operation; I discuss it in Chapter 23.

Relationships with the Massachusetts Medical Society in general, were cordial. There was only one occasion of minor disagreement. The Board wished to obtain objective evidence that every physician in the state was well educated and that no disciplinary action had been taken against him or her since his or her license last was renewed. It was most convenient and frugal to obtain this information in a brief questionnaire that each physician must answer prior to obtaining a license or a renewal. We decided to obtain the information despite objections by the MMS. Unfortunately, the information we gathered never could be analyzed in a satisfactory fashion because of lack of funds. Subsequent boards, however, have asked for considerably more information than we did.

The Massachusetts Medical Society, understandably, did not like the name ascribed to our Board by the legislature so two offending words in our title—"and Discipline"—were deleted by legislative action in 1977. Nevertheless, the most important actions of the Board consisted of disciplinary actions. They arose from complaints sent to us by patients, the Secretary of Consumer Affairs, or other physicians. Complaints varied from minor disputes concerning fees to very serious ones such as the illegal dispensing of drugs or actual crimes. We received about 200 complaints a year. We had funds to hire only one (or occasionally, two) investigators to discover and bring the facts to the complaint committee of the Board. Nearly 90 percent of the complaints were resolved by the committee. More serious complaints were brought to the entire Board, and formal hearings were held for all important cases. Eventually we revoked the licenses of approximately forty physicians, chiefly as disciplinary actions for the illegal distribution of drugs. In several cases, however, revocation was based on dangerous clinical practices.

One of the most serious criticisms directed at the Board—a fact with which we completely agreed—was that it had to act both as a prosecutor and as a judge. A hearing officer had to be chosen by the Board in each case. It was his duty to collect evidence, listen to the arguments of opposing lawyers and make a decision as to whether or not a disciplinary action should be imposed. The full Board then voted on the disposition of the case. If a disciplinary action was imposed, such as reprimand, loss of license, community service, or some other type of punishment the guilty physician had a right to appeal to the court. Economy dictated that hearing officers should be one of our members even though, as a member of the Board, he was accusing the physician. From a judicial point of view, it would be important to have a completely unbiased person act as a hearing officer. Hence in highly sensitive cases, we did obtain qualified hearing officers who had no connection with the Board.

In those cases in which we decided that the physician was guilty, a legal brief to support our action was written by the lawyer on our Board under the guidance of Garrick Cole.

Incidentally one of the recent Boards overstepped its bounds insofar as these hearing officers were concerned. The Massachusetts Medical Society objected on behalf of several of their members who had received what appeared to be unjust decisions. Such a commotion was created that the Legislature decided hearing officers can no longer be chosen from the Board. This is a wise decision. It removes from the Board one of the most important and difficult of the duties with which we had to cope and it does prevent a vengeful Board from riding roughshod over physicians.

One of our cases attracted a great deal of attention from the media—the so-called Malden case. A group of surgeons had undertaken the establishment of a center for cardiac surgery in that hospital. It was rumored in the press and elsewhere that death rates there had been unusually high. Because the case obviously was a highly sensitive one, our Board decided to obtain a hearing officer who taught at a law school and had an impeccable reputation as a jurist.

The hearing officer held many conferences. The group, however, had voluntarily stopped doing cardiac surgery just prior to these hearings. Finally, just before the hearing officer was to hold his last hearing and make his final decision he was approached with an offer to settle the case. This offer was considered to be reasonable by our lawyers, and was agreed to by the Board. The terms included the requirements that no more cardiac surgery would be done in the Malden Hospital and that all surgeons in the group be forbidden to carry out cardiac surgery in the future unless they took further training in this specialty in a university center. Although these terms might appear to be rather generous, it is important to note that the case had a chilling effect on the establishment of cardiac surgery in hospitals poorly equipped for such procedures.

Acupuncture was somewhat glamorous in 1975. The so-called benefits of acupuncture were extolled in a public hearing and an acupuncture board was proposed. Our Board's attitude was that our main function was to protect unwary patients who actually required treatment by physicians for serious diseases such as cancer. We therefore established the regulation that patients receiving acupuncture must be screened by a physician prior to treatment. After that, if a patient wished to trust his body to an acupuncturist, then it was his privilege. In recent years, however, acupuncture has lost most of its attraction, not only in the United States but also in the Peoples's Republic of China. When I saw acupuncture used in China, asepsis was minimal. The danger of sepsis is real; the needles which puncture the skin, can introduce the viruses of hepatitis and AIDs.

"Nurses practicing in an expanded role" was a phrase used to describe nurse anesthetists, midwives, and others in private practice, doctors' offices and hospitals. The legislature in 1976 directed the Nursing Board in conjunction with the Board of Medicine to prepare regulations for these individuals. For the public hearings that were held in Gardner Hall, Ann Hargreaves, R. N.—chairperson of the Nursing Board—and I were co-chairs. The meeting tended to be unruly, spiced by emotional and inappropriate remarks. Some nurses were highly disrespectful of John Figgis Jewett, an eminent obstetrician, when he spoke of the merits of having midwife-assisted deliveries take place in hospitals under the direction of a physician. But we maintained order, and eventually regulations were written. They included requirements for qualifying examinations for nurse anesthetists and for supervision by anesthesiologists when the nurses were giving anesthesia. A midwife had to have a designated physician on call to consult or to provide treatment if she should meet a complication in either a home or a hospital delivery. Considerable latitude was given to nurses practicing in regulated areas such as hospitals or doctors' offices.

There were relatively few physicians' assistants in the state at that time. We felt that the doctors or institutions hiring them were responsible for their actions. Relationships between physicians, physicians' assistants, and nurses did become strained from time to time, but we never encountered any serious problems with these interfaces. Nurses and physicians' assistants both wanted the privileges of writing prescriptions. However, our Board felt that the designation of over-the-counter drugs was becoming more liberal and that drugs designated as controlled substances should only be prescribed by physicians. The legislature listened to the Board and to the MMS, which has vigorously opposed liberalization of the statute for many years.

Continuing Medical Education (CME) is important in an age when medicine is advancing so rapidly. Physicians' licenses are renewed every two years. And in 1976 Representative Louis Bertonazzi, in a conference with members of the Board, stated that he planned to introduce a bill in the Massachusetts legislature that would make CME a requirement for renewal of licenses. At that time the Board had already decided it would recommend this requirement for renewal of a license, but we wanted to put it in the Board's regulations rather than in a statute. Fortunately, this arrangement proved to be satisfactory with the Legislature.

Although benefits from CME have never been clearly demonstrated, the Board voted to make this requirement effective in 1978. As expected, there were numerous protests, especially from elderly doctors. Eventually, nearly all fulfilled the requirements or had adequate excuses. The Board had planned to spot check a certain number of applications for renewal to be certain the physicians' statements were true, but lack of funds and personnel prevented any action.

The Board hoped that this evidence of maintenance of knowledge would increase respect for the medical profession by the public. But if any laudatory statements appeared, they never reached the Board. The Board also expressed the hope that the principle of lifelong learning would gradually become so apparent to all physicians that compulsory requirements could be eliminated and replaced by voluntary compliance. To date, that has not happened either. The MMS lost some members who disagreed with the policy when CME was made a requirement for membership in the Society shortly after the Board's action. However, this requirement for membership was revoked in 1984.

After leaving the Board, Carl Cassidy served with the Postgraduate Education Committee of the Massachusetts Medical Society and for several years prepared examinations on material that appeared in the *New England Journal of Medicine;* suitable grades were accepted as evidence of CME.

Members of the Board gained invaluable experience during these years because of their role in the very important partnership between the private sector and the government, a partnership that is certain to become more common and necessary. Compared with the MMS, whose ability to discipline its members was being sharply restricted by the Federal Trade Commission, the Board had very effective measures at its disposal, ranging from revocation of licences to less stringent measures such as censure or reprimand.

Of course, we did not realize how much of our time would be wasted by petty squabbles with political appointees and lack of funds and personnel. Many of us spent an enormous amount of time bridging the gap between the public and the profession. Under the tutelage of Garrick Cole, all of us learned about the benefits of the legal system and gained respect for many of the lawyers who appeared before us. However, we physicians never could understand the lawyers' ethics, which require them to defend individuals whom they know are guilty.

All of our decisions were made after full and frank discussion. At the end of the five years, when a new Board was appointed by a new governor, we felt that we had gained respect from the public but had made few friends because we had to be critical, at times, of physicians, and, at other times, of the public.

The Board prepared annual reports and nearly every year we gave examinations to approximately 200 physicians who had not passed the National Board Examinations and wished to practice in the state. These examinations were prepared by the Federation of State Medical Boards. Approximately half of the applicants passed each year.

We were in charge of registration and reregistration of all physicians and we also issued limited licenses to the many interns and residents who were in training programs. From our point of view it was unfortunate that the funds we received from licensing were deposited in the general fund of the Commonwealth. Consequently, we had to battle with the legislature for funds to run our programs.

Some statistics compiled by the Board during the years 1976 to 1980 may be of interest. The 1980 report is quoted as an example. In Massachusetts, 17,892 physicians were licensed to practice. The Board met twenty-four times during the year. Complaints were received from 246 individuals during the year; 63 of the 1980 complaints and nearly all that had originated in 1979 were closed.

The Board began the year with twenty-nine Orders to Show Cause; these were the serious cases in which the Board ordinarily would hold a hearing. Final action was taken on sixteen during the year; these actions included revocation of license, in five; suspension of license, in one; reprimand, in one; reprimand and settlement agreement, in five; and settlement agreement, in two.

Final actions of the Board may be appealed to the Supreme Judicial

Court. By 1990, one case—a reprimand—was still under appeal; all others in the entire five years that had been appealed were decided in favor of the Board by the court. We ascribe this unusually favorable record to the great assistance given to us by Garrick Cole.

During this same five-year period, two decisions made by the courts had effects that tended to nullify some of the changes instituted by Chapter 372. The first occurred in 1980, when the Supreme Judicial Court reinterpreted the Statute of Limitations. Instead of placing a time limit from the date of the alleged action, the court decided that "a cause of action for medical malpractice does not accrue until the patient learns, or reasonably should have learned, that he has been harmed as the result of a defendant's conduct." This decision reduced what the medical profession had interpreted as a very strict Statute of Limitations to one of relatively little temporal significance.

The Supreme Judicial Court also decided that a plaintiff was entitled to go to trial without appearing before a tribunal, provided any physician stated that the plaintiff had been injured. Such a decision essentially nullified the value of tribunals, because it was not too difficult to find some physician who would agree with the plaintiff.

The continual strife for greater financial support and more personnel consumed an enormous amount of time. Funds derived from registrations and license renewals continued to go into the general funds of the Commonwealth; budgets submitted by the Board were usually cut severely. For example, the Board's budget for 1981 was $440,000; the actual appropriation was $388,000.

As we completed our term we felt that we had helped to strengthen the cooperation between the public, the government, and the medical profession that would become progressively important in the future. Unpleasant though it had been at many times, we felt that we had done our duty.

19

Medical Malpractice

The Massachusetts General Hospital and John C. Warren, "easily the most distinguished physician in the country" according to De Ville, participated in one of the most newsworthy medical malpractice suits in the nineteenth century. Only a few months after the hospital opened, Warren tried in vain in 1821 to reduce a dislocated hip that had been treated unsuccessfully three months previously shortly after the injury by physicians in eastern Maine. A series of trials in court by the patient against the Maine physicians found Warren on the side of the patient and the famous Nathan Smith defending the Maine doctors. Eventually the patient dropped the suit, but the physicians had to pay a tidy sum for court costs. A war of vituperation by pamphlets and newspapers was waged; it was years before the altercations eventually died.[1]

These actions preceded a deluge of suits that began in 1840 and continued throughout the rest of the century. In 1920, in Massachusetts, the Massachusetts Medical Society paid the expenses of any such suits or settlements for its members. Because the dues at that time were about ten dollars per year, it seems that such litigation must have been uncommon and inexpensive at that time.[2]

Even in 1965, malpractice suits were infrequent. Now they are common and consume enormous amounts of money paid by physicians for malpractice insurance and for increased services required in the practice of defensive medicine. Reynolds, in 1990, estimated that 1989 total liability costs relating to physicians' services were $20.7 billion; much of this expense was due to practice changes in response to liability risks.[3]

The participants in this health care crisis have different opinions about its cause. Physicians complain that the public is litigious, expects perfect results from every physician-patient encounter, that the physician is held accountable when the patient dies of an incurable disease, and that lawyers and the public are greedy. Patients complain that, not only are the results of medical care poor in certain cases, but in others the patient actually is harmed by the physician. Physicians also complain that statutes of limitations are too liberal, that damages for pain and suffering are excessive, that lawyers' contingency fees are too high and that lawyers add fuel to the fire by advertising themselves as experts in medical malpractice. Physicians would prefer to have cases heard by a judge rather than by a jury. Physicians want expert witnesses to be qualified as experts only in their specific fields and not to be able to testify in others. Physicians want the collateral rule for payment applied so that any payments already paid by insurance companies would be deducted from any monetary award given to an aggrieved patient. Patients complain that they get only a small portion of any award and that a high percentage goes for court costs and lawyers' fees. Lawyers maintain it is their duty to secure justice for their clients. Insurance companies claim they are losing money and that higher premiums are necessary. Obviously these disparate points of view can never be reconciled.

Furthermore, as noted in Chapter 19, judges also have different interpretations of the law. For example, a statute of limitations adopted in Massachusetts set a time limit of five years after an occurrence (such as leaving a surgical instrument in the abdomen) for the initiation of a legal action against a physician. A judge of the Superior Court reinterpreted the statute to mean five years after the malfeasance *could reasonably* have *been discovered*.

Several events preceded the current situation. When the problem was first assuming major importance, Elliot Richardson, as Secretary of Health, Education and Welfare, appointed a commission to define the causes, costs, and potential remedies for malpractice. They published the first authoritative figures on medical malpractice in 1973. Their main conclusion was that the high costs of malpractice insurance were due to malpractice. The advice to the medical profession was, essentially, clean up your act.[4]

Thereafter, medical societies throughout the country rose in disbelief and protest. Finally, it became apparent that the conclusion of the commission essentially was correct. Corrective measures were instituted. Informed consent was obtained prior to operations. Physicians were told to avoid raising their patients' expectations too high. Meanwhile, insurance premiums continued to rise and obstetricians were held liable for abnormalities in children for many years after birth. Despite a tightening of the statute of limitations in many states, a decline in the number of obstetricians began to be noted as professional liability fees became exceedingly high. Another important change that occurred as a result of the rising insurance costs was the gradual withdrawal of general practitioners from obstetrics and surgery.

Other countries had developed other systems and seemed much less bothered by malpractice actions than we were in the United States. Physicians, seeking for reasons, considered contingency fees as an important factor. Contingency fees for lawyers (that is, payment of the lawyer by the client only when the lawyer won the case) were considered to be not only illegal but also immoral in England and Canada. These countries had very few problems with malpractice actions, and in both of them physicians' insurance rates were extremely reasonable. Also, in both countries the number of lawyers was far lower per capita than in the United States. In England all malpractice trials were held before a judge rather than a jury. Sweden had a no-fault method, whereby all patients were automatically compensated for any injury without recourse to the courts.

Several conclusions can be drawn from the preceding recital:

> The American public is contentious and expects redress for every wrong. This attitude is different from that of citizens in many countries.
>
> A total no-fault system in the United States would probably be extraordinarily expensive and increase costs of the system rather than reduce them unless some special provisions were included, such as eliminating awards for pain and suffering.
>
> Lawyers in the United States will not give up the contingency fee system easily. They maintain that this system is the only one by which a poor patient can afford justice.
>
> Our present system is grossly unfair; some patients receive inflated awards, but others who deserve recompense get nothing. The system also is slow, and only small awards go to patients, while the remainder goes to the court system and lawyers.

Professor Cloutier, in a detailed study of the entire problem, believes that crises in medical malpractice come in waves, very similar to the pattern of medical epidemics. They are abetted by the addition of more dollars in insurance funds.[5]

In recognition of all these considerations, attempts at reform were essential; they could logically be grouped as either (1) continuing reforms of the tort system, (2) no-fault insurance plans, or (3) methods of arbitration.

Historically, reform of the tort system has been the favorite method in most states to improve the situation in the past twenty years. Most of these actions have dealt with caps on compensation for pain or suffering, limits on the amounts of lawyers' contingency fees, reduction of the length of time permitted in which action can be brought after a maloccurrence, elimination of the ad damnum clause (in which the lawyer states the amount of damages he expects to claim), and better definitions of expert witnesses.

One of the great problems with reform of the tort system is that the courts found many of these statutes unconstitutional. However, in recent years, more of these changes have been supported by the courts.

Two interesting developments occurred in Massachusetts when tort reforms were made by the legislature in 1975. The first had to do with the formation of tribunals that would hear a case before it could be brought to trial. A judge, a lawyer, and a physician would review the case as a tribunal; if they decided against the plaintiff, the plaintiff could bring the case to trial but would have to post $2000 to cover some of the costs if he lost (the amount of the bond has been increased since then). One judge took the liberty of eliminating the deposit in cases he felt the patients could not afford it. As noted in Chapter 19, another judge ruled that if *any* physician stated that the defendant physician might be at fault, then the case would have to go to trial; obviously it would be no problem for a competent lawyer to find one such physician. Such a ruling can essentially wreck the tribunal system.

My first active participation in an attempt to secure some type of reform of our present system occurred in 1975. At this time Francis Moore was chairman of the Committee on Issues of the American Surgical Association. He instituted a dialogue with Attorney Tancredi of New York City. As a result, a committee was established by the American Bar Association to consider the problem of medical malpractice.[6] Further details are provided in Chapter 15. In brief we established about twenty "designated compensable events". If they occurred because of an operation the patient would be reimbursed a designated amount without entering the court system and the case was closed. We thought the method had a great deal of merit, but the lawyers rejected it.

A recent impressive study of the incidence and costs of medical malpractice was completed in 1990 by a committee with members from the Harvard Medical School and Law School under the chairmanship of Howard Hiatt. David Axelrod, Commissioner of Health for the State of New York, authorized this extremely careful, detailed statistical study because government officials in New York State were concerned about the large number of malpractice claims, the high costs of malpractice insurance, and the possibility that doctors were retiring from practice for this reason.[7]

The commission found that the number of adverse events that occurred in hospitals was much higher than they had expected and that compensation for these injuries was not fairly distributed by the tort system. In 1984, the year studied, they decided 3.7 percent of 2.7 million hospitalized patients experienced injury that was due to medical intervention and not to the underlying disease. The death of one out of seven of the injured patients was attributable at least in part to their injuries, and more than a half of the deaths were due to negligence.

The commission advocated no-fault insurance as an alternative to the present system. They believed that it would cost no more than the present system, would eliminate payments for pain or suffering, and would allow adequate, fair, and rapid settlements for injuries whether due to the underlying illness or to the negligence of physicians.

Despite the great care with which this study was conducted, several questions remain. Could the number of medical errors have been exaggerated by this retrospective study of records at a time when correct answers were clear? Doctors must make their decisions day-by-day, when the choice of therapy is much more difficult to identify. Is the experience in the State of New York typical of all states in the United States? Their conclusion that the cost of no-fault insurance would be no more expensive than the present tort system does not take into account the litigious nature of our present society and the fact that lawyers' fees were not included in their calculations.

In my opinion, it is unreasonable to expect that the great sums of money that would be thrown into a system in which all deviations from strict standards could be objects for patients' claims would not attract the attentions of patients and lawyers. Who would pay for this new method?

Another possible method of reform that has been suggested is prompt settlement by appropriate payments to injured patients who would give prior agreement to accept this payment in full. Recompense for pain and suffering would not be allowed. Decisions would be made by an adjudication group consisting of a judge, a lawyer, and a physician, who was expert in the particular field in which the defendant physician practiced. Awards would be made according to a schedule. This system is similar to workman's compensation boards. An attempt to introduce this method was made by the Massachusetts Board of Medicine in 1987. The proposal was turned down by the legislature. This method does not have many advocates at this time.

There are indications in 1990 that the malpractice problem is easing slightly and further action may soon be initiated to introduce some type of no-fault insurance. Several states have begun limited applications. The Massachusetts Medical Society presented a comprehensive bill to the Massachusetts Legislature in 1990. Barry Manuel, a recent president of the MMS, drafted the bill; he has studied the no-fault systems now in use and is convinced this method is the best. He has advocated his method vigorously both in Massachusetts and nationally.

Several auspicious signs have appeared. For the first time in history a bill approving this method has received support in the Massachusetts Legislature and has been reported out of committee. President Bush has gone on record as being interested in policy changes, insofar as professional liability costs are concerned. There appear to be fewer malpractice cases now in Massachusetts than there were a few years ago; this was reflected by a reduction in the costs of malpractice insurance in 1990 of nearly twenty-five percent for certain classes of physicians. Blue Shield, as the carrier for Medicare, has assumed responsibility for a sizable proportion of the charges for malpractice insurance applicable to Medicare patients. The Health Care Financing Administration intends to continue the policy in the future, as evidenced by recent proposed scheduled payments to physicians in the *Federal Register*.

On the other hand, there is still a great deal of evidence that the situation is far from satisfactory. The costs of medical liability insurance are overwhelming, particularly to young physicians and those in high risk specialties, such as neurosurgery and anesthesia. One of the specialties most seriously affected by the malpractice crisis is obstetrics and gynecology. A 1990 survey of members of the American College of Obstetrics and Gynecology produced important data. The average cost of malpractice insurance increased from $30,507 in 1986 to $38,138 in 1989. In 1990, at least one malpractice claim had been experienced by 77.6 percent of the sample surveyed; 23.4 percent had experienced four or more claims.[8]

These adjustments do not change the underlying problems with our present system. The high costs of malpractice insurance are deterring young people from entering medical school, and seriously inflate the costs of medical care. Deserving patients are not receiving compensation to which they are entitled. Large sums are lost in the legal and court systems that could more advantageously be applied to these needy persons. And physicians continue to suffer from the trauma of malpractice suits. It is clear that the situation at present is unstable and in need of drastic change. Any predictions concerning future action are risky except to say that there must be continued attempts at reform until some logical or reasonably workable conclusion is reached.

My personal opinion is that the present tort system should be replaced by a no-fault system. It would recompense certain specified injuries or complications similar to that involved in the designated compensable events system described earlier.

A complete no-fault system covering all unhappy events would be enormously expensive. Pain and suffering must be excluded. Any change preferably should be implemented nationwide only after a trial in one or more states has proved that the method is practical. The public should no longer tolerate the clogged tort system as it now exists—a system in which it is not uncommon for cases to mature for five or more years before they are brought to trial.

20

Years of Glory, Years of Turmoil 1950–1990

From 1950 to 1990, unusual developments in the practice of medicine were occurring in the United States. For older physicians, these changes constituted a revolution, but for the younger generation, who knew nothing different, these alterations were met with comparative equanimity.

From my own viewpoint, this period began as one entirely devoted to the practice of surgery. In 1965, with the advent of Medicare, a new era dawned for me and my colleagues. It was one in which the socioeconomic features of medicine became more and more prominent and adaptation was necessary. It was characterized by frequent change rather than by stability.

Medical practice began to be influenced by many new entities in addition to those that already were established. In fact they became so numerous that it was easy for physicians to forget that their primary duty was to care for patients. It is the purpose of this chapter to consider, albeit it briefly, some two dozen of these constraints on the practice of medicine. In many of them I played an active role.

After World War II, the medical profession led a relatively peaceful existence for nearly twenty years. The country, as well as the medical profession, was exuberant and optimistic. Guns as well as butter could be paid for by our affluent nation. There was an enormous expansion in medical facilities and research. The Hill-Burton Act became effective in 1947, and in the next twenty years the Federal Government poured billions of dollars into the construction of hospitals. In most of the country the major portion of the funds was devoted to the development of a countrywide network of small hospitals that were supposed to bring excellent medicine and surgery to outlying districts. Insurance for medical care became widespread. Physicians were in charge of many of these health-care related organizations. Hospitals were paid what they spent, and physicians were paid reasonable fees. The future appeared to be bright for the public and the medical profession alike.

Nearly a decade was required to prove that the grandiose visions of the Hill-Burton act could not be fulfilled. The supply of trained surgeons was not sufficient to man small local hospitals, nor were there enough patients in small towns to allow surgeons to maintain their skills. The phrase "acute Hill-Burtonism" crept into the surgical language to describe unfortunate complications. Many small hospitals were closed; it became wiser and cheaper to transfer patients by helicopter to larger institutions.

Research was promoted particularly by the Federal Government. The National Cancer Institute, founded in 1937, at first had relatively little financial support; it became the first major division to enter the greatly expanded National Institutes of Health (NIH) in 1944. The National Medical Library became the last of twenty organizations in 1965 to join; it was the direct descendant of the Library of the Surgeon-General of the Army, which had been founded in 1834. Some indication of the enormity of the federal contribution is shown by the budget which specified twenty-eight million dollars for the NIH in 1950, ten times that amount in 1960, and over a billion dollars in 1971. Multiple grants to institutions throughout the country, a large clinical center that opened in Bethesda in 1953, and a supportive administration kept yearly budgetary increases intact.[1]

Paralleling these advances were the large sums spent on research by industry. Drug firms were particularly active in the development of antibiotics, and drugs to control peptic ulcer, hypertension, and psychic abnormalities. Medical schools increased in number, yet prospective medical students found it difficult to gain admission. A productive partnership involving medical schools, industry, and the government appeared to be in the offing. Unfortunately, greed and dishonesty sullied this bright prospect and led to later criticisms. Investment by physicians in drug companies for which they do research or laboratories to which they can refer patients are typical examples of practices that are likely to lead to excessive use of the facilities. For several decades, the American College of Surgeons has fought against such practices as ophthalmologists prescribing and filling prescriptions for glasses, or orthopedic surgeons selling crutches or braces. Recently such excesses have continued as some physicians who owned CT scanners or magnetic resonance imaging equipment were found to prescribe such methods of diagnosis more commonly than those who did not own such machines.

Meanwhile the academic facilities in Great Britain and Western Europe had been under severe financial strain because of the extensive rebuilding of many cities required after World War II. There was also a serious brain drain from these countries. Some persons came to the United States to study but remained, while others planned to settle in this land of opportunity. Our country benefited greatly from this influx.

This enormous expansion is hard to grasp unless one actually lists all the advances that occurred in medicine during the last half-century. Although some of these changes were inaugurated just prior to or during World War II, most of them were not fully implemented until after 1945. A list of the most important contributions would run on for page after page. This list is impressive, particularly when it is compared with all that had been discovered before 1945.[2]

These were the years of glory. They were what Osler had seen coming in 1908, provided our country furnished enough funds to support America as the major shrine of Aesculapius. The United States obviously did not provide all of these advances. Actually, considering the differences in population, Great Britain has contributed about as much per capita as we have in this country. Thus, from 1941 to 1987 the United Kingdom had 42 recipients of the Nobel prize, and the United States 125.

Even more grandiose plans were on the horizon. In 1965, as noted in Chapter 12, Mary Lasker persuaded the Congress to allot funds to conquer the three major killers in the United States—heart disease, cancer, and stroke. Large centers, devoted specifically to the care of these diseases and scattered throughout the country, were believed to be the answer. Although the Regional Medical Programs, founded on the basis of this report, never accomplished the ends desired by the congressional Commission, it became apparent that the future of medicine and the care of the patient were to be determined henceforth to an increasing degree in Washington.

It was in the same year, 1965, when, with the establishment of Medicare and Medicaid, dramatic changes began in the practice of medicine. New directives appeared with increasing frequency, statutes were changed, and disciplinary bodies became more active. Under President Nixon, who took office in 1969, Federal support for research began to suffer. The days of glory were not entirely over but reimbursement for medical projects came with more difficulty. From that date onward, we entered an age of turmoil. Nor is there yet any diminution of the uncertainty in which the entire medical profession exists. Funds no longer are unlimited; restrictions on spending are on every hand. Signs of these unstable times included failure of many HMOs, proliferation of gatekeepers, competitive prices that were deleterious to patients, and multiple directives week after week; they have produced shock and instability in the medical profession. After that time, a medical practitioner was no longer in charge of his patients; he never knew what changes or directives would appear on the next day.

From 1965 onward, *it was the best of times, it was the worst of times.* Judged by advances in medicine, America continued to do very well, but our physicians began to feel they were leaving the golden era and that we were entering an era of uncertainty like that described in those famous words by Charles Dickens in his *Tale of Two Cities.* Many physicians were incredulous; to use a popular metaphor, they felt they were being drowned in a sea of alphabet soup. I shall list the important trends and organizations impinging on the practice of medicine from 1965 onward.

The focus of legislative activity that would affect medicine was rapidly turning to Washington and the Congress. Lobbying appeared to have certain advantages and began to be pursued even more actively by the AMA and its subsidiary American Medical Political Action Committee. Specialty organizations also gradually began to set up offices in the Capital City. The American College of Surgeons did this by 1980; the main function of their office was to provide actual data to Congress, and collect information for its members. This important trend—a greatly increased desire of organized medicine to provide information and be heard in Washington—was becoming apparent in 1965.

It was just over a decade later, in the mid-70s, that the Federal Trade Commission was actively investigating all medical organizations to be certain that they were not exercising a monopolistic control over prices. It became apparent at this time that the FTC would not permit any attempt to regulate competition or to fix prices; even if the practices helped patients save money, they were illegal.

Several social changes of fundamental importance became apparent. In addition to the changing relations of the medical profession and the government, the aging of the population, the entrance of women into the practice of medicine, and the decline of Aesculapian authority have had very important effects on medical practice.

Aging of the population has been obvious in the past half-century but will become even more important in the future. Increased visits to physicians, increased hospital admissions, increased utilization of acute care and respiratory wards, and increased numbers of operations such as removal of cataracts, repair of fractured hips and joint replacements will follow. This change in the population led to great alarm in Washington, because these increased demands for services by the elderly promised to bankrupt Medicare.

The emergence of women into areas formerly held to be sacrosanct for men has had a profound influence throughout the entire country. The Johns Hopkins School of Medicine admitted women from the date it opened in 1888. However, this was not the usual pattern. The first female student graduated from Harvard Medical School only in 1949. At present, between a third and a half of the medical students in the United States are women.

Women, at least in the past, were not so egotistic, abrasive, and self-centered as males. Their influence in the practice of medicine originally was directed primarily to specialties such as gynecology, anesthesia, pathology, psychiatry, and pediatrics. At a later date, however, they entered the domain of surgery and all of its subspecialties. The profession thereby has become less argumentative and more willing to accommodate to changing patterns of practice. Group practice, with opportunities for time free of professional responsibilities, has been more attractive for them than for males.

Meanwhile the public has become far better informed than it was in the past about medical care. No longer does society tolerate the empty pontifications that were common by practitioners a century ago. Such statements were based on the experience of the practitioner, rather than on scientific proof, and had been common throughout the history of medicine. The public thereby was subjected to what has been described as *Aesculapian authority*. Recent years have witnessed a decline in Aesculapian authority. There was a time, we are told, when the word of a physician was equivalent of that of a god. Those good old times, needless to say, are gone. Those doctors were assumed to be the descendants of Aesculapius and therefore endowed with such authority that their words were law; patients were not expected to understand or to reason why.

Daumier did his best to destroy this image of divinity. But it lingered on for many years. Today rebellious citizens, increasingly more interested in matters of health and educated by the media, demand a role in their fate. Not unexpectedly the impetus for change came from women. It came to a climax in Massachusetts when in the late 1970s it was clear that cancer of the breast, a tragic disease, could be treated with one of several methods. A statute endorsed by the legislature required that every woman with cancer of the breast should be apprised by her physician of all available methods of therapy.

The Board of Registration in Medicine (of which I was the chairman at that time) was required to write regulations concerning this mandate. It was apparent to us, particularly since our Board included a female psychiatrist—Dr. Kathleen Mogul—that the implications of this statute were so broad that it could bring about harm as well as good. Many patients go to doctors because they want an opinion concerning the best treatment. Psychiatric patients, as well as others, could be devastated by long discussions which might only increase their indecision and the horrors of their disease. On the other hand, for lack of time or knowledge, a doctor might be reduced to the position of a passive supporter of a patient's wishes. The doctor might end up asking a patient what she wants done, and acquiesce without argument. The Board held the opinion that doctors were more likely than the laity to know the latest evidence and that doctors should in the long run be intelligent enough to give an opinion rather than recite page after page of statistics and then ask the patient to decide which type of therapy she preferred. A refusal by the doctor to give an opinion also might trouble a woman who really wants a firm statement from a physician whom she regards as an authority.

We finally decided that if a woman did not want to discuss alternative methods of therapy and wished to abide by the doctor's advice, no further discussion was necessary. Furthermore, it was impossible for all doctors to know all of the recent data concerning treatment; instead they should provide referral to individuals skilled in alternative treatments if the patient so desired.

The practical result is that today many physicians spend an enormous amount of time discussing these problems with patients and their families. Whether or not this method of expanded communication has had any effect on the the cure rate of cancer of the breast is a problem that cannot be resolved for many years to come. But, at any rate, the patient becomes an active partner in her health care.

The requirements for preoperative discussion of all surgical procedures with patients have far wider applications. "Operative permits" are signed by essentially all patients. (Many of us believe that the "request for operation" form used by most veteran's hospitals would be far more satisfactory.) Whether or not truly informed preoperative consent has been obtained is still the basis for innumerable law suits. In one recent case, a patient testified that when he was jaundiced, the surgeon did not tell him cancer was a possible diagnosis. The jury awarded the patient a sizable sum, not because the surgeon was incapable of treating a cancer, but because, if the patient had been told, he might have decided to go to a different surgeon.

Patients now are much more knowledgeable about medical matters than they were twenty years ago. Blood cholesterol levels and mammograms are the talk of the town. Physicians no longer can cloak their ignorance as they could in the past. Aesculapian authority, unless it can be supported by facts rather than empty words, is a relic of the past.

However, this decline in physicians' authority has led to serious consequences. As an example, an army of socalled gatekeepers has been set up to keep patients out of hospitals. Physicians actually have to spend hours arguing with these functionaries while patients are suffering.

Relations between practicing physicians and the federal, state *or* local governments frequently have led to conflict. Nevertheless, from necessity, they have been growing closer as years have passed. Since the federal government is the source of funds for the payment of most professional services under Medicare, and individual states pay for Medicaid, to some extent the government is the employer of all physicians who take patients in either category.

During my career, I have received fees for the care of patients covered by Medicare and Medicaid, and I have been directly employed by the U.S. Army as a medical officer for three and a half years in World War II. I have also participated in other actions in which cooperation between physicians and the government has been valuable. Because there are differences of opinion on the ultimate success of cooperative projects with the government, it may be of interest to examine several other joint activities in which I have had a personal interest. On this basis, we can assess their results in a pragmatic fashion.

In the early 1970s the Federal Drug and Food Administration set up numerous panels to evaluate the safety and efficacy of over the counter (i.e., nonprescription) drugs. The first panel, on antacids, was chaired by Franz Ingelfinger. It was spectacularly successful, particularly because there were objective laboratory tests to measure scientifically the efficacy of different preparations.

I was the chairman of one panel that dealt with anorectal products, with tests of efficacy such as relief of pain, itching, or irritation, and with safety; all these criteria are highly subjective. We held numerous meetings, and finally produced what we considered to be the best publication ever written on the medical therapy of anorectal disease. The final work of the committee included recommendations for approval of certain preparations and disapproval of others that were on the market. Labeling also was subjected to careful scrutiny.

Before implementing the recommendations, the FDA gave industrial companies who produced the preparations time to comment on the report. That period originally was three years. However, even though our report was submitted in 1980, it was not until 1988 that the FDA's review of our recommendations was published; December 1988 was set as a deadline for final comments. The final orders of the FDA had yet (in 1990) to be published. The material that we produced is available in the Federal Register.

Even though our final monograph was excellent, it had essentially no effect on the medical profession because the final decisions could not be formulated until industry comments were obtained. The result has required an enormous amount of time to produce but upon completion should be an excellent guide. It was expensive, because costs for travel and meetings were paid by the government. It took a great deal of time for panel members, but they were happy to donate their services. It proved to be an excellent example of cooperation between the private sector and government.[3]

The Board of Registration in Medicine, of which there is one in every state, is another outstanding example of cooperation between the government and the medical profession. The Federation of State Medical Boards has prepared examinations for licensure for many years. Individual State Boards usually contain a preponderance of physicians, whose time is donated for a trivial financial return. Physicians on these Boards make very few friends; in fact, they are subject to intense criticism from the public and from other physicians. Nevertheless, medical licensure and discipline would be in a sorry state if either the physicians or the government attempted to gain exclusive control of these functions.

Professional Standards Review Organizations, or PSROs, were the original peer review organizations set up to monitor hospital care in conjunction with representatives from the Federal Government. From my point of view, the ultimate product was a large manual that included criteria for care of patients suffering from all of the common diseases seen in short-stay general hospitals.

The final criteria and the manual today may seem to be somewhat lax and flexible, but the manual represented the first cooperative attempt to carry out such a project and produced the prototype of many more detailed and critical evaluations of patient care that have appeared since that time. I would rate it an unqualified success.[4]

Professional Review Organizations, or PROs, are the successors of PSROs. They are directly under the control of the Health Care Financing Administration (HCFA) but the peer review is conducted by physicians. Governmental control has allowed the imposition of sanctions on physicians who, after peer review, have been found incompetent. Physicians, in general, have been unhappy with this system. It has proved to be extraordinarily expensive, because a high percentage of all Medicare hospital admissions are reviewed. On the other hand, unnecessary hospital admissions and stays have been reduced. In Massachusetts and in other states, quality control screens have identified numerous lapses in patient care and have served to institute corrective measures for individual physicians. It is my belief that this careful review has led to great savings for the government and much more efficiency on the part of physicians and hospitals. Very few cases of deliberate fraud have been discovered.

The Institute of Medicine was asked by Congress to evaluate PROs and the effect they have had on medical care. Their report—a comprehensive analysis published in 1990—concluded with the statement that they have not given quality of care enough emphasis, but have paid an undue amount of attention to utilization.[5] I believe that even though the results of utilization review have been good, the costs have been high. I hope that in the near future much more limited reviews of records will be sufficient.

The courts play a very important role insofar as physicians' actions are concerned. Some of their most significant decisions were concerned with abortion, withdrawal of life support in comatose patients, joint responsibility of a hospital if a staff physician is found to be negligent, and limitations of peer review. The FTC also can be involved in peer review as well as in physicians' fees. Peer review, conducted by physicians alone without statutory protection or involvement of government, may be a violation of antitrust laws. William Curran suggests that further legal protection for physicians performing peer review is necessary in many states, but there must be no possibility of control of competition by any persons concerned in the peer review. Examples of the most recent significant court decisions affecting physicians are given in the Notes.[6]

The control of graduate training and education of interns and residents in the past has been entirely in the hands of professional organizations. The Federal Government has become concerned about the relatively ineffective distribution of physicians (inner cities and rural areas do not have adequate medical care) and the drift of physicians into specialty practice that is overpriced relative to charges made by family care-practitioners.

Physician manpower therefore has become a key issue. As noted in previous chapters, a Graduate Medical Education National Advisory Committee was appointed by the Federal Government and produced a report in 1980. Their prognosis, suggesting a huge surplus of physicians in the near future (e.g., a surplus of 145,000 by the year 2000) were vigorously questioned by the American College of Surgeons, among others. GMENAC dissolved after presenting its final report. It has been succeeded by another body established by Congress—a Council on Graduate Medical Education. This council will continue for ten years. At the present moment its agenda is not clear but almost certainly will deal with manpower distribution.[7]

The ultimate value of these studies and their effect upon the medical profession are impossible to assess at this time. Other experts have denied that there will be such an increase in physicians; many physicians are troubled that the government will move a step further and attempt to control entry into certain specialties. In my opinion the primary responsibility for medical education in all of its aspects (undergraduate, graduate, and continuing) should be vested in the medical profession.

The President's Biomedical Research Panel convened in Washington for several meetings in 1975. This advisory panel included a large number of physician-scientists. In the final report, the chairman, Franklin Murphy, stressed the need for far greater support of biomedical science by the government, including better salaries for physicians and scientists working in the NIH. As a member of the panel, I was greatly impressed by their analyses and conclusions. But I have no idea whether or not this scholarly examination of the status quo and important recommendations for the future changed any programs in Washington or not.[8]

Following the report of the commission headed by Dr. Michael DeBakey that recommended the establishment of large centers for the treatment of either cancer, heart disease, or stroke, Congress passed a National Cancer Act in 1971 and gave considerable support to the establishment of such centers. Their subsequent development has been described by William Shingleton.[9] Aid has been furnished by grants to individual institutions rather than by the erection of entirely new hospitals. This decision obviously has been extremely helpful to many important hospitals.

In summary, cooperation of the government and physicians in these activities in which I have been associated generally has had a beneficial effect. This conclusion, however, does not indicate that every such project will be successful. Limits need to be drawn; control of medical education must remain in the hands of the profession. Support of medical research by the Federal Government is essential, with peer review of competing projects by organized study sections composed of physician experts. Such cooperation should not suggest that it will continue in every instance; there is every indication that in the future physicians' fees will be the center of vigorous dispute between the government and the profession.

Professional fees are important to all practicing physicians. When Medicare and Medicaid was established in 1965, payment for professional services was based on a usual, customary and reasonable charge. Both the government and physicians were dissatisfied with this method. The AMA, in combination with HCFA, then supported a pioneer study by Hsiao and colleagues who developed a new method. It based payments chiefly on the amount of work required for a given service plus overhead expenses and payment of a portion of malpractice fees, and included certain modifiers that could raise fees, as for example, services in a rural area. Despite objections from such organizations such as the American College of Surgeons concerning the methodology of the study, the House of Delegates of the AMA accepted the report with the proviso that HCFA would accept balance billing. (HCFA since then has planned to reduce balance billing to a maximum of fifteen percent by 1993.)

The Hsiao fee schedule was entitled a Resource-Based Relative Value Scale (RBRVS) and was ordered to become operative January 1, 1992. Physicians throughout the country as well as the AMA have become very unhappy about the development of the project.[10]

The Congress established the Physician Payment Review Commission in 1986 to report on the activities of HCFA. The main thrust appeared to be a fear that HCFA, in the name of economy, would alienate health care providers at all levels. The Commission, under its chairman, Dr. Philip Lee, has been assiduous in the pursuit of their mission and has voiced disagreement with HCFA's sweeping reductions in fees.

Another important player in this economic game has entered the contest. This is what has been described by Arnold Relman as the medical-industrial complex.[11] Only time will tell whether or not it will turn out to be a great danger as he suggests. There have been several ugly episodes in which desire for financial returns has led physicians to falsify the results of research. On the other hand, drug firms have promoted research for many years; done with proper safeguards, research directed toward the preservation of life or vital functions will be worthwhile, regardless of the sponsor.

Why, then, are over half of physicians in 1990 unhappy about the state of the profession? Why is it that the national pool for applicants to medical schools has dropped from 42,000 in 1974 to only 28,000 in 1990? Why have black applicants in the pool fallen from 359 in 1979 to 135 in 1990? Perhaps these students are excellent readers of the crystal ball. For prospective students, the high costs of medical education, the years spent in postgraduate training after medical school, and the imposition of high costs for medical malpractice as soon as they begin practice loom large. Desires to promote the welfare of the public become less burning when penury becomes the necessary accompaniment. Fear of AIDS also may be dissuading students from entering medical schools or internships in certain city hospitals. These young people gaze at the law profession or the financial world and the high salaries paid soon after graduation with envy; many of these prospective medical students alter their choice of profession. This decline in the number of applicants to medical schools could have very serious implications. If it continues the United States actually could have a doctor shortage by the start of the twenty-first century.

Not only prospective, but practicing physicians are unhappy. Instability of the milieu in which medicine is practiced, and decline in physicians' authority have been stressed, but much of the dissatisfaction is due to financial problems. They have seen HCFA reduce payments for Medicare patients by gradually reducing balance billing until it stabilizes at a maximum of fifteen percent. Insurance companies follow course. Meanwhile office expenses rise, and malpractice fees continue to be extremely high. The present is bad, but the future appears even more gloomy. It has become very clear that whenever funds to support welfare or hospitals for the care of uninsured patients has been promised by the government, and with state funds running low, these programs are the first to suffer.

In Massachusetts, both hospitals and physicians have been affected. HCFA is reducing fees to a point not acceptable to the Physician Payment Review Commission. In Massachusetts even the small option of balance billing allowed by HCFA is not allowed by state law. Physicians are angered by the loss of independence in professional decisions subsumed by non-professional functionaries and gatekeepers. The fact that twenty-five percent of the health care dollar now goes to administrative costs shows how extensive a bureaucracy has developed. Physicians believe they are mere pawns in the hands of grasping organizations and individuals who want to deny rights to ailing patients as well as physicians. The lack of stability of the present system is another strong factor that fans fires of discontent.

Physicians also fear the imposition of new regulations. One example is the National Practitioners Data Bank. The concept was endorsed by the Federation of State Medical Boards and by the AMA. It was designed to identify health practitioners (physicians were the most important) who committed acts that led to disciplinary actions in one state, then moved to other states. In the past, when this happened, old records were lost, and the physician started anew with a clean slate. Under the new system, all such disciplinary actions are recorded in a national computer and are available to state boards, hospitals, and disciplinary bodies. Elaborate provisions are made to protect privacy. Theoretically this should be an efficient way to promote excellence in the profession. Yet physicians fear that a young intern may make some error that leads to a minor disciplinary action, and that this action can be retained on the physician's record all of the rest of his life. Is it fair that black marks are never expunged but praise for excellence is never recorded?[12]

Thus, in 1990, the practice of medicine is carried on not only in physicians' offices but in the Congress, in the States, in the courts, by HCFA, and by insurance companies. The future of medicine depends upon them as well as the support of the public. It is my hope that this complicated interaction has been, to some extent, clarified by this chapter. However, I doubt that the situation will become relatively stable before the end of the century.

21

Massachusetts General Hospital: Nearing the End of the Century

We must remember that the strength of an institution lies in the individuals who have carried it forward. The Massachusetts General Hospital, from its beginnings until its present, has been served by men and women who, in serving it, have come also to give it their affection. It has sought and it has been sought by the best in the medical profession; its integrity has been guarded by a long line of devoted trustees, directors, and benefactors; by its staff, its nurses, its volunteers, its secretaries, its social service, and its employees. It has been generously supported by the community that it has helped to safeguard through so many years. This is the basis of its present greatness, and the foundation on which its future will rest.

I can think of no more appropriate way to begin this chapter than by quoting this tribute to the MGH from Joseph Garland, a year before he became Editor of the *New England Journal of Medicine*. It is an excerpt from his Ether Day Address at the MGH in 1946. That year marked a post bellum reshuffle of manpower and the beginning of a chronic shortage of hospital beds that was to persist for several decades. The fame of the Massachusetts General Hospital was spreading throughout the world, demands by patients were increasing, and the physical plant was aging. A complete renewal was indicated. It began slowly, but gradually gathered momentum and finally culminated in complete modernization with the erection of twin towers for patient care and preparation of adequate research facilities in MGH East. But none of it could have happened if the support of the community had not followed according to the prophetic statement made by Joseph Garland.

Modernization progressed slowly until 1956 when the new Warren Building was dedicated. Not only did it provide many floors for pathology and research, but an equal number were made into offices for the clinical staff. This was the first move to mark a coalescence of staff members about the hospital. It was followed in succeeding years by many offices in the new apartment buildings being erected along Blossom Street and, in 1981, by the Ambulatory Care Center. With the erection of the Warren Building, the MGH began a new era. But before proceeding with the narrative, it is interesting to recall two humorous incidents that occurred in 1937 and in 1964.

In the spring of 1937, when piles had been driven for the White building, a small pond of water filled the excavation made for the basement. This eyesore remained for several weeks. One morning we were astonished to see six ducks sedately paddling about in the filthy water. One was a brilliant eosin red, another gentian violet, and the others of various striking colors. It was apparent that someone had raided the pathology laboratory and secured dyes, bought white ducks, and produced a modernistic gem. James Howard Means, chairman of the department of medicine, was seen within a few hours, painting a watercolor of this unusual sight.

In 1964, at the instigation of Lamar Soutter, eight of us young surgeons gathered together, rented formal garb of the past century and posed for a portrait as if we were visiting surgeons of that era. It must be acknowledged that we made a very impressive group, although we lacked the proper paunches of our predecessors. A photograph was taken, and this portrait was hung in the surgeons' room next to the operating rooms in the White building, along with similar relics of the past. There it remained, unnoticed for over two years. We thought it never would be discovered, but one day Langdon Parsons gazed at it intently and said, "That fellow looks like Howard Ulfelder!", and, after a pause, "My God, it is Howard Ulfelder!" The portrait still hangs in the Sweet room. The participants were Gordon Donaldson, John McKittrick, Fiorindo Simeone, Howard Ulfelder, Carroll Miller, Francis Moore, CEW, and Lamar Soutter.

The next major move in the modernization of the MGH came in 1962 with the appointment of a young, brash, egocentric ex-medical resident as a director. John Knowles found that, with the exception of the Warren building, few physical changes had been made in the plant for years. He gazed out on the Bulfinch lawn, still cluttered with Nissen huts. These remnants of World War II finally were removed, leaving the view of the Bulfinch building in its pristine state.

The chiefs of the medical and surgical services were also ready to retire in 1962. Walter Bauer, chief of the medical service, was suffering from chronic pulmonary failure. Alfred Kranes assumed many of the administrative details of the medical service until Robert Ebert became Chief of the Department of Medicine in 1964.

The modern era in surgery in the MGH began with the appointment of Paul Russell as Chairman of the Department in 1962. Dr. Russell was an outstanding pioneer in the developing field of organ transplantation and was chief of surgery until 1968. His primary interest in transplantation had led to a previous year's fellowship with Sir Peter Medawar in London. He organized the department in the MGH and based it on active research and clinical practice.

It was clear at this time that patient facilities were completely out of date. Several old wards that held twenty patients and many four-bed rooms needed reconstruction. The old system of four lavatories per floor still persisted. Patients in the Baker Memorial were crowded into tiny rooms. Air conditioning was essentially secured by opening windows.

Problems were particularly acute in the operating rooms. The suite in the White building was excellent but those in the Baker and Phillips House were completely outmoded. When surgeons from other institutions visited the MGH they found surgeons scrubbing in a corner of each operating room while an anesthetist was putting a patient to sleep in the same small, crowded room only a few feet away. Visitors not surprisingly made deprecatory remarks.

I finally became so annoyed that I wrote a letter to the director of the hospital, saying the conditions in the Baker and Phillips House operating suites were at least primitive, but more accurately Neanderthal. A few days later one of the associate directors called me aside and said no letter had ever upset the administrative staff more seriously than that one.

Fortunately, by that time Paul Russell was the chief of the surgical service. He immediately recognized the problem, appointed a committee chaired jointly by Thomas Gephart and myself, and presided over the erection of a new operating suite that joined the suites in the White Building, the Baker, and the Phillips House into a single unit. This suite has functioned perfectly ever since.

During Dr. Russell's tenure, many other important developments occurred. The Shriners Burn Institute was erected, with close ties to the MGH staff; it provided many seriously ill patients and a great deal of necessary laboratory space. The subspecialties of surgery began to become more independent. Faculty appointments at Harvard, which had not received much attention from Dr. Churchill, were increased; proper recognition was given to many persons who deserved higher rank. A respiratory unit, which had originated in 1955 as a result of the efforts of Henning Pontoppidan, was strengthened. The Surgical Associates were expanded.

After Dr. Russell retired from his post as Chief of Surgery, he was able to devote the major portion of his time to the development of transplantation in the MGH. During that long period, he has built a strong service and trained many surgeons in the wards and in the laboratories. He became recognized as one of the outstanding transplant surgeons in the world. In December 1990, a large number of his colleagues and ex-students from here and abroad gathered in Boston for a two-day program that honored Dr. Russell's contributions to the specialty.

Dr. Russell continues to serve as John Homans Professor of Surgery in 1992. For some years he had served with distinction as the Secretary of the Faculty. He is continuing his service to Harvard Medical School as chairman of a major drive to augment the facilities of the Countway Library.

Dr. W. Gerald Austen succeeded Dr. Russell in 1969 as chairman after a brief interlude when Oliver Cope served as acting chairman. Under the direction of Russell and Austen, the surgical service of the MGH continued its high level of performance. Because both of them were deeply involved in developing specialties, laboratory research was routine for many in their departments. This reinvigoration of research was one of the most important contributions of both Drs. Russell and Austen. Such projects had diminished in number during the later years of the Churchill regime. Transplantation had opened the whole field of immunology for investigation. The advent of cardiac surgery also defined numerous problems that required solution in the laboratory. At this time the National Institutes of Health provided training for many young people who thereafter returned to the MGH. Research in transplantation has recently been strengthened greatly when Professor David Sachs returned from the NIH to the MGH.

Dr. W. Gerald Austen had had a fellowship in the cardiac unit in the National Institutes of Health under Dr. Andrew Morrow, and as a result, established laboratories as well as an exceptionally busy clinical unit in cardiac surgery. Under his leadership, each subspecialty in surgery became essentially independent. A surgical day-care unit was inaugurated in 1972; in 1982 it was moved to large new quarters in the Ambulatory Care Center. The operating suite was financed by the Cabot Family Trust. Teaching of medical students, residents, and practicing physicians has continued to expand. Private patients were integrated more frequently into teaching programs.

Dr. Austen also was very active for nine years in his duties as a regent of the American College of Surgeons and, in 1990 and 1991, was chairman of the board. He was elected president of the American College of Surgeons in 1991. The increasing demands of a restless surgical profession and the government have required him to make numerous appearances in Washington. Despite his administrative duties, both in Chicago and in Boston, he has been able to carry out a very active clinical practice.

Dr. Austen provided statistics describing the department of surgery in 1991. There are twelve divisions within the department—general, gastrointestinal, endocrine, burn, trauma, transplantation, vascular, cardiac, thoracic, plastic, pediatric surgery, and surgical oncology. There are sixty active surgeons, thirty-four Ph.D.s, seventy clinical and/or research fellows, and seventy-two residents.

A single group practice (the Surgical Associates) has seventy-three members, including all members of the department of surgery, and also neuro- and oral surgeons. Although membership is voluntary, all surgeons agree it is essential for survival of an academic program to have such a type of practice.

There was one Harvard professor in the Department of Surgery in 1932, and three in 1969 (Drs. Paul Russell, Oliver Cope, and W. Gerald Austen). There now are twelve (W. Gerald Austen, Paul Russell, Ronald Malt, John Burke, Patricia Donahoe, A. Benedict Cosimi, Andrew Warshaw, David Sachs, Mortimer Buckley, Hermes Grillo, Willard Daggett, and William Abbott.

Research has expanded enormously in the past two decades. Nathaniel Faxon, in his history of the MGH, noted that all departments had laboratories by 1935. The total amount expended for research, however, for the entire year was only about $50,000. Thereafter, the annual support rose to $2 million in 1955 and $4 million in 1960. Surgeons who conducted research in this period included Churchill, Cope, Stewart, Lyons, Simeone, Linton, Nathanson, Moore, Waddell, Fischer, and Cannon.

When the Huntington Hospital closed in 1942, the research facilities, which were headed by Paul Zamecnick, as well as the patients, were transferred to the MGH. More laboratory space was essential. A new science building was opened in 1951, and several floors in the new Warren building became available in 1956. Three other major expansions have occurred since then—the Shriners Burn Institute, the Wellman building, and a decade later the large space in the MGH East became available for research, particularly of cancer.

The funds for research in 1990 were over $85 million, much of it provided by government grants. A Research Committee of over eighty members has for many years included several professors from the Massachusetts Institute of Technology. The fruits of research in the MGH fill a large book of abstracts every year.

This dramatic rise in research expenditures in the past two decades indicates the emphasis that the MGH has placed on this activity. Another way to measure the quality of the research is to note the number of Nobel prize recipients. Prior to 1955 there were only two who had been connected with the MGH. George Minot's honor in 1934 was shared with the Huntington and the Boston City Hospitals; Fritz Lippmann was biochemist in the MGH when he obtained the award in 1953. Since that time, three former members of the MGH medical staff were honored—Michael Brown, Joseph Goldstein, and J. Michael Bishop.

Laboratory research is an integral portion of education in some surgical departments in the United States. David Sabiston's department in Duke Medical School is a prime example. Churchill and succeeding chiefs in the MGH have decided that the clinical service duties are so great that basic research by residents should be voluntary and require a year or two outside the regular curriculum. Funds for such projects were aided immensely by Dr. Austen when he established five endowed scholarships for this purpose. All five scholarships are used freely. Each was named for one of these five surgeons— Marshall Bartlett, Edward Churchill, Varsted Kazanjian, Robert Linton, and Claude Welch.

Finding time for laboratory research is extremely difficult for a practicing surgeon who is deeply involved in patient care. Churchill, however, convinced several individuals to devote many hours to laboratory research. Some of them later became department chiefs in other institutions, such as John Stewart in Buffalo, Champ Lyons in Birmingham, Fiorindo Simeone in Providence, and William Waddell in Denver. Francis Moore left the MGH for the Brigham. Cope, Malt, Burke, Tompkins, Warshaw, and Nathanson (until his early death) remained in the MGH. Four of Dr. Austen's residents have become chairmen of surgical departments. They are Josef Fischer in the University of Cincinnati, Robert Corry in the University of Iowa, Anthony Imbembo in the University of Maryland, and William Wood in Emory University.

Several of these surgeons have become prominent in special fields. Ronald Malt gained immediate fame when he became the first person in the world to replant a severed arm in 1962; he has continued active laboratory research in gastroenterology since then. John Burke carried out important experiments with antibiotics and aided in the development of artificial skin. Oliver Cope conducted extensive investigations of parathyroid and thyroid disease. Together with Churchill he was a pioneer in the surgery of the parathyroid glands. He also had a great interest in burns and was the head of the Shriners Burn Institute for several years. He served as chief of the surgical department when Dr. Churchill was absent during World War II. In his later years Cope devoted most of his energy to promotion of limited operations for cancer of the breast. Ronald G. Tompkins, now head of the Shriner's Burn Institute is continuing research on artificial skin and the development of an artificial liver.

Francis Moore has been one of the most productive and versatile professors of American surgery in this century. After a residency in the MGH and a short period as a visiting surgeon, he was selected at an early age as the chief of the surgical department in the Peter Bent Brigham Hospital. There he established world-famous laboratories. Fellows came from all over the United States and abroad to work with him. He has explored many surgical frontiers that included numerous studies in metabolism in surgical patients, transplantation, and socioeconomic problems.

Membership in the American Surgical Association has been a coveted prize ever since its formation by the great Philadelphia surgeon, Samuel Gross, in 1880. As noted in Chapter 15, the MGH has had a large number of presidents of the organization among its alumni. At present there are only ten recipients of the ASA Medallion for Scientific Achievement, its highest award. Three of them came from Harvard—Francis Moore, the late Robert Gross, HMS professor of pediatric surgery in the Boston Children's Hospital, and Joseph Murray from the Brigham and Women's Hospital.

The Massachusetts General Hospital, as well as all other major teaching hospitals, obviously faces a difficult future, considering the radical changes in health care that are likely to come in the next decade. However, present data show that its economic position is satisfactory. In common with all hospitals in the state, it has had to reduce expenditures because of excessive regulation and a lack of adequate payment by the state for Medicaid patients. The number of employees—10,000 in 1981—was reduced to 9,584 by 1989. Nevertheless, a capital fund drive for $165 million was oversubscribed in 1989. A twenty-three-story Ellison tower for patient care was occupied in 1990 and another smaller tower will be started in 1992. An enormous expansion of research facilities has occurred within the past two years as a result of the lease of a large building in the former Charlestown Navy Yard; this addition is now known as MGH East.

The 1990 figures show the hospital had 1,081 beds, 35,019 admissions, 19,240 inpatient operations, 7,863 day operations, 1,954 active staff, 470 residents, 270 clinical fellows, 504 research fellows, 2,285 registered nurses, operating revenues of $538,835,000 and a surplus of $6,457,000. This improvement in finances contrasted with a loss of nearly $3 million in 1989.[2]

The whole physical plant of the MGH has improved dramatically in recent years. Much of the impetus for this change has been due to the director—J. Robert Buchanan, M.D.—who was appointed in 1982. He has been aided by innumerable donors in the recent, very successful drive. The Board of Trustees and its chairman—W. Nicholas Thorndike, the Corporation, the professional staff, employees and friends, were ably assisted by Lawrence E. Martin (Senior Vice-President), Mrs. Jane Claflin, and W. Gerald Austen; all of them deserve individual credit for success of the drive. As a result, the Ellison tower now dominates the campus.[3]

Just as Joseph Garland observed a half-century ago, loyalty to the Massachusetts General Hospital appears to be a characteristic common to all who are associated with it. Our graduates demostrate persistent loyalty though they may live far away. Over three hundred persons attended a two-day meeting of past surgical residents that was hosted by Dr. Austen in 1991.

The *U.S. News & World Report* in 1990 printed a special article on the best hospitals in the country. The text was based on a questionnaire sent to 400 physician specialists in the United States. Fifty-seven hospitals were listed as the best in the country; eleven were chosen as the best of the best. They were the Mayo Clinic, Johns Hopkins Hospital, Duke University Hospital, the Massachusetts General Hospital, the University of California in Los Angeles Medical Center, the

Above: Late nineteenth-century surgeons as portrayed in 1964 by young MGH surgeons. Left to right, (sitting): Gordon Donaldson, John McKittrick, Fiorindo Simeone, Howard Ulfelder, Carroll Miller; (standing) Francis Moore, Claude Welch, Lamar Soutter. Below: Visiting surgeons, MGH, 1953–1960, (left to right) Richard H. Sweet, Grantley W. Taylor, Robert R. Linton, Edward D. Churchill (Chief of the Surgical Service), CEW, Joe V. Meigs, Marshall K. Bartlett, Oliver Cope, Leland S. McKittrick; (below) Horatio Rogers, Howard Ulfelder.

Chiefs of the MGH Surgical Service: Paul S. Russell, Chief Surgical Service MGH 1962–1968, Visiting Surgeon MGH, John Homans Professor of Surgery HMS (left); W. Gerald Austen, Chief, Surgical Service MGH 1968-, Visiting Surgeon MGH, Edward D. Churchill Professor of Surgery HMS (right).

Visiting surgeons of the MGH from the post- World War II years who served as models for the next generation. Above: Leland S. McKittrick, general surgeon, medical statesman, died 1978, (left); Oliver Cope, general surgeon with particular interest in surgery of the thyroid, parathyroid, and burns, Professor of Surgery Emeritus HMS (right). Below: Robert Linton, general surgeon who became an eminent pioneer vascular surgeon, died 1979 (left); Richard H. Sweet, general surgeon who became a distinguished chest surgeon, died 1962 (right).

Visiting surgeons, MGH and distinguished professors of surgery, Harvard Medical School. Above: Hermes C. Grillo, Visiting Surgeon and Chief of the General Thoracic Service, MGH, who first in the world made the trachea amenable to surgery (left); Ronald A. Malt, Visiting Surgeon and Chief of Gastrointestinal Surgery, MGH, a true general surgeon, scholar and savant of the arcane, and noted in particular because he was the first individual to head the team which performed the first replantation in the world of a human extremity in 1962 (right). Below: John F. Burke, Visiting Surgeon, MGH, former Chief of the Shriners Burn Institute, Helen Andrus Benedict Professor of Surgery, HMS, who performed some of the seminal investigations on the use of antibiotics in surgery, and on the production and use of artificial skin (left); Leslie W. Ottinger, Visiting Surgeon, MGH, and Associate Professor of Surgery, HMS, a true general surgeon, whose immense contributions to teaching of residents are concealed by his modesty (right).

Senior Visiting Surgeons of the MGH. Above: J. Gordon Scannell with wife Helen. Dr. Scannell is clinical Professor of Surgery Emeritus, HMS, thoracic surgeon, author and Editor of the Harvard Medical Alumni Bulletin for many years (left); Gordon A. Donaldson with his wife Elizabeth, general surgeon, who, in this picture had just delivered the Presidential Address to the New England Surgical Society, died 1983 (right). Below: Chiu-an Wang, Clinical Professor of Surgery Emeritus HMS, noted surgeon of the parathyroid glands (left); Marshall K. Bartlett with Cary W. Akins (right). Dr. Bartlett is Clinical Professor of Surgery Emeritus HMS and was an extremely busy general surgeon; Dr. Akins is one of the talented young cardiovascular surgeons, Visiting Surgeon MGH and Associate Clinical Professor of Surgery HMS.

MGH Visiting Surgeons Above: Glenn Behringer, now retired, general surgeon, with his wife Joan, in Russia where he headed a tour of American
surgeons (left); Bradford Cannon, Clinical Professor of Surgery Emeritus,
HMS, who has made numerous contributions to the budding specialty of
plastic surgery during his lifetime (right). Below: Andrew Warshaw, Visiting
Surgeon MGH, Harold and Ellen Danser Professor of Surgery, HMS, general
surgeon, but interested particularly in the pancreas and in laparascopic surgery
both in the laboratory and in patient care (left); Ashby C. Moncure, Associate
Clinical Professor of Surgery HMS, a true general surgeon, at home anywhere
in the body, whose advice is eagerly sought by residents whenever they need
help (right).

MGH Senior Visiting Surgeons. Above: Stephen Hedberg, Associate Visiting Surgeon, facile general surgeon and skilled endoscopist, whose life was ended at an early age by fulminant acute hepatitis (left); W. Hardy Hendren, now Professor of Surgery HMS and Chief of Surgery Boston Childrens Hospital, but previously Chief of Pediatric Surgery, MGH, with a particular interest in urologic problems (right). Below: Earl W. Wilkins, now retired, Clinical Professor of Surgery Emeritus HMS, thoracic surgeon for many years, and later, director of the Emergancy Ward, MGH (left); R. Clement Darling, Jr., Associate Clinical Professor Surgery Emeritus, HMS, talented vascular surgeon, MGH (right).

Above: Two HMS Nobel Laureates. Charles B. Huggins (left) and Joseph E. Murray (right). Below: Two eminent patients and friends. Thomas D. with Virginia Cabot (left) and Mrs. Louise Pierce (right).

University of Washington Medical Center, the Barnes Hospital, the Cleveland Clinic, the Columbia-Presbyterian Medical Center, the Stanford University Hospital, and the University of California in San Francisco Medical Center.

A special section was devoted to the MGH. The writers said: "The MGH philosophy stresses the human side of medicine. Patients are seen as human beings who need help, not as machines that need fixing."[4] In a subsequent note to the editors, the director of the hospital, Dr. Buchanan, pointed out that the only reason the MGH did not have first place in the listing was because of a lack of specialists in ophthalmology, otolaryngology, and rehabilitation. These deficits are meaningless because of the very close affiliation of the MGH with the Massachusetts Eye and Ear Infirmary and the Spaulding Rehabilitation Center, both of which are nearby.

In a similar report in 1991 the *U.S. News & World Report* specified ten hospitals as the most outstanding of the 6,700 in the United States. They were the Johns Hopkins Hospital, the Mayo Clinic, the Massachusetts General Hospital, the UCLA Medical Center, the Cleveland Clinic, the Brigham and Women's Hospital, the Memorial Sloan-Kettering Cancer Center, the Duke University Hospital, the Stanford University Hospital, and the University of California Hospital in San Francisco.[5]

Continued renovation in the future will be necessary to keep the hospital abreast with the demands of universal health care. Construction of the second tower is the next major task. It is projected to be completed in October, 1994. At that time twenty-one beds will be devoted to obstetrics, a specialty that has been absent from the hospital since World War II. The Hospital has recently acquired the old prison that is adjacent to one of the parking garages on Fruit street; its destiny has not yet been decided. Within another year all offices should be equipped with computers, so information will be readily available from all important departments such as laboratories, pathology, and radiology. As soon as these tasks are completed another program is sure to be on the drawing board. Improved patient care will demand continual change throughout the foreseeable future.

Despite rumors of coming financial difficulties for all hospitals, the MGH will continue to plan for the future. Hospitals are a national resource; they cannot be allowed to founder unless they fail to use their facilities efficiently. The trustees are certain that the Massachusetts General Hospital Hospital will serve the public even more effectively in the future than it has in the past.

22

Looking Backward and Forward

As I near the end of my active career and survey what I have done during my life, I wonder if my actions actually have contributed anything to the profession of medicine and whether I, personally, have done anything to make my fellow citizens happier and more productive or the Earth a better place on which to live. Maturity leads me to recognize more clearly the debt I owe to my predecessors, and to my colleagues at home and abroad for stimulating my own additions to their original discoveries. I continue to marvel at the enormous advances that have taken place in the field of medicine and surgery during my lifetime. Gazing into the future I like to speculate about possible solutions to current problems and whether or not the promises of basic science and molecular biology will be fulfilled. Such retrospective conclusions and philosophic musings form this last chapter.

First, let us recognize that we owe great debts to our predecessors and to our colleagues both in America and abroad. Many of the ideas we call our own have sprouted from seeds implanted by others. One of the most rewarding features of a surgeon's life is furnished by personal relationships with his peers; they burgeon among surgeons who throughout the world are engaged in the same duties and have the same goals. These friendships not only serve to transfer information and stimulate discovery, but are one of the most important items that attest to the fellowship of surgeons. We must marvel at the enormous advances and changes that have occurred in medicine and surgery in the twentieth century. A list of technical surgical advances alone would fill many pages. In addition there have been important socioeconomic developments. If asked to cite the twenty most outstanding in the twentieth century, I would answer with the following list:

1. A dramatic extension of the average length of life in the United States.
2. An enormous increase in the percentage of the gross national product devoted to health care.
3. The rise of scientific medicine that has led to laboratory and clinical research and the replacement of many of the methods of prevention of disease, and diagnosis and treatment of illness.
4. The entry of women into all branches of health care, including doctors of medicine in all specialties.
5. Increasing involvement of the government, the courts, and the legal system in the United States in the practice of medicine.
6. Gradual replacement of general practitioners by specialists and subspecialists.
7. Diminution in the number of solo practitioners and development of group practices, particularly in a single specialty.
8. The growth of insurance to cover the costs of medical care.
9. The concept that medical education must continue throughout the postgraduate life of a physician.
10. The erosion of Aesculapian authority, coupled with a great increase in personal health care and critical appraisal by the public of medical facts and theories.
11. An epidemic of malpractice suits.
12. The near eradication of major epidemics such as poliomyelitis, probably total eradication of smallpox, and control of many other infections.
13. The development of new diseases such as AIDS, drug dependencies, and Alzheimer's disease, which are still completely uncontrolled.[1]
14. A dramatic change in hospital activities. Lengths of patient stays have been shortened for nearly all diseases and procedures. Relatively simple operations now are done in ambulatory facilities. Expensive machines such as equipment for computerized tomography and magnetic resonance imaging are standard equipment; many hospitals have extensive research programs. Hospital costs have escalated enormously because of these factors.
15. The generous support of research by the Federal Government and to an increasing degree by industry.

16. Neonatal care requiring high technology.
17. Improved methods of anesthesia and respiratory care.
18. Cardiac surgery.
19. Organ transplantation.
20. Expansion of pharmaceuticals and instrumentation, e.g., flexible endoscopy and laparoscopic procedures.

The results of these major trends in medicine have been far more extensive than all that occurred during the previous history of medicine and much of it has occurred in the United States. Perhaps the most important measure by which the contributions of a nation to medical science can be judged is by the percentage of Nobel prize winners in each country. The United States continues to do very well in that respect.[2] Harvard has had eighteen winners in Medicine or Physiology; in surgery, it can claim Charles Huggins and Joseph Murray.

My own important activities have involved patient care, teaching, clinical research, establishment of funds to maintain such activities, promotion of all aspects of medical education, and strengthening of ties between the government, the courts, the legal profession and physicians.

One of the greatest pleasures for a clinical surgeon is to assist the recovery of patients who subsequently go on to serve the community and the nation. A large number of such individuals that I have treated personally deserve mention, but I shall list only three outstanding examples.

The first is Thomas D. Cabot, a legendary Bostonian. My first indication of his vigor occurred when, a few days after he had been discharged from the hospital following a difficult operation, he found the elevator to my office not running as rapidly as he deemed it should. In order to keep the surgeon from waiting, he walked, or ran, up the stairs—all eleven flights.

In the following years he followed the same pattern he had developed previously—independence of thought, magnificent initiative, and, above all, an overwhelming desire and ability to improve the world in which he lived. Supported in his herculean efforts by his wife, Virginia, not only Harvard University but Massachusetts Institute of Technology, Harvard Medical School, the Brigham and Women's Hospital, and the MGH have been major beneficiaries of his leadership and his ability to raise funds to support his ideals. The MGH ambulatory surgical suite was a gift from him and his wife; their portrait hangs there. His autobiography *A Beggar on Horseback*—is a stirring account of his exploits and successes.[3] He is a prime example of a person who has made Boston a community that is unique because personal gain is subordinate to community service. Even now, in his nineties, he continues to offer sage advice to many organizations, increases his illustrious contributions, and furnishes a remarkable role model for coming generations.

The second is Mrs. Louise Pierce. She has been one of my most remarkable patients since we first became acquainted over fifty years ago. Despite a long series of serious operations, her vitality and the rock-ribbed individualism typical of Vermonters has kept her vigorous and active in multiple activities despite her age and disabilities. After the death of her husband and raising her family, her youthful spirit has led her to serve others in ventures such as the Boston Opera Company. In her late eighties, she spent her spare time making a beautiful needlepoint of the Vermont state seal. This work of art now hangs in the governor's office in Montpelier. Never daunted by physical ills, she has been a model of industry, intellectual versatility, youth, and instant empathy with all whom she encounters.

The third is His Holiness Pope John Paul II. The story of his illness began on a Wednesday evening, May 13, 1981 when he was shot twice at close range by an assassin. Three days later, in the midst of a dinner party in our home, I was called away from the table several times by telephone calls from Dr. Kevin Cahill in New York City to ask me to accompany him to Rome on the following day to consult with the physicians and surgeons who were caring for the Pope. Plans were made quickly. We were met at La Guardia airport by His Eminence Terence Cardinal Cooke who took us in his car to the Kennedy airport and parked in a VIP space immediately next to the TWA terminal. We were treated royally by the airline crew. Early the following morning, in the airport near Rome, we were whisked through customs, taken first to our hotel and then driven immediately to the Gemelli Clinic of the Catholic University.[4]

We spent several hours going over all of the clinical history with Professor Castiglioni and examining His Holiness. Despite His grievous wounds—if the bullet that struck him in the abdomen had been only an inch closer to the midline, it would have been fatal—He had an air of equanimity and peace that reduced any medical problems to secondary importance. It was not long afterward that other consultants appeared from other countries. Long conferences followed and details of further treatment were outlined. Every person agreed that the Italian surgeons had done a remarkable operative procedure under very difficult circumstances, with members of the press crowding into the operating room. The consultants then spoke a few words with the Pope. We held further consultations and wrote a press release.

Dr. Cahill and I stayed in Rome for a few days, during which we visited the Pope numerous times, and also consulted with the surgeons who were caring for the two wounded Americans who were in the Sancta Spiritu Hospital near the Vatican. We were impressed not only with the professional care in both hospitals but also with the ultra-modern facilities in the Gemelli Clinic.

Some time after my return to Boston, I received a letter from Pope John Paul II; it hangs in my study and is one of my most treasured possessions. It is a remarkable tribute from the greatest spiritual leader in the world today. It says:

> To Professor Claude E. Welch:
> Now that I have almost completely resumed the normal exercise of my pastoral ministry, it gives me great pleasure to express my gratitude to you for placing your esteemed medical expertise at my disposal, in a spirit of generous collaboration, to hasten the coming of this long awaited moment.
> Dominant among the thoughts that repeatedly came to me during the period of my stay in the hospital was a sense of thankfulness to all those, like yourself, who, even at great personal sacrifice spared no effort to further my full recovery.
> I gladly avail myself of the occasion to express my esteem and to assure you of my prayers for you and your work for the good of humanity. Invoking upon you the abundant graces of Almighty God, I gladly impart to you and your family my special Apostolic Blessing.
> (Signed) Johannus Paulus II
>   Castelgondolfo, October 4, 1981

Continuing medical education throughout a physician's life is a necessity. A brief review of all the major educational organizations with which I have been involved since 1960 has strengthened my strong belief in that statement over the years. A seven-year stint on the Residency Review Committee for Surgery as a representative of the AMA and the four years I spent as the chairman of the program committee for the annual and semiannual meetings of the American College of Surgeons allowed me to contribute to this goal. In 1975 when I was chairman of the Board of Medicine, we made continuing medical education (CME) a requirement for licensure in Massachusetts, and subsequent Boards have continued the practice.

Another seven year appointment to the review committee that certifies institutions for continuing medical education (i.e., education after medical school and residency) under the Accrediting Council for Continuing Medical Education (ACCME) was my last important assignment. The ACCME now reviews several hundred organizations engaged in this process; continuing medical education has become a multi-billion dollar project.

My absorption in clinical research has also been described in previous chapters. The obligation of a surgeon to one of his residents does not end with instruction in the art and techniques of surgery. Students must be taught to be involved in such research—to study their patients, identify problems, carry out pertinent studies, prepare papers, and present them to critical audiences. I have been able to organize at least eight such studies and have them accepted for presentations by my residents before either of two prestigious organizations—the American Surgical Association or the New England Surgical Society.

I will mention two of these papers as examples. The first presentation was by John Burke, who was working with me in 1962. One of our anesthesiologists, Henning Pontoppidan, had started the first surgical respiratory unit in the United States in 1955 and surgeons were beginning to learn that respiratory failure was leading to the death of many ill postoperative patients. It was difficult for us to recognize that patients were dying of respiratory failure when their lungs appeared to be clear by X-ray. Nor was it easy to believe blood gases could be of more importance than white blood cell counts in respiratory wards.

Nevertheless we had become convinced that respiratory failure was the cause of death in many patients who appeared to be dying of peritonitis. The paper that we wrote and he gave in 1963 in the meeting of the American Surgical Association emphasized the value of intratracheal tubes in such patients. Essentially no one else had any such cases to report, but in a year or two nearly every teaching hospital had a respiratory ward and blood gases were obtainable.

Among the large number of seriously ill surgical cases referred to me from 1950 to 1960, intestinal fistulas proved to be very difficult to handle. We had antibiotics at the time but hyperalimentation via subclavian lines was not available. Together with two of my residents—Henry Edmunds and Melville Williams—we studied a large number of cases. We concluded that earlier operations to restore intestinal function were necessary to restore electrolyte balance and prevent death from starvation.

Henry Edmunds was chosen to give the paper before the American Surgical Association in 1960. Knowing that exactly ten minutes would be allowed for the presentation, he memorized the text and practiced it again and again before a professional critic. He repeated the procedure the night before he was due to appear with Phyllis as an audience, holding a stop watch in her hand, while the other members reveled at the annual dinner. He concluded his speech with acclaim the following day—in nine minutes and fifty-nine seconds.

I take great pride in the residents I helped train in the MGH. Remarkably enough, whenever they start their recollections, I am always remembered for my many operations and as a person not averse to mopping the operating room floor to prevent loss of precious time between procedures.

Finally, in the past twenty-five years, promotion of a satisfactory relationship of the medical profession with the legal profession, the courts and the government has been a major goal in my life. It has been described amply in the previous chapters as an onerous but important task.

A legacy for the future is a common concern for all surgeons. Nearly every person eventually hopes to leave one or more mementos, either minor or major, of his professional life. They may be intensely personal, such as beliefs or credos. Some can be more substantial, such as gifts or funds for various purposes. Again I will give some personal examples.

As noted in the previous chapter, in 1981 the chief of the department of surgery, W. Gerald Austen, established funds that permit five scholarships to be offered every year to surgical residents who wish to spend a year or more in surgical research. One was named in my honor.[5] Another large fund—the Claude E. Welch Fund for Surgical Research and Education—has been established from donations from hundreds of patients. It will be enlarged greatly in the future from other very generous gifts. These funds are placed in the charge of the chief of the surgical services and should furnish further opportunities for residents, either for basic research or education. Very generous contributions have been received from patients who have been close friends for many decades; Miss Ida Littlefield, Donaldson Jones, Herman Milhandler, and Henry Hermann are examples.

My other hopes for the future are very individualistic and may not be accepted by everyone, because they are based on my beliefs relating to a few major ethical problems.

I regret abortions, but I believe that a woman should make her own choice after she has been completely informed by her physician prior to any decision.

I believe retirement of a physician should not be based on chronological age but on physiologic ability. However, I recognize that in countries such as England and Scandinavia an age for retirement must be set to allow the coming generation adequate opportunity; fortunately that day has not yet arrived in the United States. Ways should be found for elderly individuals who are in robust health and normal mental status to pursue some worthwhile endeavor, preferably in a field in which they still can contribute.

I believe that aged persons with incurable diseases should be allowed to die quietly without the intervention of soulless machines. I believe physicians have the right to relieve them from pain to make death comfortable, but this right cannot be abused. Sanction by the family and some group such as an Ethics Committee is necessary before life support is refused or withdrawn.

There is already a great deal of concern with aging, and the problem promises to become even worse in the future. Some persons regard it as a disease, particularly when such persons place a heavy drain on the health resources of the nation. I believe it should be regarded in a different light. Oldsters can be very productive in society, particularly if items such as lens implantation for loss of sight or joint replacements for pain and disability are provided. On the other hand, the aged can do society and themselves a great deal of good by subscribing to a right-to-die document or a living will that can be activated in the presence of a fatal disease that has brought them into the intensive care ward of a hospital.

Economic vistas of the future are particularly hazy. I hope that physicians will have more freedom in the future than they have in these days of intense regulation when the clouds of malpractice hang low over the profession. I believe the American public is not ready (and probably never will be) for a one-tier type of medical practice in which all citizens receive the same benefits. It would not be accepted by many individuals who not only want creature comforts but also can pay for them. As a corollary, I hope that some type of balance billing will be allowed to permit extra charges for the wealthy or for difficult procedures; I believe that such a privilege will not be abused by greedy practitioners.

I think the nation is moving slowly toward some type of national health insurance. Access to care by the poor must be improved; this task means implementing a different system without the plethora of gatekeepers now in existence and it also means support of hospitals by the government. Furthermore, physicians and patients are so disgusted with the present system of checks and balances and different types of insurance, together with the enormous administrative costs that are involved (nearly twenty-five percent of all costs for health care), that they will be anxious to accept a system promising something simpler and more likely to be stable. However, the benefits that can be offered under a universal system will have to be relatively sparse or, as John Larkin Thompson has pointed out, the costs will be impossible to accept.[6]

New challenges arise every day. However, I have every hope for the future. The young surgical residents are brilliant, make few mistakes in diagnosis, and, even if not initially adept, are certain to do well if an expert anesthesiologist can provide them the necessary time and technical tutelage is available when necessary. They are far more competent than my generation was at their age. They are not aware of the advantages of what we oldsters remember as the golden age of medical practice.

Despite the present emphasis on economy, many of the institutions that we treasure must be maintained. Medical schools must stress the humanities as well as science. Hospitals must be kept solvent and intact as prime locations for care of the very ill; surgeons cannot carry out their most difficult procedures in any other locale. Nor can the education of surgical residents be done satisfactorily outside hospital walls.

At the time this book is being written, a strong wave of interest in a plan of national health insurance promises that it will not be many years before some type of coverage will be available for all citizens in this country. Congressional committees, the AMA, and the Blue Cross-Blue Shield are among the groups considering such plans. It will be expensive, and it may take some time, but it is absolutely necessary that this blot on our health care program be eliminated.

In the long run, the golden age of medicine actually lies in the future, provided that the major institutions in our present system are not allowed to wither, funds provided for research are allowed to continue unabated, and the practitioner listens to his patients rather than merely punching the keys of his computer. However, for the next decade at least, Americans, and physicians in particular, must concentrate on socioeconomic problems. Perhaps the public is asking for the impossible from our profession. Medicine cannot be expected to guarantee long lives for all of our citizens, free from pain and distress, but it must do its best.

The United States does not have a unified national system. Medicaid benefits (which apply to patients whose income is in the poverty level) vary from state to state; the Federal contribution varies as well on the basis of these benefits. Most states allow balance billing for Medicare patients; a few others, including Massachusetts, have abolished balance billing for these patients by law. Balance billing in the entire United States for Medicare patients will be reduced in a few years, according to present HCFA plans. Furthermore, reduction in the amount of money paid for a wide variety of services or procedures will be sharply reduced for Medicare patients.

The social laboratories that provide us with the greatest amount of information about systems of universal coverage are in Canada and in Great Britain.

The Canadian system theoretically allows easy access. However, several methods of rationing of health care are in effect. Many of the "big ticket" items, such as cardiac surgery and high technology items, are limited with respect to the number of patients who can be accommodated. The great majority of Canadian physicians and surgeons also appear very unhappy that they must accept fees set by government; billing for an additional amount above that given by the government (so-called balance billing) is not allowed. In other words, all recipients of government payments are treated equally; this is the so-called one-tier system of care. Restriction of funds for research could imperil necessary advances in medicine.

The British system now is undergoing spectacular readjustments on the basis of their experience in the last forty years. Established originally as a capitation system, in which every citizen was allowed something like four pounds a year for medical care, private practice has slowly but steadily become the choice for an increasing number of individuals. This change has been due to the prolonged periods of waiting for necessary operations in many localities and the fact that many people, especially those with adequate funds, wish more personal treatment than is offered by the National Service.

If all the provisions of the plan that was outlined in 1989 eventually are activated, all citizens are qualified to receive increased capitation benefits, although the amount and method of obtaining funds was not specified. The total amount spent for health care still will be far less than that in the United States.

Private surgeons performed seventeen percent of all elective operations in England in 1989; they receive the blessing of the government because they remove some of the strains on the National Health Service. In fact, it was suggested that patients who use the private sector (approximately nine percent of the population of the United Kingdom) should receive a reduction in their income taxes. It also is suggested that those patients in the National Service who want extra creature comforts when in a hospital, such as telephones or private rooms, should have them and pay for them. These measures are tacit approvals of a two-tier system of medical care; persons who want and enjoy extra benefits should pay for them, whether they be professional or comfort fees.

A remarkable provision of the plan is that individuals enrolled in the National Health Service are given free choice of the general practitioners they wish to have or the hospitals to which they wish to be admitted. This choice certainly is not the case in the United States. We are moving in the opposite direction. For example, if our patients are enrolled in an HMO or similar organization there is a strictly limited list of doctors they may see or hospitals to which they can be admitted. Patients with Blue Cross-Blue Shield coverage have a much wider choice.

According to the plan, approximately twenty-five hospitals in Great Britain would be named immediately as "hospital trusts." They will be essentially autonomous. They will be picked on the basis of excellence. They must furnish essentially immediate admission to all emergency, and most surgical and medical patients; thus the hospitals that have very short waiting lists are likely to be chosen. Presumably they would be able to audit their own activities. The number of hospital trusts will be increased as others qualify for the privilege.

Bureaucracies thrive in all health care organizations. At present in Great Britain there is an administrative body comprised of District Medical Authorities. Above them is a higher administrative tier that is composed of twelve Regional Medical Authorities; this body will be eliminated.

Competition is considered to be a key component of cost control.

Advertising by physicians and hospitals is applauded. In summary, the latest British system has many attractive features. Competition, replacement of a one-tier by a two-tier medical system that tolerates and applauds private practice, absolute free choice by individuals enrolled in the national system of local practitioners and hospitals, rewards for hospitals that accept all emergencies and eliminate waiting lists by making them essentially autonomous as Hospital Trusts, concentrating audit (or peer review) in individual hospitals, and elimination of one of the large bureaucracies in the medical system deserve commendation and, in my opinion, adoption in the United States. Assuming that the plan goes forward on schedule, both patients and hospitals could be freed of many restraints that are becoming progressively more strict in the United States.[7]

As this book nears its final pages, the reader may have noted that the text has concentrated on the MGH and on surgery rather than upon personal details. Descriptions of family life intentionally have been omitted. However, a few words are apropos because a happy family life is an important goal for every person. At the present time, Phyllis continues her work as a good samaritan. She has been intensely interested in the work of the Boston Museum of Fine Arts. She was a member of the Ladies Committee for many years, the chairman of the committee for two, and now is an Honorary Overseer of the Museum. In her spare time she has been a volunteer in the MGH and in the Belmont town library. Now she supervises the library and flower arrangements in Fox Hill Village, a retirement complex built by the MGH.

Claude, Jr., Professor of Political Economy in the State University of New York in Buffalo, recently was appointed the sole Distinguished Service Professor in the school that holds some 25,000 students. He has been very active in the Human Rights movement, is an international authority, and has written a dozen books. His first wife, Nancy Edwards, bore four children, and died at age 38 of cancer of the breast. His second wife, Jeannette Ludwig, is a Professor of French in the University.

John is a Professor of Clinical Surgery in the University of Connecticut. The most important of his numerous publications is an encyclopedic volume on intestinal obstruction. His wife, Marylouise, teaches nurses and earned a Ph. D. in that subject a year ago.

Of the six grandchildren Martha, a graduate of Harvard, is now a student in the Medical School of the University of Connecticut. Elisabeth's work has taken her over the entire world. Sarah is an ecologist and recently obtained an M.A. from the University of Washington. The three grandsons, all excellent students and athletes, are still in school.

Family contacts are very close, and are cemented by summer vacations together in our camp on Lake Winnepesaukee. It is very comforting in these days when the entire world is full of problems and changing so rapidly to realize that this beautiful lake, an emblem of stability, probably has been just as lovely as it is today for over ten thousand years.

Table 22.1   Nobel prize winners, HMS and MGH

Name	Degree	Year	Prize	Subject
George R. Minot	MD	1934	P or M	Liver for primary anemia
W. P. Murphy	MD	1934	P or M	Liver for primary anemia
Edward A. Doisy	PhD	1943	P or M	Chemistry, vitamin K
J. B. Sumner	PhD	1946	Chem	Crystallized urease
Fritz A. Lipmann	MD	1953	P or M	Co-enzyme-A (MGH)
John F. Enders	PhD	1954	P or M	Grew polio viruses
F. C. Robbins	MD	1954	P or M	Grew polio viruses
Thomas Weller	MD	1954	P or M	Grew polio viruses
Chas. B. Huggins	MD	1966	P or M	Hormonal Rx Ca prostate
C. B. Anfinsen	PhD	1972	Chem	Protein formation
D. C. Gajdusek	MD	1976	P or M	Delayed action viruses
B. Benacerraf	MD	1980	P or M	Immunology
David Hubel	MD	1981	P or M	Visual system
Torsten Wiesel	MD	1981	P or M	Visual system
*B. Lown et al.	MD	1985	Peace	Anti-nuclear war
**Michael S. Brown	MD	1985	P or M	Cholesterolemia
**J. L. Goldstein	MD	1985	P or M	Cholesterolemia
G. H. Hitchings	PhD	1988	P or M	Drug treatment principles
J. M. Bishop	MD	1989	P or M	Cells mutate to cancer
Joseph E. Murray	MD	1990	P or M	Transplantation Kidney
E. D. Thomas	MD	1990	P or M	Transplantation Marrow

P or M = Physiology or Medicine
* Joint award with International Physicians for Prevention of Nuclear War;
** Former medical resident, MGH.

Ten surgeons have received the Nobel prize; only two (Huggins and Murray) were born in the United States. Carrel was born in France; he later moved to the United States and did his important work in this country.

Table 22.2   Surgeons who received Nobel prizes

Year	Surgeon	Specialty	Country	Discovery
1909	Kocher	General Surgery	Switzerland	Thyroid surgery
1911	Gullstrand	Ophthalmology	Sweden	Dioptics
1912	Carrel	Vascular	France*	Vascular suture
1914	Barany	Otoneurology	Austria	Vestibular system
1923	Banting	Orthopedics	Canada	Insulin
1945	Fleming	Surgery	England	Penicillin
1949	Hess	Ophthalmology	Switzerland	Brain function
1956	Forssman	Urology	Germany	Cardiac catheterization
1966	Huggins	Urology	USA	Cancer prostate; hormone treatment
1990	Murray	Plastic surgery	USA	Organ transplantation

* Most important work done in United States.

For a discussion of these medalists, see J. B. Morris and W. J. Schirmer, "The 'Right Stuff': Five Nobel Prize-Winning Surgeons," *Surgery* 1990; 108: 71–80. The remaining five were added in the correspondence section in the June, 1991 issue.

Our Leaders, who provide Direction. Above: J. Robert Buchanan, Director of the Massachusetts General Hospital since 1982. Below: Lawrence Martin, Associate Director since 1971 (left); Jane Claflin, Trustee, whose intense interest in the MGH and particularly in the recent drive for new buildings has endeared her to the whole MGH Community.

Young surgical specialists assume control: Above: Richard P.Cambria, Associate Visiting Surgeon MGH, Associate Professor of Surgery HMS (left), and David C. Brewster, Visiting Surgeon MGH, Associate Clinical Professor of Surgery HMS, vascular surgeons (left); Willard M. Daggett, Visiting Surgeon MGH, Professor of Surgery HMS, cardiac surgeon (right). Below: Mortimer J. Buckley, Chief of Cardiac Surgery and Visiting Surgeon MGH, Professor of Surgery HMS, (left); William M. Abbott, Chief of Vascular Surgery and Visiting Surgeon MGH, Professor of Surgery HMS (right).

More young surgical stars. Above: A. Benedict Cosimi, Chief of Clinical Transplantation and Visiting Surgeon MGH, Professor of Surgery HMS (left); Patricia E. Donahoe, Chief of Pediatric Surgery, MGH, Professor of Surgery, HMS, the first woman appointed as Professor of Surgery (1986) in the MGH. Below: James W. May, Jr., Chief of Plastic Surgery and Visiting Surgeon MGH, Associate Clinical Professor of Surgery HMS, (left); Ronald G. Tompkins, Chief, Shriners Burns Institute, Associate Visiting Surgeon MGH, Associate Professor of Surgery HMS (right).

Family pictures: Above: Phyllis, about 1960 (left); Son John (left) and CEW (right) operating in the MGH about 1970 (right). Below: Son Claude and family 1982 (left to right, Elisabeth, Claude Jr., Sarah, Christopher, Martha, Jeannette) (left); Son John and family 1982 (left to right, Evan, John, Tyler, Marylouise) (right).

Above: CEW receiving the Trustees Medal from W. Nicholas Thorndike, Chairman of the Board of Trustees of the Massachusetts General Hospital, 1991. Below: Recipients of Trustees Medals, 1991. (Left to right) Daniel C. Tosteson, Dean of the Harvard Medical School; J. Michael Bishop, Professor of Microbiology in the University of California at San Francisco; CEW.

Phyllis and CEW with the Matterhorn in the background, Zermatt, Switzerland.

23

The Trustees' Medal

Every narrative finally must end. When this personal story was begun, the end point was specified to be January 1, 1991. However, in September, 1990 I was notified that I would be given an important award on February 25, 1991. It therefore seems appropriate to describe it in the final note.

The charter that gave permission to construct the MGH was granted by the Great and General Court of the Commonwealth of Massachusetts on February 25, 1811. In 1986, at the annual dinner commemorating the granting of the charter the Trustees, for the first time, gave Trustees' Medals to four distinguished physicians. The 180th charter year dinner, the second one in which medals were given, was held in 1991, five years after the original celebration. In accord with the previous award, "the Trustees' Medal honors those American physicians and scientists whose lifetime contributions have uniquely benefited humankind, particularly through the advancement of medical care and practice."

The original honorees were Michael S. Brown, Joseph L. Goldstein, James A. Shannon, and Norman A. Shumway. Both Drs. Brown and Goldstein were Nobel prize recipients and had been previous medical residents in the MGH. Dr. Shannon had been a distinguished investigator and educator. He had made important contributions to public health and had received some thirty honorary degrees. Dr. Shumway had done what no person had succeeded in doing before—to make transplantation of the heart a safe and effective procedure.

In 1991 three physicians were granted the medal. They were J. Michael Bishop, Professor of Microbiology, Immunology, and Biochemistry, University of California at San Francisco, former medical resident in the MGH and a Nobel prize winner in 1990: Daniel C. Tosteson, Dean, Harvard Medical School: and Claude E. Welch, Honorary Surgeon, MGH.

Professor W. Gerald Austen, Chief of the Department of Surgery, wrote my citation which was read by the Chairman of the Board of Trustees, W. Nicholas Thorndike, as follows:

> Claude E. Welch, M.D., in 1928, after gaining your baccalaureate and master's degree with great distinction, you moved from the great plains of your native Nebraska to scale new academic heights at Harvard Medical School. Four years later you began a 60-year odyssey at the Massachusetts General Hospital, and five years later, in 1937, upon completing your residency, you joined the Harvard Medical Faculty.
>
> Throughout your long and distinguished professional career your patients always came first, but your allegiance to the MGH and Harvard came next. Indeed your work as a superb clinician-teacher, careful clinical researcher and prolific author of authoritative texts has gained you world wide respect as a master physician from your patients, students and academic peers alike. This was recognized by your progressive promotion through the ranks of the MGH professional staff and those of the Harvard faculty to gain the highest status in both.
>
> In further recognition of your leadership accomplishments, you have received multiple honors including three honorary degrees; you have been elected to the Presidency of the American Surgical Association, the American College of Surgeons, the Massachusetts Medical Society, and virtually all other prominent academically-rooted surgical societies. Moreover, you have been awarded the Nathan Smith Distinguished Service Award of the New England Surgical Society, the Bigelow Medal from the Boston Surgical Society, and the Roswell Park Medal of the Buffalo Surgical Society. All these honors are still more impressive when one realized that they are most commonly awarded to the Chairman of academic surgical departments.
>
> Accordingly, as an exemplary physician, teacher, elegant and extraordinary gentle-man and as a loyal contributor to the MGH that salutes you tonight, we recognize you as an example of our very best and most admired physician who has been a life-long model for patients, students, and peers.

I had prepared a brief response to be given if necessary. I did not need to read it, but it is an appropriate conclusion to this book:

I am deeply grateful for the honor you have conferred on me this evening. But I appreciate even more the opportunities you have given to me for nearly sixty-five years both by the HMS and the MGH. The medical school endowed me with a zest for medicine and surgery, life-long curiosity, and a devotion to the profession. The MGH provided me with role models—Drs. Arthur Allen and Edward Churchill were the most famous. And, among other gifts, the MGH was responsible for the most important event of my life. It was to meet Phyllis Paton, a student nurse, who for fifty-four years has been my devoted wife, and who properly should be seated where I am today. Ever since that first meeting, our lives have been entwined with the MGH.

As one ages, he becomes more philosophical. The great surgeon, Henry Jacob Bigelow, once said that institutions cannot make a man; they can only provide opportunities for development. The MGH has done this many times over. Grateful patients, opportunities for education and teaching, and contact with other workers in the vineyard of surgery have provided excitement and satisfaction. When considering colleagues, I feel similar to a tiny droplet of water on the crest of an ocean wave. For a few moments in the eternity of time, it is privileged to shimmer in the rays of the sun. It is well to note that this position on the top of the wave would be impossible were it not for the support of thousands of similar droplets below—my colleagues, my patients, my friends—who either have sparkled in the sun before, or later will replace me. So to you in this audience, I salute you and thank you deeply for the great honor you have bestowed on me today.

Appendices

Important Dates in Surgery, 20th Century

(This list is not intended to be complete. It includes, in particular, items mentioned in the text, or of special importance to those readers interested in HMS or MGH. Data covering other aspects of American Medicine can be obtained form Bowers and Purcell in *Advances in American Medicine: Essays at the Bicentennial*, from which many of these facts have been obtained.)

1900	Carrel	Began experiments on suture of blood vessels
1901	Landsteiner	Identifies four blood groups
1906		Dedication of the new Harvard Medical School
1908	Ehrlich	Nobel prize: discovered salvarsan, cure for syphilis
1908	Miles	Introduction of combined AP resection for cancer of the rectum
1908	Kausch	First use of intravenous glucose in surgical patients
1909	Kocher	Nobel prize: surgery of the thyroid gland
1912	Hartwell, Hoguet	Dog experiments proved replacement of vomitus by salt solution given by clysis prevented death from simple intestinal obstruction
1912	Flexner	Report on education in U.S. medical schools
1912	Carrel	Nobel prize for vascular surgery and tissue transplantation
1912	Kausch	First successful resection of head of pancreas and duodenum for cancer
1913	Martin	Founding of the American College of Surgeons
1918		Start of a major influenza epidemic
1921	Levin	Introduced nasogastric intubation
1923	Banting, MacLeod	Nobel prize: insulin for diabetes
1929	Magill	Introduction of intratracheal tube for anesthesia
1930	Landsteiner	Nobel prize: discovered blood groups

1932	Wangensteen, Paine	Introduction of continuous nasogastric suction
1933	Morgan	Nobel prize for discovery of the gene
1934	Minot, Murphy, Whipple	Nobel prize for treatment of pernicious anemia with liver
1935	Kendall	Discovery of cortisone
1935	Whipple	Pancreaticoduodenectomy rediscovered
1937	Krebs	Discovery of the Krebs cycle
1937	Crafoord	First clinical use of heparin for thrombosis
1938	Murray	Experimental use of heparin for arterial anastomosis
1938	Gross	Ligation of ductus arteriosus
1939	Domagh	Nobel prize for discovery of prontosil, forerunner of sulfanilimide
1939	Dam	Nobel prize: discovery vitamin K
1939	Doisy	Nobel prize: chemical nature, vitamin K
1940	Landsteiner, Weiner	Description of Rh factor
1940	Link	Discovery of dicumarol
1941	Florey	First clinical trials of penicillin
1941	Hertz	Radioactive iodine for Graves' disease
1941	Huggins	Estrogens and orchiectomy for cancer prostate
1941	Coons	Fluorescent labeling of antibodies.
1942	Churchill	Described use of first blood banks in army
1942	Red Cross	Began collection of blood
1942		Atomic energy released and controlled in chain reaction
1942	Gilman	Description of effect of nitrogen mustard on lymphoma
1942	Griffith, Johnson	Muscle relaxants (curare) used during anesthesia
1942	Dragstedt	Reintroduction of vagotomy
1943	Papanicolaou	Cytologic smears
1943	Waksman	Discovery of streptomycin.
1943	Kolff	Introduction of kidney dialysis in humans
1944	Blalock, Taussig	Operation on blue baby
1944		Early ambulation after surgery
1944		First woman admitted to Harvard Medical School
1945	Am Cancer Soc	Incorporated
1945	Hinshaw, Feldman	Streptomycin successful against human tuberculosis
1945		Promin therapy effective against leprosy

1945	Fleming, Florey, Chain	Nobel prize: discovery of penicillin
1946	Williams, Wycott	Viruses demonstrated by electron microscope, using shading technique
1946		Synthetic penicillin
1946		Hill-Burton Act passed
1946		Communicable Disease Center established in Atlanta
1946	Rabi	Nobel prize for discovery of MRI (magnetic resonance imaging)
1947		Artificial kidney: work started in Peter Bent Brigham Hospital
1947	Bing	Catheterization of coronary sinus
1947		Chloromycetin and aureomycin synthesized
1949	Moniz	Nobel prize for prefrontal lobotomy
1950	Kendall, Hench, Reichstein	Nobel prize for discovery of cortisone
1951	Hufnagel	First prosthetic heart valve in human
1952	Waksman	Nobel prize for discovery of streptomycin
1952	Dubost	Excision of aortic aneurysm with homograft
1953	Krebs	Nobel prize: citric acid cycle in metabolism of carbohydrates
1953	Lipmann	Nobel prize: coenzyme A
1953	Gibbons	First successful use of cardiopulmonary bypass in human.
1954	Murray	Successful renal transplant in monozygotic twin
1954	Enders, Weller, Robins	Nobel prize for discovery polio vaccine can grow in different tissue cultures
1955	Pontoppidan	First respiratory unit in USA
1955	Salk	Polio vaccine introduced
1955	Conn	Decription of adrenal adenoma producing primary aldosteronism
1955	DeBakey, Creech	Replacement of aortic aneurysm with homograft; first in USA
1956	Forssman	Nobel prize for cardiac catheterization 1956
1956	Tigo, Levan	Described 48 chromosomes in man
1956	Zoll	Introduction of external defibrillation
1957	Smithwick	Vagotomy-antrectomy for duodenal ulcer
1957	Edwards et al	Vagotomy-antrectomy for duodenal ulcer

1957	Li, Hertz, Spencer	Methotrexate for choriocarcinoma
1957	Freis, Hollander	Antihypertensive effect of thiazide derivatives
1957	Hirschowicz	Fiberoptic endoscopes
1957	Bovet	Nobel prize; synthetic curare
1958		First use of closed chest massage with mouth to mouth breathing for cardiac resuscitation
1959	Ochoa, Kornberg	Nobel prize for synthesis of DNA and RNA by enzymes
1960	Rock	Introduction of birth control pills
1962	Murray, Hitchings, Elion	Imuran developed and used
1960		Introduction of laser
1960	Burnet, Medawar	Nobel prize: discovery of acquired immunity for tissue transplants
1960	Berson, Yalow	Immunoassay of hormones
1961	Good, Miller	Thymectomy in newborn prevented development of immune system
1962	Lown	Electric conversion for cardiac arrhythmias
1962	Watson, Crick, Wilkins	Nobel prize for double helix form, DNA
1962	Malt	First replantation, human extremity (arm)
1962	Chang	Replantation of human extremity (hand)
1963		Community mental health act passed by Congress
1964		Establishment of Presidential Commission on heart disease, cancer and stroke (Chairman—DeBakey)
1964	Hardy	Transplant of chimpanzee heart into human
1964		National Library of Medicine introduced Medlar system
1964	Darling v. Charleston Community Memorial Hospital	(Hospital found responsible for patient care as well as doctor)
1965		Passage of Regional Medical Programs Act
1965		Passage of Medicare, Medicaid and Higher Education Act
1965		Countway Library opened in HMS

1966	Huggins	Treatment of cancer with hormones
1966	Rous	Proved virus a cause of chicken sarcoma
1966		Passage of Comprehensive Health Planning Act
1966	Parkman, Myer	Developed rubella vaccine
1967	Favaloro	First coronary artery bypass
1967	Barnard	First cardiac transplant
1968	Cotzias	L-dopa for treatment of Parkinson's
1968	Starzl	First orthotopic liver transplants with long-term survival
1968		Dornier introduced lithotripsy
1969	Dudrick, Wilmore, Vars, Rhoads	Intravenous hyperalimentation
1969		Introduction of vaccine against rubella
1969		Man walked on the moon
1970	Khorana	Synthesis of first artificial gene
1978	Herbst, Ulfelder	Diethylstilbesterol may cause cancer of vagina in daughters
1970		Implantation of first cardiac pacemaker
1971		HMOs approved by President Nixon
1971		National Medical Care established for renal dialysis
1972		Congress extended Medicare benefits to all persons with end stage renal disease
1973		Roe vs. Wade. Supreme Court decision liberalized indications for abortion
1974		National Health Planning and Resources Development Act
1974		Report of the Secretary of HEW on medical malpractice
1975		ASA-ACS SOSSUS report
1976		AMA Criteria for Care in Short-Stay Hospitals
1978		Statute in MA requiring information of all alternative methods of treatment be given to breast cancer patients
1980	Teutsch	Synthesis of mifepristone (RU 486), an antagonist to progesterone.
1982		Acquired immunodeficiency syndrome recognized and designated as AIDS
1985	Brown, Goldstein	Nobel prize; MGH Trustees' Medal 1986

1987		Balance billing of Medicare patients prohibited by statute in MA
1987		Care of Medicaid patients made compulsory by statute in MA as a condition of licensure
1987	Wideman v. Shallowford Hospital	Constitutional right to health care denied by courts Hospital
1988	Hsaio	Introduction of value based relative value scales
1988		AMA Adopted Hsaio report as basis for indemnity payments for physicians' bills provided balance billing is preserved
1988		Patrick vs. Burget decision by US Supreme Court defined limitations of peer review
1987	Mouret	Laparascopic cholecystectomy
1988	Dubois	Laparascopic cholecystectomy
1989	Bishop	Varmus Nobel prize for discovery of oncogenes for work done in 1975
1989		Omnibus Budget Reconciliation Act of 1989 changed Medicare fee schedule from usual, customary and reasonable to a resource based relative value scale
1990	Rosenberg et al	First transfer of a gene into human
1990	Murray	Nobel prize: first renal transplant in 1954; imuran used in patient
1990	Hitchings, Elion	Nobel prize for Imuran
1990	Thomas	Nobel prize: bone marrow transplant
1990		US Supreme Court decision in *Cruzan* case established right of an individual to appoint a proxy who later could refuse medical treatment in a hopeless situation
1990		Institute of Medicine study concluded PROS should stress quality of patient care rather than utilization. than utilization.

Reference Books of General Interest

American College of Surgeons *Factbook for Surgery* (Chicago: American College of Surgeons, 1977–). These handbooks have been published yearly since 1977. They provide important data on numerous socio-economic topics of interest particularly to surgeons, as well as discussions of the relations of the ACS to other groups, and policies of the organization.

American Foundation, *Medical Research: A Midcentury Survey* (Boston: Little Brown and Co., 1955).

Beecher H. K. and Altschule M., *Medicine at Harvard: The First 300 Years* (Hanover, NH: University Press of New England, 1977).

Bowers J. Z. and Purcell E. F., *Advances in American Medicine: Essays at the Bicentennial* (New York City: Josiah Macy Jr. Foundation, 1976).

Burrage W. L., *A History of the Massachusetts Medical Society 1781–1922* (Norwood, MA: Plimpton Press, 1923).

Castleman B., Crockett D. C. and Sutton S. B., The Massachusetts General Hospital 1955–1980 (Boston: Little Brown and Co, 1983).

Churchill E. D., *To Work in the Vineyard of Surgery: the Reminiscences of J. Collins Warren* (Cambridge, MA: Harvard University Press, 1956).

Faxon N. W., *The Massachusetts General Hospital 1935–1955* (Cambridge, MA: Harvard University Press, 1959).

Fulton J. F., *Harvey Cushing: a Biography* (Springfield Illinois,: C. C. Thomas, 1946).

Garland Joseph, *A Time for Remembering* (Boston: New England Journal of Medicine, 1972).

Garland J. E., *The Centennial History of the Boston Medical Library 1875–1975* (Boston: Boston Medical Library, 1975).

Rackemann F. M., *The Inquisitive Physician: The Life and Times of George Richards Minot,* (Cambridge, Massachusetts, Harvard University Press, 1956).

Ravitch M. M., *A Century of Surgery: The History of the American Surgical Association* (Philadelphia: J. B. Lippincott Co., 1981).

Spencer E. R., Jr., *A Society of Physicians. An Account of the Activities of the Members of the Massachusetts Medical Society 1923–1981* (Boston: Massachusetts Medical Society, 1981).

Starr P., The Social Transformation of American Medicine. (New York City: Basic Books, Inc., 1982).

Stephenson G. W., *American College of Surgeons at 75* (Chicago: American College of Surgeons, 1990).

Truax R., *The Doctors Warren of Boston* (Boston: Houghton Miflin Co., 1968).

Washburn F. A., *The Massachusetts General Hospital: Its Development 1900–1935* (Boston: Houghton Miflin Co., 1939).

Wangensteen O. H. and Wangensteen S. D., *The Rise of Surgery from Empiric Craft to Scientific Discipline* (Minneapolis: University of Minnesota Press, 1978).

Notes

Chapter 1.

1. The year of my birth, 1906, was an extremely important year for Harvard Medical School. In September the five gleaming white marble buildings in the present Quadrangle were dedicated. For J. Collins Warren they marked the fulfillment of a forty year quest for the funds. On the building to the left of the entry from Longwood Avenue an engraving from Hippocrates warned the passing reader:

   Life is short
   And the art long
   The occasion instant
   Experiment perilous
   Decision difficult.

   The story of the building of the new school, its prime movers—Drs. Henry P. Bowditch and J. Collins Warren—and the major gift by Mr. J. P. Morgan that made it possible has been told in detail by Edward D. Churchill in *To Work in the Vineyard of Surgery: the Reminiscences of J. Collins Warren (1842–1927) (Cambridge: Harvard University Press, 1958), pp. 203–218.*

2. A detailed history of Stanton County and the town of Stanton was written by Meroe J. Outhouse, A History of Stanton County, Nebraska, in a privately printed master's thesis presented to the Colorado State Teachers College, Greeley, Colorado in 1944. The State of Nebraska was admitted to the Union in 1867. Stanton was incorporated as a village in 1881 and, when it grew large enough to contain two wards, as a "city of the second class" in 1893. The first railroad through the town was laid in 1879. The population of Stanton in 1910 and 1920 was listed as 1,487, in 1960 as 1,317, and in 1989 as 948.

3. The following clipping, taken from a Crete, Nebraska newspaper published in 1921, furnishes an accurate description of my father.

   J. H. WELCH VISITS CRETE AFTER SIXTEEN YEARS ABSENCE

   Those who knew Crete people in 1903 to 1905 knew J. H. Welch, the "live wire" of the Crete high school faculty. During those years our school was making records in the state that have never been forgotten and that put Crete on the educational map where it has remained. Then our grade and high school were visited by teachers from Lincoln, Beatrice and surrounding towns to observe the methods used here, and many of our visitors adopted Crete methods to the better merit of their schools.

Mr. Welch was a booster in every line. As an instructor he stood at the top. In athletics he was an inspiration and a clean forceful leader. He put basketball on a basis that built up teams that defeated nearly all opponents and proved to doubters that the game was a great one at a time when colleges and universities were skeptical of its merits. Mr. Welch organized and trained the first high school band and made it a success. He strongly supported the military company which was under command of Captain Weeks. These few features of his many activities are only an indication of his merits.

Mr. Welch accepted the superintendency of the Stanton Nebr. schools in the fall of 1905 and for some years was one of the best known and most successful educators in North Nebraska. During that time he brought the Stanton schools to the top notch in efficiency and through his splendid executive and organizing ability led the town to build a new high school building. He then laid aside school work, entered the banking business, and is one of the most respected citizens of Stanton.

4. There is only one town in the world called Primghar. The name was formed by splicing together the initials of the surnames of the eight founders of the town. It was (and is) the county seat of O'Brien County in northwestern Iowa. In the early twentieth century the population of approximately 1000 was composed chiefly of farmers, businessmen and their families.

5. Joseph Nye Welch, the youngest son of William and Martha Welch, was born on the family farm near Primghar. He attended a one-room school house where he was taught for several years by his brother (my father) John. He graduated from Grinnell College, having earned necessary funds by selling maps door-to-door to farmers and other citizens. He studied law in Harvard where he was a member of the *Law Review*.

After graduation he joined the firm of Hale and Dorr and remained with them for the rest of his life. His first letterhead that I can recall listed in that office only six lawyers. His office was adjacent to that of Mr. Hale, a courtly gentleman. Jose always worked at a standup desk. The firm now is one of the largest in Boston.

We had many pleasant times together, particularly when I was in medical school. I would drive out to his home in Walpole on an occasional Sunday; we would have a round of golf and play a little cribbage or gin rummy. He was a genius with words but less than adequate with mechanical affairs. Jose also was not very good at golf, so we made an undistinguished pair as we chewed up the local golf course. Years later, completely exasperated by his inability to get over a water hole, he picked up his clubs and silently threw them one by one into the pond; the bag then made a big splash and that was the last time he worried about golf.

Jose had enormous success as a trial lawyer. His greatest triumph occurred at the time Senator McCarthy was holding hearings in Washington. The Senator could see communists everywhere; it is hard to imagine, but even President Eisenhower had difficulty maintaining his reputation for loyalty, so strong was the Senator's influence. Hence, when McCarthy announced that the names of some members of the high command in the Army were in his black book, Secretary Stevens was called before the Committee. Jose was picked to defend the Army.

All of the proceedings were broadcast on television. The whole country hung on every word. Prior to the hearings, Jose asked all of his assistant lawyers if any of them had any matter, great or small, that might lead McCarthy to suspect their patriotism. One person stated that he had belonged to a leftish group in college. This was discussed by both Jose and Roy Cohn, the Senator's legal adviser, but both decided it was unimportant. Both sides agreed never to mention it. One day in the heat of a long argument, however, McCarthy raised the probability that Jose's young assistant was a communist; Cohn tried vainly to stop him. In fact, the attack became so violent that Jose finally rose from the table and cried, "Senator, have you no sense of decency?" The words rang around the world and down the halls of time. McCarthy was destroyed.

Chapter 2.

1. A *History of Doane College 1872–1912* was published by the College in 1957. Detailed accounts of the first 40 years of the school were followed by individual sketches of several important benefactors of the College. The dedication of the school to high educational standards and the close association with the Congregational Church (later the United Church of Christ) were salient features throughout its existence.

A more recent book is D. J. Ziegler's *A College on a Hill: Life at Doane 1872–1987* (Lincoln, Nebraska: Media Publishing, 1990). This authoritative history vividly portrays the struggles of a small college to maintain high scholastic standards despite chronic financial difficulties. Success has been measured by increased size and diversification of the student body, extension of the college by a branch in the city of Lincoln, and continued modernization of the curriculum.

About a quarter of a century after I graduated from Doane, *Life* magazine published a major article on small colleges in the United States. Doane was discussed and pictured as an excellent example.

In 1990 there are approximately 20 buildings on the Doane campus and about 800 students in the combined Crete and Lincoln campuses.

In 1955 I was given an honorary Doctor of Science by Doane. This award probably was given because of my reasonably distinguished career after graduation and my record during the college years (graduated summa cum laude, editor of the college paper, president of the class). Reception of the award involved my presence at a ceremony during the annual commencement exercises.

The school had changed considerably since I left it twenty-eight years before. There were several new buildings, including dormitories for men and women, science laboratories, and a much larger library. Some of the older structures such as the conservatory and the observatory were used for other than their original purposes. The athletic facilities had been greatly expanded.

We learned that several teaching functions during the summer kept the campus busy throughout the year. The student body had nearly tripled. The ratio of faculty to students had not changed, and the student body appeared to be very happy. The campus maintained its rustic beauty, with buildings scattered between groves of trees and small lakes.

I was also awarded an honorary Doctor of Science by the University of Nebraska in 1970. I had made several previous appearances as a speaker both at the medical school in Omaha and at other major medical meetings in the state. The exercises required my presence on the platform during all the programs for two days. Fortunately, I did not have to make a response when receiving my citation.

In 1970 Merle (Jim) Musselman was professor of surgery and chairman of the department in the medical school. He was a great friend. He had seats on the fifty-yard line for all the Cornhusker (University of Nebraska) football games and generously gave the tickets to Phyllis and me at a time I was giving lectures in the medical school. He pressed me to move permanently to Omaha and accept a professorship in the school; the medical school was in the midst of a period of growth and in 1990 is an excellent institution.

Chapter 3.

1. The relationships between the city of Boston, the Boston City Hospital, the Thorndike Laboratory and Harvard Medical School, and the two other medical schools, Boston University and Tufts, that staffed the BCH, have ranged from tortuous to acrimonious. Each of the three medical institutions rapidly acquired a tradition of excellence, but infusions of politics and the chronic problems associated with limited municipal funds tended to dim the luster that an effective coalition could have produced. A few historical details may clarify this statement.

The Boston City Hospital opened in 1864. Then there were two neat wards on either side of a domed administration building. The hospital was staffed by six seniors from Harvard Medical School. One of the early surgeons was William L. Thorndike.

Harvard entered the BCH for the next time in 1914 when the fourth medical service was assigned to it. This was the only important ward Harvard had at the City Hospital for teaching students until 1930 when the second medical service was added.

By 1919 it was apparent the Boston City Hospital was deficient in clinical leadership. Previously, a sizable bequest had been made in honor of his brother William by George L. Thorndike. This fund with accumulated interest was given to the City of Boston for erection of the Thorndike Laboratory. The trustees turned to Harvard for leadership, and the famous Francis W. Peabody became the first of a line of distinguished professors who guided it for the next half century. The building, designed for laboratory research, patient care and teaching, formally was opened in 1923.

The Thorndike Laboratory in the Boston City Hospital was the first general clinical research facility in Boston and in a municipal hospital in the United States. The Thorndike group of gifted physicians carried out investigations in infections, hematology, liver, gastrointestinal and cardiac disease.

I arrived at the Boston City Hospital with the HMS Class of '32 only five years after the Thorndike had opened. We were eager students, and stayed in the BCH for several weeks as we were introduced to medicine. I returned during my fourth year as a resident, first on the pneumonia service, and immediately afterward as a resident in pathology. This was an era when the BCH was on the crest of the wave.

The hospital then consisted of innumerable buildings, all of a different vintage and type of architecture. The wards, often spotless in the morning, were filled later in the day when cots had to be placed between the two long lines of beds to accommodate new arrivals. A fine large building had been finished only two years before for the residents. A new pathology building was dedicated to Dr. Frank Mallory in 1933.

2. Eventually there were 1410 graduates of the unit; 1082 finally held the rank of assistant professor or higher in a medical school, and 461 were full professors. The Harvard-Thorndike combination had produced innumerable papers. With the Huntington Hospital it had one Nobel prize winner—Dr. George Minot—for his discovery that liver cured pernicious anemia. Incidentally Minot's life had been saved by another pair of prize winners. He developed severe diabetes and nearly died in a few months. Just in time, Banting and Best sent him some of the newly discovered insulin and he lived nearly forty more years. The list of famous men was augmented every year by such individuals as Castle and Finland.

The story of the Boston City Hospital and the Thorndike Laboratory is a thrilling tale, filled with nostalgia but, for Harvard, ending on a melancholy note. It is the history of a rapid rise to fame, remaining on the pinnacle for a half century, and a sudden collapse. There were three reasons. A great decline in the number of BCH patients occurred because

Medicaid and Medicare provided funds sufficient for private accommodations; the mayor demanded a reduction in the hospital budget; and an Arthur D. Little study recommended amalgamation of various medical schools affiliated services including medicine and surgery. In 1973 the break was made. Most of the personnel of the Thorndike laboratory moved to the Beth Israel Hospital, and funds were divided. Boston University was the victor; the Thorndike has remained under its control since 1973.

The complete history of the institution has been written by Max Finland, who was director of the Harvard Medical Unit from 1963–1968. Maxwell Finland and William B. Castle, *The Harvard Medical Unit at Boston City* Hospital. (Boston: The Francis A. Countway Library of Medicine, Harvard Medical School, 1982).

3. The Pneumonia Service originated in 1918 at the height of the great influenza pandemic. Dr. Edwin Locke was in charge. The Service closed in 1923 but research continued under the aegis of the Thorndike. Drs. Finland and Sutliffe were the directors; Dr. John Parsons was the resident and I was the assistant resident in the year 1931–32. I believe the Service was terminated after that year.

4. Henry Knowles Beecher was not only a classmate of mine in HMS, but a colleague during our years as surgical interns in the MGH. In 1935, following the advice and strong support of Dr. Churchill, he became Anesthetist-in-Chief in the MGH and in 1941 Professor of Anesthesia in HMS. He served in Italy with the armed forces and returned to continue his activities in the MGH and Harvard. His department quickly became one of the most famous and productive in the world. He was first to be honored with a high academic appointment that was entirely free of domination by the department of surgery. In addition to his primary interest, he developed the criteria for brain death and wrote a detailed and critical book entitled *Medicine in Harvard, the First Three Hundred Years*. He retired in 1969 when he became ill from a malignant carcinoid of the intestine that had metastasized; I was able to resect all gross disease. Despite great physical disability he continued to work until 1975 on his book but finally succumbed to his cancer in 1977.

His story has been told by B. Castleman, D. C. Crockett, and S. B. Sutton, in the volume *The Massachusetts General Hospital 1955–1980* (Boston: Little, Brown and Co., 1983). To items published in it by Buckman McPeek and John Hedley-White and notes from a Memorial Minute published in the Harvard University Gazette in January, 1978, I am adding a few personal details.

During our medical school days Harry was several steps ahead of his fellow students. While we were attending classes, he was carrying out advanced research. Professor Zinsser was a great friend and guided him in some of these efforts. As a student in the MGH, his studies on so-called postoperative pneumonia proved that it actually was caused by aspiration of gastric contents. This was a major argument in favor of intratracheal anesthesia—a great advance inaugurated by Samuel Meltzer in 1909.

As surgical house officers we worked together but never saw each other outside the hospital. He was not a particularly dextrous surgeon, but he was superb in development of the department of anesthesia. He combed Europe to secure outstanding persons for his service. He not only was interested in research but administered a large percentage of anesthetics for my patients over the years after World War II.

During the war he spent several weeks on the Anzio beachhead, which was one of the most dangerous spots in the battle against Germany. In that small area, shells from German batteries on the heights to the east of the town rained down day after day, night after night, and week after week. Not only did Henry show great personal bravery as he spent weeks giving anesthesia under those trying conditions, but produced important scientific observations. He found that wounded soldiers were given too large doses of morphine in first aid stations; as a result anesthesia became much more dangerous. Directives from headquarters soon righted this problem.

The six major accomplishments of the Department of Anesthesia in the MGH under his direction were listed by McPeek and Hedley-White as follows:

• It established the first research laboratory devoted exclusively to the study of anesthetics.
• It was the first department of anesthesia in the world to apply the modern technology of resuscitation to the wounded.
• It was the first to demonstrate and use quantitative measurements of subjective responses to drugs.
• Professor Beecher, on behalf of his department, became a vigorous proponent for human rights in science.
• It was a pioneer in establishing scientific principles for the ethical study of drug effects in man, the motivating force for the establishment of the first human study committees at Harvard.
• In the later 1960s the department became the major driving force behind the first formal enunciation of brain damage, a major advance in human transplantation efforts.

To this list must be added the development of the first formal respiratory care unit in the U.S.A. in 1955 under the direction of Dr. Henning Pontoppidan.

Thus Beecher was in the vanguard of the developing sciences of anesthesia and also of medical ethics that was to blossom a decade later.

I found him to be a very effective anesthesiologist. He brooked no delays in the operating room; we were two of a kind. If the patient was sluggish in efforts to breathe after an intratracheal anesthesia he would remove the tube and wait for the increase in carbon dioxide in the lungs to permit the body to resume respiratory function. Although this method was decried by other members of the department it did save a great deal of time and it was a rare occurrence to have to replace the tube.

He also trained over 250 anesthesiologists and at least twenty chairmen of departments. He was the first anesthesiologist to become a member of the American Surgical Association.

Harry Beecher was described in the Harvard University Gazette in these words: "In science he was a Cyclops; in social life a Bacchus." I am sure that was an exagerration. Nevertheless he did have a complex personality. Grantley Taylor called him the true Renaissance Man. I agree.

5. Carl W. Walter, "Finding a better way," *Journal of the American Medical Association* 1990; 263:1675–78. In this biographical sketch, Carl described the many problems he encountered during his school days, and the early years as a physician and surgeon.

Chapter 4

1. M. R. Lipp, *Medical Landmarks USA* (New York: McGraw-Hill, 1991), pp. 44–47.
2. R. Truax, *The Doctors Warren of Boston* (Boston: Houghton Miflin Co., 1968).
3. Frederick A. Washburn, *The Massachusetts General Hospital* (Boston: Houghton Miflin Co., 1939), p. 546.
4. M. R. Lipp, *Medical Landmarks USA*, p. 44.
5. Edward D. Churchill, *To Work in the Vineyard* of *Surgery*, p. 146.
6. Frederick C. Shattuck, "Arthur Tracy Cabot M.D. (1852–1912)," *Proceedings of the American Academy of Arts and Sciences* 1918; 53:793–798.
7. Walter L. Burrage, *Guide to Boston for Physicians.* (Cambridge: Harvard University Press, 1921), p.93.
8. The battle to replace empiricism with scientific medicine and surgery has been a long struggle. The entire history has been described and annotated in the delightful volume written by Owen and Sally Wangensteen (see general references). John Hunter (1728–1793) generally has been regarded as the prime example of a true medical scientist; his numerous contributions were based chiefly on anatomical observations. However, experimental surgery did not achieve an important role until near the middle of the twentieth century.
9. A. Flexner, *Medical Education in the United States and Canada.* (New York: Carnegie Foundation, 1910).
10. H. K. Beecher and M. Altschule criticized Flexner and defended the Harvard system of teaching medical students. (See *Medicine at Harvard: The First 300 Years,* (Hanover, N. H.: University Press of New England, 1977), pp. 176–184.

Altschule extended his defense of humanism and gave a detailed discussion of the impact of Flexner's report in his *Essays on the Rise and*

Decline of Bedside Medicine (Philadelphia: Lee and Febiger 1989). The focus of his book was to praise the personal contacts involved in the doctor-patient relationship, and to subject medical science to a secondary role both in medical education and medical practice.

Altschule also criticized Flexner because he failed to give credit to the AMA for its vigorous attempts to improve medical education (pp. 375–403).

11. E. D. Churchill, "Science and humanism in surgery," *Annals of Surgery* 1947; 126:381.

12. H. B. Clapesattle, *The Doctors Mayo* (Minneapolis: University of Minnesota Press, 1941). Ms. Clapesattle has written the definitive history of this remarkable family and the world-famous clinic that they founded.

   O. T. Clagett, *General Surgery at the Mayo Clinic 1900–1970* (Rochester, Minnesota: privately printed by O. T. Clagett, 1980). This book contains a series of profiles of all of the general surgeons associated with the Mayo Clinic from the time of its origin until 1980. Written by one of the most skilled general and thoracic surgeons of his age, this brief volume by Jim Clagett awakens memories of many of his colleagues and of other surgical giants.

13. W. Kausch, "Uber intravenöse und subcutane Ernährung mit Traubenzucker," Deutsche medinzinisch Wochenschrift, Leipzig 1908; 37:8.

14. W. Kausch, "Das Carcinom der Papilla duodeni und seine radikale Entfernung," *Beiträge zur klinische Chirugie*, (Tübingen) 1912; 78:439–486.

15. A. O. Whipple, W. B. Parsons, and C. R. Mullins, "Treatment of carcinoma of the ampulla of Vater," *Annals of Surgery* 1935; 102:763–779.

16. J. A. Hartwell, J. P. Hoguet, "Experimental intestinal obstruction in dogs with especial reference to the cause of death and the treatment by large amounts of normal saline solution," *Journal of the American* Medical Association 1912; 59:82–87.

   F. D. Moore, "Hartwell and Hoguet reviewed sixty-eight years later," *Surgical Rounds* 1980 (May), pp. 39–42. Discussing their paper many years later, Francis Moore pointed out that they emphasized water loss although electrolytes also were partially replaced, and that the fluid was given by clysis rather than by the intravenous route.

17. E. A. Codman, *A Study in Hospital Efficiency*. This small volume, privately printed, is available in the Rare Books Section of the Countway Library in the Harvard Medical School, Boston and in the Treadwell Library of the MGH.

18. D. B. Adams, "Mandatory exploration of abdominal wounds," *Archives of Surgery* 1991; 126:115. This brief letter indicates that early exploration of penetrating wounds of the abdomen was proved to be valuable in World War I.

   G. W. Beebe and M. E. DeBakey, *Battle Casualties* (Springfield, Illinois: C. C. Thomas 1952), p. 83. Abdominal wounds in the Army of the USA were followed by death in 32% of the cases in World War I and 18% in World War II.

19. John F. Fulton, *Harvey Cushing—A Biography.* (Springfield, Illinois: Charles C. Thomas, 1946.) This delightful biography of the father of neurosurgery is extraordinarily detailed. Fulton obviously admired Cushing not only as a surgical genius but also as a man of letters. It remains a miracle how Cushing could accomplish so much, such as writing his biography of Osler, filling his notes with appropriate sketches, traveling frequently in this country and abroad, and spending long hours in the operating room.

Harvey Cushing, *From a Surgeon's Journal 1915–1918* (Boston: Little Brown and Co., 1936). This book is concerned more with descriptions of the country and of the tactics of World War I than with actual details of his operative procedures. Nor is much said about the tiffs with his superiors that nearly led this independent soul to be courtmartialed.

Harvey Cushing, The Life of Sir William Osler. (Oxford, Clarendon Press, 1925). This biography was selected for the Pulitzer prize in 1925.

20. W. Osler, "Vienna after thirty-four years," *Journal of the American Medical Association* 1908; 50: 1523–1525.

Chapter 5.

1. F. W. Washburn, *The Massachusetts General Hospital* (Cambridge: The Riverside Press, 1939).

2. C. E. Welch, "A student becomes a surgeon: 1932," *Journal of the American Medical Association* 1988; 259:3168–70. Excerpts have been used from the original article by CEW by permission of *JAMA*.

3. Every institution has a tradition that permits the survival of certain phrases that are incomprehensible except to the indoctrinated. In the following delightful poem Lewis Thomas described *Allen Street*—a thoroughfare which no longer exists. The street ran behind the Bulfinch building when it was erected in 1821. In 1874 the MGH built a mortuary and in 1896 a pathology building along one side of the street. The other side was lined by houses and tenements and numerous curious residents. Allen Street is now that portion of Blossom Street lying immediately between Emerson Place and the Gray building of the MGH.

The street side of the pathology building was essentially a solid red brick wall. There were only two openings, a small door through which the workers passed and a larger one, which accommodated hearses and periodically opened to disgorge them and their resident corpses. To me, the rear end of the hospital suggested a set of thrombosed hemorrhoids and the attendant discharge of effluvia. To "go to Allen Street" therefore meant to be covered with a sheet and taken to the morgue.

Allen Street

This piece by Lewis Thomas first was published in the *Aesculapiad*, the
Yearbook of Harvard Medical School, 1937. Later it was published in
Lewis Thomas's book *The Youngest Science.**

Canto I: Prelude

Oh, Beacon Street is wide and neat, and open to the sky—
Commonwealth exudes good health and, never knows a sigh—
Scollay Square, that lecher's snare, is noisy but alive—
While sin and domesticity are blended on Park Drive—
And he who toils on Boylston Street will have another day
To pay his lease and live in peace, along the Riverway—
A thoroughfare without a care is Cambridge Avenue
Where ladies fair let down their hair for passers-by to view—

Some things are done on Huntington, no sailor would deny,
Which can't be done on battleships, no matter how you try—
Oh, many, many roads there are, that leap into the mind
(Like Sumner Tunnel, that monstrous funnel, impossible to find!)
And all are strange to ponder on, and beautiful to know,
And all are filled with living folk, who eat and breathe and grow.

Canto II

But let us speak of Allen Street—that strangest, darkest turn,
Which squats behind a hospital, mysterious and stern.
It lies within a silent place, with open arms it waits
For patients who aren't leaving by the customary gates.
It concentrates on end results and caters to the guest
Who's battled long with his disease and come out second best.

For in a well-run hospital, there's no such thing as death.
There may be stoppage of the heart, and absence of the breath—
But no one dies! No patient tries this disrespectful feat.
He simply sighs, rolls up his eyes, and goes to Allen Street.
Whatever be his ailment—whate'er his sickness be,
From "Too, too, too much insulin" to "What's this in his pee?"
From "Gastric growth", "One lung (or both)," or "Question of
    Cirrhosis"
To "Exitus undiagnosed," or "Generalized Necrosis"—
He hides his head and leaves his bed, and covered with a sheet,
He rolls through doors, down corridors, and goes to Allen Street.

And there he'll find a refuge kind, a quiet sanctuary
For Allen Street's that final treat—the local mortuary.

Canto III

Oh, where is Mister Murphy with his diabetic ulcer,
His orange-red precipitate and coronary? Well, sir,
He's gone to Allen Street.
And how is Mr. Gumbo with his touch of acid-fast,
His positive Babinskis, and his dark luetic past?
And what about that lady who was lying in bed 3,
Recently subjected to such skillful surgery?
And where are all the patients with the paroxysmal wheezes?
The tarry stools, ascitic pools, the livers like valises
The jaundiced eyes, the fevered cries, and other nice diseases:
Go! Speak to them in soothing tones. We'll put them on their feet!
We'll try some other method, some newer way to treat—
We'll try colloidal manganese, a diathermy seat,
And intravenous buttermilk is very hard to beat—
We'll try a dye, a yellow dye, or different kinds of heat—
But get them on their feet—
We'll find some way to treat—
    I'm very sorry, Doctor, but they've gone to
    Allen Street. . . .

Canto IV

Little Mister Greco, lying on Ward E,
Used to have a rectum, just like you or me—
Used to have a sphincter, ringed with little piles,
Used to sit at morning stool, face bewreathed with smiles
Used to fold his *Transcript*, wait in happy hush
For that minor ecstasy, the peristaltic rush. . . .
    But in the night, far out of sight, within
      his rectal stroma,
    There grew a little nodule, a nasty
      carcinoma.
Oh, what lacks Mister Gricco?—Why looks he incomplete?
What is that aching, yawning void in Mister Gricco's seat?
Who made that excavation? Who did this foulest deed?
Who dug this pit in which would fit a small velocipede?
What enterprising surgeon, with sterile spade and trowel,
Has seen some fault and made assault on Mister Gricco's bowel?
And what's this small repulsive hole, which whistles like a flute?
Could this thing be colostomy—this shabby substitute?
Where is this patient's other half! Where is this patient's seat!

Why, Doctor, don't you recollect: It's
gone to Allen Street.

Canto V. Footnote

At certain times one sometimes finds a patient in his bed,
Who limply lies with glassy eyes receding in his head.
Who doesn't seem to breathe at all, who doesn't make a sound,
Whose temperature is seen to fall, whose pulse cannot be found.
And one would say, without delay, that this is a condition
Of general inactivity—a sort of inanition—
A quiet stage, a final page, a dream within the making,
A silence deep, an empty sleep without the fear of waking—

But no one states, or intimates, that maybe he's expired.
For anyone can plainly see that he is simply tired.
It isn't wise to analyze, to seek an explanation,
For this is just a new disease, of infinite duration.
But if you look within the book, upon his progress sheet,
You'll find a sign within a line—"Discharged to Allen Street."

4. During the years from 1932–37 in the MGH the interns and residents had
no formal assignments in laboratory or clinical research. This is true in
1990 as well. Laboratory research is elective; when it is chosen, the
individual adds another year or two to his period of postgraduate education. Several fellowships are available to aid in financing. Some medical
schools include a year of laboratory research in every residency; Duke is
a prime example.

5. My operative list during the years as assistant resident and resident in
1936 and 1937 shows a total of 725 operations, of which 426 were major
and 299 minor. The major operations: Appendectomy simple 75, ruptured
44; hernia, 82; thyroidectomy, 29; cholecystectomy, 25; hysterectomy,
supravaginal 40, total abdominal 17, vaginal 5; other major pelvic operations, 29; mastectomy, radical 14, simple 4.

Gastric resections and colon resections for cancer were not common and
were done by visiting surgeons. Diverticulitis was exceedingly rare. Vascular surgery was restricted to operations for varicose veins, post-phlebitic
ulcers and amputations. Open chest surgery was rare; resection of the
lower lobes of the lungs was done chiefly for bronchiectasis.

6. The details of the controversy between the ABS and the ACS and its final
amicable settlement have been recorded by Ravitch. See M. M. Ravitch,
A Century of Surgery (Philadelphia: J. B. Lippincott, 1981), pp. 1542–1546.
Nearly fifteen years before the founding of the ABS, the famous Chicago surgeon and a powerful member of the AMA, Arthur Dean Bevan,
had attempted to form a similar organization but had failed. Thus three
organizations were involved in negotiations concerning surgical training.
In the final delineation of functions, the ABS set standards of education

and training, while the ACS became the prime provider of education, particularly by means of annual meetings. Furthermore, a tripartite Residency Review Committee, with members from the AMA, the ABS, and the ACS, was formed. I discuss this committee in more detail in chapter 13.

When the American Board of Surgery was organized in 1937 the certificates that it issued to qualified candidates had no limit insofar as time was concerned. Beginning in 1976 the ABS made it's certificates valid for only ten years; therefore a recertifying examination is required every ten years. At the present time, the qualifications required for an applicant are specified in great detail.

A candidate in 1990 must have primary responsibility in diagnosis and preoperative, operative, and postoperative management in the following areas: alimentary tract; abdomen and its contents; breast, skin and soft tissue; head and neck; vascular system; endocrine system; comprehensive management of trauma; complete care of critically ill patients; and a variety of endoscopic techniques. In addition the candidate must have experience in all subspecialties of surgery.

These standards are set at a high level. In the recent past many institutions have found it difficult to provide experience in all of these fields to many candidates. A minimum of five years is required to provide eligibility for the examinations, which are both written and oral. The failure rate at the present time is about twenty-five percent.

Chapter 6

1. Dr. Allen's contributions to the American College of Surgeons were made chiefly during the years 1949–1951 when he was Chairman of the Board of Regents. They were described in detail by Loyal Davis in his book *Fellowship of Surgeons* (Chicago: American College of Surgeons, 1988).
2. Dr. James Thoroughman in 1972 wrote his own epitaph. A copy was sent to me by his family after his death. He was a fine surgeon, a great gentleman, and a friend of Dr. Allen. I am sure he would be pleased that I quote it because it applies so well to Dr. Allen. Jim wrote:
    Death Comes to the Physician
    Who speaks thus:
    "Enter, Death, my old acquaintance! I will not call thee friend for we have been adversaries these fifty years. Success at times has been thine, and failure likewise—when victory has been mine. Neither can I deem thee wholly evil, for at times thou has brought surcease from suffering in those whom my poor skill could not ease. When the shadow of thy presence hovered over those whom thou didst not touch, was this to test the mettle of their souls or to challenge me to greater endeavors? Thou dost not answer?
    So thou has come for me. I know thee too well to fear thee. Come,

let us walk arm in arm down the long corridor until I enter the portals of eternity, from whence thou art forever barred."

3. This loneliness was expressed beautifully by John Mann Astrachan. He said:

Waiting

I kiss her eyes and smell her hair,
she lifts her mouth and we linger.
She tells me to try and not worry too much
and touches her wedding band,
secured to her finger by a small gauze tie.
I bend close to her, once more,
and we speak our love.

She lies on a rolling stretcher
in front of an elevator
where an orderly made of soft green and smile
asks if she is comfortable before he wheels her
to the place where she will sleep
and where the surgeon readies himself
for what he may have to do.

The elevator door closes
and a desperate quiet settles as waiting begins.
I think of her, so brave and afraid,
hearing the thing growing inside her,
hurting her,
so different from what grew inside her from us,
long ago, not long ago.

The people in their comings
and goings, early morning city sounds,
the colors of the autumn leaves on the hospital lawn
are vivid, yet unconnected to what little remains of me.
Weariness comes on the heels of the quiet,
A black apprehension about us, magnifies the world.

I go home and I wait, helpless,
for the telephone to ring bringing
words from the doctor;
words that will tear, perplex or comfort
in a way that cannot be fathomed
except by those who have had to wait,
wait for words.

John Mann Astrachan, "Waiting," *New England Journal of Medicine* 1984; 310:601. (Poem reprinted by permission of the *NEJM.*)

4. Ashok R. Vankitaraman described this unconscious expression of a doctor as follows:

Frustration

The stethoscope dropped unnoticed to my side.
I straightened to meet her gaze—
Her eyes a soft brown,
An unasked question, an unspoken fear
Buried in their depths.

And something else?
Faith? Understanding?
And compassion . . . for me?
My eyes, holding the power to dispel her fear,
To quiet that foreboding,
Faltered.
I could not meet her gaze.

A burst of anger at myself
Six and a half years of hard-earned knowledge:
Fine print and bulky textbooks.
Chemicals and cadavers,
Heart sounds and spleens.
Long days, and nights that never seemed to end
All this, naught before her.

My lips, full of inept platitudes,
Of clumsy comfort.
In my mind, just two words,
Inoperable cancer.
"What could I say that my eyes had not told her?"

Ashok R. Venkitaraman, "Frustration," *Pharos* 1982 (fall issue). This poem was written by a final-year medical student at the Christian Medical College in Vellore, India. (Poem reprinted by permission of *Pharos*.)

5. Rosalie Walsh Honel has shown how difficult it may be for physicians to assume this role, with these words:

Alzheimer's Disease

On summer days
He walks or sits outside to pass the hours
    empty monotonous hours—
    weeks and months of present moments—
    hollow moments.
His eye may catch upon a misplaced garden tool

perhaps an empty flower pot, discarded,
or a branch blown by a recent storm.
Carefully he places them just so,
or brings them in,
to guard them from the grasp of thieves.
He may walk around the fenced-in garden,
trying to get in,
becoming caught in chicken-wire and compost
green tomatoes tempting.
And red geraniums.
The brilliant flower clusters call
some earlier day perhaps
when, time-laden,
he sprouted them and nurtured them through winter
in rusted tin-can pots.
Geraniums, so radiant of hue,
he bends arthritic hips and knees,
defying loss of balance,
drawn by hypnotic color
selecting, choosing
this one.
To the door he shuffles,
opening carefully, slowly,
grasping frame with one hand,
flower in the other,
studying through blurred vision as he
steps up, over, into the house.
Traumatic for geranium clusters
they float gently down,
under his feet, leaving
walked-on stains of red
here and there.
Here's something
something good.
You take it.
His demand sets me on edge,
seeing red marks on the floor
I want to say, "Don't pick the geraniums,"
and then I know,
He's just a two-year old
bringing me flowers."
Rosalie Walsh Honel, "Alzheimer's Disease," *New England Journal of
Medicine* 1983; 309:1524. (Poem reprinted by permission of the *NEJM*.)
6. Francis Weld Peabody, "The Care of the Patient" *Journal of the American
Medical Association* 1927; 88:877–882. In this long essay the author, one

of the most famous physicians of the Boston City Hospital, emphasized the need to understand a patient's socioeconomic status in order to evaluate his functional and organic problems. This analysis is much more likely to be accurate if it is done in the patient's home or the doctor's office rather than in the hospital.

The last phrase in his paper is quoted frequently. "The secret of the care of the patient is in caring for the patient." For a memoir of Peabody, see Oglesby Paul *The Caring Physician: The Life of Dr. Francis W. Peabody* (Boston: Distributed by Harvard University Press for Countway Library, 1991).

7. J. E. Dunphy, Annual Discourse—"On Caring for the Patient with Cancer," *New England Journal of Medicine* 1976; 295:313–319.
8. H. Zinsser, *Spring, Summer & Autumn. Two Sonnets II* (New York: Alfred A. Knopf, 1942), p. 89.

Chapter 7

1. F. W. Washburn *The Massachusetts General Hospital* pp. 530–537.
2. T. R. Goethals, "The War Effort and the 6th General Hospital." In N. W. Faxon, *The Massachusetts General Hospital 1935–1955.* (Cambridge. Harvard University Press 1959), pp. 365–386.
3. W. A. Shriver, The Story of the 6th General *Hospital* (Boston: 1945.) This brief summary was published privately. It contains many interesting statistics, some of which are recounted here.

15 May, 1942. Departure by train from Boston for Camp Blanding, Florida.

19 January, 1943. Departure by train from Camp Blanding to Camp Kilmer, New Jersey. (The 160th Station Hospital had been separated from us in June, 1942. They shortly afterward were stationed in England.}

7 February, 1943. Departure by the *Brazil*, the Argentina, and the *Uruguay* for an unknown destination. We were in a convoy guarded by a battleship, an aircraft carrier, a cruiser and ten destroyers.

20 February, 1943. Arrival in Casablanca. En route the *Uruguay* was involved in a collision at sea, had to stop in Bermuda for repairs, and arrived in Casablanca nearly a month later.

27 February, 1943. First patients arrived in the hospital.

14 May, 1944. Admitting office closed. Over 18,000 patients had been admitted during the stay in Casablanca. 8,747 patients were treated on the surgical wards with 12 deaths; several other persons were dead on arrival. Of the 8,747 surgical patients about 3,000 were battle casualties, about 3,000 had other injuries, and the remainder had surgical diseases. Deaths were due to severe head injuries in 7; accidents, in 6; burns, in 2; gas gangrene in 1; liver abscess in 1; accidental machine gun wounds, in 1; and suicide in 1.

30 June, 1944. Hospital opened in Rome. Over 3,000 patients were admitted in July. The maximum number of patients in the hospital at any one time was nearly 3,000; 6,432 patients were admitted on the surgical wards; 4,731 returned to duty after an average stay of 39 days in the hospital; fourteen patients died.

22 December, 1944. Admitting office closed. Over 8,000 patients had been admitted during that time. Frequently as many as 150 operations were done in a single day.

9 May, 1945. Hospital opened in Bologna. Over 2700 patients were admitted in less than three months. The majority were German prisoners, but many other nationalities were represented. Complete statistics are available only to June 1. By that time there had been 796 surgical admissions, 393 operations, and 10 deaths, only 1 of whom was an American.

21 July, 1945. Hospital closed.

15 September, 1945. Hospital deactivated in Leghorn Italy, exactly forty months following its activation.

Among the officers in the 6th General Hospital none died or received disabling injuries. Dr. Philip Giddings, from the MGH, who was working with the Second Auxiliary Surgery Group, received a perineal wound which required a temporary colostomy. Major James Townsend was hit in the heel by shell fragments as he dived into a foxhole. Both men recovered uneventfully.

Chapter 8.

1. J. Gordon Scannell, *Wanderjahr. The Education of a Surgeon: Edward D. Churchill* (Boston, Mass.: Francis A. Countway Library of Medicine, 1990).

    Dr. Churchill kept a detailed diary in the years 1926 and 1927, when, as a Moseley Travelling Fellow, he visited many of the important surgical and research institutions in Europe. Dr. Scannell has edited these recollections into a comprehensive, exciting travelogue and commentary.

2. J. Gordon Scannell, "Samuel Robinson, Pioneer Thoracic Surgeon (1895–1947)," *Annals of Thoracic Surgery* 1986; 41:693–699.

3. Colonel Churchill wrote the following tribute to the surgeons of the Mediterranean Theater. It appeared originally in the last issue of the *Medical Bulletin of the Mediterranean Theater of Operations* in June, 1945 and was reprinted in The Excelsior Surgical Club Yearbook which was printed privately.

    A Tribute to the Surgeons of the Mediterranean Theater In the Surgical Management of the Wounded in this Theater has:

    Demonstrated that military surgery need not be a crude departure from accepted surgical standards—but may be a development of the science of surgery to carry out a specialized and highly significant mission.

Established continuity in the professional procedures that govern the management of the wounded soldier from the time the missile strikes to the complete repair of the damage it has caused.

Shown that the essentials of wound treatment are found in prompt emergency treatment, complete initial surgery and early reparative surgery.

Introduced the concept of reparative surgery—a new and far reaching development of wound management.

Originated the transfer of selected cases of the most seriously wounded to a surgical (Field) hospital adjacent to the divisional clearing station and established the highest standards of surgical treatment at this forward point.

Maintained the strength of the fighting force by prompt and expert surgical treatment of the lightly wounded combat soldier within the Army area.

Clarified the nature of shock in wounded men and demonstrated that an adequate supply of fresh whole blood for resuscitation from shock is essential to forward surgery.

Designed and trained blood procurement and distribution organizations that have provided over 70,000 pints of whole blood from within the Theater.

Introduced the new agent penicillin into large scale use in military surgery as a potent adjunct to wound management.

Eliminated the scourge of infection as a common complication of war wounds.

Developed and standardized effective, comfortable and safe methods of transportation splinting.

Reduced the incidence of crippling and permanent disability in wounds of major joints and bones by early and radical operative treatment combined with penicillin.

Dispelled the fear of gas gangrene as any but a rare complication of severe wounds.

Changed the focal center in wounds of the chest from the treatment of severe complications of these formidable injuries to a rapid and complete re-expansion of the lung and early restoration of the functional integrity of the respiratory system.

Reduced the mortality rate and incidence of complications in all special fields of surgery—abdominal, cranio-cerebral, maxillo-facial, etc.

Pioneered in the large scale evacuation of wounded by C-47s establishing thereby a close link between forward and rear hospitals.

Introduced sodium pentothal as one of the three most important anesthetic agents of military surgery by a clear definition of its limitations and a reduction of the hazards that initially attended its use.

Standardized for military use a simple, comfortable and effective treatment for burns.

Collected and recorded technical data under the pressure of heavy
loads of routine work in order that this data might be made available
to other theaters of less experience.

(He also paid tribute to the support staff and the military organization).
A detailed analysis of data collected from the Mediterranean Theater
was published by G. W. Beebe and Michael E. DeBakey, *Battle Casualties:
Incidence, Mortality, and Logistic Considerations* (Springfield, Ill: C. C.
Thomas, 1952).

4. E. D. Churchill, *Surgeon to Soldiers*, (Philadelphia, J. B. Lippincott Co.
1972).

During World War II, Colonel Churchill kept a careful diary of his
experience in the Mediterranean Theater. The book contains a wealth of
information. It was written somewhat hurriedly and lacks Churchill's
usually meticulous editing. However the content more than atones for
the style, and if a reader wants to know exactly what happened on the
surgical battle front this book is an excellent source.

5. Dr. Churchill delivered two important addresses to the American Surgical
Association. The first was given in 1944; in it he described the conditions
in the Mediterannean Theater of World War II. This paper was followed
by General Rankin's enthusiastic discussion. The second paper on humanism was his presidential address; it was given in 1946. E. D. Churchill,
"Surgical Management of the Wounded in the Mediterranean Theater at
the Time of the Fall of Rome," *Annals of Surgery* 1944; 120:268–283.
"Science and Humanism in Surgery" *Annals of Surgery,* 1947; 126:381–
396.

6. Churchill, E. D. *To Work in the Vineyard of Surgery.*

7. Churchill's interest in wound healing continued throughout his life. He
delivered a Harvey Memorial Lecture at Yale in 1963. In this historical
survey he identified John Hunter as the first surgeon who employed
practical science rather then empiricism. E. D. Churchill, "Healing by
First Intention and with Suppuration," *Journal of the History of Medicine
and Allied Sciences* 1964; 19(3):193–214.

8. In 1954 Dr. Churchill presented an address on *The Surgeon and The University* in Queen's University in Kingston, Ontario on the occasion of the
100th anniversary of the foundation of the faculty of medicine. This
address combined a historical perspective of the relationship of surgeons
to the university with many of his own philosophical comments. It was
typical of his interests in the later stages of his professional life. He viewed
surgeons as scholars as well as technicians.

His conclusion was that surgeons finally have established their rightful
position not only in the faculty of medicine but in the university. (I have
his origianl manuscript. I believe the text later was published privately.)

9. E. D. Churchill, "Evarts Graham—Early Years and the Hegira," *Annals
of Surgery* 1952; 136:3–11.

10. These papers, including a curriculum vitae and a list of publications by
Dr. Churchill were published in the *Annals of Surgery* 1963; 158:731–914.

Chapter 9

1. My personal biography lists nearly 300 publications excluding innumerable book reviews. The articles usually were concerned with state-of-the-art presentations at various meetings. Some were detailed retrospective clinical studies. Others were review articles on abdominal surgery published serially for nearly forty years in the *New England Journal of Medicine*. The most important articles included studies on the use of catheter duodenostomy after Billroth II gastric resections for duodenal ulcer; on diverticulitis of the colon; on intestinal fistulas; on long-term follow-up after gastric resection alone for duodenal ulcer; on operations for combined intestinal obstruction and peritonitis; and on cancer of the colorectum. An early series of papers analyzed the life expectancy of all cases of cancer seen in the Huntington and Pondville hospitals. Many late papers were concerned with socioeconomic issues or peer review.

Four books are listed. The first, *Surgery of the Stomach and Duodenum*, was devoted chiefly to techniques and was filled with excellent illustrations by Muriel McLatchie. It was a medical best-seller; roughly 50,000 copies were sold. It had five revisions and was translated into several foreign languages. The next, *Intestinal Obstruction*, appeared at the same time as Owen Wangensteen's book on the same subject and was not nearly as popular. The third, *Polypoid Disease of the Colon and* Rectum, went through two editions; they appeared just prior to the great revolution brought about by the invention of the fiberoptic colonoscope. Stephen Hedberg, who unfortunately died a few years afterward from hepatitis, was a coauthor of the second edition. The fourth book, *Surgery of the Colon and Rectum*, with Leslie Ottinger and John Welch, was a handsomely illustrated volume. It won the first prize in a competition held annually by the Association of Medical Illustrators; its numerous original water color illustrations by Robert Gallo were spectacular. It was published by Springer Verlag, which also published a later revised edition in German. The books cited above were: C. E. Welch, *Surgery of the Stomach* and *Duodenum* (Chicago: Year Book Medical Publishers, 1951). C. E. Welch, *Intestinal Obstruction*, (Chicago: Year Book Medical Publishers, 1959). C. E. Welch, *Polypoid Lesions of the Gastrointestinal Tract* (Philadelphia: W. B. Saunders Co., 1964). C. E. Welch, L. W. Ottinger, and J. P. Welch, *Manual of Lower Gastrointestinal Surgery* (New York: Springer-Verlag, 1980).

In the late 1960s I was asked to be the editor of a new annual publication called *Advances in Surgery*. A small editorial board was appointed. I served as the editor for six years. We then decided to rotate the arduous editorship every few years. This venture has proved to be very successful. I have remained on the board as a founding member for over twenty-five years, while other members have been replaced after serving for a period of five to ten years. Other less time-consuming editorial duties included service on the Editorial Board of *Surgery* and the *American Journal of* Surgery for many years.

My duties as chairman of the Committee on Publications of the Massachusetts Medical Society that supervises the publication of the *New England Journal of Medicine* will be described in detail in Chapter 12.

2. This was the first major venture by Harvard Medical School members into large scale commercial projects. The problem became much more difficult in later years when some products of questionable value were supported by members of the HMS faculty. Strict guidelines were established in 1990 after considerable discussion.

3. Daniel C. Tosteson *Dean's Report Harvard Medical School, Bicentennial 1782–1982* (Boston, 1982, pp. 4–6.

In this report the Dean discussed his plans for changes in the curriculum and the "New Pathway" for about twenty-five students for the M. D. degree. In large part because of the "New Pathway," Dean Tosteson was given the 1991 Abraham Flexner Award for Distinguished Service to Medical Education by the Association of American Medical Colleges.

4. *U.S. News and World Report*, March 19, 1990, pp. 64–67.

5. H. K. Beecher and M. D. Altschule, *Medicine at Harvard:* the *First 300 Years* pp. 341–343. Reprinted by permission of the University Press of New England.

6. The only other scholar surgeon described by Beecher and Altschule was Dwight Harken who had consistently successful results in the removal of shell fragments from within the heart during World War II. His biography as well as a succinct history of the development of cardiac surgery is recorded in L. Wertenbaker, *To Mend the Heart* (New York: Viking Press, 1980).

Chapter 10

1. W. S. Halsted, quoted by M. M. Ravitch in *A Century of Surgery*, p. 367.

2. F. S. Dennis cited these figures in his Presidential address in 1895. Ravitch. p. 163.

3. M. M. Ravitch, p. 163

4. M. R. Lipp, *Medical Landmarks USA*. (New York: McGraw-Hill, 1991). This book gives an excellent brief description of the important cancer centers in America.

5. Nancy Bucher, "Dr. Aub, Huntington Hospital and Cancer Research," *Harvard Medical Bulletin* Fall-winter 1987, 46–51.

F. M. Rackemann, *The Inquisitive Physician: The Life and Times of George Richards Minot* (Cambridge, Massachusetts, Harvard University Press, 1956), pp. 109–113, 254–255.

6. G. W. Stephenson, *American College of Surgeons at 75* (Chicago: American College of Surgeons, 1990), pp. 111–130.

7. These statistical studies combined the total experience of each type of cancer in thousands of cases that had been treated in the Huntington and Pondville Hospitals.

The papers contained an original method of providing an actuarial estimate of life expectancy that was approved by the head of the Harvard Cancer Commission. It was based upon the principle that the life expectancy of any patient with the specific type of cancer in any given year after treatment would be the same as the average of all others who were living at the same interval after treatment and who had been followed five or more years. For example, some cases of cancer of the breast had been followed for 4 years after therapy but still had not reached the fifth year. Their expectancy was considered to be similar to the average of all patients who were alive at least four years after therapy. This method made no allowance for a possible remarkable improvement in the more recent cases who had been followed for a brief time; actually there were no such dramatic improvements that invalidated the method. Dr. Nathanson and I flipped a coin to decide the priority of authorship of the first paper and alternated thereafter. They were published in the *American Journal of Cancer* in the following series: cancer of the breast—1936; 28:40–53; oral cavity—1937; 31:238–252; gastrointestinal tract—1937; 31:457–466; genito-urinary tract—1937; 31:586–597; other areas—1937; 31:598–608.

8. These data are available in a report prepared by Dr. Ernest M. Daland and made to the Massachusetts Department of Public Health in 1960. The report is entitled *Pondville Hospital 1927–1960*.

9. American Cancer Society, *CA—A Cancer Journal for Clinicians*. 1991;40 (January/February):16. The annual death rate for females with cancer of the breast in 1930 was 25 per 100,000. It remained essentially on the same level thereafter. In 1985 (the last available figure), it was 27 per 100,000.

10. G. W. Stephenson, American College of Surgeons at 75, pp. 111–130.

11. B. Castleman, D. C. Crockett, and S. B. Sutton, *The Massachusetts General Hospital 1955–1980*, pp. 332–350.
    A comprehensive review of the activities of the MGH related to cancer in the years 1955 to 1980 is given in this volume.

12. In 1988 the MGH acquired a large building in the old Charlestown Navy Yard, which it has converted to research laboratories. Dr. Isselbacher and his group have generous quarters there.

13. W. W. Shingleton, "Cancer centers—origin and purpose," Archives of Surgery 1990; 124:43–45. (See Chapter 23, Note 9 for further discussion.)
    Some of the early and major cancer hospitals included the following institutions:
    1898 Roswell Park Memorial Institute Buffalo New York
    1906 Memorial Hospital New York City (became Memorial Sloane-Kettering Cancer Center in 1939)
    1912 Huntington Memorial Boston (moved to MGH in 1942)
    1925 Massachusetts General Hospital Boston, MA
          First in-hospital cancer clinic

1925   Pondville Wrentham, MA
        Closed in 1969; converted to local hospital
1937   National Cancer Institute   Bethesda, MD
        (NIH Cancer Center)
1941   M. D. Anderson Cancer Center   Houston, Texas
1942   Massachusetts General Hospital   Boston
        acquired laboratories from Huntington Hospital
1947   Childrens Hospital Research Center   Boston (forerunner of
        Dana-Farber Cancer Institute, 1969)
1982   Duke U. Medical Center   Durham (prototype of modern
        cancer centers)

(This incomplete list shows representative insitutions.)

The Roswell Park Memorial Institute is one of the oldest and most famous centers for cancer research and therapy in the United States. It was named in honor of one of America's great surgeons. His name also is perpetuated by the Roswell Park Medal. The award was first given in 1948 to Allen Whipple and has honored one person every year since that time. Honorees are elected by the membership of the Buffalo Surgical Society, which initiated and has continued to support the entire project.

I received the medal in 1986. My program included a very interesting morning with Lewis Flint. He was then a relatively new chairman of the department of surgery in the medical school and rapidly was developing an excellent teaching program, integrating many of the institutions that previously had scarcely thought of cooperation. Dr. Flint also reduced the teaching staff and the total number of residents. His close cooperation with the Buffalo branch of the State University of New York bodes very well for the future of Buffalo surgery. Later I discussed several cases and gave the Roswell Park lecture on the influence of politics on the practice of medicine around the world.

Chapter 12

1. The MMS was incorporated in the State of Massachusetts in 1781. It enjoys the longest continued existence of any American medical society. The only history of its early years was written by Walter M. Burrage, at that time Secretary of the MMS. It is entitled *A History of the Massachusetts Medical Society with Brief Biographies of the Founders and Chief Officers, 1781–1922* and was privately published in 1923 by the Plimpton Press in Norwood, MA. The two-hundredth anniversary in 1981 was celebrated, in part, by the publication of a second volume by the MMS—*A Society of Physicians* by Everett Spencer, Jr. The choice of an author to write this volume had been subject to protracted discussion by the Committee on Publications. The final selection was made when I was chairman. It was a fortuitous choice, because Spencer, as executive vice-president, had an intimate knowledge of the Society. The result was a sprightly volume,

highly readable, full of facts. Many dramatic incidents have been recounted in full. Life in the MMS has never been dull.
2. Joseph E. Garland, *The Centennial History of the Boston Medical Library*
   (Boston: Trustees of the Boston Medical Library, 1975).
3. A detailed history of the *NEJM* can be found in E. R. Spencer, Jr., *A
   Society of Physicians* (Boston: Massachusetts Medical Society, 1981),
   pp. 141–211. In addition to the information in the text some salient facts
   should be cited.

   Successive editors have been Walter Bowers (1928 to 1937), Robert
   Nye (1937 to 1947), Joseph Garland (1947 to 1967), Franz Ingelfinger
   (1967 to 1977), and Arnold Relman (1977 to 1991). The circulation in
   1929 was 6,048; in 1948, 24,770; in 1967 105,978; and in 1979 for the
   first time, over 200,000.

   The Committee on Publications of the MMS was established in 1921
   at the time the *Boston Medical and Surgical Journal* was purchased by the
   MMS. In the ensuing years the *NEJM* was the poor dependent of the
   MMS and required financial support from the MMS. Homer Gage was
   the first chairman of the committee. Succeeding chairmen have been
   Roger I. Lee, Frank H. Lahey, Richard M. Smith, James Faulkner,
   Claude E. Welch, William Sweet, and James McDonough.

   A Time For Remembering, the autobiography of Joseph Garland, the third
   editor of the NEJM, was published by the Massachusetts Medical Society
   in 1972. It was the fifth book authored by this remarkable man. The
   interest in and the superb care he gave his pediatric patients for many
   years made it unlikely that he would ever forsake his medical practice.
   But he did, and in 1947 began another career that brought him even
   greater fame.

   Franz Ingelfinger, his successor, said in the introduction to Garland's
   chronicle:

   > When Joe Garland retired as editor of the NEJM in 1967 he
   > bequeathed to his successor a journal that during the Garland regime
   > of 20 years had quadrupled its circulation, had expanded its influence
   > from regional to international dimensions, and was rarely mentioned
   > in the press without the adjective "prestigious." Major ingredients of
   > this success were the obvious ones: wise selection of topics, carefully
   > evaluated reports, fastigious editing, and a dependable publication
   > schedule. But a journal cannot live by prestige alone. Joe Garland
   > also endowed the *Journal* with the quality of his personality. Although
   > its pages could speak with sharp anger, its general approach was that
   > of tolerant wisdom. Whimsical understatement persuaded the reader
   > rather than bald exaggeration. Literary allusions and quotations
   > graced the editorial section. Scientific excellence, in brief, was leav-
   > ened by humanity.
4. Other comments on Joe Garland and Franz Ingelfinger:
   R. O'Leary, "The Luminous Autumn—The Journal and Joseph Garland," *New England Journal of Medicine*, 1967; 277:18–21.

C. E. Welch, "Franz Ingelfinger, Editor Emeritus," *New England Journal of Medicine,* 1977;296:1415–1416.

A. S. Relman, "Franz Ingelfinger 1911–1980," *New England Journal of Medicine,* 1980;302:859–860.

5. This letter was published in Spencer, *A Society of Physicians,* pp.177–179.
6. Arnold S. Relman, "The New England Journal of Medicine; Editor-in-Chief's Report 1977–1991." This report was presented at the MMS Council meeting on May 17, 1991.
7. Franz Ingelfinger, "The Distinguished Services of Claude E. Welch, M. D.," *New England Journal of Medicine,* 1976; 295:503. (Reprinted by permission of the *NEJM.*)
8. In 1984 Grant Rodkey nominated me to be Orator of the MMS for the annual meeting in 1985. This task is not highly competitive; it carries no laurels except the honor of nomination. At any rate, being unopposed, I began to search for a topic.

All of the titles of the orations from their origin in 1804 are listed in Spencer's history. The speakers dealt chiefly with professional problems. I decided to change the pattern and consider the mythology that led to the cult of Aesculapius and the relationship between his life and that of the MMS. This choice appeared to be particularly appropriate because the official seal of the MMS consists of a figure of Aesculapius; the first version appeared in 1783 and was reapproved in 1980 after several other variations had been used temporarily and discarded. In addition, it was easy to consider the vicissitudes of Aesculapius until he finally was received into the pantheon of gods, to compare his trials to those of the medical society, and to express the hope that the medical society might eventually earn similar immortality.

As it developed, the speech was interesting. I illustrated it with numerous slides and was ready to present it at the appointed time during the annual meeting—2 P.M. We had been warned previously that there might be some type of public demonstration against the MMS at that hour. The meeting was on Cape Cod in Dunphy's Inn. It was in this very area that patients had complained that no private medical care was available for Medicaid patients and that Medicare patients were neglected; some of their complaints appeared to be justified. Meanwhile, the dramatic increase in the population of Cape Cod had exhausted many of the physicians, so emotions ran high on both sides.

Finally, after a long business meeting, all of the officers had left the platform and it was my time to ascend to the podium. Just as I had finished my first paragraph, there was a tremendous banging on the iron doors just behind the stage. The barrage was sufficient to open the doors, whereupon several dozen demonstrators burst into the hall. The atmosphere became tense. But I calmly invited them in, asking them to be seated and listen to my speech, after which they would be given the privilege of the platform. I was very glad no officers of the Society were on the stage, because if anyone had become angry, there could have been a serious confrontation. Much to my relief, there was no commotion. The uninvited audience proved to be very orderly and interested in my address. Thereafter they presented short, appropriate criticisms of the medical care they were receiving. The Society officers listened to their complaints and met with them later.

My oration "Aesculapius—Can We Learn from Your Example?" was published in the *Massachusetts Physician* 1986; 1:30–35.

Chapter 13

1. When any member of the AMA or a state society wishes to bring a matter before the AMA, a resolution is prepared, forwarded to headquarters, and distributed to the delegates of the House well before one of their two yearly meetings. Usually over a hundred resolutions appear; each one is assigned to a reference committee which then holds hearings on all resolutions assigned to it. At the hearings of the reference committees everyone is given opportunity to speak on any subject that is on the agenda before the committee. The number of facts and the amount of wisdom that is displayed in the presentations are phenomenal. The committee then digests the comments, writes a report, or edits a resolution, and presents it to the full House where the resolution is accepted, amended or rejected.

2. W. D. Holden, "Graduate Medical Education," In J. C. Bowers and E. F. Purcell, *Advances in American Medicine: Essays at the Bicentennial* (Baltimore: Port City Press, 1976), pp. 313–344.

Holden has described the historical development of the regulatory agencies that have affected medical education in the United States. He observed that the AMA first took an active leadership role in 1904, when it established the Council on Medical Education largely as the result of the remarkably effective energy and vision of the great Chicago surgeon Arthur D. Bevan. Originally composed of members from medical schools and the AMA, the Liaison Committee for Medical Education (LCME), which exerts a regulatory function on medical schools, now is composed of members from the American Association of Medical Colleges, the AMA, a Canadian representative, representatives of the Federal government and students. The Accreditation Council for Graduate Medical Education (the ACGME, which exerts a similar function insofar as interns and residents are concerned) now includes members from the American Board of Medical Specialties, the American Hospital Association, AMA, American Association of Medical Colleges, the Council of Medical Specialty Societies, the Federal Government, and the public. The present organization pattern dates from 1981.

In 1978 a great impetus developed for continuing medical education (i.e., education following internship and residency and extending through-

out a physician's life—now known as CME). The AMA again assumed
an organizational initiative. After a lively exchange with many other groups
who were interested in the same function, the Accreditation Council for
Continuing Medical Education (ACCME) was established in 1981. It now
contains members from the American Board of Medical Specialty Societies, American Hospital Association, AMA, American Association of
Medical Colleges, Council of Medical Specialty Societies, Federation of
State Medical Boards, Association for Hospital Medical Education, the
Federal Government and the public. In a final compromise, the AMA
retained authority for approval of State Medical Societies and their subsidiary groups for CME if their activities essentially were local and restricted to one state or neighboring states; the Council has authority over
approval of organizations that provide this function for national audiences.

ACCME today is extremely important because of the recent proliferation of institutions that aspire to create an accredited department of
continuing medical education. The review committee judges all applications on the basis of the following factors:

1. A written statement of the mission of the organization
2. Established procedures for identifying needs and interests of prospective participants
3. A statement of explicit objectives for each activity
4. A design of educational activities conforming with the objective
5. Evaluation of its program by the sponsor and use of such material in
   future planning
6. Management and resources adequate to fulfill the mission
7. A sponsor must be responsible for the content of any activity that it
   cosponsors.

By June 1990 ACCME had accredited nearly 500 institutions that had
developed programs designed for national audiences. Individual state
medical societies (and Canadian provincial medical societies) had accredited nearly 2000 institutions; the great majority of them catered to groups
that originated from a single state, or from closely adjacent states. Most
of this dramatic development occurred between 1970 and 1990. The costs
obviously have been enormous. The effects have not been evaluated, nor
will it be possible to do so. However, the popularity of the entire process
indicates the great interest the medical profession has in this project. The
public has not responded with acclaim or praise for physicians but many
other professions have instituted similar programs.

A designated amount of continuing education has been made a requirement for licensure in many states. However, CME, as a requirement for
membership in a state medical society, has been far less popular.

3. I was asked in 1963 by Leland McKittrick, the Chairman of the Council
   on Medical Education of the AMA, to serve as a member representing
   the AMA on the Residency Review Committee (RRC) for Surgery. This

relatively small group has been very powerful because approval of all programs in general surgery for education or training of residents has rested since 1950 in their hands. The influence of this Committee has grown with the years as it has become increasingly difficult to fulfill the requirements of the American Board of Surgery.

After the Residency Review Committee for Surgery was founded in 1950, similar committees for surgical specialties that had approved boards followed the same pattern as they were formed. In 1950 there were three members each appointed by the AMA, the ACS and the ABS. The chairmanship rotated between the ACS And the ABS; the AMA provided staffing and most of the necessary on-site staff reviews. In the early years of the RRC there was great interest in establishing satellite programs in busy community hospitals. More recently, most of these satellite programs have been abandoned, and even residencies with excellent programs have suffered a reduction in the number of their residents.

In recent years the chairman of the committee has been elected by the committee; the last two have been AMA appointees. Claude Organ has observed that forty percent of the committee members have been graduates either of Harvard or Johns Hopkins. In the forty year period ending in 1990 a total of eighteen chairmen and seventy-eight members have served on the committee. The term of office is six years.

Roughly 100 programs are approved each year. Approximately the same number of ongoing programs must make changes in their program. Approval generally is for three years. If a decision of the RRC is appealed by a residency program, the Liaison Committee on Graduate Medical Education makes the final decision. Further information may be obtained from: C. H. Organ, Jr., "Forty Years of the RRC in Surgery," *Archives of Surgery* 1990; 125:1251.

J. T. Boberg, "Procedures and Staff Support for the Surgery Residency Review Committee," *Archives of Surgery* 1990; 125:1246–1250.

G. W. Stephenson, *American College of Surgeons at 75*, pp. 50–53.

4. For a detailed history of this episode, see E. R. Spencer, Jr., *A Society of Physicians*, pp. 283–293.

5. Ibid, p. 292. The quoted phrase was taken from *Newsweek* July 1, 1968.

6. C. E. Welch, "Professional Standards Review Organizations—Problems and Prospects," *New England Journal of Medicine* 1973; 289:291–295.

   In addition to worrying about "cook-book medicine" some delegates feared that lawyers might seize the material in the *Sample Criteria for Short-stay Hospital Review* and use the printed criteria against a physician who did not follow them to the letter. Neither of these worries came to pass.

7. C. E. Welch, "PSRO: Guidelines for Criteria of Care," *Journal of the American Medical Association*, 1975; 232:47–50. This article described the joint AMA-HEW project in detail.

8. See Chapter 12, Note 7.

Chapter 14

1. At least four important histories of the ACS have been written:
   Franklin H. Martin, *Fifty Years of Medicine and Surgery* (Chicago: Surgical Publication Co., 1934).
   Loyal Davis, *Fellowship of Surgeons: A History of the American College of Surgeons* (Springfield, Illinois: American College of Surgeons, 1960). This extremely detailed history of the ACS describes the events leading up to the formation of the College and the history of the organization until 1955.
   C. R. Hanlon, *The American College of Surgeons 1970–1986* (Chicago: American College of Surgeons, 1988). This book is a compendium of the memoranda that were written by Dr. Hanlon and appeared in monthly editions of the *ACS Bulletin* during the years 1963 to 1986, when he was director of the ACS.
   G. W. Stephenson, *American College of Surgeons at 75*. This concise volume contains innumerable facts concerning the ACS. Dr. Stephenson has played a major role in the organization ever since he joined the staff shortly after World War II. He received the Distinguished Service Award in 1973 for his major services to the College. This book represents his last major contribution to the College prior to 1990.
2. G. W. Stephenson, *American College of Surgeons at 75*, pp. 131–143.
3. C. Rollins Hanlon is one of the great surgeons of the twentieth century. He forsook an enviable career as a cardiac surgeon to become director of the ACS in 1969. In the seventeen years he spent in this position he exerted a powerful influence on medical care as he guided the evolution of surgical practice in the United States and in the world. He maintained the independence of the College and aided the consolidation and collaboration of all of the surgical specialties in the organization. He built one of the most important educational programs in the medical profession. One must read his director's memos to discover and to gauge the scope of his wide interests. Above all, he is a scholar, widely versed in ethics and philosophy, as well as in linguistics and literature of the past and present. Never at a loss for words, he chooses the correct ones with canny precision, whether his remarks are spoken or written. He chose an able group of associate directors. Drs. George Stephenson and Frank Padberg were extremely capable in their posts, dealing with admissions, liaisons with specialty societies, and many other tasks. Dr. Stephenson, instead of retiring, spent the last few years as historian of the College. Edwin Gerrish, in charge of the programs, and Fred Spillman, who engineered the two large annual meetings without problems, also deserve special commendation. Dr. Hanlon, in addition to many other awards, became president of the College and of the American Surgical Association. Having reached retirement age, he was succeeded by Dr. Paul Ebert in 1986.
4. The concept of SOSSUS was conceived in the American Surgical Asso-

ciation. However, the ACS was deeply involved from the outset. If the ACS had not been a partner, the whole project would have been judged to be only an ivory tower production and would have been doomed.

One of the main conclusions of the SOSSUS study was that there would be an excess of surgical manpower by the turn of the century. Hanlon never agreed to this statement. He felt that too many other factors were involved to make a sound prediction. In 1990, there were several indications that Hanlon was correct.

5. C. Rollins Hanlon, "The delusion of unity," *Bulletin of the American College of Surgeons* 1986; 71(11):18–26.

6. The Council of Medical Specialty Societies was formed in 1965 by the American College of Obstetricians and Gynecologists, the American College of Physicians, and the American College of Surgeons. It now contains twenty-four member societies.

7. C. E. Welch, "Quality care, quasi-care, and quackery," *Bulletin American College of Surgeons.* 1973; 58(11):1. In this essay I predicted that in order to maintain competence as a surgeon or specialist in surgery, recertification would be required within a decade, and that multiple pathways to recertification should be considered.

8. The American Board of Medical Specialties, founded as a consortium of four existing boards, has gradually expanded and now includes twenty-three member boards. It is concerned with the education of physicians, particularly at the level of interns and residents. It also publishes a list of certified specialists in each specialty.

9. Carl Schlicke was a member of the JCAH for many years prior to its reorganization as the JCAHO as a representative of the ACS. In his presidential address before the Western Surgical Society in 1972, he surveyed the history and the future prospects of the JCAH. He considered the JCAH to be one of the most important contributions of voluntary medicine to the public. At that time 71 percent of the 7,123 hospitals in the United States were accredited by the Commission; the others usually were small proprietary hospitals or had been refused accreditation. C. P. Schlicke, 1973. "American Surgery's Noblest Experiment," *Archives of Surgery* 1973; 106:379–385.

Chapter 15

1. M. M. Ravitch, *A Century of Surgery*, p. 1.
2. Ibid, p. 5.
3. Ibid, p. 15.
4. Ibid, p. 1072
5. C. E. Welch, "Presidential address: Surgical competence in a changing world," *Annals of Surgery* 1977; 186:233–240.
6. T. S. Chitteden, *Designated compensable event system: A feasibility study* (New York: American Bar Association, 1979.) Chittenden was Chairman of the

Medical Professional Liability Committee of the American Bar Association.

7. American College of Surgeons and American Surgical Association, *Surgery in the United States: A Summary Report of the Study on Surgical Services for the United States* (Chicago: American College of Surgeons, 1975–1976). The study was published in three volumes.

8. Ibid, p.85.

9. C. E. Welch, "SOSSUS Revisited," In M. M. Ravitch, *A Century of Surgery*, pp. 1556–1561. (Reprinted with permission of Lippincott.)

SOSSUS Revisited

In 1972, two major surgical organizations—the American Surgical Association and the American College of Surgeons—began a comprehensive survey of surgical practice in the United States. The initial impetus for the study had been furnished by the American Surgical Association and its president in 1969, Dr. Owen Wangensteen.

The project was organized with Dr. George Zuidema as chairman and Dr. Francis Moore as chairman of the Subcommittee on Manpower. The work was accomplished with the aid of many committees, the Department of Preventive Medicine, Harvard Medical School, and innumerable individuals. Financial support was obtained by grants from foundations and the government. This report, unique because of its scope, was published in summary in 1975 and was followed a year later by the completed volumes. Meanwhile, during this period a method of estimation of surgical workloads devised by Hughes was followed by a series of papers by Moore, et al, that included extensive compilations of data and computer projections. Today it is possible to appraise the early effects of the Study on Surgical Services for the United States (SOSSUS). It should be emphasized that this summary represents an individual point of view and does not imply specific approval by the sponsoring societies.

First a few words about the content of the report are in order. Ten subcommittees submitted recommendations. Subsequently some of their statements received relatively little attention. For example, one suggestion that surgeons should cooperate with other professionals and join in local and governmental health planning was received without adverse criticism. One particularly important chapter contained documentation of major contributions of surgical research in the last thirty years. However, attention has been focused particularly on the sections that are concerned with the issues of surgical manpower, of financing, and with the quality of surgical care.

The main thrusts of the report were to suggest that there are too many individuals engaged in the practice of surgery in the United

States, that at present approximately a third of them are less than fully qualified by adequate training, that costs of surgical care can be reduced, and that the quality of care is capable of improvement. The most important objectives that were suggested by the study were:

1. The number of training programs should be reduced and identified more closely with university centers, (i.e., "affiliated hospitals" were to be upgraded or eliminated).

2. Ultimately, the total number of persons entering practice with Board certificates in general surgery and the surgical specialties should be reduced to provide a total of 1,600 to 2,000 yearly in the next ten years. Though not examined in detail in the report, it is obvious that as a corollary, the total number of persons in training would need to be reduced to an appropriate level.

3. Ideally, surgical procedures should be carried out only by individuals with appropriate training, continued activity and proficiency in their fields. In order to attain these goals individual hospital staffs should grant surgical privileges only to well-trained individuals, and should continue to monitor their performances.

4. Academic manpower must be strengthened. Research activities and teaching are in a precarious condition because of lack of adequate personnel and financial support.

5. Costs must be controlled; such experiments as ambulatory clinics, development of surgical teams in which reliance is placed on non-M.D. members, and prepaid programs furnish possible methods.

6. Quality must be improved by stricter peer review.

10. Estimates concerning medical manpower in future years have varied considerably. The SOSSUS report (jointly sponsored by the ASA and the ACS) was the first comprehensive study of a specialty by its own members. It should not be surprising that the Federal Government might consider itself to be less biased and duplicate or expand such efforts. Obviously, the selection of individuals could have a very important influence on the final decisions of any appointed committee or commission. In 1980 a final report was delivered by the Graduate Medical Education National Advisory Committee (GMENAC). It had studied the problem for four years, and ended its life with this report. Their prediction was that there would be a physician surplus of 90,000 in 1990 and of 145,000 by 2000. They advised (1) reduction in the number of United States medical graduates and a sharp reduction in the number of foreign medical graduates allowed to practice in the United States; (2) cessation of the production of nonmedical assistants until another study confirms a need for them; (3) an increase in the number of general (or family) practitioners and a decrease in the number of specialists, and surgeons in particular. The conclusions of the Graduate Medical Education National Advisory Committee were disputed hotly by many groups, particularly the ACS. At the time this note was

written the only positive action that has followed has been a sharp restriction in the number of licenses given to foreign medical graduates.

The Graduate Medical Education National Advisory Committee now has been succeeded by the Council on Graduate Medical Education. This is an advisory body established by Congress as part of the Consolidated Omnibus Budget Reconciliation Act known as (COBRA) that was passed in 1986 and is found in Public Law 99–272. It is to report to the Congress, the Secretary of Health and Human Services (DHHS) and the public. Its duty is to investigate supply and distribution of physicians, both in toto and by specialty, problems related to foreign medical graduates, and issues concerned with medical education and financing of undergraduate and postgraduate programs. Membership is heavily weighted to nonfederal individuals (fourteen to three). The project will run for ten years. One glaring weakness of the Council is its meager budget. The reader should consult N. A. Vancelow, "The Council on Graduate Medical Education: First Report to Congress," *Federation Bulletin* 1989 (1); 76:1–13 for an excellent discussion; much of the material in this note is obtained from this reference.

11. Moore has conducted three studies on board-certified physicians in the United States. They now cover the years 1971–86, a 15-year period. The last paper updates the material from 1980 to 1986. In this last period there is a surprising leveling off of U.S. medical graduates and a fall in the number of foreign medical graduates. This has happened despite a continued linear rise in the U.S. population. The conclusion of the authors is that the nonlinearity of growth and massive changes in the epidemiology and treatment of disease render predictions about the need for or the number of physicians a decade hence unreliable.

Other data of interest include an increase in the number of board-certified surgeons of 21.69 per 100,000 population in 1971 to 34.57 in 1986. See: Moore F. D. and Priebe, C., "Board-Certified Physicians in the United States 1971–1986," *New England Journal of Medicine* 1991; 324:536–543.

12. Calvin H. Plimpton, "The Future Is Not What It Used to Be," *Proceedings of The Charaka Club* 1985; 12:105–119.

13. M. M. Ravitch, *A Century of Surgery*, p. 10.

Chapter 16

1. Bradford Cannon's *The Boston Surgical Society History and Bylaws* was published privately in 1978 by the Society. It contains excellent historical sketches of the Society from the time of its organization in 1911 and of the Bigelow Medal. In addition, the Presidential Address given by Gordon Donaldson in 1976 is included; it was entitled "The First Team of the

Boston Surgical Society" and described the contributions of nine of the founders. The history was updated by Dr. Cannon in 1991.

2. A list of Bigelow Medalists follows:

Recipient	Year	Location and Reason for Honor
Mayo, W. J.	1921	Rochester: founder Mayo Clinic
Keen, W. W.	1922	Philadelphia (Jefferson): neurosurgeon, author
Matas, R.	1926	New Orleans (Tulane) endoaneurysmorrhapy
Jackson, C.	1928	Philadelphia (Temple): endoscopy
Turner, G. G.	1931	Newcastle and London: esophageal cancer
Finney	1932	Finney, J.M.T. 1932 Baltimore (Johns Hopkins): pyloroplasty
Cushing	1933	Cushing, H. 1933 Boston (Brigham's): neuro-surgeon, author
Archibald, E. W.	1937	Montreal (McGill): founder ABS
Whipple, A. O.	1941	New York (College of Phys. and Surgeons, Whipple operation, triad
Lahey, F. H.	1946	Boston (Lahey Clinic): thyroid, abdominal surgery
Cutler, E. C.	1947	Boston (Brigham's): heart, general surgery
Graham, E.	1951	St. Louis (Washington U.) pneumonectomy for cancer
Churchill, E. D.	1955	Boston (MGH): surgery pericardium, parathyroid, trauma
Allen, A. W.	1956	Boston (MGH): abdominal surgery
Crafoord, C.	1961	Stockholm (Karolinska): aortic coarctation
Blalock, A.	1964	Baltimore (Johns Hopkins): pulmonary-subclavian shunt
Dragstedt, L. R.	1964	Chicago (U. of Chicago): vagotomy
Huggins, C.	1967	Chicago (U. of Chicago): hormone-cancer relationship
Gross, R. E.	1970	Boston (Children's Hospital) surgery infants and children
Moore, F. D.	1973	Boston (Brigham's) surgical metabolism; economics
Dunphy, J. E.	1978	San Francisco (U. of California): wound healing
Kirklin, J. W.	1983	Birmingham (U. of Alabama): cardiac surgery, computers

Welch, C. E.	1986	Boston (MGH): abdominal surgery, so-cioeconomics
Starzl, T. E.	1989	Pittsburgh (U. of Pittsburgh): trans-plantation
Murray, J. E.	1992	Boston: transplantation; immunology

3. C. E. Welch, "From Mayo to Kirklin: Riding on Bigelow's Coattails," *American Journal of Surgery* 1986; 152:245–251. (Permission to reprint has been granted by the American Journal of Surgery.)

Chapter 17

1. B. Eiseman and J. C. Thompson, "The visiting professor," *New England Journal of Medicine* 1977; 296:845–850.
2. The New England Surgical Society, founded in 1917, and one of the oldest regional surgical societies, was less than thirty years old when I became a member. At that time the meetings were primarily devoted to scientific discussions. Members were drawn from cities in all of the New England states, although Boston, Hartford, and New Haven dominated the list. Gradually wives began to appear much more frequently, and social activities became slightly more prominent. Although I presented a fair number of papers at the annual meetings, other duties often prevented me from attending, and I never was an officer in the Society.

   In 1977 Gordon Donaldson (Butch to all of his friends) devoted his presidential address at the New England Surgical Society to a description of the life of Nathan Smith. Dr. Smith had aided in the foundation of Dartmouth, Yale, Bowdoin, and the University of Vermont medical schools after he gained his own M.D. degree from Harvard. Thus he had a profound influence on medical education in all of the New England states, although, as pointed out by Donaldson, his only relationship to Rhode Island was that he had lived there. This address beautifully cemented the ties of the five states in surgery and medical education. It made a deep impression on the audience. See: G. A. Donaldson, "The Legacy of Nathan Smith," *Harvard Medical Alumni Bulletin* 1981; 55, no. 1:20–28.

   Eight years later, the Society, under the presidency of John Braasch, established the Nathan Smith Award. It was designated as a honor to be bestowed on members of the Society who had made significant contributions to the Society and to surgery. I was notified in July 1985 that I was to be the first recipient of the award to be given at the annual meeting at The Balsams in Dixville Notch, New Hampshire.

   The presentation was brief. On the same program, the first Samuel Jason Mixter lecture was given. This event, named in honor of one of the founders of the Society, was delivered by our good friend—Lord

Smith of Marlow. Both Rodney and his wife, Lady Sue, were present to receive this honor.

In 1989 the second Nathan Smith Award was made. The recipient, Francis Moore, had for many years been the chief of surgery in the Peter Bent Brigham Hospital. Undoubtedly one of the few great surgeons of the twentieth century, he made enormous contributions to the science of surgery. His studies in metabolism, in transplantation, and in socioeconomic problems were preeminent. His discussions were models of lucidity. (See Chapter 21, and Chapter 21, Note 1.)

When Joseph Murray won the Nobel Prize in Medicine or Physiology in 1990, it appeared that he was certain to receive the third Nathan Smith Award at the time of the September, 1991 meeting. This major event was celebrated by Brownell Wheeler, president of the New England Surgical Society, and Francis Moore, who delivered an address on surgeons who had won the coveted prize.

3. C. E. Welch, "China Report," *PRISM* 1975; 3:25–30 & 53. (Reprinted with permission of the *Journal of the American Medical Association.*)

4. A list of the top twenty-five spots that we have seen include the following, not necessarily arranged in order of preference. Some of these locations are not readily available to visitors at the present time.

1. The Taj Mahal, India. In the dry season, coming from the brown sere fields about Agra, this serene pure white monument, accentuated by reflecting pools is like a vision of Heaven.

2. Manchu Picchu, Peru. Magnificent mountains produce an unbelievable vista for this site of Incan civilization.

3. Kirche im Wiese, Germany. The exterior is uninteresting; the interior is an extravaganza in the Mannerist style. It was cited by Sir Kenneth Clark in his series on *Civilisation*. When we were there, a visiting male chorus was singing beautiful cantatas.

4. Kalat Semen, Syria. Man has attempted to destroy the Earth about this enormous cathedral. The Earth has retaliated; earthquakes have reduced the man-made structure to lonely ruins affording spectacular views of the blue Turkish mountains far away.

5. Baalbeck, Lebanon. Only ruins remain of the temples dedicated to Jupiter and to Bacchus; they were among the most imposing in the world and still retain remnants of their ancient glory.

6. Corfu, Greece. There is a beautiful bay on the island where balmy breezes caress the sun-dappled wavelets and the nearly nude bathers. Is this the isle where burning Sappho loved and sung?

8. Heidelberg, Germany. From across the Neckar, the ruins of the castle remind us of the city's noble past.

9. Vigeland Park in Oslo, Norway. Some say there are too many figures, but the sculptures were the work of a lifetime, and when examined in detail, often are dramatic.

10. Salisbury Cathedral, England. From a site across the Avon, the unique spire soars into the clouds.

11. Angkor Wat, Cambodia. A massive remnant of a former civilization, being slowly devoured by the jungle.

12. Mount McKinley, Alaska. A magnificent view of the entire range from the Alaska railroad, with a moose in the foreground.

13. The Jungfrau, Switzerland. This perfect mountain is assaulted time and again by climbers but regains the white symbol of her virginity with every snowfall.

14. The Matterhorn, Switzerland. One of its kind, often forbidden by menacing clouds to the eyes of tourists.

15. The Blue Mosque, Turkey. A great sense of beauty and spaciousness in the midst of the hurly-burly of Istanbul.

16. The Great Wall in China. It stretches 1500 miles, climbs hills, descends into valleys, and is steep even for horses.

17. Temples in Bangkok, Thailand. Golden spires are surrounded by acolytes.

18. Houseboats in Srinagar, Kashmir. Floating on a glassy lake, almost in clouds, with mighty mountains beyond, they are a symbol of the old British Raj.

19. Pyramids in Gizeh, Egypt. Everybody knows them; they are enormous, and frightening if you crawl inside.

20. Auschwitz, Poland. Forbidding, with its stark memories and an entering railroad that led to death.

21. Kaiser Wilhelm Kirche in Berlin, Germany. Germans adore ruins; this is one of the most poignant of World War II.

22. Mount Fuji, Japan. This imposing mountain rises above mists and clouds. No wonder it is revered by the Japanese.

23. Lions in Kenya. Interesting to see several of them looking at you curiously when you are only a few feet away in an open car.

24. The Grand Canyon, Arizona. From Artist's Point, in the deep canyon castles and fortresses appear and disappear as the sun rises and shadows come and go.

25. Lake Winnipesaukee, New Hampshire. The most perfect lake in the world.

Chapter 18

1. See Chapter 19, Note 5.

Chapter 19

1. Kenneth Allen de Ville, *Medical Malpractice in Nineteenth-Century America: Origins and Legacy* (New York, New York University Press, 1990).
   The author states that there were few malpractice actions in the courts

in the United States before 1840. He found there were 216 appelate decisions from 1790 to 1900. After 1840 there were hundreds of cases, directed particularly against surgeons.

2. Walter L. Burrage, *Guide to Boston for Physicians*, (Cambridge, Harvard University Press, 1921), p. 93.

   From June 6 to 10, 1921 the AMA met in Boston. Walter Burrage prepared a charming guidebook for the visitors. It contained a full description of the medical landmarks of the city. He referred to Dr. Bigelow as "the deity" of the MGH. Among other items in this 189-page description of the Boston medical scene in 1921 are the statements that the dues of the MMS were $10 a year, and that all malpractice actions against members of the Society were handled by the MMS free of charge. (MMS annual dues in 1990 were $300.)

3. R. A. Reynolds, *The Cost of Medical Professional Liability in the 1980s* (Chicago, Illinois, Center for Health Policy Research, American Medical Association, 1990). (Quoted by G. D. Malkasian, Jr., "1990 ACOG Survey: Professional liability and the delivery of obstetrical care," *Bulletin of the American College of Surgeons* 1991; 76 (6):6–37.)

4. *Report of the Secretary's Commission on Medical Malpractice* (Washington, Government Printing Office, 1973). DHEW Publication No. (OS) 73–89.

   This very detailed and comprehensive report was drawn up by a blue-ribbon commission under the direction of the Secretary of HEW, Elliot Richardson.

5. Charlotte B. Cloutier, "Medical Malpractice: Social Program versus Political Crisis," Doctoral dissertation. Northeastern University, Boston, Mass., 1988.

   This thesis contains a mass of data pertaining to the recurrent problems of medical malpractice from the 1960s to the present. Particular attention is paid to the actions in Massachusetts. She concludes that crises occur in cycles and, to the time of the thesis, each episode appeared to be more troublesome than the previous one. She predicts the next crisis will come in 1992 unless some major corrective action is taken prior to that time.

6. J. R. Boyden, and L. R. Tancredi, "Identification of designated compensable events (DCEs)," pp. 32–34. In American Bar Association Commission on Medical Professional Liability, *Designated Compensable Event System: A Feasibility Study*. (Chicago, Ill. American Bar Association, 1979), pp. 32–34. This report is difficult to find. A recent publication dealing in the same way with obstetrics is readily available: R. R. Bovbjerg, L. R. Tancredi, and D. S. Gaylin, "Obstetrics and Malpractice: Evidence on the Performance of a Selective No-fault System," *Journal of the American Medical Association*, 1991; 265:2836–2843. In this feasibility study Tancredi and coworkers explore the possibilty of expanding a system very similar to the application of no-fault insurance for designated compensable events. These "accelerated-compensation events" can easily be developed, can cover two-thirds of currently paid claims, would save time and

expense, and probably would not introduce an unmanageable number of large new claims.

7. Harvard Medical Malpractice Study. *Patients, Doctors, and Lawyers: Medical Injury Malpractice Litigation, and Patient Compensation in New York. Report to the State of New York.* (Boston, 1990). This report, reproduced from typescript, was the product of a team brought together by Deans Howard Hiatt of the Harvard School of Public Health and James Vorenburg of the Harvard Law School, and known as the Harvard Medical Practice Study, to investigate the current malpractice problem and the tort litigation system.

8. Malkasian, 1990 ACOG Survey, p. 9, Note 3.

Chapter 20

1. Mider noted that from 1963 to 1976 the federal government has subsidized almost two-thirds of all the medical research done in the USA. G. B. Mider, "The Federal Impact on Biomedical Research" in J. C. Bowers and E. F. Purcell, *Advances in American Medicine: Essays at the Bicentennial.* (New York, Josiah Macy Jr. Foundation, 1976), pp. 806–871.

2. All subspecialties in surgery demonstrate long lists of technical advances. The *Physicians Desk Reference*, which lists and describes available drugs now covers nearly 2500 pages.

3. Public advisory committees have been appointed for many years by the FDA. A series of approximately twenty-five were formed in the late 1970s to review over-the-counter (OTC, or non-prescription) drugs.

   I was appointed as chairman of a panel to review hemorrhoidal (ano-rectal) drugs in 1977. Other professional members of the group included Judith Jones and Eugene Castiglia (internists), Thaddeus Grosicki (pharmacologist), Winston Gaskin (pharmacist), Leon Banov (proctologist and medical historian), and Jean Golden (surgeon). We reached a consensus on nearly every drug and on claims that could be made for labeling.

4. C. E. Welch, "PSRO's—Pros and Cons," *New England Journal of Medicine,* 1974; 290:1318–1322.

5. K. N. Lohr, *MEDICARE—A Strategy for Quality Insurance* (Washington: National Academy Press, 1990).

   The Congress of the United States commissioned the National Academy of Sciences to "design a strategy for quality review and assurance in Medicare" in conformity with Section 9313 of the Omnibus Budget Reconciliation Act of 1986. The studies were carried out by expert committees from the National Academy of Sciences and the Institute of Medicine, and were supported by the Health Care Financing Administration.

6. Important court decisions include the following:

   a. In 1973 the US Supreme Court gave its opinion in Roe v Wade. Annas has called it "the most important, most controversial and most well-known US Supreme Court decision in recent history". Prior to that time, the legality of abortion had rested in the individual states. This variation, for example, had required many women in Massachusetts who wanted an abortion to go to New York State where it was legal for several years prior to 1973. The Supreme Court decision allowed abortion to be a matter of the woman's choice, except in the last trimester of pregnancy when the fetus was deemed to be viable, abortion could be legal only if continuing the pregnancy would imperil the life of the mother. (See G. J. Annas, *Judging Medicine* Humana Press Clifton, N.J., 1988, pp. 147–179 for a complete discussion of the original decision and further challenges that reached the US Supreme Court).

b. A Massachusetts case—*Brophy v New England Sinai Hospital*-was concerned with a comatose patient who ultimately was kept alive for three years by means of a gastrostomy tube. Despite evidence from Brophy's wife that his preference would have been to die, his case ground slowly through the courts. Finally the Massachusetts Supreme Court overturned a lower court's decision that he had to be continued on tube feedings. He was transferred to another hospital; the tube was withdrawn; he died eight days later. (See G. J. Annas, op cit., pp. 302–308).

c. The legal relationship of physicians and hospitals was never accurately defined until the *Darling v Charleston Community Hospital* case in 1965 established the shared liability of a hospital with a surgeon with privileges in that hospital if a malpractice suit against the physician was settled in favor of the plaintiff.

d. The case, *Patrick v.Burget* involved a physician (Patrick) who, by peer review carried out by members of the clinic in which he worked, was dismissed from the clinic and received no further referrals from members of the clinic. Patrick claimed enormous pecuniary damages against the clinic physicians based upon FTC regulations. After 10 years of ritual passing through various courts, the U.S. Supreme Court finally decided in favor of Patrick. As a result, the members of the clinic have moved out of the state and all are subject to huge financial assessments.

The case with all of its intricacies was considered in an exhaustive review by Curran. (W. J. Curran, "Legal Immunity for Medical Peer Review Programs", *New England Journal of Medicine* 1989:320; 233–235). His conclusions were that the verdict is final, that the State had not been involved sufficiently by statute or action to prove the "peer review" process had actually been one of true peer review rather than an activity motivated by restraint of trade. He has pointed out the importance of legislative action as evidence of participation of the public that is imperative to preserve the values of peer review.

e. It should be noted that an Ad Hoc Committee from Harvard with Dr. Henry Beecher as chairman in 1968 published the criteria of brain death in the *Journal of the American Medical Association*. The Committee not only specified the criteria which have remained inviolate until the present time, but also stated there was no need for legal statements to buttress this position because the Courts had always recognized the medical profession's definition of death.

7. See note 10 in Chapter 15.

8. In 1964 the Congress established this Panel to review and assess the management of the NIH and the National Institute of Mental Health. Franklin Murphy was appointed as chairman. Roughly 75 members were appointed to the Panel, which had a life span of 15 months.

 The final report was presented to the President in April, 1976. Over 80 recommendations were made. Increases in salary and appropriations, more flexibility for the directors, and more stability for research by increasing the time limits of research grants were among the most important. I served as a member of the Overview Cluster which considered the recommendations made by the separate task forces. I am not certain that the Panel influenced the final disposition of federal funds, but it documented clearly the financial stringencies of these agencies compared with the benefits that could be gained by employment in the private sector.

9. "Cancer centers" are not clearly defined. In general terms they provide for basic research, clinical care and interaction with the public and are staffed by a wide range of specialists that cover the spectrum of malignant disease. Some are free standing but the great majority are connected with university hospitals. The number of cancer centers in the United States has increased dramatically in the past decade.

 The American College of Surgeons has maintained intense interest in the treatment of cancer since it was organized. Accreditation of cancer clinics by the College has continued; by 1947 the reporting of end results was emphasized. In 1965, to provide for input from other persons than surgeons, the name of the Committee was changed to the Commission on Cancer. Boston chairmen over the years included Robert Greenough, Grantley Taylor and Richard Wilson; in addition Ernest Daland was Chairman of the Committee that developed the methods of reporting end results. By 1988, the Commission had approved 1204 programs and the budget for the year was over $1,700,000.

 The American Society for the Control of Cancer was organized in 1913; the name was changed to the American Cancer Society in 1945. It has raised large amounts of money some of which has helped to sponsor the programs of the College.

 The Federal Government has played an increasingly important role in support of the battle against cancer. The National Cancer Institute was established in 1937, and it became the first organization to enter the National Institutes of Health in 1953. The first important action of the Congress—to establish the Regional Medical Program for cancer, heart disease and stroke—never became organized. But the National Cancer Act of 1971 was a great success and provided funds for the rapid development of cancer centers. By 1963 there were 12 such centers, and 57 in 1988. W. W. Shingleton, "Cancer centers—origin and purpose," *Archives of Surgery*, 1989; 124:43–45.

10. Relations between the AMA and HCFA cooled considerably when HCFA refused to retract their opposition to balance billing and also published a fee schedule that made wide reductions in Medicare fees for both physicians and surgeons. The wave of protests that inundated Washington after publication of the first schedule has led to substantial revision. Initial enthusism for the project was announced in the following articles:
   W. C. Hsiao, P. Braun, D. Yntena, E. R. Becker, "Estimating Physician's Work for a Resource-Based Relative-Value Scale," *New England Journal of Medicine* 1988; 319:835–841.
   P. R. Lee, P. B. Ginsberg, "Physician Payment Reform: an Idea Whose Time Has Come", *Journal of the American Medical Association* 1980; 260:2441–2443.
   J. S. Todd, "At last, a Rational Way to Pay for Physicians' Services," *Journal of the American Medical Association*, 1988; 260:2439–2441.
   Three years later the opinions of these men had changed completely. Dr. James Todd, vice-president of the AMA, was especially bitter. See:
   P. R. Lee, P. B. Ginsburg "The Trials of Medicare Physician Payment Reform," *Journal of the American Medical Association* 1991; 266:1563–1565, and J. S. Todd, "Whom Can We Trust?" *Journal of the American Medical Association*, 1991; 266:1566.
11. Arnold Relman, in an editorial, sounded a warning against corporations who were promoting medical care for profit. He regarded this development as a threat to medicine as it traditionally has been practiced in non-profit and government hospitals. Dialysis centers had been in the vanguard of this change and had reaped a financial bonanza. A.S. Relman, "The New Medical-Industrial Complex", *New England Journal of Medicine*, 1980; 303:963–968.
12. D. Schneidman, "The National Practitioner Bank: What Surgeons Should Know," *American College of Surgeons Bulletin* October 1990; 75 #10: 14–18.

Chapter 21

1. F. D. Moore, "Surgical Professor for Three Eventful Decades," *Journal of the American Medical Association* 1990; 264:3185–3188. This article gives a summary of his accomplishments.
2. Massachusetts General Hospital, *Annual Report*, 1990.
3. The White building (opened in 1939) has been completely renovated during the past few years. Other buildings remaining on the site and their dates of completion are the Warren building (1956), Research building (1951), Bartlett Hall (1953), the adjacent Shriners Burn Institute (1968), Gray and Bigelow-Jackson Towers (1969), Cox Cancer Center (1975), the Wang Ambulatory Care Center (1981), Wellman Research Building (1984), the expanded Treadwell Library (1989,) and the MGH Corporation office building (1989). The MGH East was leased in 1988.

4. *U.S.* News *& World Report*, April 30, 1990, pp. 51–86.
5. U.S. News & World Report, August 5, 1991, pp. 36–71.

Chapter 22

1. The onset of the epidemic of AIDS early in the 1980s rudely shattered any complacency concerning the ability of medicine to readily determine the cause of and develop a cure for new diseases. The succeeding decade has been dominated by the problems of the human immunodeficiency virus (HIV), the acquired immunodeficiency syndrome (AIDS), and the AIDS-related complex (ARC).

The cause of the disease—a retrovirus—has been determined by 1982 by independent investigators in France and the United States. Methods of transmission were clear—unprotected sex, particularly anal sex in male homosexuals, intravenous drug use with nonsterile needles, and contaminated blood products. Identification of the virus by laboratory tests shortly became highly (although not completely) reliable. Thus methods of prevention of AIDS and identification of persons with HIV were clear. However, by 1990 many children were born with the disease and heterosexual transmission was not infrequent, so other factors for transmission were introduced.

In the year 1982, 912 cases of AIDS were reported in the United States. In 1989, 35,238 cases of AIDS were reported in the United States, an increase of 9.4 percent from 1988. The epidemic is still spreading despite an apparent recent reduction in the yearly rate of increase in homosexual males. Once the syndrome had developed, it was uniformly fatal.

The disease has very serious connotations, especially for surgeons, because of the opportunities for infection due to such injuries as needle pricks or lacerations in the operating room. Infection also can occur from body fluids of an infected patient. Since twenty-five percent of all patients admitted to some emergency rooms have the virus, extreme precautions are necessary throughout hospitals. Conflicting personal, ethical, legal, and medical viewpoints have led to considerable argument insofar as methods of reporting and control are concerned. By 1988, the AMA had established a code of action stating that all doctors must care for AIDS patients, regardless of personal danger. In 1989 the Harvard Medical School faculty adopted a similar code of ethics requiring all medical students to care for AIDS patients. Obviously extensive protective measures must be employed with all patients known to have or suspected of having the disease. Inasmuch as over a million persons in the United States were estimated to be HIV positive in 1990, this means that protective measures must be taken with all workers and patients in hospitals. The expense is enormous.

By 1990, drugs that apparently slow the course of the disease are in use but no cures have occurred. Is it possible to hope that the human body may prove more resilient and adaptable than we expect and that the disease eventually will wane and disappear?

A few of innumerable references are listed. The Centers for Disease Control published reports from Los Angeles and New York City in 1981 and numerous ones thereafter.

The first papers on AIDS appeared in the *New England Journal of Medicine* in 1982. Two articles in Science sparked a controversy that still continues concerning the discovery of the causative agent. They are:

F. Barré-Simovis, J. C. Chermann, F. Rey, et al., "Isolation of a T-lymphotrophic retrovirus from a patient at risk for acquired immuno deficiency syndrome," *Science* 1983; 220: 868–871.

M. Popovic, M. C. Sarngadharan, E. Read, and R. C. Gallo, "Detection, isolation and continuous production of cytopathic retroviruses (HTLV-III) from patients with AIDS and pre-AIDS ," *Science* 1984; 224; 497–500.

The final report of the Harvard Medical Center AIDS committee was published in *Focus*, December 11, 1989.

Hope that the AIDS epidemic might disappear spontaneously is expressed in:

D. J. Bregman, A. D. Langmuir, "Farr's law applied to AIDS projections," *Journal of the American Medical Association*, 1990; 263: 1522–1525.

2. There are several important prizes that reward medical scientists for their important contributions. The foremost is the Nobel prize in physiology and medicine. Examination of the natinality of recipients shows that the United States ascended to first place a half century ago and has continued to hold this position. Out of 29 prizes by 1930 in physiology and medicine, the United States had only one recipient—Landsteiner. Successive figures show six out of thirteen from 1931 to 1940; eight out of seventeen from 1941 to 1950, fourteen out of twenty from 1951 to 1960, fourteen out of twenty-six from 1961 to 1970; seventeen out of twenty-five from 1971 to 1980, and fourteen out of twenty-two from 1981 through 1990 were United States citizens. Only ten of the entire 152 were surgeons.

The Crafoord prize, also based in Sweden and honoring the name of their eminent vascular surgeon, was founded in 1982; it has been held by Americans every year since then.

In the United States, the Mary Lasker fund is another source of prestigious awards. Michael DeBakey has been chairman of the committee that selected winners of these awards for many years. Among the winners one of the most remarkable is the columnist, Eppie Lederer (Ann Landers). Her advice, given daily to millions throughout the world, is sound and authoritative.

The American Surgical Association presents a medallion for scientific achievement at irregular intervals. Recipients have included Dragstedt, Gross, Wagensteen, Zollinger, Moore, Murray, Rhoads, DeBakey, Varco, and Starzl.

Harvard Medical School alumni and faculty members have received a total of 18 Nobel Prizes. The recipients and their contributions have been described in detail in three issues of *Harvard Medical School PERSPECTIVES*. See the 1990 autumn and winter editions and the 1991 spring edition. In 1990 Joseph Murray received the medal.

3. Thomas D. Cabot, *Beggar on Horseback* (Boston: David R. Godine, 1979).

4. Kevin Cahill, internationally known physician, consultant to the World Health Organization, and author of several books, was the personal physician of Cardinal Cooke. He had received a potential list of several American surgeons and was assured his choice would be accepted. Dr. Cahill has served many important persons in the Catholic church.

   After we had examined the Pope and watched him for a few days, we returned. A short time later, a puzzling fever developed. Dr. Cahill returned to Rome and remained until this complication has been resolved.

5. Surgical fellowships widen the careers of gifted doctors. *MGH News*, 1981; 40 (4): 7–8.

6. John Larkin Thompson, president of the Massachusetts Blue Cross-Blue Shield, in an editorial in the *Boston Globe* in 1990, has cited many of the dangers of a national health plan. He said the reality is that if we want universal access to health care, control over health-care costs, and competitiveness of American business we must face up to the underlying causes of health-care inflation: increasing medical research and technology costs, escalating malpractice premiums, excess institutional capacity, an aging population, and, most important, a level of expectation on the part of all of us that the system can address every illness and problem that falls within the unlimited definition of health care. He cited Massachusetts; an attempt is being made to establish such a universal system of access in that state but the state already owes $488 million for unpaid Medicaid bills for the past three years. The Blue Cross-Blue Shield organizations in the United States in 1991 formed a committee to consider a health care system. Thompson is chairman of the committee.

7. In a comparison of the salient features of the Canadian, British, and American systems, several other facts require brief discussion. They include:

   Costs. Approximate costs in 1990, in percentage of the gross national product: United States, twelve; Canada, nine; Great Britain, six.

   Expenses. Administrative costs: United States (estimated) twenty-five percent of all health care costs; Canada, five percent. The United States has other special charges that are not sustained by other systems. They include:

   Professional liability insurance. In the United States, professional liability insurance charges, including fees of lawyers and court-proceedings as well as the necessity of practicing defensive medicine, which leads to the ordering of a large number of unnecessary tests, combine to cause an annual outlay of an estimated ten to twenty billion dollars.

Contingency fees. Both in Canada and Great Britain, it is unethical for lawyers to take cases with contingent fees (where the lawyer is paid only if he wins the case); in the United States lawyers believe that contingency fees are ethical, and they have been supported by the courts.

Gatekeepers. One feature of medical care in the United States in recent years is the institution of "gatekeepers." Even if a patient has insurance and needs to go into a hospital for an operation, several conditions must be met; permission usually must be granted by a third-party payer who provides insurance. A second option as to whether or not an operation is indicated often must be obtained from a panel appointed by the payer. The number of days allowed for hospital stay, and often permission for a one-day hospital stay for a patient prior to a serious operation, must be decided and granted as well as assurance that the insurance is in order. All these decisions m ay be in the hands of several functionaries who may be clerks or nurses in an insurer's office. The physician must conquer all of these obstacles before these gatekeepers are satisfied and his patients receive proper care.

Second opinions. Second opinions by other surgeons are required by some insurance companies before they agree to pay for this prospective procedure. Despite the fact most of these opinions are not cost-effective, they still are used widely.

Peer Review. In the United States expenses related to the peer review demanded by HCFA for a substantial percentage of Medicare patients and by various other third-party payers add a very sizable amount to medical costs. Such audits are minimal or non-existent in other countries. Peer Review Organizations form part of the large bureaucracy that is required for the HCFA audits. The United States may wish to consider the method of audit used in Great Britain where it is given to hospital trusts as a more cost-conserving practice.

Continuing medical education. In the United States continuing medical education throughout the life of a physician is regarded as one method to maintain excellence in the profession. Many states also require it for licensure. The procedure is estimate to cost at least a billion dollars annually, and probably it is very much higher. Other countries do not require similar education.

Coverage. In the United States, it is estimated that twenty-five to thirty million individuals have no health insurance and therefore no coverage for professional or hospital care. Coverage in Canada and Great Britain was designed to be universal and costs were covered by the state. However, long waiting lists and lack of coverage for certain procedures have tended to diminish or even negate the value of universal coverage. The British White Paper of 1989 praises the growth of private insurance in Great Britain as an antidote, because fewer individuals will have to be covered under the national plan.

Index

Brief Biography, Claude E. Welch

1906:	Born in Stanton, Nebraska
1923–27	Doane College (graduated summa cum laude)
1927	Columbia University Summer School
1927–28	University of Missouri
1928–32	Harvard Medical School (graduated magna cum laude)
1932–37	Massachusetts General Hospital (Internship through residency)
1937:	Married to Phyllis Heath Paton, in Montreal, Quebec

Children:
Claude E. Welch, Jr.: Distinguished Service Professor, State University of New York, Buffalo, NY
John Paton Welch: Clinical Professor of Surgery: University of Connecticut, Surgeon, Hartford Hospital

Academic and professional appointments:
Massachusetts General Hospital:
Visiting Surgeon, 1953;
Chief of Tumor Clinic, 1957–1966,
Senior Surgeon, 1972
Harvard Medical School:
Clinical Professor of Surgery, 1964
Clinical Professor of Surgery Emeritus, 1972

President:
Massachusetts Medical Society, 1966
Boston Surgical Society, 1966
Society for Surgery of the Alimentary Tract, 1966
New England Cancer Society, 1969–70
Harvard Medical Alumni Association, 1972–74
American College of Surgeons, 1973–4

American Surgical Association, 1976–7
American Chapter, International Society of Surgeons,
1978–80

Honors and Awards:
Alpha Omega Alpha
Army Commendation Ribbon
Bigelow Medal, Boston Surgical Society
Distinguished Service Award, American Medical Association
Leaders in American Medicine Award (Countway series)
Nathan Smith Award, New England Surgical Society
McLaughlin-Gallie Visiting Professor, Canadian Medical Schools
Orator, Massachusetts Medical Society
Roswell Park Medal, Buffalo Surgical Society
Special Award, Sloan-Kettering Hospital, NYC
Trustees Medal, Massachusetts General Hospital